EQUALITY

TRANS FORMED

SOCIAL PHILOSOPHY & POLICY CENTER

EQUALITY

A Quarter-Century of Affirmative Action

TRANS FORMED

Herman Belz

transaction

Transaction Publishers
New Brunswick (USA) and London (UK)

Published by the Social Philosophy and Policy Center and by Transaction
Publishers 1991. Third printing, 1994

Library of Congress Cataloging-in-Publication Data

Belz, Herman.
    Equality transformed : a quarter-century of affirmative action /
Herman Belz.
        p. cm.—(Studies in social philosophy & policy ; no. 15)
    Includes bibliographical references and index.
    ISBN 0-88738-882-5 (pbk.)—ISBN 0-88738-393-9 (cloth).
    1. Affirmative action programs—Law and legislation—United
States—History. 2. Discrimination in employment—Law and
legislation—United States—History. 3. Affirmative action programs—
United States—History. I. Title. II. Series.
KF3464.B45   1991
344.73'01133—dc20
[347.3041133]   90-10176
                               CIP

Cover Design: Kent Lytle

For Valerie

Series Editor: Ellen Frankel Paul
Series Managing Editor: Dan Greenberg

The Social Philosophy and Policy Center, founded in 1981, is an interdisciplinary research institution whose principal mission is the examination of public policy issues from a philosophical perspective. In pursuit of this objective, the Center supports the work of scholars in the fields of political science, philosophy, law, and economics. In addition to the book series, the Center hosts scholarly conferences and edits an interdisciplinary professional journal, *Social Philosophy & Policy*. For further information on the Center, write to the: Social Philosophy and Policy Center, Bowling Green State University, Bowling Green, OH 43403.

Contents

Acknowledgments

I wish to thank the Earhart Foundation for its generous support during the research and writing of this book. The University of Maryland General Research Board and Department of History provided assistance for which I am grateful. The study was begun at the urging of Michael P. McDonald of the Center for Individual Rights, Washington, D.C., and was first presented as an article in the Washington Legal Foundation monograph series. Phil Lyons of the U.S. Equal Employment Opportunity Commission, Earlean McCarrick of the University of Maryland, Earl Maltz of the Rutgers University School of Law at Camden, Robert Eden of Hillsdale College, and the late John Wettergreen of San Jose State University read portions of the manuscript and provided valuable criticism. Hugh Davis Graham of the University of Maryland, Baltimore County, and James Sharf of the U.S. Office of Personnel Management gave me the benefit of their knowledge of the development of affirmative action. Ellen Frankel Paul of the Social Philosophy and Policy Center, Bowling Green State University, provided exceedingly valuable criticism of the manuscript for which I am grateful.

Introduction

When the Supreme Court modified the legal doctrines supporting race-conscious affirmative action in a series of decisions in 1989, leaders of the civil rights establishment denounced the rulings as a repudiation of the Civil Rights Act of 1964 and an attack on the principle of equality itself. The Court "in its mischievousness . . . gutted Title VII of the Civil Rights Act," said Althea Simmons of the National Association for the Advancement of Colored People.[1] Eleanor Holmes Norton, Chairman of the Equal Employment Opportunity Commission (EEOC) in the Carter Administration, wrote: "During the Court's last term, for the first time in memory those seeking equality lost repeatedly." Referring to the damage done by the Court, she declared: "This can only be fixed by a Congress with a commitment to Title VII."[2] On the other side of the issue, critics of affirmative action were encouraged by the decisions. According to former federal judge Robert Bork, the Court merely insisted on the traditional rule that discrimination must be proved, not assumed.[3] William Bradford Reynolds, Assistant Attorney General for Civil Rights in the Reagan Administration, stated that the Court's decisions "remove invidious racial preferences from affirmative action."[4]

As these reactions indicate, the basic meaning of the anti-discrimination principles of Title VII of the Civil Rights Act of 1964 remains legally contested and politically controversial a full generation after its enactment. Statutory language that was intended to confer an individual right to equal opportunity in employment without distinguishing by color has for many years been interpreted as authorizing government officials and

1

private employers to adopt preferential practices benefiting designated racial and ethnic groups. A similar transformation has occurred in the second major source of employment discrimination policy, the federal contract program, in which the government through executive orders establishes the conditions of doing business with it. Labor Department officials have changed President Kennedy's 1961 executive order requiring contractors to take affirmative action to ensure equal employment opportunity—intended as a procedural guarantee of nondiscriminatory recruitment and hiring practices—into a substantive demand for employment of minorities in accordance with numerical goals that make race and ethnicity decisive considerations.

This transformation of employment discrimination law under Title VII and the federal contract program, and its parallels in other areas of civil rights policy, was effected by administrative regulations and court decisions based on the disparate impact theory of discrimination. Although rejected by Congress in the Civil Rights Act, this theory was asserted by the EEOC as soon as Title VII went into effect and adopted by the Supreme Court as the authoritative interpretation of the law in *Griggs v. Duke Power Co.* in 1971. The theory holds that discrimination is not an individual act of injury or denial of rights caused by racial prejudice (as it had traditionally been conceived of in civil rights law), but is rather the sum of the unequal effects of employment procedures and business practices on racial groups. Persistent and widespread application of disparate impact theory after the *Griggs* decision gave employers a powerful incentive to engage in hiring quotas in order to avoid liability and costly litigation.

Race-conscious affirmative action developed under both Democratic and Republican administrations from 1961 to 1980; it was approved by the Supreme Court in a series of reverse discrimination cases in the late 1970s. The Reagan Administration, in contrast, challenged the system of racial group preference in significant respects and tried to enforce Title VII in accordance with the original understanding of equal employment opportunity. In the mid-1980s the Supreme Court, rejecting the anti-quota interpretation of Title VII advanced by the Department of Justice, gave broad approval to race and sex employment preferences. At the end of the decade, however, in yet another round of cases dealing with the meaning of discrimination and the propriety of race-conscious remedies, the Court began to reconsider the affirmative action settlement reached only a few years earlier. The affirmative action controversy thus continued: attention redounded upon Congress, where legislation to override the comparatively recent decisions was introduced.

This book seeks to illuminate this continuing conflict by studying the redefinition of equality that has resulted from over two decades of race-conscious affirmative action. Examining the path of the law reveals the tension not only between rival theories of discrimination and equal opportunity, but also between forward-looking and backward-looking conceptions of social change. At one level, everyone involved in the affirmative action controversy agrees that progress toward a non-racist society requires Americans to overcome their past. Like earlier generations of American reformers inspired by the revolutionary principles of liberty and equality, the twentieth-century civil rights movement long believed that the best way—indeed, the only realistic way—to overcome the past was to create equal opportunity for individuals. Civil rights reform aimed at the removal of discriminatory racial barriers so that individuals could exercise their rights and pursue their interests, according to their personal talents, abilities, and qualities. The removal of barriers and impediments was remedial, but the remedy concerned the present and looked to the future. Social reform was not backward-looking: it did not focus on historical wrongs and injustices as a source of inspiration, but rather on the principles of liberty and equality. Even less was reform backward-looking in the sense of being designed to compensate for specific acts of injury and wrongdoing; it did not focus on giving individuals—not to mention entire racial and ethnic groups—the material benefits and status they would have had if they had not been injured or oppressed. Reform calculated to correct the errors, contingencies, and prejudices of the past was not attempted because it was not liberating and progressive, and because it was believed impossible to attain. Better to work for change in the future than to try to alter the past, which it was thought could not be changed.

Fundamentally, however, race-conscious affirmative action is oriented towards and based on the past. It attempts to do what the Supreme Court, in a major employment discrimination decision in the 1970s, said federal courts were required to do in enforcing Title VII: namely, to "recreate the conditions and relationships that would have been had there been no unlawful discrimination." Referring to the details of a specific employment situation involving thousands of employees, the Court modestly conceded: "This process of recreating the past will necessarily involve a degree of approximation and imprecision."[5] Applied broadly in judicial doctrines and agency regulations, affirmative action elevates "approximation" and "imprecision" into a national policy for rectifying the past. Courts and administrative agencies assume that they can order virtually any policy they please on the theory that it is a remedy for some wrong or injustice in the past. Moreover, the idea of re-creating and correcting the past, when used as the basic rationale for civil rights policy, reinforces categorical assumptions of guilt and innocence that undermine progress toward the goal of racially impartial equal rights.

Such is the appeal of the equal rights principle in public opinion that proponents of racial preference are forced to agree, in a highly abstract and superficial sense, with the opponents of affirmative action on the proposition that race is an unsound principle of political and social organization. For example, Eleanor Holmes Norton observes: "There is no denying that, however necessary, race and sex-conscious remedies are inherently problematic."[6] Yet in terms of concrete political and social attitudes, the historical justification of affirmative action—the argument that it is "simple justice" needed to compensate for the effects of slavery—perpetuates the racial thinking of the past.[7]

The removal of exclusionary racial barriers in the Civil Rights Act of 1964 and the Voting Rights Act of 1965 was politically motivated in a positive sense: the desire of the majority to promote its interests led it to protect the rights of the minority and thus to promote the public interest. Moreover, insofar as the laws were intended to place civil rights protection on an impartial, racially neutral basis, they were also intended to remove the legal process of rights enforcement from the controlling influence of political partisanship and ideology. Under race-conscious affirmative action, however, civil rights policy has been politically motivated in a negative sense: it has been based on irrelevant and superficial racial characteristics. It is used to promote partisan interests at the expense of the common good; it is in patent contradiction of the ideal of common citizenship. Measures that confer benefits on groups according to race and ethnicity reflect obvious political choices, rather than recognition of a standard of common citizenship that guarantees individual rights on an impartial basis, as required by the Constitution and the civil rights laws.

As racial barriers fell in the 1960s, blacks gained access to the political, social, and economic institutions and associations through which individuals participated or were represented in the design of public policy. By reason of occupation, profession, or market situation in an economic sense, and by virtue of citizenship in a political sense, the black minority was in a position to be integrated into the system of interest-group pluralism that characterizes twentieth-century American government. The pluralist solution in some respects can itself encourage tendencies that challenge the constitutional ideal of general policies or legislation based on common citizenship and directed toward the good of the community as a whole. However, whereas pluralistic class legisla-

tion, such as that relating to labor organizations in the 1930s, arguably had a defensible economic rationale, race-conscious affirmative action has transformed blacks into a monolithic racial interest group that can claim no rational justification or functional purpose. Indeed, affirmative action is dysfunctional to the extent that it perpetuates racial stereotypes that invert the relationship between the individual and the group that characterizes pluralism in the United States. Any argument for the historical justice of affirmative action is contradicted by this basic fact.

Instead of the individual being the primary social unit, on the basis of which groups are formed, under affirmative action policies the group becomes primary and is the source of rights for the individual. Moreover, blacks were *the* prototype for the proliferating assertions of group rights that in the 1970s and 1980s introduced a debilitating factionalism into American politics and government. As the original "discrete and insular minority," to use the language of constitutional law, blacks' claim to preferential treatment based on the collective victimization of slavery has become politically entrenched, making reform of contemporary minority group factionalism all the more difficult. A critic of affirmative action asked in 1967: "Once the special interests of racial and ethnic groups in preferential employment are recognized, will our political leaders have the courage to abandon the program, particularly since it is called a 'fair employment practice' program . . . ?"[8] A supporter of preferential remedies worried in 1973 that government Equal Employment Opportunity agencies, and the civil rights lobbyists and legal professionals bound to them in a symbiotic relationship, might have an incentive to perpetuate the problem of discrimination rather than end it.[9] The politics of affirmative action in the 1980s tends to confirm the accuracy of these warnings.

Affirmative action is viewed as a temporary policy needed to wipe out the effects of past societal discrimination. Defenders of the policy such as Eleanor Holmes Norton continue to assert that race-conscious remedies "will . . . remain transitional and fall into disuse once the job is done."[10] After more than two decades, however, it is pertinent to ask what conception of civil rights and what kind of society affirmative action is a transition to. The rhetoric of affirmative action professes the goal of a color-blind society, but the political and social reality is increasingly that of a racially balanced society, regulated by courts and administrative agencies enforcing systems of proportional representation.

More than we care to acknowledge, preferential policies have been adopted in the belief that individual rights and equal opportunity do not lead to social progress and sustained in the fear that civil rights policy based on these principles will result in "social and racial chaos."[11] Motivated by these convictions, civil rights policy makers—in the words of a former government official who helped establish affirmative action in the early 1970s—have undertaken an "illusive" search "to develop a doctrine that accommodates the paradox of using race or sex considerations to achieve a color- or gender-blind society."[12] This book is an analysis of that illusive search, which has so profoundly altered the meaning of American equality.

1

From Equal Employment Opportunity to Affirmative Action: 1961 to 1969

In the Civil Rights Act of 1964, Congress guaranteed the right of equal employment opportunity in private industry to every individual. Title VII of the act declared it an unlawful employment practice for companies and labor organizations with 25 employees or members to fail or refuse to hire, to exclude or expel, or to limit, segregate, or classify its employees or members in any way that would deprive any individual of employment opportunities because of race, color, religion, sex, or national origin. Despite extensive government intervention into the free market, private employment relations before 1964 (with the exception of the National Labor Relations Act and the Fair Labor Standards Act) remained beyond the reach of federal regulation. During and after World War II the federal government tried to curb employment discrimination through the federal contract program, and many states created fair employment practices commissions. These efforts produced few results, and civil rights advocates were unsuccessful in attempting to place the issue of job bias on the national political agenda.

The political situation began to change after the *Brown v. Board of Education* school desegregation decision in 1954. With Republicans and northern Democrats competing for the political support of blacks, the question of civil rights was increasingly recognized as an issue demanding action by the federal government. A decisive breakthrough occurred in 1957, when Congress passed the first civil rights legislation since Reconstruction. The act established a Civil Rights Commission, created the Civil Rights Division in the Justice Department, and prohibited attempts to intimidate or prevent persons from voting. In 1960 another act was passed requiring the preservation of state records of federal elections and providing for the appointment of voter-referees by federal courts to receive complaints from any person allegedly denied the right to vote. These measures signified the weakening of the southern veto over civil rights legislation, paving the way for the Civil Rights Act of 1964. In this historic measure, civil rights organizations successfully revived and enacted a controversial proposal to prohibit job discrimination that, in all likelihood, could never have been passed had it been introduced as a separate bill. By hitching it to more widely supported proposals to ban discrimination in public facilities and accommodations, elections, and public education, they succeeded in penetrating the sphere of private employment relations.

The Civil Rights Act created instruments of judicial and administrative power that promptly were used to transform the legal definition of employment discrimination and the meaning of equal opportunity in broad areas of American life. By 1970, federal courts and the Equal Employment Opportunity Commission acting under Title VII, and executive branch officials acting under a revised federal contract program, introduced into national civil rights policy concepts radically at odds with the individual rights/nondiscrimination principle of the Civil Rights Act. Establishing policies of race-conscious affirmative action and compensatory preferential treatment, courts and agencies posited group rights and equality of result as the new meaning of equal employment opportunity.

I

At the time the Civil Rights Act was passed, equality of opportunity was a concept that, as much as is possible in political life, had an agreed-upon if not self-evident meaning. The word "opportunity" refers to a favorable or advantageous combination of circumstances for accomplishing something; it has a prospective, active, forward-looking connotation. In this sense the term is not readily associated with traditional hierarchical societies, which were organized on the basis of distinctions defined by race, religion, social rank, or family that conferred legal privileges on some persons and disqualified others from a wide range of political and social activities. Modern liberal societies like the United States created equality of opportunity by abolishing, or refusing to establish at the outset, systems of legal privilege and disqualification.

In liberal societies, the legal order allows individuals to compete on the basis of their interests, abilities, and efforts under the right of common citizenship. In his account of American society in the early nineteenth century, the French philosopher and political theorist Alexis de Tocqueville described the widespread equality of condition that he observed in his travels in the United States. What he meant by equality of condition was that, in the United States, the great majority of its citizens were able to achieve independence and attain a good and decent standard of living because of the existence of equality of opportunity, defined as the absence of legally defined political and social privilege. Notwithstanding the existence of slavery, the defining principle of American nationality was the idea of equality of opportunity and common citizenship under republican government.

A century later, this same idea guided and informed the civil rights movement and the adoption of the Civil Rights Act of 1964. "Our historic and universal acceptance of equality of opportunity, justice and liberty as the standards of the American way of life," declared an analyst of employment discrimination in 1947, "has bred a struggle to square the national conscience with the fact that minority racial and religious groups, so prevalent in our nation, do not find this 'a land of equal opportunity for all'."[1] Fair employment laws were intended to abolish race as a legitimate factor in private employment decision-making. Under them lay the idea that, if given an equal opportunity, blacks would be able to pursue their interests as individuals and achieve a level of economic independence and prosperity determined by their ability and efforts.

Decades of racism, institutionalized under the theory of racial group rights on which the segregation doctrine of separate-but-equal was based, made civil rights advocates acutely aware of the meaning of equality of opportunity. The concept of equal opportunity is exemplified in impartial procedures that treat individuals equally—that is, that create a situation where they can compete on the basis of ability and be judged according to achievement, rather than irrelevant criteria over which they have no control. As public policy, equal employment opportunity consists of procedural requirements that, through the prohibition of specific racially motivated practices, have the positive result of expanding the sphere of individual liberty. Equal opportunity is a persuasive and appealing social philosophy because it offers the prospect of individual advancement and progress. In policy terms it is concerned with forms, rules, procedures, and practices that are directed toward the end of enabling individuals to demonstrate personal effort and merit.[2]

Equality of opportunity is the social philosophy of modern industrial market societies. It is individual-regarding and presupposes a single class based on common citizenship. Civil rights organizations in the 1950s were especially clear in underscoring the individualist character of equal opportunity. Objecting to arguments for racial quotas advanced by some supporters of civil rights in the latter part of the 1950s, Jack Greenberg of the NAACP stated that "civil rights groups do not aim to perpetuate their group interest since the group interest itself is to eliminate the socially enforced group identity." Greenberg recognized that a theory of group rights cannot guarantee equality for individuals. "The chief problem with quotas," he wrote, "is that they introduce a potentially retrogressive concept into the cherished notion of individual equality." "If groups are admissible," he asked, "when do we stop considering whether the group is sufficiently represented and commence weighing whether the individual is not?" Because the NAACP was seeking to establish equality of opportunity, Greenberg questioned a policy that would "give the group concept a secure foothold," promoting "corporate as distinct from individual concepts of individual human rights."[3]

Race-conscious affirmative action is philosophically grounded on the group rights concept that Greenberg and other civil rights leaders rejected in the 1950s. It aims at equality of condition rather than equality of opportunity. Affirmative action's supporters argue that the abolition of race, religion, sex, and national origin as legal qualifications for employment or other activities in society does not create equal opportunity. When these disabilities are removed, it is contended, individuals still differ in significant ways with respect to talent, interest, ability, determination, and other personal qualities. According to proponents of affirmative action, opportunity does not consist of the forms and procedures that create circumstances where individuals can demonstrate merit. Opportunity is substantive in nature, consisting of the social and cultural factors that produce or determine what has traditionally and erroneously been labeled individual merit and ability. Equality of opportunity can therefore only exist, according to the theory of affirmative action, when the conditions that determine the qualifications of individuals are equal. Equality of opportunity thus becomes equality of condition or result.

Stated in this form, affirmative action is a theory of equality that requires comprehensive and systematic social engineering in order to eliminate or negate the natural differences between individuals. It seeks the utopian goal of making all persons equally qualified for engaging in the various activities covered by the civil rights laws. As a means of dealing with the differences between individuals that the rule of equal opportunity recognizes and permits to exist, affirmative action tends toward one or both of what James Madison in *Federalist* No. 10 said were the two methods of removing the causes of faction: "the one, by destroying the liberty which is essential to its existence; the other, by giving to every citizen the same opinions, the same passions, and the same interests."[4] Affirmative action policymakers have not sought, or have been unable, to create equality of result through systematic policies of social and cultural conditioning and economic control. Using the instruments of the regulatory welfare state, they have adopted a less coercive solution that regards private employment as a public utility and seeks to control the outcome of the employment process as a problem in industrial relations.

Through legal doctrines and administrative regulations that will be examined subsequently, affirmative action policy forces employers to give jobs and other employment benefits to blacks and other protected groups. Under the legal theory of affirmative action, the only way an employer can successfully resist government requirements of race-conscious preferential treatment under Title VII of the Civil Rights Act is to claim that its existing employment practices are justified by business necessity. (Not the least significant result of affirmative action is thus to reduce the idea of business freedom and entrepreneurial liberty to a legal demonstration of necessity.) Regulated by affirmative action rules and measured in terms of racial group proportionality or balance, the results of the employment process are then submitted as evidence that the procedural requirements of equal opportunity, which are written into Title VII and other civil rights laws, have been satisfied. In this way group-based equality of result is substituted for equality of opportunity.

Congress adopted equal opportunity as the rule for employment relations in the Civil Rights Act because it offers the best basis for securing the rights of life, liberty, and the pursuit of happiness set forth in the Declaration of Independence for the mutual benefit of both individual citizens and the community as a whole. Equal opportunity based on individual rights, by making individuals responsible for themselves, enables them to gain the rewards of dignity, pride, and self-respect that come from individual achievement. Grounded in a realistic understanding of human nature, equal opportunity recognizes the importance of autonomy and independence for each individual in a framework of ordered liberty. Moreover, by accepting differences between people and rejecting the possibility of perfect equality of condition or achievement among individuals or groups, it permits the recognition of other essential social values, such as personal liberty, the family, voluntary associations, and economic incentives.[5] Equality of opportunity reconciles individual rights and interests with the common good in a way that is impossible under affirmative action, which proposes to distribute social goods and resources according to schemes of racially proportionate equality that deny the natural rights of individuals on which a prosperous and free society rests.

II

The origin of equal employment opportunity as a legal right lies in the Thirteenth, Fourteenth, and Fifteenth Amendments and the civil rights laws adopted after the Civil War to integrate the freed slaves into society on the basis of legal and civil equality.[6] In addition to protecting rights of personal liberty, access to the legal system, and domestic relations, these measures secured rights of entrepreneurial freedom and employment opportunity. The Civil Rights Act of 1866, for example, conferred the right to purchase, lease, sell, hold, and convey real and personal property and to make and enforce contracts. Although blacks used these rights to create a new system of labor relations and improve their socioeconomic status, the employment opportunities opened to them in the decades after Reconstruction were in no realistic sense equal to those of whites.[7] This condition was in large part the result of Jim Crow policies in the southern states; by the early twentieth century, with the approval of the national government, they had effectively disenfranchised and denied the civil rights of black citizens.

In time the interpretation of the Constitution that permitted this system of race relations to exist, epitomized in the "separate but equal" rule of *Plessy v. Ferguson* (1896), came to be recognized as erroneous. Guided by Justice Harlan's dissenting opinion in *Plessy* that the Constitution was color-blind, the twentieth century civil rights movement sought to abolish legalized racial discrimination and guarantee equal protection of the laws in the areas of voting, jury service, office-holding, public facilities, government services, and public education. Equal employment opportunity, however, occupied a different status in the civil rights reform program. While the Fourteenth Amendment declared that no state shall deprive any person of life, liberty, or property without due process of law, it did not prohibit private discrimination. Accordingly, private employers could lawfully differentiate among applicants or employees on the basis of race, color, religion, education, ability, performance, or any other reason that suited them.[8]

Although deeply embedded in the public philosophy, equal opportunity in employment was not a legally recognized or actionable right. In a political sense, an individual's interest in freedom from discrimination in employment could be viewed as part of his broader interest in freely disposing of his labor, and occasionally courts endorsed the notion that the right to work was a natural right rooted in the common law and protected by the Constitution. In 1943, for example, a New Jersey court stated that "the right to earn a livelihood is a property right" guaranteed by the Fifth and Fourteenth Amendments.[9] As a practical matter, however, this right amounted to the right to seek a job and perform it if the employer was willing to hire the individual. In legal terms, the right to work was merely a right to contract for the sale of one's labor. In the absence of contract an employer could interfere with any individual's "right to work" as far as his business was concerned, under what courts described as its absolute discretion in matters of employment practice. Federal and state courts thus recognized the right of an employer to hire at will and set the terms and conditions of employment.[10]

In addition to employers, organized labor was a major source of discrimination in private employment prior to Title VII. Labor unions were defined under state law as private voluntary associations and protected by the common law rule which held that private individuals could not be forced into association against their will. Accordingly, unions were permitted to discriminate in their membership policies and organizational practices. In the early twentieth century, racial discrimination was a basic, structural feature of the development of organized labor. Through a process referred to as occupational eviction, blacks were excluded from national craft unions by explicit provisions or tacit agreement. Industrial unions that organized unskilled labor admitted blacks to membership, but placed them in segregated units and separate lines of seniority and job assignment according to race. In the legal framework of collective bargaining established by the National Labor Relations Act (NLRA) of 1935, employers accepted racial segregation and discrimination as a basic demand of organized labor.[11] In effect, the NLRA legalized and made the federal government a party to the discrimination practiced by the union movement.

By giving organized labor formal recognition in national law, the act also made it possible to apply anti-discrimination pressure on the unions when job bias became an issue of civil rights concern in the 1940s. Under the Railway Labor Act of 1926, the NLRA, and the Taft-Hartley Act of 1947, unions were prohibited from unfair labor practices. The statutes also imposed a duty of fair representation that arguably required unions to abandon racially discriminatory practices. Even under the fair representation strategy, however, membership policies were exclusively under union control. Before the Civil Rights Act of 1964, it was not possible for a person excluded because of race to force a union to accept him through a federal judicial or administrative agency order.[12]

The first serious attempt to establish equal employment opportunity as a national policy occurred during World War II. In response to a threatened black protest march on Washington, D.C., in June 1941 President Franklin D. Roosevelt issued Executive Order 8802. The order prohibited discrimination in government employment and declared it to be the duty of employers and labor organizations to provide for the full and equitable participation of all workers in defense industries, without discrimination because of race, creed, color, or national origin. To enforce the order, Roosevelt created a Fair Employment Practices Committee (FEPC) with authority to receive and investigate complaints of discrimination and resolve them through negotiation with the aggrieved individual and the employer. In 1943, under Executive Order 9346, the president extended the anti-bias ban to government contractors and reconstituted and strengthened the FEPC, giving it authority to hold public hearings and issue findings of fact concerning discriminatory employment practices. Although the wartime FEPC had little permanent impact on employment practices and was terminated by Congress in 1946, it put employment discrimination on the civil rights agenda and pioneered the approach to ending job bias that was eventually embodied in the Civil Rights Act of 1964.[13]

The immediate background of equal employment opportunity policy in the 1960s was the fair employment practice legislation adopted by numerous states after World War II. Between 1945 and 1964, 26 states passed laws against job discrimination and established fair employment practice commissions. These measures typically declared it unlawful to refuse to hire or otherwise discriminate against an individual because of race, color, religion, or national origin. They were enforced through voluntary compliance and individual complaint resolution, backed by regulatory action. State fair employment practice commissions received and investigated complaints of discrimination from individuals; if they found the complaint to have merit, they attempted to persuade the employer to offer the applicant or employee the first available job for which he was qualified and to stop discriminating. If conciliation failed, the commission could hold a public hearing to consider evidence of alleged discrimination, make a finding of unlawful practice, and issue an order to cease and desist from the practice. The commission could also order the employer to remedy its discriminatory action by hiring, reinstatement, or upgrading (with or without back pay), and it could order a union to admit an individual to union membership.[14]

The federal background of equal employment opportunity policy in the 1960s consisted of a series of executive orders beginning in 1948 that required nondiscrimination in government contracts and in the federal civil service. Government contract committees were authorized to publicize, persuade, and conciliate disputes, but not to impose sanctions for noncompliance. Contracting officers in executive departments and agencies, more concerned with procuring goods and services than with ending discrimination, had the power to enforce the nondiscrimination requirement. Consequently, little progress was made against job bias. As support for civil rights enforcement spread in the 1950s, however, the potential of the federal contract program for creating employment opportunities and actually increasing minority employment began to emerge. The President's Committee on Government Contracts, under the direction of Vice-President Richard Nixon, conducted surveys of the racial composition of the federal work force in several cities, gathering statistical data that raised questions about possible discrimination and indirectly pressuring contractors to hire blacks. In a few instances the Nixon government contracts committee forced employers to hire blacks, using a tactic that would later be described as preferential treatment. At the end of the Eisenhower Administration, the Nixon-led committee considered a policy requiring government contractors to supply monthly racial surveys of their minority hiring performance, with timetables for increasing black employment.[15]

At the start of the 1960s, equal employment opportunity law and policy were less developed than other areas of civil rights concern. Experts agreed that legislation prohibiting racial discrimination in employment was necessary. Unlike issues such as voting rights and school desegregation, however, it was believed that job discrimination could be ended most effectively by an administrative agency exercising the authority to order an employer to cease and desist, rather than by judicial enforcement of an anti-discrimination law. The state experience with fair employment practice laws, as well as liberal ideological commitment to social and economic regulation by government agencies, justified this approach to employment discrimination.

Equal employment opportunity policy rests on the legal principles defining discrimination in employment practices. To discriminate is to make a distinction among individuals or treat someone differently from someone else. State law on fair employment practices declared it unlawful for employers to treat individuals differently on account of race. Although prejudice and discrimination are legally separate things, they are related in the sense that the latter, an overt social act, is believed to be caused by the former. Because the same act can be based on a variety of motives, an essential element of discrimination in the legal context is the mental process or state of mind of the alleged discriminator.[16] Difficult to establish even as a general proposition, proof of an individual's state of mind is especially elusive in an employment situation—compared, say, to the denial of voting rights. In the latter area, where qualifications are readily established and are less likely to be a reason for distinguishing among individuals, it is relatively easy to determine racial prejudice as the cause of black exclusion.[17] In employment, however, it is a bit different: the number of jobs is limited, qualifications of and differences between individuals are highly relevant, and numerous business considerations are legitimate. It is more difficult there to determine the motivation behind a decision.

In the absence of an overt discriminatory barrier—for example, an explicit policy against hiring blacks, or hiring only for low-level jobs—proof of discrimination under state law before Title VII consisted in a showing that an individual who was rejected was qualified, and that the employer's reasons for rejecting him were illegitimate or a pretext for discrimination. The possibility of a statistical group approach to proving discrimination was recognized but rejected. For example, the absence of blacks from a work force in a community with a ten percent black population was believed to be an insufficient basis for drawing an inference of discrimination, because it was impossible to predict the number of blacks that could be expected in the absence of discrimination. Prediction of an expected number depended on so many factors other than the percentage of blacks in the community—on the number of qualified blacks, the number of applicants, the number of jobs available—that its validity was doubtful.

Discrimination was also hard to prove in the 1940s and 1950s because some companies operated on a covert quota system which, while giving the appearance of nondiscrimination, actually concealed unequal treatment of individuals.[18] There was no doubt among employment law analysts that a quota system based on an outlawed standard such as race was just as discriminatory and illegal as complete exclusion because of it. This judgment also applied to so-called positive or benign quotas demanded by some black groups, which the Supreme Court disapproved in a 1950 case involving picketing.[19] In the absence of direct evidence, however, it was difficult to distinguish a carefully constructed quota system from the results of a chance distribution. Indeed, some legal commentators believed that the enactment of anti-discrimination laws might result in more widespread use of quotas as a means of concealing race-conscious practices. Moreover, it was thought that the desire to avoid the appearance of discrimination and the risk of an investigation by a state fair employment practice commission might lead employers to recruit and hire a certain number of blacks. However, the "paradox of the enactment of anti-discrimination statutes leading to the use of discriminatory quota systems," as one commentator expressed it, could be countered by insisting that the hiring of minority group individuals not be considered conclusive evidence that a qualified individual was not discriminated against.[20]

The evidentiary problems inherent in proving discrimination, combined with the general belief that prevention of discriminatory actions (rather than punishment after the event) was the purpose of fair employment practice laws, led civil rights advocates to support the regulatory approach to ending job bias. Administrative enforcement of equal employment opportunity had several disadvantages. The government, rather than private individuals, bore the burden and expense of investigating and carrying forward the charge of discrimination. Educational efforts to shape public opinion and encourage voluntary compliance were possible, and sanctions could be imposed on recalcitrant employers. A means of reconciling the interests of employee and employer, administrative enforcement of anti-discrimination law aimed at guaranteeing each individual equal opportunity while maintaining the employer's right of free choice and entrepreneurial liberty.[21]

III

The Civil Rights Act of 1964 was intended to establish color-blind equal employment opportunity through a combination of voluntary compliance, agency conciliation, and judicial enforcement in civil litigation of the personal right of individuals not to be discriminated against because of race. Under the pressure of direct action political protest and social upheaval in the late 1960s, federal courts and the civil rights bureaucracy abandoned this policy. They fashioned an administrative-judicial enforcement scheme that forced employers to give preferential treatment to racial and ethnic minorities under a new theory of discrimination based on the concepts of group rights and equality of result.

It is often assumed that affirmative action began as a color-blind individual rights policy, and it was gradually superseded by race-conscious measures only as it became clear that equality of opportunity was inadequate to the needs of the times.[22] Although not entirely inaccurate, this view ignores the extent to which racial preference was an objective of liberal equal employment opportunity policy throughout the 1960s. From the start of the Kennedy Administration in 1961, federal officials pursued race-conscious affirmative action by applying government pressure to hire members of favored minority groups, justifying the action by reference either to an explicit charge or an implicit perception of discrimination, which was defined as racial imbalance in the work force. This pressure can be sufficiently moderate to be compatible with the concept of voluntary compliance and employer autonomy, as it had tended to be under the government contract program before 1965. On the other hand, affirmative action pressure can be applied so forcefully as to constitute thinly disguised preferential treatment and reverse discrimination, as it was in the late 1960s and the 1970s. Affirmative action, which was created under the Kennedy Administration's revised contract program in 1961, acquired a statutory basis in Title VII of the Civil Rights Act. This law provided the long-sought federal fair employment practices measures by which, against its sponsors' intentions, equal employment opportunity was transformed into racial group equality of result.

To fulfill his campaign promise to improve on the civil rights record of the Eisenhower Administration, President Kennedy chose in 1961 to revise the government contract program rather than seek civil rights legislation. This strategy was dictated by the strength of southern Democrats in Congress who opposed any civil rights measures and by the fact that contract compliance put pressure directly on businessmen rather than organized labor, a key Democratic constituency. Executive Order 10925, issued in March 1961, confirmed the nondiscrimination requirement of previous executive orders dealing with the government contract program. The Kennedy order imposed a new obligation, however, directing federal contractors to "take affirmative action to ensure" that individuals were treated without regard to race, creed, color, or national origin.[23]

Soon to become the symbol of a new concept of racial equality, the term 'affirmative action' had occasionally been used with reference to remedial measures in labor relations and employment discrimination situations.[24] In Executive Order 10925, it referred to requirements that contractors post notices and make announcements of their nondiscrimination obligation and agree to furnish information and reports about their employment practices, including work force statistics. The Kennedy order created the President's Committee on Equal Employment Opportunity (PCEEO), which had the authority to enforce the affirmative action obligation by imposing sanctions in the form of contract cancellation or contractor debarment. Charged with monitoring equal opportunity in the federal government, the PCEEO was also required to review and publicize statistical surveys of the federal work force which departments and agencies were directed to conduct.

The President's Committee subordinated individual complaint processing and conciliation to group-based preferential hiring pegged to statistical patterns of minority underrepresentation. Plans for Progress, a program of voluntary compliance that exempted corporations from routine contract compliance enforcement, was the main instrument of the new approach. Over 250 companies signed agreements with the PCEEO in which they promised to conduct racial surveys of their work force and improve their practices to ensure employment equality. Strongly supported by Vice-President Johnson and approved by organized labor, Plans for Progress was the preferred Democratic solution to the problem of job bias from 1961 to 1964. Although attacked by the civil rights lobby as meaningless voluntarism, it anticipated what was later called "systemic" anti-discrimination policy. By drawing businessmen into anti-bias efforts, it also helped prepare the way for the Civil Rights Act of 1964.[25]

While PCEEO could not ignore complaint processing, it regarded work force profiles based on racial canvassing that showed underutilization of minority groups as the most important feature of the contract compliance program. Informed of the statistical impact of their employment practices, government contractors were expected to take affirmative action to correct any problems. The real object of affirmative action, according to the PCEEO, was pervasive institutional discrimination in society, discrimination beyond the formal barriers existing in the employment office or union hiring hall, that denied blacks education, training, and the personal initiative and motivation needed to compete.[26] A Civil Rights Commission staff member expounded the emerging theory of affirmative action. He stated that while employers might be guilty of "unconscious discrimination" by using traditional sources of recruitment, it was a waste of time to try to prove that discrimination existed. The government should provide equal opportunity; to do so, it should consider adopting preferential treatment. Asserting that past discrimination must be rectified by permitting blacks to participate fully in society, he said this goal could be achieved by "imaginative, wise and compassionate administration" of anti-discrimination laws and affirmative action programs.[27]

Proposed regulations of the Bureau of Apprenticeship and Training in the Labor Department of 1963 illustrated the tendency toward preferential treatment as the new meaning of equal opportunity. The regulations stated that apprenticeship selection should be by objective examination. In the absence of objective standards, however, labor-management councils had to prove the existence of equal treatment by accepting a significant number of minority group applicants or by setting aside a significant number of openings for such applicants. In acting upon existing application lists, moreover, councils were required to offset the effects of previous practices that resulted in discriminatory employment patterns. Unions and contractors objected that the regulations set up a quota system, arguing that the government was defining discrimination as industrial practices, rather than as prejudicial acts denying equal treatment to individuals. Adopted with slight modifications, the Labor Department regulations contained two additional features that anticipated subsequent affirmative action. They denied any intent to select applicants according to the population percentage of any racial group and stated that apprentices could be selected "in any manner that assures equality of opportunity and which is acceptable to the Administrator."[28] In other words, affirmative action meant whatever the government said it meant.

The Kennedy Administration supported race-conscious affirmative action in the context of the national controversy over preferential treatment that formed the background for the congressional debate over Title VII in 1964. The administration's outlook reflected the belief of black protest leaders that civil rights policy should no longer profess racial impartiality. Expressing the new view, a National Urban League official told a congressional committee in 1961:

> I am sick and tired of people saying they are color-blind so they do not have to give up any information . . . I think the time has come where the problem is so great that being color-blind for an official of government is no longer a virtue. What we need to be is positively color conscious and go to work on this job of color and know what we are doing.[29]

The same strategy was applied in private industry. In 1962, for example, the Congress of Racial Equality made compensatory preference for blacks the object of protests against job bias. Asserting that businessmen had a responsibility to find qualified blacks or provide on-the-job training to those who were unqualified, civil rights spokesmen argued that in the absence of discrimination, blacks would have acquired the skills and experience needed to compete in the labor market. They contended that representative numbers of blacks should be employed in each job category and that blacks should be given an advantage over equally qualified whites. While agreeing with critics that quotas were illegal and morally unacceptable, civil rights lobbyists denied that their proposals amounted to quota hiring or preferential treatment. They were simply seeking special treatment to overcome the negative special treatment imposed on blacks in the past. Roy Wilkins of the NAACP reasoned that blacks should be placed in the positions from which they were excluded until racial imbalance was corrected.[30]

Meanwhile, civil rights attorneys devised a strategy for promoting minority preference that would avoid the evidentiary problems of proving discrimination in court. The essential element of the strategy was the contention that a *prima facie* charge of discrimination should be based on the absence or scarcity of blacks in the work force. Employers who were uncertain about rebutting the charge, and who wanted to avoid the appearance of discrimination, could then be persuaded to hire a specific number of blacks while not admitting to unlawful practices. This approach (soon to be conceptualized as the disparate impact theory of discrimination) offered a promising alternative to individual complaint processing, which fair employment lawyers were convinced was inadequate for achieving employment equality. The disparate impact approach supplied the new standard for defining discrimination that the civil rights lobby considered necessary to eliminate deeply entrenched patterns of job bias and establish rules for permanent compliance with affirmative action by employers.[31]

Many companies responded favorably to black demands for compensatory preference in employment. The business press in the early 1960s reported intensive recruiting of black applicants, relaxed hiring standards, less reliance on objective tests, and willingness to take into account educational deficiencies and cultural disadvantages of black candidates. Influenced by changing public opinion, black protest demands, and the threat of federal contract cut-off, leading corporations chose not to make equal employment opportunity a fighting issue. Unlike southern state governments, businessmen were not "massing for the defense" as the struggle for civil rights enforcement increased in intensity.[32]

Although supported by some business groups, preferential treatment provoked strong opposition. Critics attacked it as a contradiction of the equal rights principle, arguing that it exacerbated racial tension and was inherently unjust. Noting state fair employment practice proposals to investigate racial imbalance in the work force, opponents warned against government bureaucrats who, in the guise of enforcing anti-discrimination laws, would treat individuals as " 'ethnic groups' to be manipulated according to some sociological dictum." Unqualified blacks, it was charged, would be hired "to sit by the door" merely to satisfy demands for preferential employment, but would remain outside the economic mainstream. Ultimately, critics contended, a requirement of "equal representation of every segment of the population in every working force would . . . mean the end of freedom."[33]

Preferential treatment became sufficiently controversial in 1963 to provoke comment from President Kennedy. Stating that the past could not be undone and that most blacks wanted equal rather than special treatment, the President said in a press conference: "I think we ought not to begin the quota system." Kennedy put a gloss on the equal rights principle, however, that could accommodate the informal race-conscious practices that the administration at the time was engaged in supporting. Urging that every qualified individual be given an opportunity, he advised employers to "look over our employment rolls, look over areas where we are hiring people and at least make sure we are giving everyone a fair chance. But not hard and fast quotas."[34]

IV

Southern intransigence and escalating black protests forced the Kennedy Administration to change its civil rights policy in 1963 to support comprehensive anti-discrimination legislation. Among the proposals considered, equal employment opportunity legislation, which had long been opposed by the southern Democrat-conservative Republican coalition as a threat to entrepreneurial freedom, faced the largest obstacle. Deciding how to draft a bill against job bias proved no less problematic.

The favored liberal solution was to declare equal employment opportunity a public right enforceable by an administrative agency with powers to initiate investigations, make charges of discrimination, and seek a settlement through conciliation. If negotiation failed, the agency could make findings of unlawful practices. It could then issue a cease and desist order that would eliminate the discrimination and provide a remedy for the complainant. This method avoided waiting for individual complaints, and it found discrimination in routine industrial practices rather than in specific acts denying equal treatment because of race. A bill introduced by Senator Hubert Humphrey and reported by the

Senate Committee on Labor and Public Welfare in 1963 was illustrative. It proposed to equalize disparities in "[a]ll of the incidents and conditions of employment opportunity," including not only hiring, promotion, transfer, and seniority, but also recruitment, apprenticeship, access to employment facilities, and other things "necessary to the achievement of equality as an existing reality in the operation of the national job market."

According to the Labor and Public Welfare Committee, this bill was intended to find employers in violation "not only if they overtly discriminated against Negro job applicants but also if their employment practices in collateral areas of employment opportunity denied equality of treatment." Explaining the broad scope of the measure, Senator Humphrey asserted that "willful discrimination is often commingled with many impersonal institutional processes which nevertheless determine the availability of jobs for nonwhite employees."[35] Providing for enforcement by an agency with cease and desist powers, the Humphrey bill proposed to remove barriers to equal opportunity. If these barriers were to be defined with reference to institutional discrimination reflected in patterns of disparate racial impact, however, as seemed likely, the measure implicitly pointed to group rights and equality of result— employment equality rather than equality of opportunity—as the goal of employment bias policy.

From 1961 to 1963, liberals had no success in pursuing job discrimination bills. When the administration decided to support civil rights legislation, House liberals added to the omnibus administration bill a proposal for a new national FEPC with cease and desist authority. This was substituted for the administration's recommendation that the President's Committee on Equal Employment Opportunity be retained and given statutory recognition. The House liberals' bill was too radical, so a new measure was drafted. Dropping cease and desist powers, the new bill created an agency to receive and initiate complaints, investigate and seek conciliation, and file discrimination charges in court. The bill declared it unlawful for private employers to fail or refuse to hire, to limit or classify, or otherwise discriminate against or adversely affect an individual's status because of race, color, religion, or national origin.[36] The civil rights bill containing this employment discrimination title passed the House in February 1964.

In the Senate, the moderate House job bias title was still considered too radical and another version—the Dirksen-Mansfield substitute amendment—was introduced. This measure, Title VII as enacted, contained the same nondiscrimination requirement, but it denied the Equal Employment Opportunity Commission (EEOC) the power to go to court to enforce the act. If EEOC conciliation failed, only the individual complainant was permitted to file a suit charging unlawful discrimination. EEOC authority was further weakened by a provision allowing state commissions to preempt the federal agency in dealing with discrimination complaints. To balance this dilution of agency power, the Senate substitute gave the Attorney General authority to initiate what were called pattern or practice discrimination suits. The term "pattern or practice of discrimination" had not been used in any previous fair employment legislation, and its meaning was obscure. Liberals said it referred to the actions of an individual employer or company that consistently or avowedly denied rights in a routine or generalized way, while conservatives believed the language would be applied collectively to employers in an industry, community, or area.[37]

Title VII was intended to settle the controversy over quotas and preferential treatment that existed in the early 1960s. This intent was mainly expressed in the nondiscrimination principle that was the heart of the bill. It was clarified and reinforced by a series of amendments provoked by opponents' fears that the law would be used to require race-conscious preferential treatment.

Several southern Democrats and northern and midwestern conservative Republicans asserted that Title VII could be interpreted to establish quotas based on the percentage of blacks in the local population. Noting that the bill did not in express terms define discrimination, critics said EEOC would regard racial imbalance in the work force as evidence of discrimination and would pressure employers into quota hiring in conciliation proceedings. In order to avoid statistically-based discrimination charges, employers would in turn engage in preferential minority hiring of their own accord. Opponents contended that civil suits would produce the same result. Courts would accept racial disparity in the work force as sufficient for a *prima facie* case, shifting the burden to the employer to prove in effect that his practices were free of bias and did not discriminate. According to critics, the bill failed to require proof of intent to discriminate, a necessary element in traditional discrimination law and a major part of the plaintiff's burden. It was suggested that this omission would permit courts to impute intent to an employer under the tort law doctrine that a person intends the natural and probable consequences of his actions.[38]

The sponsors of Title VII unequivocally rejected the view that it was in any way intended or capable of being interpreted to promote race-conscious preferential practices. They stated that under the act, according to the universal understanding, discrimination was unequal treatment of individuals in a procedural sense, motivated by racial bias.

Denying that racial imbalance could be considered evidence of discrimination, supporters said that the plaintiff would have the burden of proof, intent was a necessary element in proving discrimination, and courts, upon finding a violation, could only order an end to the unlawful practice as well as reinstatement and back pay for the individual. A court could not order quotas or preference for a racial group. Title VII, said its sponsors, was prospective rather than retrospective legislation; it did not reach pre-act discrimination. The act did not intend to correct for the past; cultural and educational disadvantages, such as might be reflected in a minority candidate's low test performance, were not relevant to the determination of unlawful discrimination. Judicial enforcement of Title VII thus presented no possibility of preferential treatment, and the EEOC was even less cause for concern in this respect. With no rulemaking or adjudicatory power, the commission could merely receive or initiate complaints, investigate, and seek voluntary conciliation. It could not require employment practices to achieve racial balance.[39]

Responding to criticism, the authors of Title VII accepted several amendments intended to protect employer prerogatives and to preclude preferential treatment and quotas. Employers were permitted to make distinctions among employees in accordance with a bona fide seniority or merit system, provided such differences were not the result of an intent to discriminate. Employers were also authorized to use any professionally developed ability test, provided its administration and actions based on test results were not designed, intended, or used to discriminate because of race. A third amendment stated that nothing in Title VII was to be interpreted as requiring an employer to grant preferential treatment to any individual or group on account of racial imbalance. Furthermore, the section providing for judicial remedies was amended to clarify the fact that the act was concerned with intentional discrimination, not racial imbalance or disparate impact (which would reflect societal discrimination). As amended, it stated that judicial relief could be ordered upon a finding that an employer intentionally engaged in an unlawful employment practice.

As finally enacted, then, Title VII declared it an unlawful practice for an employer or labor union with 25 or more employees or members to fail or refuse to hire, to exclude or expel from membership, or otherwise discriminate against any individual in the terms and conditions of employment because of race, color, religion, sex, or national origin. The act also declared it unlawful to limit, segregate, or classify employees or union members in any way that would deprive any individual of employment opportunities or otherwise adversely affect his status as an employee because of his race or other prohibited characteristics. Title

VII created a five-member Equal Employment Opportunity Commission, authorizing it to receive complaints of discrimination from individuals, investigate, and (upon determining there was reasonable cause to believe the charge was true), seek to eliminate the alleged unlawful practice by informal negotiation, conciliation, and persuasion. If EEOC conciliation failed, the individual complainant could bring a civil action against the employer or union. The act provided that if a court found an employer guilty of intentional discrimination, it could require the unlawful practice to be discontinued and order such affirmative action as might be appropriate, including reinstatement or hiring with or without back pay. Finally, the attorney general could bring a civil action if he had reason to believe a person or group of persons was engaged in a pattern or practice of denying rights secured by the act.

Read in the light of its legislative history, Title VII constitutes a clear rejection of the demand for preferential treatment raised by the civil rights lobby in the early 1960s. Because the rule of law requires courts to apply statutes as written and intended by the legislature, the subsequent introduction of race-conscious affirmative action, purportedly under authority of the Civil Rights Act, makes the purpose and intent of Title VII a pertinent and contested issue. Supporters of affirmative action argue that preferential practices are necessary to carry out the goal of improving economic conditions of blacks and other minority groups by guaranteeing a right to equal employment. Critics contend that the purpose of Title VII is to improve the economic status of blacks by guaranteeing equal employment opportunity based on the nondiscrimination principle. The latter view is not only more accurate historically, but it is also more consistent with the principles of individual natural rights and equality before the law on which national civil rights policy rests.

The intent of Title VII is to be found in its express provisions and legislative history. In ascertaining legislative intent, the views of the supporters of Title VII are to be accorded more weight than those of its opponents. The latter predicted that, in a practical sense, discrimination would as an evidentiary matter be defined in the same racial group terms that characterized the segregation system. More broadly, they held that the logic of race relations—and of any anti-discrimination law—was that of racial balance, group rights, and proportional equality of result. The proponents of Title VII, said Senator Stennis of Mississippi, "do not want a quota system." They "do not dare put [quota provisions] in the bill" because "such proposals draw blood and a quick response" in the north, where they were opposed.[40] Yet opponents believed the provisions of the law would result in *de facto* racially proportionate hiring or quotas in the South, the principal target of the Civil Rights Act. The southern critics' arguments forced the supporters of Title VII to accept anti-preferential provisions, and to assert their disapproval of quotas more clearly and emphatically than they otherwise might have. These professions of anti-quota purpose and intent can be accepted as genuine, without denying that supporters of Title VII were aware of, and were probably willing to accept, *de facto* quotas that might result from administrative and judicial enforcement of the law.[41] Nevertheless, Title VII requires equal opportunity based on individual rights and is intended to prohibit race-conscious employment practices.

V

The redefinition of American equality under the concepts of group rights and equality of result, modestly begun by the Kennedy Administration's government contract program, accelerated with the start of Title VII enforcement in 1965. The Equal Employment Opportunity Commission was the unlikely instrument of this transformation. Denied authority to issue cease and desist orders against discriminatory employers, the EEOC could not even take alleged violators to court. With respect to formal powers, it was weaker than the state fair employment practice commissions, which were themselves increasingly regarded in civil rights circles as inadequate for dealing with the problem of job bias. The EEOC's limited powers included investigating individual and commissioner-initiated charges, making findings of reasonable cause to believe discrimination had occurred, and conciliating disputes between the complainant and the employer. The commission could also issue procedural interpretations of Title VII and file *amicus curiae* briefs in individual discrimination cases. Despite the very limited nature of its authority, however, the EEOC revised the basic principles of employment discrimination law and began the transformation of equality of opportunity into equality of result.

Congress conceived of individual dispute resolution as the principal function of the EEOC. The civil rights organizations that were the Commission's major constituency believed this policy to be essentially futile; instead, they proposed to attack statistically defined patterns of discrimination. For political as well as statutory reasons the EEOC decided it had to process individual complaints, which were far more numerous than expected and created a virtually perpetual backlog. Its central focus, however, reflecting the outlook of the civil rights lobby, was to promote minority hiring by identifying patterns of institutional discrimination.

A White House conference on employment discrimination in August 1965, a month after the Commission came into existence, indicated the direction of EEOC policy. Commissioners, staff, and clientele groups agreed that discrimination should be defined as patterns of social and economic disadvantage caused by employment practices and social institutions in general, in relation to which complaint processing and case-by-case litigation were irrelevant. The conference envisioned a policy requiring employers to conduct racial surveys, generate and publicize profiles of under-representation problems, and hire minorities. This could be done through conciliation after the filing of a commissioner complaint or through class action suits based on racial disparity in the work force. A *prima facie* charge thus having been made, the burden of proof would shift to the employer, in all likelihood disposing of the case and leading to affirmative action hiring as a remedy for discrimination. The Commission's constituent groups further proposed that past discrimination, especially in the operation of seniority systems, be brought within the scope of Title VII and that objective tests be examined for discriminatory impact and required to be job-related.[42]

EEOC policy from 1965 to 1970 followed the course thus outlined. Executive director Herman Edelsberg reported after one year that the Commission viewed discrimination not as "an act of individual malice but more an element of a pattern of customary conduct." Employers might not consciously intend to discriminate, but "traditional attitudes and patterns of conduct in business . . . may have the effect of barring minorities from employment opportunities as surely as overt discrimination itself." Edelsberg observed that although affirmative action in the form of expanded recruitment was widely accepted, this might "not produce affirmative results, and it is results that are needed." Where a pattern of discrimination was determined, the remedy should "require specific results, immediate hiring and promotion of Negroes . . . rather than procedures that offer them equal opportunity in the future." In a practical sense, he wrote privately to civil rights leaders, "the name of the game in EEOC is jobs." Unable to file court charges, the EEOC conducted racial surveys of the drug, petroleum, textile, insurance, publishing, banking, travel, and communication industries, and held public hearings attacking patterns of discrimination. Avoiding the procedural difficulties of complaint resolution, it pressured employers into minority hiring. EEOC chairman Clifford Alexander stated in 1968: "We . . . here at EEOC believe in numbers . . . our most valid standard is in numbers . . . in a variety of categories, not just total numbers . . . The only accomplishment is when we look at all those numbers and see a vast improvement in the picture."[43]

Although lacking substantive rule-making authority, EEOC advanced new principles of employment discrimination law through its power to make reasonable cause findings, issue procedural regulations, and file *amicus* briefs. Rather than mediate conflicts between employees and employers, it consistently took the plaintiffs' side in matters ranging from technical requirements for filing complaints to the problem of defining the legal meaning of discrimination. The Commission treated Title VII as broadly remedial and retrospective in nature, rather than simply prospective. Pre-act practices could be reached under the doctrine that the present effects of past discrimination were unlawful. Asserting this 'present effects' doctrine in seniority desegregation cases, the EEOC argued that victims of discrimination were entitled to the position they would have occupied in the absence of discrimination. Civil rights leaders referred to this as the moderate 'rightful place' theory of relief; it was contrasted to the radical 'freedom now' theory that would have blacks displace whites, and the conservative 'status quo' theory that would simply end discrimination in the future. The EEOC also issued guidelines on employment testing intended to force employers to eliminate or modify the use of tests that had a disparate impact on minority groups and were not specifically job-related.

Because they neither conformed to notice and comment requirements of the Administrative Procedure Act nor rested on administrative law fact-finding, EEOC guidelines and reasonable cause determinations were not legally binding.[44] Nevertheless, in the atmosphere of social crisis typical of the late 1960s, they were given great deference by the judiciary as an interpretation of Title VII. Moreover, while the EEOC had no direct legal enforcement authority, employers responded to government pressures. Unwilling to appear opposed to civil rights or fearful of urban riots, many companies engaged in preferential practices.[45]

VI

While the EEOC developed theories of employment discrimination law that formed the basis for subsequent judicial revision of Title VII, the government contract program had more immediate significance in establishing preferential practices in industry. In response to demands from the civil rights organizations to strengthen contract compliance, in September 1965 President Johnson issued a new executive order. Reaffirming the affirmative action obligation of President Kennedy's 1961 order, Executive Order 11246 abolished the President's Committee on Equal Employment Opportunity and transferred its function to the Secretary of Labor, who created the Office of Federal Contract Compliance (OFCC). Although contract compliance continued to be decentralized in the executive departments and agencies that awarded federal contracts, the OFCC issued regulations imposing more stringent requirements on contractors. This tendency reached a climax in the Philadelphia plan of 1969, requiring quota hiring in the construction industry in a major metropolitan area.

Affirmative action in contract compliance was directed at collective social and institutional discrimination, rather than individual discriminatory acts defined as denial of equal treatment in a procedural sense. Implicitly resting on the theory of disparate impact discrimination, the executive order program constituted a simpler and more direct form of government coercion than Title VII enforcement because it was not concerned with the legal question of the meaning of unlawful discrimination. Whereas under Title VII judicial relief could not be ordered except on a finding of unlawful practices, the executive department agencies that awarded government contracts operated under no such limitation. They could require affirmative action as a condition of doing business with the government, and could define it to mean whatever they pleased. If employers wanted to retain or bid on federal contracts, they had to accept the government's view of affirmative action or be found in noncompliance.

The OFCC faced the same employment discrimination problems as the EEOC, including seniority system desegregation, transfer rights, upgrading, apprentice selection, testing, and racial canvassing of the work force. Although the executive order program was intended to be prospective, the OFCC believed it could focus either on preventing discrimination in the future or on eliminating the effects of past discrimination. Under pressure to keep up with the more ideologically militant EEOC and overcome a reputation for being soft on contractors, the OFCC adopted a remedial rationale based on concepts of institutional racism and systemic discrimination. OFCC director Edward C. Sylvester told a congressional committee in 1968, for example, that while overt discrimination was declining, racial discrimination was increasingly defined in terms of structural impediments rather than discrete prejudicial actions.[46]

To convince skeptics in the civil rights lobby that it had a tough enforcement policy, the OFCC emphasized "result-oriented" affirmative action. One contract compliance officer explained the new approach thus: "All that is needed is to take the employer to the cliff and say, 'Look over, baby.' "[47] Critics of affirmative action objected that under OFCC policy, contrary to the statutory and regulatory requirements governing public contracting, the precise scope and content of the affirmative action obligation was unclear. As conceived by the OFCC, however, affirmative action was intended to be vague and imprecise. Only in this form could it be successful, for to specify the meaning of affirmative action in terms of minority hiring results was believed to constitute a quota policy in violation of Title VII.[48] In order to avoid the prohibitions of the statutory nondiscrimination principle, the government in a basically under-handed way forced contractors to take affirmative action.

Director Edward C. Sylvester explained that the OFCC did not insist on a strict statistical approach to affirmative action because it regarded numbers merely as a measurement of equal employment progress. Conceding that contract officials pressured employers to hire blacks if demographic data provided the basis for an expectation of minority access, he said: "We really prefer that the contractor determine himself what affirmative action he can take." Sylvester told a conference of government contractors: "I don't pretend to have a definition of affirmative action that is going to satisfy everybody here." The obligation would vary according to the situation—"from day to day, from place to place, from escalation to escalation"—depending on the local labor market and the kinds of businesses in the community. But in "a general way," he declared, "affirmative action is anything that you have to do to get results."[49]

Pressure both from the civil rights lobby, which sought more rigorous enforcement of the contract obligation, and from critics of affirmative action, who sought to stop the trend toward race-conscious practices, led the Johnson Administration to adopt "hard and fast" quotas instead of the strategy of coerced yet non-specific minority hiring.

Quotas developed as a technical requirement of contract compliance. In public contracting, the concept of "contractor responsibility" refers to the technical and financial capability, professional character and integrity, and tenacity and perseverance of firms seeking to win government contracts. These are general qualifications that enable the government to have confidence that a contractor will perform well. The ability to meet the nondiscrimination requirement of Executive Order 11246 was considered an aspect of contractor responsibility. The concept of "bid responsiveness," on the other hand, refers to the ability of the contractor to meet the specific requirements and specifications of a particular contract.[50] In 1966, the OFCC started a policy of pre-award compliance reviews that shifted the affirmative action obligation from the area of contractor responsibility to that of bid responsiveness. Before the actual award of a contract, the low-bid contractor was required to satisfy the government that it could meet the affirmative action obligation. This in effect made affirmative action an additional requirement of the contract, without identifying it in the bid specifications or stating specifically what it consisted of.

As part of the pre-award policy, written affirmative action plans were mandated in 1968. The Department of Labor required contractors with $50,000 in contract work or 50 employees to submit written affirmative action plans based on a "utilization evaluation" identifying problem areas in minority employment. The evaluation was to depend on analysis of minority group "representation" in all job categories, as well as a review of recruitment sources, testing, upgrading, and transfer and promotion actions. If deficiencies were revealed, specific goals and timetables were to be submitted to achieve full and equal employment opportunity. The OFCC said the purpose of having written plans was to make sure affirmative action was dealt with like any other aspect of business enterprise.[51]

Racial discrimination in the construction industry provided the occasion for introducing quotas in the form of goals and timetables as a requirement of affirmative action in the Philadelphia plan of 1969. In 1967, federal contractors in Cleveland and Philadelphia were told they had to submit, under the pre-award policy, affirmative action plans assuring minority group representation in all trades in all phases of the work. A "manning table" stating the number of minority employees to be hired was the key feature of an affirmative action plan. Federal officials informed contractors that although the choice of methods was their own, an affirmative action plan "must have the result of producing minority group representation."[52] Simultaneously, the OFCC prepared to extend the manning table requirement to all federal agency and federal-aid construction projects.

The Johnson Administration's more coercive policy was intended to appeal to the civil rights lobby without antagonizing organized labor, which attacked affirmative action as reverse discrimination. Attempting to placate the construction unions, the heart of the opposition to race-conscious policies, Secretary of Labor Willard Wirtz said the manning table requirement was more symbolic than substantive. It was justified as a response to a specific problem, "But it isn't right as a general policy and it won't work," he explained.[53] The situation was one which Republicans could exploit politically. If the administration acknowledged or could be shown to be using a quota policy, it would alienate the construction unions. If it backed down from a more aggressive insistence on quotas, it would provoke criticism from the civil rights lobby. Either way, a split between key Democratic party constituent groups would be encouraged, to Republicans' advantage. In these circumstances a southern Republican, Representative William C. Cramer of Florida, attacked the Johnson Administration's incipient quota policy by requesting the General Accounting Office (GAO) to investigate the legality of OFCC's manning table requirements.

The GAO is an agency in the legislative branch charged with auditing and determining the legality of the expenditure of public funds by the departments and agencies of the executive branch. Politically accountable to Congress, it is not likely to act contrary to the policy of the party that controls that body. Since Congress was then under Democratic control, the GAO's decision to intervene at Cramer's request shows that the party was divided on affirmative action. On its own initiative, moreover, as part of an ongoing bureaucratic struggle with the executive branch in which it sought to establish its final authority to review the legality of federal expenditures, the GAO was reviewing the pre-award policy aimed at minority hiring even before contractors complained about it. Accordingly, in both May and November of 1968, the GAO advised the Department of Labor that pre-award negotiations on affirmative action, as in the Cleveland and Philadelphia plans, were inconsistent with the rules of competitive bidding. The rules required that invitations to bids offer equal and unambiguous terms and conditions to all bidders; under the OFCC policy, though, government contract agencies did not state the minimum standards for equal employment opportunity. The GAO therefore concluded that a contract could wrongfully be denied to the low bidder based on the arbitrary decision of a contract compliance officer.[54]

In response to the growing opposition to race-conscious policy, Congress tried to stop the practice of pre-award affirmative action bargaining. In the Federal-aid Highway Act of 1968, it directed the Secretary of Transportation to obtain compliance with Executive Order 11246 by the use of state-wide, pre-bid, standardized affirmative action plans signed by all contractors, rather than through pre-award negotiations with the low-bid contractor. According to the Committee on Public Works, the purpose of this act was to make the nondiscrimination requirement a matter of contractor responsibility rather than bid responsiveness and to prevent the development of a quota system. The act did not expressly prohibit manning tables or goals, however, and the Department of Transportation simply ignored it. The Federal Highway

Administration shifted minority hiring negotiations from the pre-award phase to the pre-bid qualification stage of the contracting process. In other words, it insisted on specific affirmative action commitments as a condition of becoming a responsible bidder. Yet the head of the Federal Highway Administration continued to deny that the policy in any way constituted a "quantitative treatment" or "quota method" of enforcing contract compliance.[55]

VII

The intensifying if clandestine pursuit of preferential treatment under Executive Order 11246 was part of an increasingly race-conscious civil rights policy which the Johnson Administration left to the incoming Republican administration of Richard M. Nixon in January 1969. For several years the Office of Education, contrary to the intent of Congress, had interpreted Title VI of the Civil Rights Act to require racially balanced integration of public schools.[56] In the electoral area, the concern of the Voting Rights Act of 1965 to eliminate barriers to the ballot box was being transformed by the Department of Justice into a concern to prevent dilution of minority votes that rested on the logic of proportional representation.[57] After four years of race riots and black power threats growing out of the civil rights movement, Nixon's election appeared to signal a return to law and order, a lessened emphasis on civil rights, and the restoration of more traditional equal rights concepts. At the same time, however, it was an article of liberal (and, to some extent, bipartisan) faith, expounded in official commission reports, that the ghetto riots were caused by racism and discrimination. This conclusion was the basis on which more rigorous civil rights enforcement could be demanded to prevent renewed urban violence. In such a preventive strategy, enforcement of equal employment opportunity was seen as especially important.

By 1969, the bipartisan consensus on which the Civil Rights Act rested had collapsed, and civil rights was a bitterly partisan issue. The Democratic party, moving steadily to the left, was politically identified with the views of the civil rights lobby. Trying to retain the support of organized labor and middle class opinion, however, it concealed and obfuscated its growing commitment to race-conscious measures, provoking the intraparty conflict seen in the controversy over quotas in the federal contract program. This division was temporarily healed by the election of Nixon, whose call for law and order and an end to the riots was dismissed as a code word for opposing civil rights enforcement.

Far from being an opponent of civil rights, Richard Nixon was a strong supporter of them. As chairman of the Government Contracts Committee in the Eisenhower Administration, he showed a willingness to press the issue of employment equality.[58] Political reasons reinforced President Nixon's tendency to focus on this area of civil rights policy. Democratic unity on civil rights was fragile, especially with respect to employment discrimination—where the black lobby and organized labor were potential enemies. As noted above, Republicans might have been able to gain politically by forcing the job bias issue and driving a wedge between key constituent groups in the Democratic coalition. At the same time, the Nixon Administration had political reasons for relaxing civil rights enforcement in the field of school desegregation. Heavily dependent on southern support for his election, Nixon had to accommodate white opposition to racially balanced school integration. These conflicting pressures led the Nixon Administration to take a more conservative position on race-conscious remedies in school desegregation and a more liberal one on preferential treatment in employment discrimination policy.

In employment discrimination, the Administration proposed to curb bureaucratic excesses while continuing to regard affirmative action as a minority job program. Instead of attacking quotas and preferential treatment, Nixon officials promised greater administrative efficiency and reduced paperwork. The Department of Transportation, for example, dealt with the pre-award controversy by accepting standardized, multi-employer affirmative action plans in the highway construction industry, as contractors had urged. It said its purpose was to make contract requirements more explicit and definite, in accordance with GAO recommendations. Denying that the administration was relaxing enforcement pressure, the Secretary of Transportation told hostile congressional Democrats: "Paperwork and pious words do not achieve equal opportunity results, and results are what we are after."[59]

The Nixon Administration focused its civil rights enforcement energies on the issue of affirmative action in the construction industry and the Philadelphia plan inherited from the Johnson Administration. The Comptroller General's November 1968 pronouncement against minority group manning tables discouraged, but did not eliminate, pre-award affirmative action bargaining by federal contract agencies. In March 1969, therefore, the GAO renewed and escalated its criticism of the policy. A series of discussions followed with the executive departments, members of Congress, and civil rights spokesmen, in which the GAO again stated that affirmative action requirements had to be made explicit. It argued further that government specification of the level of minority hiring violated both the nondiscrimination requirements and the ban on preferential treatment in Title VII.[60] Liberal congressmen and the civil rights lobby urged continuation of the Philadelphia plan as a program of black economic assistance that was needed to avert a renewal of ghetto rioting. The Departments of Labor and Justice then decided to revise and implement the plan, giving it the formal specificity that the GAO said was required by public contracting law.

In June 1969, the Department of Labor announced the revised Philadelphia plan. It required contractors to choose a specific goal within stipulated minority hiring ranges, which were included in the invitation for bids. The hiring ranges were based on the availability of minority group applicants, the need to supply persons for training programs, and the impact of minority hiring on the existing labor force. Compliance review would occur after the award of a contract; if a goal was not met, the contractor would be given an opportunity to demonstrate that he had made a good faith effort to meet his obligation. The plan disclaimed any intention of discriminating against any qualified individual because of race.[61]

The revised Philadelphia plan turned a minor dispute involving technicalities of government contracting into a major political controversy with implications for civil rights policy in general. Defending congressional authority to audit executive branch spending, Comptroller General Elmer B. Staats issued an opinion stating that while the revised plan satisfied the requirements of specificity in government contract law, it constituted a racial hiring order in violation of the Civil Rights Act. The plan was an attempt to spend funds in a manner not authorized by Congress.[62]

The Nixon Administration held that it could require affirmative action plans going beyond the requirements of Title VII, provided they were aimed at the purposes of the law: eliminating discriminatory practices and promoting employment equality for blacks. Responding to the Comptroller General, Attorney General John Mitchell said the legal definition of discrimination was changing and Title VII did not absolutely bar taking race into account. Citing recent Title VII judicial decisions, he argued that the "obligation of nondiscrimination . . . does not require and in some circumstances may not permit obliviousness or indifference to the racial consequences of alternative courses of action which involve the application of outwardly neutral criteria." But did not the use of race-conscious practices mean that employers would be forced to discriminate because of race? Furthermore, while a contractor failing to meet his minority hiring goal could claim a good-faith-effort defense, the Philadelphia plan did not state what this consisted of. Thus, no fair method of resolving questions of compliance was provided. In other words, the government would still be able to define affirmative action subjectively and arbitrarily. Attorney General Mitchell did not deny these facts, but simply said any such argument was premature and speculative. There was no reason to believe the OFCC would not tell contractors what was expected in the way of a good faith effort. "We cannot assume," he said, "that a contractor will be forced, as a practical matter, to choose between non-compliance with the affirmative action obligation and violation of Title VII."[63]

The controversy over the Philadelphia plan reached a climax in December 1969, when the Senate Appropriations Committee attached a rider to a supplemental appropriations bill prohibiting any government funds from being spent on contracts disapproved by the Comptroller General. Declaring the issue to be one of congressional authority over appropriated funds, the committee secured Senate approval, 73-13, and sent the bill to a conference committee. President Nixon and other Administration officials publicly opposed the rider. Defending the Philadelphia plan as an equal opportunity measure, Nixon described the impending House action as "an historic and critical civil rights vote," and threatened to veto the appropriations bill if it contained the rider. Privately the President spoke of forcing "the civil rights people," apparently referring to liberal Democrats, to take a stand either for labor or for civil rights. Criticizing Democrats as "token oriented," he said the administration was "job-oriented." The White House rescue operation of the revised Philadelphia plan worked. The House rejected the rider, 208-156, and the Senate receded from its earlier vote, 39-29.[64]

The jurisdictional dimension of the conflict complicates evaluation of the substantive views of affirmative action involved in the controversy over the Philadelphia plan. If congressional critics and the Comptroller General had objected only when the Nixon Administration took up the plan, one might conclude that partisan motives were at work, denying the Republican executive control over the contract program that they were willing to let Democratic presidents exercise. In fact, however, opponents of the Philadelphia plan criticized it under both Democratic and Republican auspices, and the votes on the rider cut across party lines. It is true that Comptroller General Staats said the real issue was congressional authority over executive branch spending, which the civil rights aspect obscured. Yet it is significant that the authority he ultimately relied on was Title VII of the Civil Rights Act.[65]

Instead of obscuring the main issue, the interdepartmental conflict might be seen as making debate on affirmative action possible after several years of surreptitious development. Widespread anxiety over race relations, apprehension about ghetto riots, white guilt about past discrimination, and fear of appearing racist in the face of civil rights claims that were regarded as presumptively valid all tended to inhibit debate about preferential treatment. It was politically beneficial and useful therefore that the ideological passions involved in the debate over the meaning of equality and discrimination raised by the Philadelphia plan should be modulated by the necessity of dealing with it in the context of a struggle over separation of powers.

If there was one central meaning of the Civil Rights Act as it was understood at the time of its adoption, it was that quotas and preferential treatment were prohibited by Title VII. Everyone involved in anti-discrimination policy also believed that the federal contract program, which was increasingly administered so as to result in minority preferential hiring, was bound by the requirements of Title VII. Accordingly, the Comptroller General's formulation of the jurisdictional dispute posed precisely the issue that was expected to arise. And since affirmative action under Executive Order 11246 did not need to be justified as a remedy for unlawful discrimination but was imposed simply as a contractual obligation, the Title VII ban on preferential treatment on account of racial imbalance seemed all the more applicable.

Reading the debates on the Philadelphia plan as a reflection of civil rights attitudes, it is clear that President Nixon's action gave decisive support to the concepts of disparate impact discrimination, preferential treatment, and group equality of result that were transforming anti-discrimination policy. The minority hiring plan was near extinction when the Administration intervened to preserve and elevate it to national prominence as a supposedly essential civil rights policy. Organized labor opposed the plan because it was aimed at discrimination in the construction trades, and the civil rights lobby, dependent on labor for much of its financial support, initially stayed out of the fight. Black leaders were evidently prepared to accept defeat of the plan for the sake of liberal unity against the Nixon Administration. The White House lobbying effort produced few results and attracted little attention, until Nixon's assertions about the civil rights issues involved convinced members of Congress that the Philadelphia plan could not be regarded as a parochial labor question.[66]

The administration acted for a combination of political and ideological reasons. Critical of what they considered utopian Democratic promises, Republicans stressed results over rhetoric. Fearful of continued urban violence, they hoped to give blacks a greater stake in society through economic development plans. Accused by liberals of being opposed to civil rights, they wanted to demonstrate their civil rights credentials. The

Philadelphia plan provided an issue on which the Administration could condemn trade union discrimination, promote black economic interests, and perhaps win some black political support. Defense of the plan put labor leaders in the awkward position of appearing to be against civil rights and forced liberal Democrats to choose between their trade union allies and the civil rights lobby. Moreover, President Nixon acted to defend a rich source of executive patronage in the government contract program that Democratic administrations had enjoyed and that he was determined to use for his own purposes.

If Richard Nixon was genuinely committed to the principle of color-blind equal opportunity, as he often professed to be, his action on the Philadelphia plan was a case of all tactics and no strategy. By formalizing and protecting the emerging policy of quota preferences, the administration took a decisive step toward legalizing preferential treatment. Defeat of the appropriations bill rider was immediately taken to signify congressional approval of quotas as consistent with Title VII, and courts began to cite the congressional action and the Philadelphia plan as complementary authorities supporting quota remedies under it. The political motives behind the Philadelphia plan, however, though characteristically vigorous and shrewd in the Nixon manner, should not be seen as producing unintended long range consequences, but rather as reinforcing Nixon's genuine tendency to support preferential treatment.

We have noted that, as chairman of the Government Contracts Committee, Vice-President Nixon put pressure on contractors to hire minorities. In 1969, along with the Philadelphia plan, he revised the federal government's equal employment opportunity policy in the direction of preferential treatment. White House minority affairs advisor Robert J. Brown, a black businessman, proposed a civil service affirmative action plan involving "quantitative targets" and "agency quotas" that would in effect make it possible to create a "test class" of minority employees, who could be advanced rapidly to supervisory positions.[67] In August 1969, President Nixon issued Executive Order 11478; it established "a continuing affirmative program" for recruitment, employment, development, and advancement of members of the civil service. Specific steps to be taken included full use of the present skills of each employee and "maximum feasible opportunity to employees" to gain the skills necessary to advancement. Although not necessarily inconsistent with color-blind equal opportunity, the Nixon in-house equal employment opportunity program contained obvious potential for preferential treatment.[68]

The Philadelphia plan illustrated the politicization—or repoliticization—of civil rights policy under the imperative of race-conscious affirmative action. In a modern constitutional state, government is impartial: its purpose is to protect the natural rights of individuals. Civil rights are legally guaranteed to each citizen against denial based on political interests or ideology. In the era of segregation, the civil rights of black Americans were sacrificed to the interests of southern and northern politicians representing white majorities. The twentieth century civil rights movement has been aimed at depoliticizing government regulation of individual rights by eliminating race, a superficial and irrelevant consideration, as a criterion in political and social decision making. The Civil Rights Act of 1964 comprehensively asserts this purpose, establishing individual rights and equal treatment irrespective of color as a rule of action in public life generally. From the outset, however, implementation of the act and enforcement of parallel executive orders containing the nondiscrimination principle proceeded on the belief that the principle of color-blind equal opportunity is inadequate for securing civil rights and achieving racial equality in contemporary American society. This belief constitutes a political judgment contradicting the decision of Congress to insist on the equal rights principle in the Civil Rights Act. It provides the ground for race-conscious affirmative action, an invention of courts and administrative agencies that lacks democratic legitimacy; it makes the exercise of civil rights, as in the era of segregation, contingent on expedient political considerations and interests.

It can be argued, as supporters of affirmative action still do, that preferential treatment combines justice and expediency, and that, despite appearances to the contrary, it is actually an effective way of enforcing the color-blind equal rights principle. Since the nondiscrimination principle of Title VII and the executive orders was in large measure abrogated from the outset in the 1960s, it is impossible to say with certainty that things would have been better had equal opportunity been enforced as intended. The fact is that it has never really been tried. Yet it is questionable that the politicization of civil rights under race-conscious affirmative action saved the country from social convulsion, or conversely, that enforcement of equal opportunity as intended would have propelled blacks into social revolution. The one clear result of acquiescing in demands for minority preference is to provide an incentive for the conferral of further benefits based on racial criteria to an extent undreamt of in the early days of affirmative action. It is hard to see how this tendency protects individual rights or promotes justice and the common good.

To say that the urban disorders of the 1960s that provided the rationale for affirmative action were caused by white racism, as official commissions at the time declared, is to acknowledge that the problem was not that the equal rights principle was tried and found wanting. Race-conscious policies were adopted by federal officials at the urging of the civil rights lobby without seriously attempting to implement the equal rights principle. A political decision was made to revive race as a criterion of public policy in the belief that race-based decision making, when employed in the service of a good cause and used not to stigmatize or offend those whose rights are thereby denied, has no corrupting effect, but rather is consistent with democratic justice. Combined with practical political considerations, this was the underlying rationale of the Nixon Administration's defense of the Philadelphia plan.

Congressional defeat of the attempt to kill the Philadelphia plan was taken as an endorsement of quota hiring and a legislative determination that it did not conflict with Title VII.[69] In March of 1970, a federal district court ruled the Philadelphia plan valid under Executive Order 11246, stating that goals and timetables do not violate Title VII.[70] This decision was in turn cited by courts in Title VII litigation to support the view that preferential treatment, including quota remedies, is not prohibited by the provision of the act that was specifically intended to preclude any interpretation of a court or government agency that required preferential treatment because of racial imbalance. The Philadelphia plan thus contributed to an emerging policy of judicial approval of quota relief which formed the centerpiece of the effort to rewrite the Civil Rights Act that began with the first Title VII decisions in 1966.

2

The Law of Employment Discrimination: 1965 to 1975

If the political impulse to redefine equality came from the civil rights bureaucracy and the civil rights lobby, the legal rulings that confirmed race-conscious affirmative action in public policy were the product of judicial government. In performing this function, courts did not merely register the opinions of government administrators. The judiciary made its own political judgments about the inadequacy of the equal rights principle and the need to revise the basic concepts of the Civil Rights Act to meet what it considered the public policy needs of the later 1960s and 1970s.

Anti-discrimination law was a fertile field for judicial activism in the 1960s. Prior to the congressional legislation of the mid-1960s, civil rights policy concerning the desegregation of schools and public facilities and the guarantee of voting rights rested largely on judicial interpretation of the Constitution. Directed at intentional, state-mandated unequal or disparate treatment of black citizens, civil rights jurisprudence sought to end discriminatory practices, thereby remedying the effects of past discrimination. Compared to the management of elections or the operation of public schools and public facilities, private enterprise was a fundamentally different type of activity. Nevertheless, after the passage of the Civil Rights Act, courts proposed to apply the same legal principles to eliminate discrimination in both areas. Racial discrimination was viewed as essentially the same phenomenon wherever it appeared, to be dealt with according to the same injunctive and remedial techniques.

In a 1965 voting rights case, the Supreme Court declared: "the Court has not merely the power but the duty to render a decree which will as far as possible eliminate the discrimination of the past as well as bar like discrimination in the future."[1] Although dealing with situations basically different from denials of voting rights, courts in employment discrimination cases cited this dictum as authority for ordering far-reaching remedies beyond the intended scope of Title VII. Judicial decisions ignored the fact that deprivation of the suffrage had been unconstitutional since Reconstruction, while discrimination in private employment was not unlawful prior to the Civil Rights Act. Judges also disregarded the fact that in employment the number of jobs is limited and that legitimate business considerations—including the qualifications of applicants—need to be taken into account in determining the existence of unlawful practices. By contrast, with respect to voting, public education, and public facilities and accommodations, there is an unlimited number of goods available—that is, ballots to be cast or places to be occupied—and qualifications of applicants and competing policy considerations are less likely to enter into the problem of defining discrimination.

Congress ultimately entrusted Title VII enforcement to the judiciary.[2] Although this grant of authority necessarily implies a degree of technical interpretive discretion, the rule of law requires courts to conform to the purpose, intent, and basic principles of anti-discrimination law written into the statute. In applying Title VII, however, the judiciary revised or redefined virtually every key provision in the act. Rejecting the even-handed dispute resolution that Congress identified as a principal means of guaranteeing equal employment opportunity, the judiciary transformed Title VII into a one-sided pro-plaintiff measure. It initially expressed this tendency in decisions concerning the procedural requirements governing the complaint process and anti-discrimination suits under Title VII.

I

Procedural disputes were resolved in favor of plaintiffs in order to facilitate litigation by individuals and circumvent the backlogs of EEOC complaints that quickly built up when Title VII went into effect. Although it was unfair to take the side of the employee automatically, at least these procedural rulings reflected the traditional concept of equal opportunity as the removal of barriers. However, with respect to class action suits, the major procedural issue, judicial construction of Title VII went well beyond congressional intent and implemented the group-rights, equality-of-result approach to anti-discrimination law.

Class action suits are used to expedite the administration of justice when many individuals with the same interest can be represented by a single party. In the 1950s, class actions were sometimes employed in school desegregation suits to confer a group right of equal protection on blacks and impose on state governments an affirmative duty to promote integration and eliminate the effects of segregation. Title VII authorized class action suits in the form of attorney general pattern or practice suits, but Congress probably did not intend private class actions. Plaintiffs' attorneys in early Title VII litigation, however, gave high priority to the certification of class action causes. They were not disappointed.

Courts approved broad use of class action suits on the theory that racial discrimination was by definition class discrimination. If it existed in any form, whether as an avowed employment practice or an individual action, it applied throughout the class and was a "Damoclean threat" to every black.[3] Declaring the individual plaintiff to be a "private attorney general," courts said class actions were private in form only. Through the class action device, the judiciary in effect transformed the Title VII personal right of equal employment opportunity into a collective public right, as proponents of a national FEPC with cease and desist powers had originally intended. "Across-the-board" class actions were certified, in which large numbers of minority individuals in a firm were assumed to be in the same fact situation and to have the same interest, irrespective of differences in the circumstances and qualifications of individual jobs. A group rights concept of employment equality developed as appellate courts, especially in the southern Fourth and Fifth Circuits, so consistently ruled against employers as to establish a virtual presumption of discrimination whenever a Title VII charge was filed.[4]

Substantive interpretation of Title VII was equally one-sided. Although Congress based Title VII on the disparate treatment concept of discrimination required by the concept of equality of opportunity, the EEOC and the civil rights lobby viewed the law as having no fixed content and thus definable without reference to its legislative history. By the time the first substantive cases reached the courts in 1968, the disparate impact theory of discrimination had gained wide currency in civil rights circles and was advanced by the plaintiffs' bar. Affirmative action theorist and EEOC staff member Alfred W. Blumrosen argued that if discrimination were narrowly defined to require a hostile intent to injure minority group individuals, as the disparate treatment concept required, it would be difficult to prove that unlawful practices existed. The exclusion of minorities would then have to be explained in policy terms with reference to problems in education, housing, domestic life, and other areas that would take years to overcome. If, however, discrimination could be defined legally as "all conduct which adversely affects minority group employment opportunities," Blumrosen reasoned, if Title VII could be interpreted so that discrimination could be found "at every turn where minorities are adversely affected by institutional decisions . . . which are subject to legal regulation," then compensatory remedies in the form of job benefits could be ordered. The problems of race relations and black economic deprivation could be promptly resolved.[5]

Provisions of Title VII that were thought to have a clear and unequivocal meaning in the debate on the Civil Rights Act were redefined by the plaintiffs' bar and the judiciary at will. Civil rights lawyers now claimed that in identifying unlawful employment practices in the statute, Congress did not define discrimination. Moreover, they contended that no generally accepted concept of discrimination existed at the time the law was enacted. The way was clear, therefore, to assert the theory of disparate impact discrimination. This was manifestly untrue, for Congress plainly wrote the concept of intentional disparate treatment discrimination into the act.[6] Plaintiffs' bar sought to evade this obstacle, however, by invoking the tort law doctrine that a person intends the consequences of his actions.

In the new disparate impact theory of employment bias, discrimination was any differentiation by an institution without sufficient social and economic justification. Civil rights lawyers claimed to find a textual basis for this interpretation in Section 703(a)(2) of Title VII, which states that employers may not limit or classify employees in any way that may "adversely affect" their status because of race. The phrase 'because of race' was the historic touchstone of national civil rights protection from the Reconstruction period. It limited the scope of federal intervention since only deprivation of rights motivated by racial prejudice, or because of race, was prohibited. The disparate impact theory of discrimination deprived the legal concept 'because of race' of its ordinary meaning: prejudicial animus or deliberate and willful intent. If the objective of the Civil Rights Act was to give jobs to blacks, asked one employment discrimination analyst, "Why is intent any part of this process? Is not *result* the only relevant factor?" Result-oriented affirmative action forced employers to assume responsibility for societal discrimination by hiring underprivileged minority group individuals. According to civil rights strategists, it showed the irrelevance and injustice of applying the equal rights principle in conditions of social and economic inequality.[7]

The first step in rewriting Title VII was to make the law retrospective. Title VII went into effect on July 2, 1965, a year after the Civil Rights Act was passed. As of that date, specific employment practices that discriminated against individuals because of race were unlawful. Practices occurring before the effective date were not unlawful because Congress was not trying to make up for the past or revise industrial relations to place individuals in the position they would have occupied in the absence of discrimination. Section 703(h) of Title VII expressed this non-retrospective or non-remedial outlook. It states that it is not an unlawful practice to differentiate among employees pursuant to a bona fide seniority system, provided the differences are not the result of an intent to discriminate because of race. According to the sponsors of Title VII, this meant that while racial criteria had to be eliminated, seniority arrangements based on collective bargaining and rights and expectations of employees deriving therefrom need not be abolished or revised, even if they had a discriminatory effect on black employees after the removal of racial classification.

The plaintiffs' attorneys simply disregarded the legislative history and argued that Title VII should be applied retrospectively because Congress did not anticipate the problems that were created when racial barriers were removed. The question arose, for example, whether blacks transferring to a new department should be permitted to carry their plant seniority with them or be required to start at the bottom of the ladder in their new department, inferior to whites with less plant seniority. Asserting that the debate over Title VII did not address this question, the plaintiffs' bar contended that a seniority system that permitted racial distinctions to persist in this way was not bona fide. The present effects of past discrimination were unlawful and required a remedy, typically one in the form of plant seniority being credited toward departmental seniority. This was called the 'present effects' doctrine of Title VII liability. It was justified under the 'rightful place' theory of relief, which civil rights advocates touted as the moderate approach to the problem of remedies. They contrasted it to the radical 'freedom now' theory that would allow blacks to replace whites so they could have what was due them, and the conservative 'status quo' theory that would simply apply the color-blind principle prospectively and hence leave blacks in a position inferior to that of whites with less plant seniority. A consultant to EEOC on seniority desegregation argued that an interpretation of Title VII that did not permit the courts to address pre-act practices "unnaturally bifurcates the pattern of discrimination that has existed."[8]

District courts disagreed over retrospective application of Title VII, but appellate courts accepted the present effects doctrine. In *Quarles v. Philip Morris* (1968), a district court decision that on appeal became the leading precedent for retroactive enforcement of the law, Judge John D. Butzner said Title VII condemned all racial discrimination without excluding present discrimination originating in seniority systems devised before the effective date of the act. The court rejected the view that a remedy permitting blacks to carry plant seniority into a departmental transfer was unlawful preferential treatment. "It is . . . apparent," Judge Butzner declared, "that Congress did not intend to freeze an entire generation of Negro employees into discriminatory patterns that existed before the act."[9]

While it is true that Congress did not intend to freeze blacks in traditional patterns of inequality, it is inaccurate to assume that prospective enforcement of the nondiscrimination principle had no significant effect on discriminatory patterns. Yet this was the assumption on which courts accepted the present effects doctrine. The result was to transform Title VII into what one federal judge later described as "nothing more than remedial legislation enacted for the purpose of correcting problems of discrimination and abuse."[10] In the atmosphere of social crisis that prevailed in the late 1960s, judicial interpretation of Title VII expressed the political judgment that prospective application of the nondiscrimination principle would be unjust and unwise as public policy.

Retroactive application of Title VII was used by Nixon Administration officials to justify preferential treatment for blacks in the Philadelphia plan.[11] Trade union exclusion of minorities, the target of the Philadelphia plan, had been formally and explicitly prescribed earlier in the twentieth century. When these formal barriers were removed, racial segregation persisted; it seemed so deeply entrenched as to appear to illustrate the force of societal or institutional discrimination. In a superficial sense, the Title VII present effects cases, in which relief was awarded to individual blacks as victims of discrimination in desegregated seniority situations, presupposed the intentional disparate treatment concept of discrimination. Yet in a deeper political sense, the retrospective application of Title VII to pre-act union discrimination through the present effects doctrine shifted the focus of the law's enforcement to unintentional societal discrimination. Eliminating the effects of past discrimination through the award of compensatory remedial seniority credit or other employment benefits became the preferred means of ending discriminatory practices. In erasing the distinction between past and present, lawful and unlawful, intentional and unintentional, and individual and collective discrimination, retrospective enforcement of Title VII paved the way for judicial acceptance of the concept of disparate impact discrimination resting on the theory of group rights and equality of result.

Cases concerning standardized employment tests were the vehicle for explicitly introducing disparate impact theory into Title VII law. Section 703(h) of the statute authorized employers to give and act on the results of a professionally developed ability test, provided such action was not designed, intended, or used to discriminate because of race. EEOC and the plaintiff's bar, citing the Commission's 1966 guidelines on testing, contended that tests that had a disparate impact on minority groups were unlawful unless they were shown to be specifically job-related and justified by business necessity. Although this interpretation had no basis in the text or legislative history of Title VII, several courts adopted it. Tests passed by whites at a substantially higher rate than blacks were declared discriminatory if their effect was exclusion of blacks and if employers could not show the test predicted job performance. The controlling principle of Title VII, said a district court in a leading case, was that an employment practice that had the effect of significantly preferring whites to blacks was unlawful unless the employer could demonstrate a business necessity for it.[12]

The present effects doctrine and disparate impact theory were concepts of liability. Both implied preferential treatment, insofar as the employer's interest in averting discrimination charges based on statistics showing racial imbalance provided an incentive to engage in racially preferential programs. This preferential effect, identified by fair employment analysts before the enactment of the Civil Rights Act as an inevitable consequence of any anti-discrimination law, formed a third feature of emerging Title VII jurisprudence.

In the Senate debate on Title VII, the bill was amended to allay fears that federal officials would define discrimination as racial imbalance and order preferential minority hiring as a remedy for unlawful practices. Section 703(j) was therefore added, stating that nothing in the statute was to be interpreted to require preferential treatment for any individual or group on account of racial imbalance between the number of minorities in the work force and the number in the local population. Civil rights lawyers knew that this provision reinforced the basic prohibition of racial decision making, and that if taken literally and applied broadly it would restrict judicial remedial powers.[13] Although in some early cases courts recognized and gave effect to the anti-preference provision, by 1970 the trend of judicial decisions was clearly toward the nullification of Section 703(j).[14]

Accepting the arguments of the civil rights lobby, courts interpreted the ban on preference as concerned only with the definition of a violation. That is, it simply meant that racial imbalance could not be declared a violation of the law; it had no bearing on the relief a court could order upon a finding of unlawful discrimination. In 1969, for example, the Fifth Circuit held that a district court remedial order admitting blacks to union membership, and requiring work referrals based on 1:1 ratio between blacks and whites, was not preferential treatment.[15] In 1970 the Sixth Circuit, finding racially neutral union admission and referral rules unlawful under the present effects doctrine, said Section 703(j) merely meant that preferential treatment could not be required "solely because of an imbalance in racial employment." The court concluded that to interpret Section 703(j) as a limitation on affirmative relief "would allow complete nullification of the stated purposes of the Civil Rights Act of 1964."[16]

Negation of the ban on preferential treatment in Title VII cases occurred at the same time that the Nixon Administration was forcing federal contractors to adopt preferential minority hiring goals. Both actions were emblematic of the belief that prospective application of the nondiscrimination principle was inadequate to secure equal employment opportunity. The argument might be made that, in seniority cases, justice for individual blacks required an expansive interpretation of Title VII under the disparate treatment concept of discrimination. It was clearly contrary to the requirements and intent of the law, however, to apply it retroactively, and to nullify the prohibition of preferential treatment by divorcing it from the judicial determination of unlawful practice and appropriate remedies for proven violations under the disparate impact theory of discrimination.

In the disparate impact situation, racial imbalance is for all practical purposes held to be unlawful discrimination. A *prima facie* charge based on statistics of racial imbalance shifts the burden to the employer to show the job-relatedness or business necessity of the challenged employment practice. This burden is heavy and often proves dispositive. In disparate impact cases, moreover, the judicial remedy, unrestricted by Section 703(j), was often a quota order benefiting minority group individuals who had not been discriminated against. Quota relief was based on the idea that the racial group as a whole was the victim of discrimination, so that a benefit for any member of the group, regardless of his or her circumstances, was a proper remedy. Based on the idea of group rights and the equality of result, this concept of remedy was antithetical to the provisions and intent of Title VII and was refuted by its legislative history. Quota remedies, divorced from specific injury to identified individuals and made possible by the nullification of the ban on preferential treatment, pointed to the establishment of specific racial balance, rather than the creation of equality of opportunity, as the end of employment discrimination policy. Although liberal theorists denied it, this was the direction of affirmative action law in the 1970s.[17]

II

The emerging strands of employment discrimination law came together in 1971 in *Griggs v. Duke Power Co.*, the first Title VII case to reach the Supreme Court. In a sweeping opinion, Chief Justice Burger for a unanimous Court adopted the disparate impact theory of discrimination as the central principle of Title VII. *Griggs* shifted civil rights policy to a group-rights, equality-of-result rationale that made the social consequences of employment practices, rather than their purposes, intent, or motivation, the decisive consideration in determining their lawfulness. The decision supplied a theoretical basis for preferential treatment as well as a practical incentive for extending race-conscious preference: employers' desire to avoid charges, based on racial imbalance, of discrimination.

Griggs was a class action by employees of Duke Power Company charging that racially neutral hiring, transfer, and promotion policies that required a high school diploma and a passing performance on an objective test were racially discriminatory. The North Carolina company's practices, which had been adopted in 1965 when it ended a policy of racial segregation that confined blacks to the least skilled jobs, was open to challenge as being unlawful either in the sense of continuing the effects of past discrimination or having a disparate impact on black employees as a class. NAACP lawyers representing the plaintiffs made both arguments, but emphasized that the selection standards disproportionately screened out blacks, whether or not malicious intent existed. The company based its defense on Section 703(h) of Title VII and the legislative history, contending that ability tests were permitted as long as they were not used to discriminate.[18]

For such a momentous decision, the Court adopted a surprisingly superficial and imprecise approach to the problem of proving disparate racial impact. No evidence was introduced concerning the educational attainments or test scores of the thirteen black plaintiffs. Indeed, the

NAACP attorneys who argued the case were not concerned with the abilities and performance of their clients as individuals; they acknowledged at oral argument before the Supreme Court that they did not know which employees, white or black, had taken and failed the test used by the company. Their argument was that the test was "patently discriminatory," so that facts concerning individual employees were irrelevant. What mattered was the impact of the test on blacks as a group. The Supreme Court agreed, accepting the view that the black plaintiffs were incapable of passing the test because blacks in general were known to perform less well than whites on measurements of intelligence and educational achievement. Accordingly, as evidence of disparate impact discrimination, the Court cited statistics from the 1960 census showing that whereas 34 percent of the white population in North Carolina had graduated from high school, only 12 percent of the black population had. Further evidence of disparate impact used to invalidate the company test were the test scores reported in an unrelated EEOC decision (supplied by the EEOC in an *amicus curiae* brief), in which 58 percent of whites achieved a passing score compared to only 6 percent of the blacks. Since the plaintiffs in the *Griggs* case were black, these results were presumed to apply to them. Furthermore, the Court said the results were "traceable to race" in the sense that blacks had received an inferior education in segregated schools, preventing them from developing their intelligence in a way that could be demonstrated in a testing process.

In other words, blacks were the victims of societal discrimination in the educational system. Employers were not responsible for this discrimination, but they were to be held accountable for it because Congress, according to Chief Justice Burger, "has now required that the posture and condition of the job-seeker be taken into account." "The Act proscribes not only overt discrimination," the Court declared, "but also practices that are fair in form, but discriminatory in operation." The "touchstone" of the act was business necessity. "If an employment practice which operates to exclude Negroes cannot be shown to be related to job performance," the Chief Justice observed, "the practice is prohibited." He added that the "absence of discriminatory intent does not redeem employment procedures or testing mechanisms that operate as 'built-in headwinds' for minority groups and are unrelated to measuring job capacity." Disparate impact theory appeared further in Chief Justice Burger's assertion that "Congress directed the thrust of the Act to the *consequences* of employment practices, not simply their motivation."[19]

Chief Justice Burger described business necessity, the "touchstone" of Title VII, in various ways. He said the act contained a requirement that employment practices be shown to possess "business necessity," that they fulfill "a genuine business need," that they be "related to job performance," and that they bear "a manifest relationship to the employment in question" or "a demonstrable relationship to successful performance of the jobs" in question.[20] He did not explain the difference between these formulations, but used them synonymously. In a practical sense, however, the Court defined business necessity by reference to the EEOC guidelines on testing, which it said expressed the will of Congress and were entitled to great deference. The guidelines stated that employers using tests should have data available "demonstrating that the test is predictive of or significantly correlated with important elements of work behavior which comprise or are relevant to the job or jobs for which candidates are being evaluated."[21] Chief Justice Burger purported to find support for the EEOC standards in references in the legislative history to employers using tests to ascertain the qualifications of employees. In fact, "job-relatedness" and "business necessity" were judicial inventions that transformed an accepted rule in pre-Title VII state employment discrimination law: that an employer might be asked to explain the legitimate business reasons for an employment practice to show it was not a pretext for discrimination. By judicial fiat, this metamorphosed into a requirement that an employer prove the absolute indispensability of a challenged practice if it had a disparate racial impact. If taken at anything like face value, this requirement imposed an extremely heavy burden on the employer.

Revolutionary as the decision was, the Court could not simply dismiss equal opportunity and the disparate treatment concept, if only because most people still conceived of employment discrimination in these terms. Accordingly, Chief Justice Burger also asserted the traditional right of equal opportunity for individuals. Although the social conditions of job applicants were to be taken into account, Burger wrote, Title VII did not guarantee a job to every person regardless of qualifications. The act did not command that any person be hired simply because he was formerly the subject of discrimination or a member of a minority group. "Discriminatory preference for any group, minority or majority, is precisely and only what Congress has proscribed," he declared. "Far from disparaging job qualifications," he observed, "Congress has made such qualification the controlling factor, so that race, religion, nationality, and sex become irrelevant." Nevertheless, tests "must measure the person for the job and not the person in the abstract." Because the tests used by the company did not do this, they constituted unlawful discrimination against the class of black employees.[22]

Griggs gave the civil rights lobby a stunning (if publicly unheralded) victory, far exceeding their wildest expectations.[23] Citing no lower court Title VII decisions, the Court appeared to have made anti-discrimination law out of whole cloth.[24] An affirmative action policymaker approvingly observed that "the Supreme Court exhibited the creativity and boldness necessitated by restrictive lower court decisions to reach for a new concept if Title VII was to have any real effect."[25]

Insofar as the Court tried to ground its decision in prior case law, it relied on a recent voting rights decision. Indeed, it adopted a southern strategy for writing disparate impact theory into Title VII.[26] The southern setting of the case, the fact that the company had practiced racial segregation until it adopted impartial selection criteria, and the presumption that societal discrimination in the South was related to or dependent on official, state-imposed racial classification invited the inference that, in *Griggs*, the Supreme Court really objected to intentional disparate treatment discrimination. Instead of deciding the case under the theory of intentional disparate treatment discrimination, as it probably should have, or under the present effects doctrine, as it might have, the Court went all the way to disparate impact theory. Moreover, the Justices failed to recognize the difference between a literacy or intelligence test in voting, which serves little if any purpose in modern government, and an aptitude or ability test in private employment, which serves the purpose of promoting safe and efficient business operation. From the standpoint of public perception, the circumstances of the case obscured the significance of the adoption of disparate impact theory as the new meaning of Title VII. Indeed, the Court's references to the importance of qualifications and its professed denial of preferential treatment for any group gave disparate impact theory the appearance of being merely a strong means of enforcing traditional equal opportunity.

The subsequent wholesale adoption of the *Griggs* effects test by the courts and the civil rights bureaucracy to support race-conscious affirmative action in the 1970s showed that disparate impact theory was not just another way of upholding individual rights. *Griggs* was used to attack a wide range of recruitment, hiring, assignment, testing, seniority, promotion, discharge, and supervisory selection practices. Courts struck down such selection standards as arrest and conviction records, previous work record, and wage garnishments as not job-related. Furthermore, *Griggs* was applied in public employment, which was not covered by Title VII until 1972, and cited in a wide variety of discrimination cases outside the employment area. Courts defined the 'business necessity' test stringently, requiring employers to validate or show the job-relatedness of practices that had disparate impact, or rejecting business reasons offered as justification for challenged practices on the grounds that alternatives were available that had less racial impact.[27]

Griggs provided a theoretical rationale for the liberal impulse to rectify past racist sins, an impulse manifested in preferential policies that had no other justification except the feeling that they were "necessary" to make the Civil Rights Act meaningful. If the threat of liability was a possible incentive to quota hiring under the disparate treatment concept of discrimination,[28] minority preference was practically required in order to protect against charges of disparate impact discrimination. The logical premise of disparate impact theory was group rights and equality of result. Discrimination 'because of race' came to mean actions based on nonracial purposes that could be shown to be correlated with a racial-group pattern. Correlation was deemed proof of causation, a dubious proposition in a legal order based on individual rights and responsibilities.[29] Contrary to the traditional concept of justice, under disparate impact theory employers were held accountable for societal discrimination, although they were not responsible for it.[30] Fear of renewed racial violence, the tendency to regard all questions of racial discrimination in unified moral and legal terms, and the liberal assumption that property rights were distinguishable from civil rights and could routinely be redefined led the judiciary to adopt a theory of discrimination entirely contradictory to the requirements and intent of the Civil Rights Act.

III

The theory of disparate impact liability rationalized the political and legal tendency toward preferential treatment evident in the affirmative action policies of the civil rights bureaucracy and the Title VII judicial decisions. As lower courts applied the *Griggs* effects test in the 1970s, they extended the scope of preferential remedies, including quotas.

Legal analysts defined a strict quota as an absolute numerical preference which was racially exclusive, and a consensus existed that such a measure was illegal and unconstitutional. Although the reasoning behind this conclusion was rarely articulated, it appears to have been that an absolute preference denied the rights of those who were not members of the preferred group and whose qualifications were superior on unacceptable racial grounds.[31] A non-absolute quota, stipulating a specific ratio of black and white employees, was no less racial in character and also conflicted with the color-blind requirements of Title VII and the Fourteenth Amendment. It was considered legal and constitutional, however, because it was thought not to deny the rights of persons not in the protected group as clearly or directly. Contrary to constitutional standards, a partial abridgment of rights on this view became acceptable. Similarly, courts said a permanent quota would be invalid while a temporary one would not, without explaining why the legal disability of the former did not afflict the latter.[32]

The implicit premise of affirmative action policy was that a public emergency existed that justified otherwise unconstitutional or illegal race-conscious measures. In political terms, this was expressed in the argument that although quotas were intrinsically unsound, under the circumstances they were valid because they were politically and socially necessary. More specifically, quotas were legal when ordered as a judicial remedy for discrimination, the legal form the public emergency assumed in equal employment litigation. The corollary was that quotas could not be ordered to overcome racial imbalance *per se*, which could not be found a violation.[33] The inherent contradiction, if not deliberate deception, of affirmative action appeared in the fact that although courts said racial imbalance was not a violation, under the disparate impact theory racial imbalance was in fact a violation if an employer could not justify a racially adverse effect by showing the business necessity of a challenged practice. Moreover, in order to avert disparate impact charges, employers and unions adopted preferential practices. Yet there was an underlying consistency in affirmative action. It was expressed in the proposition, as one court put it, that since the discrimination was racial, the remedy must be racially conditioned.[34] Under affirmative action, the history of racism paradoxically became a justification and source of legitimacy for preferential treatment that took race into account and thus sanctioned that practice.

The tendency to unify past and present through the use of racial criteria was paralleled by the desire to unify all contemporary employment discrimination problems by extending the *Griggs* statutory definition of discrimination into the area of constitutional interpretation. Preferential remedies that are the logical consequence of disparate impact theory raise questions about the violation of individual rights, but under Title VII it is practically impossible to challenge race-conscious practices by introducing individual rights claims based on the equal protection component of the Constitution. Title VII is based on the constitutional power of Congress to regulate interstate commerce. This power has been so broadly construed in modern constitutional law that legislation predicated upon it is virtually always upheld. Alleged violations of individual rights under Title VII—for example, a claim by a white employee that an employer action or a judicial quota order is reverse discrimination and a denial of individual rights—are viewed by the courts as presenting simply a question of statutory interpretation concerning the validity of the exercise of the commerce power on which Title VII rests. Under the expansive interpretation of the commerce power that has prevailed since the New Deal, courts uphold the statute and are at liberty to define the meaning of unlawful discrimination—and hence the meaning of the nondiscrimination or equal opportunity principle—without having to consider the requirements of the equal protection principle. In other words, Title VII is viewed as raising only questions of congressional power, not individual rights under the Constitution. Although Title VII confers on "any individual" the right not to be discriminated against in employment, this right is not grounded in the Constitution. In effect, the exercise of the commerce power by Congress excludes any consideration of constitutional civil rights, other than the property right of the employer which, under the broad interpretation of the commerce power referred to, is held not to be improperly denied by legislation such as Title VII.[35]

Whether the *Griggs*-Title VII concept of discrimination would control employment discrimination problems under the Constitution was a major issue in the early 1970s. Title VII applied only to private employers. Public employers, with the exception of the U.S. Congress, were brought under the coverage of the statute in 1972.[36] Before that date, discrimination in public employment was dealt with under Sections 1981, 1982, and 1983 of the U.S. Code. These provisions were the codified version of the Civil Rights Acts of 1866 and 1870, which were based on the Fourteenth Amendment. The question that arose in public employment cases was whether discrimination under the Constitution was the same thing as discrimination under Title VII.

Under the Constitution, discrimination had long been interpreted and defined as intentional disparate treatment. Indeed, segregation and discrimination enacted by state law (that is, *de jure*) were by definition intentional and deliberate. The tendency to unify problems of racial discrimination led courts to apply disparate impact theory in public employment. State practices having a disparate impact on minority groups were held to establish a racial classification. When these questions arose in the late 1960s, racial classification under the equal protection clause of the Fourteenth Amendment was regarded as suspect. This meant that it triggered strict judicial scrutiny, rather than the more relaxed type of judicial review known as the rationality test, and was thus unconstitutional unless justified by a compelling governmental interest or purpose. In applying the strict scrutiny/compelling interest approach to public employer practices under Section 1981, courts translated the substance of the Title VII disparate impact-business necessity standard of *Griggs* into its constitutional idiom.[37]

Courts also ordered quota remedies in public employment cases. Employment quotas were justified by analogy to voting rights and school desegregation decisions where race-conscious remedies were used. For example, the Fifth Circuit asserted the principle that "until all traces of discrimination against blacks were removed, blacks would be accorded the same treatment as that accorded whites in the era of discrimination." In order to achieve equality, "blacks had to be dealt with as blacks."[38] In another case the Fifth Circuit described a quota as "a temporary remedy that seeks to spend itself as promptly as it can by creating a climate in which objective neutral employment criteria can successfully operate to select public employees solely on the basis of job-related merit." The court concluded that when "an environment where merit can prevail exists," the color-blind principle of equal access would satisfy the constitutional requirement.[39] Until then, the Constitution permitted (if it did not require) quota preferences based on the concept of group rights and equality of result.

Quotas were inherently divisive, however, and as the sense of crisis in race relations subsided in the early 1970s, judicial resistance to preferential treatment began to appear. Some courts rejected absolute numerical preference, quota-based layoff plans, permanent (as opposed to temporary) quotas, and promotional (as opposed to hiring) quotas.[40] A test for evaluating race-conscious remedies emerged at the circuit level, holding that racial quotas would be tolerated "only when past discrimination has been clear-cut and the effects of 'reverse discrimination' will be diffused among an identifiable group of unknown, potential applicants rather than upon an ascertainable group of easily identifiable persons."[41] According to the Second Circuit, quotas created reverse discrimination, contradicting the basic assumption that individuals are to be judged as individuals, not as members of particular racial groups. Other circuit courts disputed this view and upheld quotas, and this disagreement forced the Supreme Court to go farther to supervise and protect the emerging law of racial preference in employment.[42]

IV

Griggs was a broad decision under which the Supreme Court let the lower courts shape employment discrimination law. As affirmative action became more politically controversial, however, it was necessary for the Court once again to intervene. In a series of cases in the mid-1970s, the Supreme Court modified, without in any way repudiating, the emerging structure of race-conscious equal employment opportunity policy based on disparate impact liability.

Griggs so dominated fair employment policy that, for a time, it was questionable whether the disparate treatment concept of discrimination that Congress wrote into Title VII would even be recognized. The civil rights lobby and plaintiffs' bar resisted such an interpretation, but at length the Supreme Court affirmed the disparate treatment theory of job bias, which helped to restrict the expansion of *Griggs*.

In *McDonnell Douglas v. Green* (1973), the Court overturned a circuit court ruling. The lower court had ruled that a company's refusal to hire a former employee who had engaged in unlawful protests against it was discriminatory, because it had a disparate racial impact and was not job-related. Rejecting the disparate impact theory as irrelevant in this situation, Justice Powell said the issue was the order and allocation of proof in an individual private discrimination suit under Title VII. For a unanimous Court, Powell stated that an individual could make a *prima facie* charge by showing that he belonged to a racial minority, had applied for a job, had met the qualifications, and was rejected despite them, and that the employer continued to seek to fill the job. The burden then shifted to the employer to "articulate some nondiscriminatory reason" for rejecting the plaintiff. In this case, the refusal to hire because of unlawful conduct was deemed a legitimate business reason. The Court added a step to the traditional trial procedure by stating that after the employer rebutted the *prima facie* charge, the plaintiff must be given the opportunity to show that the proffered reason was a pretext for discrimination. Justice Powell did not disavow disparate impact theory; he wrote that statistics could be used to determine whether an individual employment decision conformed to a pattern of discrimination. Nevertheless, the chief significance of *McDonnell Douglas* was its recognition of intentional disparate treatment as a valid concept for Title VII enforcement. In refusing to extend *Griggs*, the Court affirmed the traditional view that an employer could make business decisions for any reason he liked, provided he did not act on the basis of race.[43]

Although *McDonnell Douglas* showed that there were limits to the application of the *Griggs* effects test, in other decisions the Supreme Court confirmed the tendency to transform Title VII into an instrument of minority preference. This development rested on broad exercise of judicial equitable powers to order remedies for unlawful discrimination.

The question of remedies was not a major issue in early Title VII litigation. Termination of discriminatory practices by judicial order was the main form of relief envisioned by Congress. In the present effects cases involving seniority desegregation, courts also ordered modification or establishment of new seniority systems, merging of unions, and objective criteria for union membership. Although Section 706(g) of Title VII authorized reinstatement or hiring of an individual with or without back pay, the plaintiffs' bar initially did not press back pay demands. It pursued a moderate strategy focusing on procedural and substantive questions defining the scope and content of the anti-discrimination principle. Successful on these issues, the plaintiffs' bar expanded the reform agenda in a seemingly reasonable and moderate way by seeking to obtain extensive monetary relief in the form of back pay awards. This effort was so successful that by 1975 Title VII was principally perceived as a remedial measure for eliminating the effects of past discrimination.

Under Title VII, the award of back pay was not mandatory upon a finding of unlawful practices. The statute made back pay discretionary, on the theory that the public interest in fair resolution of disputes between employer and employee might in some situations require the denial of back pay. Asserting the principle of complete remedial relief for victims of discrimination, the plaintiffs' attorneys argued that back pay should ordinarily be awarded unless special circumstances made it unjust. While some courts accepted this view, others held that back pay was discretionary. They reasoned that the trial court should be guided by concern for the interests of both employee and employer while taking into account good-faith efforts to comply with Title VII. In *Albemarle Paper Co. v. Moody* (1975), the Supreme Court accepted the pro-plaintiff view of judicial remedial authority and the back pay problem. Concerned with desegregation in a southern paper mill, the case originally involved remedies such as plant-wide seniority credit. Four years after the suit began and the employer made good faith compliance efforts, back pay was added as a class demand. The district court denied back pay. The circuit court reversed, and the Supreme Court affirmed, 7-1. Justice Stewart said for the majority that although under the statute back pay was discretionary, equitable power had to be exercised in accordance with the purposes of Title VII. These purposes, said the Court, were to remove barriers that operated in the past to favor an identifiable group of white employees over others and to make victims of discrimination whole again. Properly understood, equitable power under Title VII required the award of back pay. It could only be denied, Justice Stewart said, "for reasons which, if applied generally, would not frustrate the central statutory purposes of eradicating discrimination throughout the economy and making persons whole for injuries suffered through past discrimination."[44]

In *Albemarle*, the Court adopted the make-whole theory of relief long advocated by the plaintiffs' bar. Going beyond the 'special circumstances' rule used to award back pay in some circuits, the Justices made back pay virtually mandatory by equating it with fulfillment of the objects of Title VII.[45] Asserting that only the threat of back pay forced employers to comply with the law, the Court ignored the fact that most Title VII compliance occurred without the threat of monetary relief. It held that the district court's denial of back pay, on the ground that the employer made a good faith effort to comply, was inconsistent with the *Griggs* principle that Title VII was concerned with the results of employment practices, not their intent or motivation. *Albemarle* in effect meant that equitable powers should be exercised to promote the interests of plaintiffs over those of employers. Judicial remedial authority was formally discretionary, but it was to operate in only one direction.

Albemarle reinforced *Griggs* in a second sense: it was a disparate impact case in which the Court found the use of objective aptitude tests discriminatory under the EEOC guidelines on testing. *Griggs* held that selection standards having disparate impact on minorities had to be shown to be specifically job-related, but left open the question of precisely what such a demonstration entailed. In *Albemarle*, the company tried to validate its tests by showing a rational relationship to job performance. The Court found the test policy unlawful because it failed to meet EEOC guidelines. Declaring the guidelines "entitled to great deference," the Court accepted them as the administrative interpretation of Title VII, despite the fact that the Commission had no substantive rule-making authority and its statements about Title VII were merely opinions that lacked the force of law.[46] The Court also added a step to the order and allocation of proof in a disparate impact case. It ruled that if the employer validated its tests, the plaintiff had an opportunity to prove the test policy was a pretext for discrimination by showing that other tests with less racial impact would serve the employer's business purpose. *Albemarle* thus elevated to a position of primacy government guidelines that made validation so difficult that they effectively forced employers to drop objective tests.

The Supreme Court further expanded the scope of judicial remedial authority in *Franks v. Bowman Transportation Company* in 1976. As a remedy for the company's failure or refusal to hire them, a class of blacks sought (among other things) seniority credit to the date of their application for employment. Appellate courts had refused to award this type of relief, considering it to be preferential treatment rather than a rightful remedy and thus beyond the scope of judicial authority under Title VII. The liberal Fifth Circuit stated that to give constructive or fictional seniority to newly hired employees would change the competitive standing of incumbent employees and was contrary to the protection of bona fide seniority systems provided in Title VII.

The Supreme Court rejected this limitation on judicial power. Justice Brennan stated for the 6-3 majority that the purpose of the seniority provision was to prevent differences in treatment of employees under a seniority system from being found in violation of the act. Where a violation was determined, however, the provision placed no limit on judicial remedial authority, which the statute in another place said could order any equitable relief deemed "appropriate." Appropriate relief was relief that fulfilled the objectives of Title VII. Using the language of 'rightful place' theory for the first time in a Supreme Court opinion, Justice Brennan declared that an award of constructive or retroactive seniority served the Title VII purpose of making victims of discrimination whole and giving them their rightful place. Observing that retroactive seniority was still incomplete relief because it did not deprive whites of seniority earned during the time when discriminatory practices existed, he said the interests of arguably innocent white employees were not a valid consideration in fashioning remedial orders. Establishing a presumption in favor of rightful-place seniority relief, the Court in effect held that in the exercise of their unlimited discretionary authority, district courts were required to award fictional seniority.[47]

In *Franks*, the Supreme Court took a significant further step toward a clear-cut policy of preferential treatment. Heretofore each revision of Title VII—its retroactive enforcement under the present effects doctrine, the adoption of disparate impact theory in cases involving southern companies with a history of racial discrimination, the elevation of the remedial function to a paramount position as an objective of the act—was approved virtually unanimously. This consensus might be seen as reflective of public willingness to stretch the traditional concepts of discrimination and equal opportunity to their limits in order to help blacks make economic gains. *Franks* marked the point where judicial revision of Title VII ceased to have even a remote connection to equal opportunity and unambiguously began to promote outright preferential treatment. This change was registered in the first significant division within the Court in a Title VII case. Three Justices dissented, objecting that the decision favored minorities over innocent whites and elevated remedies for past discrimination to a higher priority than the end of present discriminatory practices.[48]

Franks conferred benefits on non-employees who were discriminated against by being rejected for employment. In the opinion of equal employment opportunity strategists, the case pointed toward further decisions benefiting minority group individuals who did not apply for employment, but who nonetheless could be considered victims insofar as they were discouraged from seeking a job by the employer's reputation for discrimination. As the award of fictional seniority rested on unwarranted assumptions about the ability of an individual to hold a job and advance in the absence of discrimination, so the logic of *Franks* blurred the distinction between actual and putative victims of discrimination. The decision reflected the tendency of affirmative action theorists to regard all blacks as victims of discrimination, regardless of individual circumstance. In *Franks,* the Supreme Court shifted Title VII enforcement more decisively to a group rights/equality of result perspective. Its holding encouraged affirmative action strategists to anticipate further decisions approving the denial of innocent white employees' rights or their displacement by blacks.[49]

Reservations about preferential treatment expressed by the *Franks* minority gained sufficient support to command a 5-4 majority in *Washington v. Davis* (1976), a decision that interrupted the Court's virtually automatic acceptance of the views of the civil rights lobby on employment discrimination. This was not a Title VII case, but was brought under Section 1981 of the U.S. Code, which itself was derived from the Civil Rights Act of 1866. It thus involved the meaning of the Fourteenth Amendment. At issue was the constitutionality of a verbal ability test used to select police trainees for the District of Columbia police force. The Court held the test to be job-related and nondiscriminatory, despite the fact that it had a disparate racial impact and failed to meet the EEOC guidelines on testing. Noting that the District of Columbia police force had a large proportion of blacks as a result of an affirmative action program, the Court implied that the lawfulness of an employment policy should be judged in light of an employer's overall success in bringing blacks into the work force, even if one component of the selection process had a disparate impact on minorities.

The chief significance of *Washington v. Davis* lay in the Court's refusal to extend the *Griggs* disparate impact theory into constitutional law. Overruling numerous appellate court decisions in public employment cases, Justice White stated for the majority that proof of intent to discriminate was required in bringing discrimination charges under the equal protection component of the Constitution. If disparate impact theory were used for constitutional purposes, he predicted, it would possibly invalidate a wide range of tax, welfare, public service, regulatory, and licensing statutes that might be shown to be more burdensome to blacks than to whites.[50] Because public employers were brought under the coverage of Title VII in 1972, and because the decision did not interpret the meaning of Title VII, *Washington v. Davis* did not alter federal employment discrimination policy under the Civil Rights Act. The Court seems mainly to have acted with a view toward stopping the disparate impact theory of discrimination in the employment field from expanding into the realm of state government activities in general. Nevertheless, by reasserting the intentional disparate treatment concept of discrimination, a majority of the Justices implied that they had doubts about the general validity of disparate impact theory as an approach to civil rights law.[51]

Washington v. Davis complicated the already confused and ambiguous question of the principles of anti-discrimination law and policy. On the one hand, it permitted the disparate impact theory of discrimination announced in *Griggs* to continue as the dominant approach to public and private employment bias under Title VII, with the disparate treatment concept relegated to a subordinate role. On the other hand, *Washington v. Davis* asserted the intentional disparate treatment theory for constitutional cases generally, outside the employment field. The civil rights lobby feared the decision augured the overruling of *Griggs*. Yet in a practical sense, the court's action had the effect of insulating Title VII enforcement under disparate impact theory—and affirmative action preferences logically related to it—against challenges based on constitutional equal protection and individual rights standards. Although the Civil Rights Act was based on the Fourteenth Amendment and the commerce power, when it was upheld against constitutional challenge the Supreme Court interpreted only the commerce clause as a source of authority.[52] Under the commerce power Congress has authority to regulate private employment, as in Title VII, and it is virtually impossible for an individual to bring constitutional rights to bear in this legal context to challenge private employment decisions that have the sanction of congressional authority. Thus, although *Washington v. Davis* cautioned against the indiscriminate spread of affirmative action driven by disparate impact theory, it protected and permitted the future expansion of preferential treatment in public and private employment.

V

A decade after the color-blind equal rights principle was confirmed and reasserted as the foundation of national civil rights policy in 1964, it was in process of being repudiated in favor of the concepts of group rights and equality of result. In public and private employment, race-conscious affirmative action had advanced far beyond what the most optimistic civil rights activists could have imagined when the Civil Rights Act was passed. In the field of political rights, the congressional intent to protect the right of individual access to the ballot in the Voting Rights Act of 1965 was transformed into a policy aimed at preventing the dilution of electoral power of blacks as a group.[53] In school desegregation, the Supreme Court approved the use of racial remedies to achieve racially-balanced integration in public education in the North, as well as the South.[54] The principle that had virtually served as a categorical ban on race-conscious government decisions—namely, that race is a suspect classification which triggers strict scrutiny and is acceptable only when justified by a compelling governmental interest—was transformed into an almost routine instrument of racial preference aimed at ending discrimination or eliminating its incalculable effects.

Acquiescing to the demands of the civil rights establishment, courts and government agencies adopted preferential policies as a politically expedient response to the race riots of the 1960s. Although it was rarely acknowledged, in the opinion of civil rights policymakers preferential measures were the price society had to pay to prevent further violence in the black community.[55] Considered in the abstract, few Americans then or now accept the notions of group rights and equality of result. The radical transformation of civil rights policy on this basis was politically feasible only in the context of southern racism and state-ordered discrimination. Against this background and in disregard of obvious evidence of social change resulting from society's acceptance of the nondiscrimination principle as embodied in the Civil Rights Act, proponents of preference argued that result-oriented affirmative action and proportional representation were the only effective means of overcoming institutional racism and societal discrimination. Through the use of race-conscious means, they contended, racially impartial individual rights and equality of opportunity could be achieved. The presumption of necessity and the threat to the public safety on which affirmative action rested obscured the fact that, in reality, it repudiated equal rights principles.

Commentators at the time acknowledged that courts adopted race-conscious measures in the absence of reasoned discussion, essentially on the grounds of political and social necessity. Since the crisis conditions that justified it were by definition not permanent, some civil rights theorists, aware of the bias in public opinion toward traditional equal opportunity, sought a more principled justification of preferential treatment.[56] They recognized in particular, as the equal employment opportunity strategist Alfred Blumrosen candidly observed, that justification of "numerical standards . . . for participation by minorities . . . in employment opportunities" was the "one major conceptual problem in the law which must be further explored to have meaningful implementation of Title VII."[57]

Yet, in the early 1970s, no defense of racial preference was offered other than the unexamined claim of necessity. Affirmative action theorists searching for a principled explanation of judicial acceptance of quotas fell back on the same reasoning used by the courts, which were criticized for making unprincipled, expedient decisions. The nondiscrimination principle was seen as inadequate because social conditions of blacks were unequal to those of whites. The Civil Rights Act, if not clearly a failure, could not achieve its goals without permitting racial decision making. Above all, since past discrimination was race-based, remedies aimed at ending it and overcoming its effects must be race-based.[58] A theoretical justification by a former EEOC staff attorney, intended to show that preferential remedies were not simply pragmatic and result-oriented, concluded that although quota relief was "punitive," it was necessary in cases of extreme employer recalcitrance. Furthermore, where a court could not determine, under disparate impact theory, which practices in an institutional setting caused discrimination, it was practical and equitable simply to require quota hiring.[59] Pragmatism—or political expediency—was thus a pervasive rationale for race-conscious measures.

Although they either failed to recognize or refused to admit it, the real justification for affirmative action, in the view of its apologists, was the belief that group rights, racial proportionalism, and equality of result are correct principles of social organization that deserve to be established as the basis of civil rights policy. This is the inference to be drawn from civil rights leaders' insistence on racial group proportionalism, in the face of evidence in the late 1960s and early 1970s that employer acceptance of the nondiscrimination principle removed barriers and enabled blacks to advance economically. As discriminatory practices ended and opportunities were opened to minorities, the civil rights lobby changed its tune. Now it complained that discrimination was a subtle and continuous social process constituting a complex web of institutional relationships that required new strategies of attack. As one legal commentator on affirmative action put it, discrimination became "a term of art" that was "developed by the courts in ways that are not intuitively obvious."[60] Under the concept of disparate impact discrimination, it became an unquestioned assumption of public policy, contrary to reason and empirical observation, that jobs and other social benefits in the absence of discrimination are distributed in proportion to the percentage of the total population constituted by a racial or ethnic group.

The legal meaning of discrimination, and hence of equality of opportunity, was divorced from the ordinary meaning of intentional unequal treatment used in political and social life. Group rights and equality of condition were introduced into public opinion as a new public philosophy that distinguishes among individuals on racial and ethnic grounds and that ultimately denies the existence of a common good. The consequence was to inject political and ideological motives and a tendency toward legalistic manipulation and underhandedness into civil rights policy. Such an infusion weakens personal responsibility in race relations and erodes the moral consensus on which the nation agreed to abolish racial discrimination in the Civil Rights Act of 1964.[61]

Would the race problem in the United States be resolved in accordance with the color-blind equal rights principle contained in the Constitution and confirmed in the Civil Rights Act? Or would the race question be used by reformers hostile to this principle to repudiate equality and expand government power at the expense of individual freedom and entrepreneurial liberty? Judicial interpretation of Title VII from 1965 to 1975 clearly tended toward the latter outcome. This might have been justified, as a defender of affirmative action argued at the time, if judicial decisions contributed to social unity, interracial harmony, and minority progress based on recognition of individual rights, thus fulfilling the goal of the Civil Rights Act.[62] Whether Title VII enforcement in the 1970s tended toward this result, however, is highly debatable.

Title VII makes racial decision-making irrelevant in employment relations in order to give equal opportunity to individuals. The question is whether race-conscious remedies, especially those unrelated to specific acts of discrimination that give preference to blacks because of historic societal discrimination, advance American society toward that goal. Critics of affirmative action contend that racial preference reinforces and institutionalizes racial thinking and decision making. Defenders of preference, appealing to a dialectic that has become an article of liberal faith, hold that the best way to show the irrelevance of race and promote racial understanding is to use race-conscious policies to give blacks jobs alongside whites.[63]

By the mid-1970s, judicial decisions on employment discrimination generally supported the liberal dialectic. In the pattern of shared responsibility that characterized the development of affirmative action, judicial policymaking in turn influenced the political departments and the civil rights bureaucracy. Not to be outdone, these executive agencies, oblivious to public opinion, extended and institutionalized racial preference in the business practices and corporate culture of our society.

3

The Title VII Amendments of 1972 and the Nixon Administration EEOC

The Civil Rights Act of 1964 and the Voting Rights Act of 1965 were bipartisan measures that recognized the political significance of the black vote. Such legislation was intended to guarantee the individual rights of black citizens as members of the governing majority. Although these laws were politically motivated insofar as both parties sought to appeal to black voters, they were nonpolitical in a deeper sense: they were an attempt to promote the common good by eliminating race as a legitimate classification in public policy and in private employment. Scarcely before the ink dried on this historic legislation, however, federal administrative agencies and courts decided that the color-blind nondiscrimination principle embodied in it was inadequate for achieving the equal rights goal. Both laws were promptly implemented as remedial measures conferring preference on blacks as a designated minority group requiring affirmative discrimination.[1]

Particularly, Title VII of the Civil Rights Act was used to assert a new social theory—the theory of disparate impact discrimination—that provided the ground for repudiating and redefining American equality. Under the concept of disparate impact, the cause of racial inequality was found in societal discrimination rather than individual prejudice, and group rights and equality of result were assumed as foundational principles of civil rights policy. Disparate impact theory, which was to be adopted by the Supreme Court in *Griggs v. Duke Power Co.* as the central meaning of unlawful discrimination under Title VII, rationalized and supplied a legal incentive for the preferential practices that the Equal Employment Opportunity Commission (EEOC) and the Office of Federal Contract Compliance (OFCC) required employers to adopt in the 1960s as the substance of affirmative action.

Preferential treatment politicized civil rights policy in a destructive sense: it legitimized the use of racial and ethnic criteria for conferring or denying the rights of individuals according to political expediency or ideology. When civil rights policy passed from Democratic to Republican control in 1969, it became further politicized. Bipartisanship did still exist to some extent; neither party could afford to appear opposed to civil rights or unsympathetic to measures for improving the socioeconomic condition of blacks as a disadvantaged minority. Instead of eliminating race from politics, however, as the Civil Rights Act intended, affirmative action bipartisanship during the Nixon Administration broadened the use of race in public policy. Although the administration opposed racial balancing in school desegregation, it supported extension of the Voting Rights Act and national application of the idea that the black vote should be protected against "dilution." In the employment field, the Nixon Administration extended the Philadelphia plan quota policy from the construction industry to the entire federal contract program. Moreover, it supported the long-standing effort of the civil rights lobby, commencing with the enactment of Title VII in 1964, to strengthen the enforcement authority of the EEOC.

Like his Democratic predecessors, Richard M. Nixon approached the administration of equal employment opportunity policy partly with a view toward the partisan benefits it could produce. Particularly, the federal contract program, along with the program for businesses owned by disadvantaged persons that was created by Congress in 1967 and operated by the Small Business Administration as a minority set-aside policy, formed a source of patronage that could help win black political support for the Republican party. Liberal criticism of President Nixon as an opponent of civil rights reinforced the tendency inherent in executive administration of equal employment opportunity policy to politicize the issue.

Despite vigorous Republican expansion of preferential treatment under the affirmative action policy begun by the Johnson Administration under Executive Order 11246, liberals in Congress and the civil rights lobby attacked the Nixon OFCC for failing to enforce the affirmative action obligation. Similarly, despite EEOC's success in securing judicial adoption of the disparate impact theory, liberals attacked the commission as a powerless agency that failed to eliminate job discrimination. Seeking to strengthen the EEOC, they proposed not only to give it cease and desist authority but also to transfer the OFCC's contract compliance function to it. Continually placed on the defensive and threatened with denial of a source of patronage that had been an executive prerogative for nearly three decades, President Nixon responded to liberal criticism by extending the sphere of OFCC affirmative action and supporting amendments to Title VII expanding the powers of the EEOC. Under both Executive Order 11246 and Title VII, the Nixon Administration strengthened the ability of the civil rights bureaucracy to promote race-conscious equality of result in the name of equal opportunity.

I

Giving EEOC enforcement authority was an item of unfinished business from the liberal agenda of 1964. As though oblivious of the development of Title VII law in the courts, liberals clung to the idea that EEOC should be an independent regulatory agency with cease and desist authority. Regarding the compromise that created the Commission as a tactical maneuver that imposed no political or moral obligation, they rejected the idea that Title VII represented a fundamental consensus on the nature of discrimination and the proper scope of government interference with business autonomy. Clifford L. Alexander, the EEOC chairman in the Johnson Administration, stated that the employment discrimination structure set up by Title VII was merely an interim device to be eventually superseded by the creation of an agency with cease and desist power. Liberal Republican Senator Jacob K. Javits of New York similarly observed that the compromise denying EEOC enforcement authority was tactically necessary to overcome the southern filibuster in 1964, and was not a bar to giving the agency effective authority to act against employment inequality.[2]

While EEOC and the courts developed the pro-plaintiff disparate impact theory of discrimination, congressional liberals from 1965 to 1972 introduced several proposals to reform federal employment discrimination policy in general and strengthen the EEOC in particular. Although differing in details, the measures conferred cease and desist authority on the EEOC, extended Title VII to employers with eight or more employees and to state and local governments and educational institutions, transferred authority over pattern and practice suits from the Department of Justice to the EEOC, shifted the federal equal employment opportunity function from the Civil Service Commission to the EEOC, and transferred the contract compliance program from the

OFCC to the EEOC. Bills containing several of these features were passed by the House in 1966 and the Senate in 1970. In June of 1971, the House Education and Labor committee reported a bill that included all the enumerated reforms except transfer of the federal equal employment opportunity function to the EEOC. In revised form this bill became the Equal Employment Opportunity Act of 1972, more commonly known as the Title VII amendments of 1972.

The issues involved in amending Title VII essentially arose from the debate over the Philadelphia plan. The only difference was that organized labor and the civil rights lobby were now more agreed on a common course of action against the Nixon Administration. Liberal Democrats and their allies in the civil rights organizations wanted a strong EEOC with independent regulatory authority. Centrist and conservative Democrats, representing organized labor, saw an opportunity to strike at the Nixon Administration and satisfy the anti-quota demands of their constituents by shifting the contract compliance program from the OFCC to the EEOC. The Nixon Administration's dual objectives were to show support for civil rights by giving the EEOC direct law-enforcement authority and to maintain control of the executive order program by keeping contract compliance in the OFCC. In protecting its administrative prerogatives, the Nixon executive branch once again rose to the defense of race-conscious affirmative action.

Liberals argued that the EEOC should have cease and desist authority to deal with the subtle and complex sort of discrimination, involving "systems" and "effects" rather than intentional wrongs, that Title VII was now said to be concerned with. The Senate Labor and Public Welfare Committee explained in 1970 that since employers did not conceive of discrimination in the language of the social sciences, it was first necessary to establish "the technical perception that a problem exists . . . and that the system complained of is unlawful." The committee argued that a full-fledged regulatory agency with the power to hold hearings, make findings of discrimination, and issue cease and desist orders could do this while achieving far more success than the judiciary in eliminating this new type of discrimination.[3] Mainly, however, liberal Democrats supported the regulatory approach because it was a fixture of civil rights ideology.

Denying that progress in civil rights had occurred as a result of the removal of what were now called "overt" discriminatory barriers, liberals treated anything less than the establishment of a full-scale regulatory agency as unworthy of consideration by those who truly cared about civil rights. "If there is one thing that is clear in the history of this subject," declared Joseph Rauh of the Leadership Conference on Civil

Rights, "it is that everybody who has been for civil rights has been for cease-and-desist powers, and everybody who has opposed us in our quest for civil rights has been against cease-and-desist powers."[4] According to Representative William Clay of Missouri, a black Democrat, the question of Title VII reform boiled down to the issue of whether the opinion should be followed of those who had devoted their lives to civil rights or those who had opposed them. Warnings of ghetto violence if blacks were not given an agency with cease and desist powers showed the political nature of the liberal proposal for Title VII revision even more clearly. Testifying in support of legislation to give the EEOC cease and desist power, Clarence Mitchell of the NAACP declared: "What we are in need of is a massive infusion of confidence which will let the country know and which will let the unhappy people and the dissident elements know that we are really serious about this effort of trying to eliminate job discrimination." Mitchell contended that if the EEOC was only given power to file discrimination changes in court, as the Nixon Administration proposed, "the man in the street will see that he is getting the runaround from the government." The NAACP lobbyist said that while he himself would never join the forces of violence, he was realist enough to know that "you can't answer the man about to throw a Molotov cocktail if we say 'We are not going to give you cease and desist powers. . . . What we are going to give you is a chance to have a different set of lawyers.' "[5]

Faced with the political necessity of supporting stronger Title VII enforcement powers, the Nixon Administration fell back on the proposal to give the EEOC the power to go into court and file discrimination charges, which liberal Republicans had insisted be included in the civil rights bill passed by the House of Representatives in 1964, but had been struck out in the compromise on Title VII in the Senate. Although the EEOC's regulatory powerlessness had not kept it from radically revising the meaning of discrimination under Title VII, good reasons existed to give the Commission direct law enforcement authority. As long as the EEOC could only conciliate and the individual complainant alone could file suit, employers could defeat meritorious claims by stalling.[6] While sound in principle, the argument that EEOC powers should be expanded for the sake of fairness and due process ignored the fact that courts were then systematically interpreting Title VII to favor plaintiffs. The Nixon Administration and its business allies were so preoccupied with opposing the grant of cease and desist authority to the EEOC that they uncritically accepted and even defended judicial supervision of Title VII enforcement, notwithstanding the drastic revision of the law that was then taking place.

Having decided that it was not politically feasible to withhold support for a civil rights bill strengthening the authority of the EEOC, the administration had little choice but to promote the court enforcement option for the Commission. The Republicans repeatedly emphasized the superior objectivity and value of adversary proceedings under judicial regulation as a means of securing fair resolution of discrimination disputes. Moreover, they could console themselves with the thought—which assumed the status of an article of faith—that an anti-business regulatory agency with cease and desist power would be the worst alternative.[7] So strong was the appeal of the emerging affirmative action ideology, however, that the Republican administration desired an impartial and equitable Equal Employment Opportunity Commission no more than did the liberals and the civil rights lobby. For example, a National Urban League official approvingly observed that an effective anti-discrimination policy required having officials who were not impartial in employment bias disputes.[8] Similarly, EEOC Chairman William H. Brown III, conceding the pro-plaintiff bias of the Commission, said such an attitude was appropriate in a judicial setting where the courts had the final word in settling employment discrimination disputes.[9]

The issue that aroused the deepest passions in the debate over the amendments to Title VII concerned control over the executive order affirmative action program. Organized labor and the civil rights establishment, key Democratic constituent groups, continued to disagree on preferential treatment, but they could cooperate on the proposal to strip the administration of control of contract compliance affirmative action. Despite the OFCC's decisive efforts to require preferential practices, congressmen identified with civil rights concerns attacked it for failing to make the Philadelphia plan effective and for lacking civil rights commitment.[10] Representing the view of labor, where the plan to transfer OFCC functions originated, mainstream Democrats denounced goals and timetables as reverse discrimination and proclaimed their intent to bring the contract program under the Title VII ban on preferential treatment.[11] These anti-quota arguments were political in nature; they could not be taken seriously in view of the pro-quota decisions of the federal judiciary under Title VII. By then, the issue was not affirmative action preferences versus color-blind equal employment opportunity. Rather, it was quotas administered by the Nixon Labor Department as against quotas under the control of the EEOC, with its political ties to the civil rights lobby and under congressional oversight.

The 1972 debates are nevertheless of interest as a further illustration of the coequal if not leading role played by the Republican Party in establishing racial preference. As in the controversy over the Philadelphia plan, the Nixon Administration was concerned about controlling the contract program as a source of patronage while satisfying the political demand to support civil rights. Administration officials boasted of pressuring contractors to go beyond the passive nondiscrimination requirements of the Civil Rights Act without getting bogged down in problems of law enforcement, including the difficulty of proving discrimination.[12] Criticizing a Democratic anti-quota amendment to the pending legislation as a mere political gesture to the trade unions, Republican congressmen defended Philadelphia plan quotas and the discretionary authority on which they rested. The power was not based on constitutional or statutory rights, they explained, but on the ability of the executive to control the practices of companies wishing to do business with the government.[13]

The Title VII amendments came up first in the House, where the Committee on Education and Labor in 1971 reported H.R. 1746 transferring OFCC functions to the EEOC. The bill also shifted jurisdiction over pattern or practice suits to the EEOC and extended Title VII coverage to state and local governments and to firms with eight or more employees. The anti-quota amendment already referred to was proposed on the floor, along with a two-year limitation on back pay. Before these could be voted on, however, the Republicans introduced a substitute bill. It authorized the EEOC to initiate discrimination suits, limited back pay to two years, required timely service of EEOC charges on employers, and limited class actions to individuals who were named or joined the suit.[14] These provisions indicated a desire to limit the extent of pro-plaintiff enforcement of Title VII without questioning the basic direction of race-conscious policy. Democrats attacked the Republican substitute measure as a quota bill because it preserved OFCC control of executive order affirmative action, derisively calling it "a phantom Civil Rights Act" that was not supported by the civil rights lobby. They urged passage of the committee bill as "a symbol that we . . . are still firmly opposed to racism and that we want to end it using the most vigorous mechanism we can."[15] Nevertheless, the House approved the Republican substitute, 200-195.[16]

In the Senate, liberal Democrats clung with unthinking conviction to the concept of an independent regulatory commission. Republicans and business lobbyists, however, citing liberal affirmative action strategists like Alfred Blumrosen who relied on disparate impact theory and numerical remedies, succeeded in breaking the perception that conferring cease and desist authority on the EEOC was the only correct civil rights position.[17] During the debate, a number of scholars committed to civil rights were reported to be critical of congressional liberals'

knee-jerk reaction against the Republican bill. The Republican measure, the scholars pointed out, confirmed the exercise of judicial
authority in Title VII cases in a manner that accepted the views of the
civil rights lobby.[18] The *New York Times* reflected the administration's
success in winning over liberal opinion when it announced its support of
the Republican bill. The *Times* praised the bill as a moderate alternative
that sought to achieve "nonpartisan enforcement of the law . . . through
reliance on the courts [rather] than upon a politically appointed
commission."[19]

Accordingly, when the Senate Labor and Public Welfare Committee
in January 1972 reported a bill to transfer OFCC functions and give
cease and desist authority to the EEOC, it ran into opposition.
Southerners filibustered and proposed the Republican substitute that
had passed the House, while centrist Democrats decided that independent regulatory authority for the EEOC was not worth fighting for. The
Senate rejected the transfer of OFCC functions, 49-37, and then
approved an amendment to the Labor Committee bill giving the EEOC
power to file discrimination charges, 45-39.[20] A conference committee
was appointed, and its report was adopted as the Equal Employment
Opportunity Act of 1972.

The amendments to Title VII contained in the 1972 act authorized the
EEOC to bring civil suits for violation of the act, extended coverage of
the law to firms with fifteen or more employees and to educational
institutions and state and local governments, and gave the EEOC
concurrent jurisdiction of pattern or practice suits with the Department
of Justice. It also provided that, after two years, the EEOC would have
exclusive jurisdiction. The act strengthened judicial remedial authority
by adding language to Section 706(g) authorizing a court to order, in
addition to affirmative action, "any other equitable relief as the court
deems appropriate." The act also authorized the Civil Service Commission to enforce equal employment opportunity in the federal service and
created the Equal Employment Opportunity Coordinating Council.
Comprising the EEOC, the Department of Labor, the Department of
Justice, the Civil Service Commission, and the U.S. Commission on
Civil Rights, the council was instructed to formulate a uniform approach
to enforcing Title VII and Executive Order 11246.[21]

In the 1972 debate on Title VII, the Senate rejected two anti-quota
amendments introduced by Senator Ervin of North Carolina.[22] Like the
defeat of the 1969 rider against the Philadelphia plan, this action has
been regarded by proponents of affirmative action as constituting
statutory approval of preferential treatment. The votes cannot properly

be regarded in this light, however, since they merely rejected proposals to prohibit quotas. At most, the Senate action expressed a political opinion supportive of the developing administrative and judicial policy of preferential treatment. The Title VII amendments have similarly been interpreted as a statutory approval of the disparate impact theory of discrimination on the basis of references to the *Griggs* decision by several lawmakers.[23] This, too, is an untenable argument. Congress did not reenact Title VII and amend the testing provision with which *Griggs* was most concerned. In fact, it rejected a proposal, requiring that tests be job-related and removing the intent requirement for proving a violation of Title VII, that would have expressly affirmed the *Griggs* ruling. In a political rather than in a legal sense, Congress may be said to have approved the Supreme Court's acceptance of disparate impact theory, but this expression of opinion did not alter the legal requirements of Title VII.[24]

II

Because Congress did not revise the substantive requirements of Title VII, the fundamental contradiction that had developed in employment discrimination policy since 1965 continued to exist. The law created an individual right not to be discriminated against in employment because of race, ethnicity, national origin, religion, or sex. It provided means by which individuals could file complaints of discrimination against employers and secure equal treatment through EEOC conciliation or civil litigation. Yet from its inception, the EEOC was mainly concerned with societal discrimination defined in terms of racial groups. Focusing on patterns of exclusion and underrepresentation, the Commission conducted and required racial surveys of the work force in order to pressure employers into hiring minorities. The basic assumption on which this policy rested was that statistical disparity was evidence of discrimination. Of course, since Title VII so plainly looked to individual complaint resolution, the EEOC could not ignore this aspect of the situation, despite the fact that employment equality policymakers considered it unproductive. The complaint backlog in 1971 was 30,000—a 60 percent increase from 1970—and it continued to expand throughout the decade.[25] The inescapable requirements of Title VII thus imposed a huge administrative burden on the EEOC that constituted a continuing political liability. In a theoretical sense, moreover, complaint processing and the backlog it generated forced the EEOC to recognize the disparate treatment concept of discrimination, based on individual rights, that civil rights liberals saw as an obstacle to their attempt to redefine American equality.

Indicative of the priorities of the civil rights lobby, EEOC Chairman William H. Brown III ignored the issue of individual rights in a public appraisal of the 1972 Title VII amendments. Interpreting the statutory changes as reflecting the disparate impact theory of discrimination, Brown said they showed how far the concept of employment bias had advanced from the naive and simplistic notions prevalent in 1964, when discrimination was thought to be the result of specific actions caused by the prejudice of an individual or organization. Brown explained that employment discrimination was now known to be the result of institutional systems and effects associated with personnel structures such as seniority, lines of progression, and the perpetuation of past practices in present requirements. Most important, proof of the intent to discriminate was no longer a prerequisite for a finding of unlawful practices.[26]

EEOC staff member Phyllis A. Wallace, in a 1973 analysis, elaborated on the detrimental effect of the individual rights approach to employment discrimination policy. Wallace criticized federal policy as a cumbersome system that was bogged down in a steadily expanding backlog of complaints from individuals and expensive litigation efforts. She recommended that the EEOC put a one-year moratorium on complaint processing and spend 90 percent of its budget on identification of patterns of discrimination. In addition to class actions, she proposed "multi-defendant" suits under the Commission's new court enforcement authority as a way of streamlining and reducing the costs of litigation. In fact, the objective of affirmative action strategists like Wallace was to skip the litigation process entirely and force employers to adopt hiring policies set by the government. Wallace recommended eliminating the confidentiality provisions of Title VII that protected employers from unfavorable publicity stemming from unfounded accusations of discrimination. "If the minority employment data from some of the largest companies and unions was made available to the public," she wrote, "such organizations might be induced to alter their employment practices." Wallace further proposed quota systems to overcome the limitations of Title VII. She supported a plan under which large corporations, the federal government, and universities would recruit, train, and promote minorities and women over a ten-year period in proportion to their representation in the local labor market. "If it appears that a quota system can be set for jobs with status, power, and money," she asserted, "this might be sufficient to induce other employers to comply with the weaker provisions of Title VII," which she admitted prohibited quotas.[27]

Further advice on how to overcome the individual rights bias of Title VII came from Alfred W. Blumrosen, a leading theorist of disparate impact discrimination and an EEOC staff member in the Commission's early years. Like other civil rights experts, Blumrosen criticized the EEOC for doing what the law required: investigating complaints, finding reasonable cause, conciliating, and filing discrimination charges under its new litigation authority. As an alternative, he proposed that the Commission pursue selected major employers, using temporary injunctions based on findings of reasonable cause produced by its investigations. Blumrosen believed that with the *Griggs* decision, anti-discrimination law was at a crossroads. It could either be bureaucratized with an emphasis on individual litigation or expeditiously applied against strategically located corporations to end employment discrimination throughout the economy. Blumrosen would threaten large employers with disparate impact charges, forcing them to bring minorities into the work force on a reasonable numerical basis. Yet he feared that the result-oriented managerial or corporatist approach to employment equality that he favored would be frustrated by an expanding and legalistic bureaucracy, linked in a symbiotic relationship with civil rights organizations and equal employment opportunity consultants, who for reasons of self-interest would perpetuate the discrimination problem.[28]

Blumrosen, always candid, was prophetic in his understanding of the political consequences of the institutionalization of employment discrimination policy. Bureaucratic sub-governments are inherently unsound in a republican constitutional order, and the one described by Blumrosen is especially threatening because it directly challenges the principles of individual rights and equality of opportunity. There was little awareness or appreciation of this fact in the early 1970s, however, because proponents of race-conscious measures, protected by the presumptive validity of any civil rights claim that was made against the historical background of southern racism, were able to obscure the real meaning of the redefinition of equality implied in the disparate impact theory of discrimination.

A perceptive analysis by economist Dale L. Hiestand clarified the basic issues at stake in anti-discrimination policy. Civil rights leaders and policy makers, Hiestand observed, were increasingly committed to the view that discrimination and any meaningful remedies for it must be conceived in group or class terms. The rhetoric of anti-discrimination enforcement and the concept of the labor market, however, were concerned with individual rights. As a result, the remedial policy of Title VII focused on individual complaints and discrimination charges—precisely what the civil rights establishment believed was useless for solving the social problems comprehended in the theory of societal discrimination.[29]

Civil rights policymakers therefore had to persuade the public and mainstream politicians to support or accept racial-group remedies against the public philosophy of color-blind equal opportunity expressed in the nondiscrimination principle and embodied in the Civil Rights Act and Executive Order 11246 according to their original purpose and intent. More specifically, this meant allocating jobs according to racial and ethnic criteria, instead of the methods then in use, including referral unions, veteran preference, seniority, and individual merit based on education, tests, and licensing criteria. Hiestand observed that the latter methods were all socially approved, especially merit selection based on tests, which was simply considered to be "good common sense." What would happen, however, he asked, if tests and other objective screening devices could not be used because of failure to meet EEOC standards of job-relatedness? Hiring decisions would become a kind of lottery, and Hiestand predicted that, under these conditions, affirmative action goals would become a source of comfort to employers because they represented a legally approved selection instrument where none other was available. Yet hiring goals were really quotas, and quotas were not socially approved. "The crucial question," Hiestand concluded, "seems to be whether legitimacy will develop for a sense of socially allocating jobs on the basis of belonging to a group . . . which is subject to unfavorable discrimination."[30]

III

Writing in 1973, Hiestand obviously thought racial criteria were not then generally accepted as legitimate. This perception makes clearer the decisive role of the Nixon Administration in establishing affirmative action preference.

In the 1960s, the EEOC tried to make racial group membership rather than individual merit the critical factor in employee selection practices. Equipped with the power to take discriminatory employers to court and initiate pattern or practice suits, the Nixon EEOC confirmed and expanded this approach. Starting in 1972, it undertook a major campaign against what it called institutional or systemic discrimination, based on disparate impact theory. It adopted the view that all employers, not simply federal contractors bound by the executive order, were obligated to go beyond passive nondiscrimination and merit hiring practices.[31]

The EEOC scored a major victory in its effort to make systemic discrimination the principal focus of Title VII enforcement in the A.T. & T. settlement of 1973. The case began in 1970, when A.T. & T. filed a request for a rate increase with the Federal Communications Commission, and the EEOC petitioned to intervene on the grounds that the company had violated equal employment opportunity requirements of the Federal Communications Act and the Civil Rights Act. This strategy, initiated before EEOC was given direct enforcement authority, was intended to test employment discrimination law in the arena of administrative litigation before a regulatory agency. Because 5 percent of the EEOC's complaint backlog involved A.T. & T. grievances, the Commission's intervention was also intended to reduce this burden. The principal concern, however, was to obtain a consent decree that could serve as a model to be applied on a system-wide or national scale to other industries. In public hearings and private negotiations with the company, the EEOC focused on institutional discrimination against women and racial and ethnic minorities. It attacked practices that perpetuated the effects of past discrimination, regardless of whether the acts occurred before the adoption of Title VII. The Commission held that Title VII provided whatever remedies were needed to end discrimination and make the victims whole; at one point it estimated that $175 million in back pay would be necessary.[32]

The EEOC appeared as David against Goliath in this test of power between the civil rights bureaucracy and a major national corporation. A.T. & T. had a good equal employment opportunity record by prevailing standards. In the previous three years, one-fourth of A.T. & T.'s new employees had been minorities, minority employment had increased 52 percent, and the number of minorities in management positions had increased 157 percent.[33] The company, represented by N. Thompson Powers, formerly the EEOC executive director, argued that the Commission's interpretation of Title VII went beyond existing law and expressed what the agency wished the statute to say, rather than what it actually required. Asserting that the major issue was whether the company was making a good-faith effort to comply with Title VII, A.T. & T. accused the EEOC of shifting the focus of the law to equal representation rather than equal opportunity. It further contended that the EEOC improperly and unfairly declared practices discriminatory that occurred before the enactment of Title VII, using standards not approved by Congress or the Supreme Court. John W. Kingsbury, an A.T. & T. vice-president for human resources development, rebuked the Commission for failing to recognize that the company's principal purpose was to provide communications service to the public, "not merely to provide employment to all comers, regardless of ability." Accusing the EEOC of pressuring the company to lower its selection standards, Kingsbury attacked the Commission's policy as "a misguided form of paternalism."[34]

A.T. & T. lost the battle with the government, in large part because it got caught in the toils of the contract compliance program and bureaucratic political infighting. While negotiating with the EEOC, A.T. & T. complied with OFCC requirements to submit a written affirmative action plan to the General Services Administration (GSA). The GSA, breaking an earlier agreement with the EEOC, accepted the plan without consulting with the Commission. The EEOC promptly attacked the affirmative action plan, complaining that the methodology used to calculate goals and timetables was flawed, that job and departmental transfer procedures were inadequate, and that no attempt was made to identify affected classes, thus avoiding the back pay issue. Many of these were questions having to do with Title VII that arguably did not arise under the strictly prospective affirmative action mandate of Executive Order 11246. Nevertheless, the EEOC prevailed. The Department of Labor decided that the GSA had not acted in the best interests of the contract compliance program and took jurisdiction of the A.T. & T. case. Negotiations ensued among the Department of Labor, the EEOC, and A.T. & T., and a settlement was reached. The key to it was the unified reaction of the government agencies to the proposed GSA accord with the company.[35]

The A.T. & T. consent decree was filed in the U.S. District Court for Eastern Pennsylvania in January 1973. The decree contained an affirmative action plan with goals and timetables; guidelines for intermediate targets and time frames; upgrading and transfer arrangements; and pay adjustments in the amount of $15 million in back pay to 13,000 women and 2,000 minority men, and $23 million to be paid annually to 36,000 minority and female workers as a result of real wage adjustment. A second consent decree was filed in May of 1974 that covered $30 million in back pay for 25,000 management employees. A.T. & T., by entering the agreement, did not legally admit to any discrimination. This was small consolation, however, considering that the outcome was similar to what might have resulted from actual litigation. From the

EEOC point of view, the A.T. & T. consent decree appeared to be a model negotiated settlement that struck a balance between voluntary compliance and court litigation as an enforcement procedure. EEOC staff regarded it, in effect, as a collective bargaining agreement for attacking institutional discrimination.[36]

Following the A.T. & T. settlement, the EEOC undertook an aggressive enforcement policy that focused resources on broad charges of discrimination and targeted a number of the nation's largest corporations. In April and May of 1973, it filed ninety discrimination suits against companies and unions. In September, it charged General Motors, Ford, Sears Roebuck, and General Electric with discrimination, as well as the United Auto Workers, the United Electrical Workers, and the International Union of Electrical, Radio, and Machine Workers. The Commission filed 300 suits against the country's largest corporations from 1972 to 1974, concerning wages, benefits, terms and conditions of employment, promotion, training and testing programs, and layoff and seniority procedures. The new systemic approach typically consolidated hundreds or even thousands of individual complaints into a single company-wide case. Among the more notable results was the steel industry consent decree, involving nine steel companies and the United Steelworkers. The decree awarded $30.9 million in back pay to 40,000 female and minority workers and provided transfer rights, wage retention, seniority provisions, and goals and timetables. Back pay awards of seemingly staggering proportions attracted the most attention, but the costs of restructuring transfer and promotion systems and revising personnel and industrial relations systems amounted to millions of dollars as well.[37]

The EEOC selected corporations as targets that had good civil rights records in the period before 1972, when equal employment opportunity was generally handled by personnel departments rather than lawyers and was considered a matter of enlightened social policy.[38] In the period initiated by the Title VII amendments and the A.T. & T. suit, equal employment opportunity was viewed as a financial threat and was dealt with by the corporation's legal department. Corporation executives complained that despite a good minority hiring record in the period of essentially voluntary compliance before 1972, they were targeted for aggressive EEOC enforcement. Conceding the applicability of the disparate impact theory of discrimination, they contended that companies should be judged on the basis of their success in overcoming racial imbalance. Corporate officers also worried that result-oriented anti-discrimination policy would lead to quotas in place of standards of merit. They feared that pressure to adopt affirmative action plans in order to avoid Title VII liability would open them to complaints of past discrimination from minority employees as well as charges of reverse discrimination from white male workers.[39]

William H. Brown III, the chairman of the EEOC, summed up the administration policy in stating that since it was obvious that not all employers would voluntarily comply with Title VII, the best way to get results was to threaten to take them to court. John H. Powell, Jr., Brown's successor as chairman, defended the targeting of leading corporations as a better allocation of resources than a plan of concentrating on individual complaints. "Once we get the big boys," Powell declared, "the others will soon fall in line." In pursuing its systemic policy the EEOC acquired a reputation for heavy-handed coercion. Assuming a hostile, take-it-or-leave it attitude, EEOC conciliation staff rejected the notion of trying to find a middle ground between two opposed positions and insisted that a settlement was possible only on the terms of the charging party. According to one EEOC representative, the Commission believed that "Title VII rights are not negotiable." "There are many ways to fulfill those rights," he explained, adding, "We negotiate over the *ways* to fulfill Title VII. Respondents invariably insist on negotiating the *rights* themselves! We justifiably take a *very* hard line on that issue."[40]

On the basis of interviews with over a dozen equal employment opportunity corporate managers, one industrial relations expert described EEOC staff thusly:

> Young people with no work experience . . . adversary conscious . . . Lack of understanding . . . Young, well educated, antagonistic to business . . . Lack business experience . . . Cynical distrust of industry and the union . . . Good faith? They say *we* define good faith . . . Demanding, at times threatening and usually egocentric . . . Activists who view each case as part of an ongoing movement.

According to an EEOC spokesman, the Commission interpreted the 1972 Title VII amendments to mean that "Congress said the EEOC view [of the law] was correct and gave us the power to *force* employers and unions to adopt *our* view!" Against the employer argument that compliance should be judged in relation to improvements in minority hiring and future projections, an EEOC lawyer said the pertinent question was: "Has the respondent done enough? We define 'enough' as being everything that's possible!"[41]

From the business standpoint, the EEOC's bureaucratic and legalistic approach was an obstacle to equal opportunity progress. It meant that judges, lawyers, and government administrators would decide complex questions in industrial relations despite lack of knowledge and experience with seniority systems, ability testing, and other features of the industrial system. Corporate leaders feared the EEOC attack on patterns of discrimination would undermine merit standards in executive hiring and promotion. There was no assurance, moreover, that after a consent decree was signed new demands would not be made by the government. These were all reasons to oppose EEOC policy. Yet the A.T. & T. example was instructive. It caused most large corporations to acquiesce in the Commission's policy, because the cost in bad publicity and the expense of litigation in resisting it were too high. Companies now began to create internal equal employment opportunity bureaucracies to comply with the government's affirmative action demands.[42]

John W. Kingsbury, the A.T. & T. executive who publicly accused the EEOC of "hyperbole of monstrous proportions," later recanted. Confessing that the company had failed to understand the need for formalized procedures to facilitate equal employment opportunity progress, he said that A.T. &. T. was acting to correct the situation by building the responsibility to meet affirmative action obligations into each supervisor's job. The company now understood that equal opportunity performance was as important as meeting service standards, budget, and productivity objectives. Kingsbury said reverse discrimination continued to be a problem, in the sense that no matter how hard corporate officials tried to explain the difference between goals and quotas, most employees believed they were the same thing. The company nevertheless insisted that ability and qualifications were the decisive factor in its employment practices. It further conceded that to achieve equal employment opportunity, it was necessary to acknowledge and compensate for past practices that were now considered discriminatory. A.T. & T. only hoped, in conclusion, that the government recognized there were limits to the burden business could carry in fulfilling national equal employment opportunity policy.[43]

Reflecting on the 1972 Title VII amendments, business pundits conceded that they erred in failing to anticipate the consequences of giving the EEOC direct enforcement power. Business lobbyists had thought it most important to deny the Commission cease and desist authority. To gain the votes needed to reject the regulatory approach, however, it was necessary to give the EEOC the power to sue employers. This created a situation, in the words of one corporation lawyer, where "Every company is now wide open." Under disparate impact theory, good-faith efforts, intention, and relative improvement in minority hiring were irrelevant in determining unlawful discrimination. If anything, equal employment progress was rewarded by the imposition of more systematic racial hiring requirements. The only way to remain in compliance, corporate equal employment opportunity advisors concluded, was to have the company work force reflect the minority population of the local community.[44]

The Nixon EEOC thus confirmed and expanded the race-conscious policies begun by the Democratic administrations of the 1960s. In a general sense, the failure to implement Title VII as intended is attributable to the fact that the political coalition that produced the compromise on equal employment opportunity enforcement did not last beyond the enactment of the law. This is not to exculpate courts and administrative agencies, but to call attention to the ultimate responsibility of Congress and the President for capitulating to the radical protests and social violence of the 1960s by rejecting the principle of color-blind individual rights as the basis of civil rights policy. From the moment Title VII went into effect, civil rights administrators, reflecting the views of the civil rights lobby, directed its enforcement machinery at past societal discrimination under an implicit theory of proportional representation. At the same time, congressional liberals proposed legislation to revise the law—or, in their view, to complete the task of reform begun in 1964—by giving the EEOC full regulatory authority, which was intended to be used to promote race-conscious affirmative action.

The systematic introduction of group rights and equality of result in place of equality of opportunity provoked a variety of critics and opponents. Organized labor, contractor associations, the National Association of Manufacturers, and the U.S. Chamber of Commerce at various times in the late 1960s and early 1970s publicly opposed the emerging policy of racial preference. These groups were unable, however, to organize an effective political opposition. In part, this was because the redefinition of civil rights policy was effected by seemingly minor and obscure bureaucratic regulations. Their practical significance was not understood, but in the political atmosphere of the time they were accepted by high level government administrators, politicians, and the courts as a legitimate fulfillment of the promise of equal rights contained in the Civil Rights Act.[45] At a deeper level, the failure to mount an effective opposition to quotas was the result of the willingness of the Washington political establishment to accept the view that compensatory racial preference was justified by past discrimination. This perception discredited the objections to quotas raised by organized labor and southern politicians like Senator Ervin of North Carolina. Business and industrial opposition to preferential treatment was more clearly based on principles of equal rights and entrepreneurial freedom, and did not bear the stigma of past discrimination. Yet business critics of quotas were unable to gain recognition and support from the Republican-controlled executive branch, which might have been expected to oppose the erosion and abandonment of equality of opportunity.

The Nixon Administration, despite efforts to slow down southern school integration, chose to make its mark in civil rights policy by requiring quotas in the construction industry under the revised Philadelphia plan and by protecting it against bipartisan congressional attack. The administration then joined battle with civil rights liberals on the question of Title VII reform. It succeeded in winning direct law enforcement authority for the EEOC, which in effect confirmed the judicial interpretation of Title VII and the affirmative action strategy of the plaintiffs' bar. Although placing some restrictions on back pay claims and class actions, the 1972 Title VII amendments agreed to by the administration expanded the sweep of the law and strengthened judicial remedial authority, which was being vigorously exercised to transform the statute into a redistributive public policy measure. Using its new powers, the EEOC gave priority to systemic enforcement based on statistically defined patterns of discrimination as a means of promoting race-conscious employment practices. Within the Nixon EEOC, only one dissenting voice was heard, that of black Republican Commissioner Colston A. Lewis, who objected to the anti-business thrust of the systemic enforcement strategy and to the policy of treating blacks as a distinct class to be viewed categorically as victims of discrimination.[46]

The Nixon Administration also succeeded in keeping control of the executive order anti-discrimination program against trade unionists' efforts to shift it to the EEOC. Race-conscious preferences were then greatly expanded by the Department of Labor under Executive Order 11246, the operational center of affirmative action that had the widest practical effect on employment practices.

4

The Office of Federal Contract Compliance and Affirmative Action in the 1970s

While Title VII enforcement agencies must develop remedial rationales under disparate impact theory to evade the manifest requirements of the nondiscrimination principle, the Office of Federal Contract Compliance (OFCC) employs coercive tactics that more clearly reflect the nature of affirmative action as a politically motivated policy of racial preference. Operating outside the legal-judicial process that (at least in theory) imparts fairness into Title VII proceedings, the OFCC is under no obligation to make findings of discrimination in order to require affirmative action. It simply demands that federal contractors adopt minority preference as a condition of doing business with the government. By broadening the labor pool, the affirmative action requirement of Executive Order 11246 is intended to lower the cost of procurement to the government. In reality, preferential practices often increase the cost of goods and services. These increased costs are contrary to the provisions of the Federal Property and Administrative Services Act of 1949, the nominal authority on which executive order affirmative action is often justified. This has never become an issue, however, mainly because affirmative action has usually been viewed as an instrument of social policy resting on inherent executive authority. Few are willing to challenge such authority as long as it is exercised on behalf of minority interests.

Although the OFCC could act largely without fear of legal challenge, it encountered greater political obstacles than did Title VII agencies claiming statutory or constitutional authority. On the one hand, labor unions and contractors continued to criticize the OFCC for establishing racial quotas. On the other hand, civil rights organizations charged it with lax enforcement of affirmative action for its failure to cancel contracts and put enough pressure on executive agency contract officers, who were said still to give priority to the government supply function rather than to employment equality for minorities. Despite its beleaguered position within the structure of civil rights politics, the OFCC in its freewheeling administrative discretion was the quintessential affirmative action agency. Operating in relative obscurity, it more directly affected a larger number of employers than the EEOC. Furthermore, although it was not required to, the OFCC found it politically expedient to employ a remedial rationale to justify preferential treatment. Unconcerned with the legal definition of discrimination, the OFCC, by acting on the basis of statistics of racial imbalance in an informal and non-theoretical way, put the concepts of societal discrimination and equality of result based on proportional representation into practice.

I

First ordered by President Kennedy in 1961, the affirmative action requirement was reaffirmed by President Johnson in Executive Order 11246 in 1965. In 1968, the OFCC required contractors to submit written affirmative action plans, without specifying the precise nature of their obligation. At the same time, it imposed minority hiring goals on the construction industry in a few cities, defining the affirmative action requirement more precisely. Philadelphia was the principal focus for this administrative innovation, giving rise to the controversy over the Philadelphia plan in 1969. Although President Nixon was able to save the plan from congressional attack, political opposition to quotas thereafter led the OFCC to pursue minority preference in the construction industry through less controversial 'hometown' plans 'voluntarily' adopted by contractor groups, labor unions, and local civil rights organizations. Counteracting this tactical retreat, however, the OFCC dramatically expanded the quota policy introduced in the Philadelphia plan. In November 1969, during the fight over the Philadelphia plan, the Labor Department issued OFCC Order No. 4, implementing Executive Order 11246 and applying to all federal contractors outside the construction industry. This order was to become famous (or infamous) in the world of employment discrimination policy as the linchpin of affirmative action. As initially promulgated without hearings and without notice, comment, or publication in the *Federal Register*, the order stated that, when administering affirmative action programs, "The rate of minority applicants recruited should approximate or equal the rate of minorities to the applicant population in each location." The order was altered slightly after Senator Ervin, smarting from his defeat in the battle over the Philadelphia plan, discovered and attacked it in January of 1970.[1] Order No. 4 was then reissued by the Secretary of Labor in February of 1970. It required non-construction federal contractors to submit affirmative action plans containing goals and timetables. In December of 1971, in the revised Order No. 4, the OFCC included women along with minorities as a protected group and beneficiary of the affirmative action obligation.

Like the affirmative action requirement dating from 1968, Order No. 4 applied to each prime contractor or subcontractor with fifty or more employees and a contract of $50,000 or more. It set forth the classic statement of affirmative action, couched in bureaucratic doubletalk designed to obscure the requirement of racial-group preferential hiring that was its main purpose. "An affirmative action program," the OFCC directive declared, "is a set of specific and result-oriented procedures to which a contractor commits himself to apply every good faith effort. The objective of those procedures plus such efforts is equal employment opportunity."[2] "Procedures without effort to make them work are meaningless," the order elaborated, "and effort, undirected by specific and meaningful procedures, is inadequate."

The traditional view of equal opportunity had always been that it was procedural in nature. It involved making available, or breaking down barriers that obstructed access to, forms and procedures by which individuals could exercise and pursue their natural rights and interests. The purpose of having procedures, of course, was to achieve results, but the outcome of practices based on the procedures was not predetermined. Rather, the outcome depended on the ability and effort of those individuals who exercised the right of equal opportunity. Order No. 4, by contrast, explicitly introduced the notion of "result-oriented procedures" as an expression of its racial-group redistributionist ethic. "An acceptable affirmative action program," the order stated, "must include an analysis of areas within which the contractor is deficient in the utilization of minority groups . . ." An affirmative action program also had to include "goals and time tables to which the contractor's good faith efforts must be directed to correct the deficiencies, and thus to increase materially the utilization of minorities at all levels and in all segments of the work force where deficiencies exist."

Order No. 4 defined under-utilization as "having fewer minorities in a particular job category than would reasonably be expected by their availability." Contractors were instructed to determine whether under-utilization existed by performing an eight-factor analysis. Factors to be considered were: (1) the minority population of the area surrounding the facility; (2) the size of the minority unemployment force there; (3) the percentage of minority work force there as compared with the total work force; (4) the general availability of minorities there that have the requisite skills; (5) the availability of minorities having requisite skills in an area in which the contractor can reasonably recruit (presumably one with a larger radius); (6) the availability of promotable minority employees within the contractor's organization; (7) the existence of training institutions capable of training minorities in the requisite skills; and (8) the degree of training which the contractor is reasonably able to undertake as a means of making all job classes available to minorities.[3] Order No. 4 said goals, timetables, and affirmative action commitments must be designed to correct any identifiable deficiencies. Where deficiencies existed, "and where numbers or percentages are relevant in developing corrective action, the contractor shall establish and set forth specific goals and time tables." Where the contractor did not establish a goal, his affirmative action program had to analyze each factor in the eight-factor analysis to explain the reasons for failing to set a goal.[4]

It will be apparent that the OFCC regulation, on the surface so precise and systematic, actually just listed a series of considerations relevant to employment without indicating how reliable data were to be obtained and proper weight given to each factor in order to determine whether a deficiency existed. Presumably, ascertaining relevant data under each factor and combining them through some formula or equation would reveal whether under-utilization existed. Advice on exactly how the eight-factor analysis was to be used to arrive at goals and timetables was therefore offered in language that stated:

> The goals and time tables should be attainable in terms of the contractor's analysis of his deficiencies and his entire affirmative action program. Thus, in establishing his goals and time tables the contractor should consider the results which could be reasonably expected from his good faith efforts to make his overall affirmative action program work.[5]

This advice or guidance, however, did not clarify the problem of how to proceed with the eight-factor analysis. In the end, Order No. 4 said in essence that under-utilization or a deficiency was to be determined in relation to a reasonable expectation of available minorities. Goals and timetables to correct the deficiency, while showing a relationship to the analysis of deficiencies, were to be based on what could reasonably be expected to result from "good faith efforts." It is little wonder that employers found Order No. 4 hopelessly vague and confusing. The order purported to make one thing unequivocally clear, however: quotas were not to be permitted. Invoking the formulation that was intended to obscure the reality of federal equal employment opportunity policy, Order No. 4 declared: "Goals may not be rigid and inflexible quotas which must be met, but must be targets reasonably attainable by means of applying every good faith effort to make all aspects of the entire affirmative action program work."[6] Consistent with this injunction, the order stated that each contractor's compliance status was to be judged not by whether he met the specified goals, but by reviewing the contents of his program, the extent of his adherence to it, and "his good faith efforts to make his program work . . .".[7]

Businessmen did not pay much attention to Order No. 4 when it was issued in 1970.[8] The construction industry was the focus of concern in the early battles over quotas in the Philadelphia plan; it continued to be controversial as unions, contractors, civil rights organizations, and government officials clashed over the hometown plans instituted by the Labor Department after it dropped the Philadelphia plan as a prototype. In fact, neither the Philadelphia plan nor the hometown plans achieved much minority hiring in the construction trades.[9] However, the Philadelphia plan did not have to work in any practical sense in order to achieve its goal. It had only to succeed in a political sense: it had to acquire symbolic value as a "civil rights" program sufficient to establish the legality of racial hiring quotas and to suggest that its critics were opposed to civil rights and economic improvement for blacks. Ineffectual as social policy, the OFCC quota policy accomplished this political purpose and prepared the way for Order No. 4. By broadening the application of numerical racial hiring requirements, the OFCC's expanded affirmative action policy in turn contributed to the national debate over quotas that occurred in 1972.

II

The quota question, as we have seen, was discussed in Congress during the framing of the Equal Employment Opportunity Act of 1972. At the same time, courts in Title VII cases were ordering quota remedies, providing civil rights advocates with arguments to refute the widespread belief that preferential treatment for minorities was unconstitutional.[10] The decision of the Democratic Party to adopt racial, ethnic, and gender quotas for its 1972 convention had the further effect of placing the issue on the national agenda. When millions of Americans saw delegates on television who had been selected according to strict affirmative action rules, it stimulated fears that jobs and education would also be apportioned on the basis of quotas rather than merit.[11] Moreover, while businessmen may have been slow to perceive the threat, many academics and intellectuals were vocal in their denunciation of the quota system portended by OFCC Order No. 4.[12] Although busing to achieve racial balance was the dominant issue in civil rights politics in 1971, by the summer of 1972 affirmative action quotas were prominently discussed in national politics.[13]

As in earlier phases of the struggle to define American equality, there was superficial agreement that quotas as a general policy were unwise, unconstitutional and illegal. There was disagreement, however, about what constituted a quota. Critics said the OFCC goals and timetables were quotas. Supporters of affirmative action invoked the distinction between goals and quotas, insisting that good-faith efforts were required for employers to be in compliance with equal employment opportunity standards and denying that specific numbers of minorities had to be hired. Once again, semantic sparring over the consequences to the employer of preferential racial hiring obscured or deflected attention from the fact that hiring by race was prohibited by Title VII and Executive Order 11246. The paradoxical and perverse result of Nixon Administration policy was that good-faith efforts *to hire according to race* were seen as protecting employers against the penalties imposed by law for discriminatory racial hiring.

President Nixon preached equal rights for individuals, while consolidating and extending preferential policies for minority groups. In his State of the Union message in January 1972, he stoutly defended the principle that each citizen must be given "an equal chance at the starting line and an equal opportunity to go as far and as high as his talents and energies will take him." To illustrate this approach he pointed to the Philadelphia plan, the model for "fair hiring standards" in the federal contract program, and to stepped-up hiring efforts within the government that resulted in a 20 percent minority employment rate throughout the federal service. President Nixon also noted a threefold increase in federal aid to minority business enterprise.[14] In fact, Nixon was too modest. The administration's expansion of set-asides for black businesses under the Small Business Administration Section 8(a) program appears to have been much greater than he suggested: it increased from

$8.9 million in 1969 to $208 million in 1973. Moreover, President Nixon extended the minority assistance policy by issuing an executive order in 1970 directing federal departments and agencies to increase black representation in the award of contracts.[15]

As preferential treatment became more politically controversial later in the year, President Nixon adjusted his rhetoric accordingly. He vigorously condemned quotas, while leaving government policies of minority preference in place. In August 1972, President Nixon and Democratic presidential nominee George McGovern both expressed opposition to quotas in letters to the American Jewish Committee.[16] In a Labor Day message, the President pursued the issue of quotas. "In employment and in politics," he said, "we are confronted with the rise of the fixed quota system—as artificial and unfair a yardstick as has ever been used to deny opportunity to anyone." He added: "Quotas are intended to be a shortcut to equal opportunity, but in reality they are a dangerous detour away from the traditional value of measuring a person on the basis of ability."

Instead of stopping with this categorical rejection of quotas, however, Nixon in effect set up a distinction between the Democratic party's political use of racial preference, and his administration's economic use of same. He defined the future of civil rights as a contest between the two policies. In an eerie and distorted echo of Abraham Lincoln's house-divided speech in the slavery struggle before the Civil War, Nixon said the country could not have it both ways. "You cannot be for quotas in limiting political opportunity," he admonished, "and against quotas in limiting economic opportunity." The implication was that liberal Democrats and labor leaders could not logically support political participation quotas while simultaneously attacking the Republican administration for establishing employment quotas. Ultimately, the issue for President Nixon was not the use of racial criteria, but the role of government in promoting the use of racial criteria. "Shall we become a people who place our individual welfare in the hands of Government bureaucrats, limiting each other's opportunity by race, religion, sex, age, national origin?" he asked. "Or shall we continue to try to erase false restrictions, judging each person by the quality of his work and the reach of his mind?"[17] If President Nixon saw the Democrats as the party of bureaucratic government, as he surely did, then he regarded the policies of his administration, including minority goals and timetables and business set-asides, as a non-bureaucratic, essentially voluntary means of erasing false restrictions and creating equal opportunity for individuals.

At the same time that he spoke out against quotas, President Nixon instructed department heads, for purposes of the federal equal employment opportunity program, not to interpret goals as quotas. This action was viewed in industrial circles as opening "a fresh can of worms," since although in theory there had never been quotas in employment, goals and timetables were commonly regarded as a euphemism for quotas. The respected construction industry trade journal, *Engineering News-Record*, asked whether, in banning quotas in government equal employment opportunity programs, the Administration was actually banning goals and timetables. If so, companies with government contracts would argue that they, too, should be released from such requirements. If not, "the entire squabble over quotas can be interpreted as an exercise in political semantics that would have no effect on actual opportunity practices in the government."[18]

An exercise in semantics and political maneuvering was indeed what the quota controversy of 1972 amounted to. Labor union officials seized on the President's statements enthusiastically, predicting that the administration would try to find ways other than "goals" to encourage minority hiring. Civil rights lobbyists confirmed this impression by criticizing administration pronouncements as a signal that the government had decided to abandon the Philadelphia plan. Sustaining the illusion of a get-tough policy against quotas, the Department of Labor said that contract compliance affirmative action programs were to be reviewed to ensure that goals did not turn into quotas. In September, the Department reminded the heads of executive departments that OFCC regulations did not require quotas of proportional representation, noting that goals and timetables might have been misinterpreted or misapplied. This flurry of anti-quota announcements was intended to provide reassurance that the administration did support traditional equal employment opportunity standards. That it had this effect could be seen in the NAACP's attack on the administration for retreating on equal employment opportunity policy in order to placate the labor unions. Yet the Department of Labor, in an effort to maintain its civil rights reputation, simultaneously barred a contractor for noncompliance with the Philadelphia plan, announced the adoption in Chicago of a hometown minority hiring plan, and denied that 'imposed' plans of the Philadelphia type were being eliminated. Affirmative action plans were here to stay, a Labor Department official declared.[19]

At the start of his administration, President Nixon advised that with respect to civil rights matters, his critics should pay attention to what the government did, not what it said.[20] The quota controversy in the 1972 campaign illustrates the truth of the President's assertion. While the government's rhetoric suggested opposition to racial hiring, it actually continued the quota policy announced in OFCC Order No. 4 uninterrupted.

III

Although things appeared otherwise to defenders of segregation, the Civil Rights Act signaled a bipartisan intention to place civil rights beyond political maneuvering and manipulation. Under the rule of affirmative action, however, the exercise of basic civil rights was politicized once again. Choices were made about the allocation of resources and the distribution of benefits to groups and individuals that were essentially political in nature. Yet the political character of these decisions was obscured by calling them civil rights issues.

Anti-discrimination policy under the executive order was political in two senses. First, the affirmative action obligation was a free-floating, open-ended requirement; its practical meaning depended largely on the political relationship, broadly conceived, between the contracting agency and the government contractor. The eight-factor analysis for establishing goals under Order No. 4, for all its seeming objectivity, did not alter this fact. Contract compliance was also political in a second, more partisan sense, owing to the conflict from 1969 to 1976 between the Democrat-controlled Congress and the Republican-controlled executive branch. Democrats unsuccessfully tried to shift OFCC functions to the EEOC in the early 1970s. Reluctant to give up an instrument of partisan advantage, President Nixon understandably resisted this change. By the mid-1970s, political motives and pressures caused the equal employment opportunity system to be internally contradictory and inconsistent in many respects, the object of conflict and criticism from civil rights groups on the left and employers and business lobbyists on the right.

The Republican approach to equal employment opportunity was to promote preferential racial hiring by emphasizing results, while acknowledging problems inherent in affirmative action and proposing to modify its administration to make it more acceptable to business executives. Secretary of Labor John T. Dunlop told a congressional panel in 1975 that the basic problem was balancing the right of a contractor to be reasonably certain of his contract commitments against the inherent uncertainty involved in establishing goals and timetables. He referred to the uncertainty in determining the appropriate labor market area in relation to which goals should be set, as well as the question of when, if ever, the affirmative action obligation should cease for contractors who had successful minority hiring records. Further-more, the government could tell contractors to set goals and timetables, but "there is no inherent requirement that they be achieved and therefore that creates some uncertainty as to whether they will be achieved." "The very concept of goals and time tables," the Secretary of Labor said, "is one which does not make for certainty of results." There was "great difficulty in knowing precisely whether the particular goal and time table was reasonable," and whether good faith efforts had been made.[21]

This assessment might be interpreted to imply that if equal employment opportunity policy was to become truly effective, goals and timetables ought to be replaced by real quotas. If that was the underlying point, it was politically unrealistic to act upon it. Less drastic changes were therefore suggested to improve the equal employment opportunity delivery system. In September 1976, Assistant Secretary of Labor John C. Read told the House Education and Labor Committee that OFCC was revising its regulations to preserve the philosophy of affirmative action while de-emphasizing mechanical requirements and report making. The purpose of equal employment opportunity reform, said OFCC director Lawrence Z. Lorber, was to concentrate on enforcing substantive nondiscrimination requirements, rather than compliance with "a paper review process."[22]

Assistant Secretary Read's analysis of affirmative action theory showed the convergence of sources of authority of equal employment opportunity policy, as well as confusion about them in the minds of federal policymakers. Executive Order 11246 was prospective in nature and did not require proof of discrimination as the basis of affirmative action. It was not, therefore, remedial. Nevertheless, Read referred to the "broad remedial purposes of the Executive Order" and the need to assure that contractors took affirmative action to correct patterns of employment disparities. He explained that the concept of disparity included the present effects of past discrimination, a Title VII judicial doctrine, and he noted that the courts were developing new areas of rights and remedies under the Civil Rights Act that the OFCC intended to apply in the contract program.[23]

Read stated that the OFCC wanted generally to focus on larger employers in order to achieve more substantial results. Proposed regulatory changes toward this end included increasing the minimum requirements for a written affirmative action program to firms with one hundred employees and contracts of $100,000 or more (an increase from fifty employees and $50,000 contracts in the existing regulations), increasing the limit for pre-award compliance reviews from one-million to ten-million-dollar contracts, and eliminating pre-award compliance review if a compliance review had been conducted in the previous two years. Moreover, instead of seeking nondiscriminatory practices to ensure equal treatment of individual employees and applicants, the proposed regulations focused on potential and apparent disparities in hiring and employment conditions and on determination of whether a contractor had developed an affirmative action program that fully met the requirements of Executive Order 11246. Secretary Read said the proposed rules reflected a better understanding of the private employer's situation without relaxing the commitment to affirmative action goals. The regulatory changes were intended to generate "some informed and rational discussion," Read observed, "as to how one should go about the business of defining affirmative action and quantifying it."[24]

To admit publicly ten years after Executive Order 11246 went into effect that the government was still trying to figure out what affirmative action meant was to confirm the contract compliance program's confusion and incoherence. Few were concerned enough to dwell on this fact, however, and this was especially true for those who were trying to shape the policy toward their own ends. The civil rights lobby, for example, despite the OFCC's consistent support of preferential treatment, attacked the contract program as a failure because contracts were almost never canceled or companies disbarred for noncompliance. Civil rights spokesmen opposed the proposed OFCC regulations as a "disastrous regression" that signified a sell-out to business. Although professing sympathy for companies facing equal employment opportunity red tape, black lobbyists opposed every suggested revision in compliance review and complained of having been excluded from the drafting process.[25]

Business lobbyists were no more inclined to challenge the basic tenets of race-conscious affirmative action than the civil rights establishment. Business critics supported administrative simplification of the contract program. A reduction in paperwork, said a contractors' attorney in the House equal employment opportunity hearings, "would . . . improve everybody's attitude toward affirmative action, because I think in industry generally today there is good feeling about affirmative action. I think we are over the hump and on the right track."[26] Yet business spokesmen criticized the proposed 1975 OFCC regulations for not guaranteeing due process to contractors who were declared non-responsible bidders.[27] They also objected to the OFCC's proposed adoption of back pay remedies, introducing Title VII concepts and judicial rulings into the jurisdiction defined by the executive order.[28] Business lawyers pointed out that the executive order was prospective in nature; it did not authorize the OFCC to seek affected class or back pay relief. A contractor who agreed to a back pay settlement with the OFCC was not protected, moreover, against a subsequent EEOC back pay suit because the courts could rule that a conciliation under Executive Order 11246 was not binding on the judiciary in a Title VII suit. "That is probably the most important thing to American business in these regulations," declared an industry lobbyist. Contractor representatives thus urged OFCC to stick to goals and timetables, not to get involved in questions of back pay. Showing the limited horizon in which they acted and their narrow conception of long-term consequences, business lobbyists simultaneously praised private civil rights attorneys and the courts for devising remedies for past discrimination under Title VII that they agreed were effective in causing management to take stronger affirmative action measures.[29]

Despite persistent criticism and occasional rhetoric about the need to unify federal employment discrimination policy, affirmative action by 1975 had become increasingly functional. It served the interests of competing interest groups and government agencies sufficiently to maintain and extend itself. Federal administrators could agree that a coordinated approach, as in the A.T. & T. case, produced significant results, but they were unwilling to make the necessary political concessions in the Equal Employment Opportunity Coordinating Council (the continuing intra-governmental panel created by Congress in 1972) to reach agreement on a uniform policy. Everyone felt compelled to support affirmative action, because the political costs of not appearing to do so were high. In a very real sense, everyone involved in employment discrimination policy could support affirmative action—precisely because the concept could mean so many different things. The one clear meaning it possessed was racial group preference, yet few were willing to challenge affirmative action in these terms.

Equality of opportunity based on the nondiscrimination principle was thus further redefined by Republican administrations in the 1970s to be group rights and equality of result based on proportional representation. To do this under Title VII, as we have seen, required the virtual rewriting of the law in terms of retroactive enforcement and disparate impact discrimination theory, manifestations never intended by its authors. To establish racial hiring under Executive Order 11246 was a simpler matter, because it depended on administrative fiat.[30]

Affirmative action in the Nixon-Ford period was more bureaucratically elaborate, but it remained essentially the same arbitrary and politically manipulative process it was in the 1960s. The eight-factor availability analysis required by OFCC Order No. 4 was the basis for

measuring a contractor's utilization of minorities. The government contracting agencies, however, refused to tell contractors how to perform the analysis; to have done so would inhibit agency discretion in defining affirmative action. In 1976, no agency memoranda existed to advise contractors on where information for the eight-factor analysis was to be found, how it was to be measured, what the relative significance of the factors might be, or how they were to be combined. The compliance agencies approached the analysis differently, with some of them ignoring the enumerated factors altogether in determining under-utilization by a contractor. If disparate impact theory was to be used, the key issue was the standard in relation to which minorities could be said to be disproportionately represented or under-utilized. The reasonable comparison to determine whether discrimination existed was between the proportion of minorities in the contractor's work force and the proportion of the minority group having requisite skills in the immediate labor market area. It was not clear, however, what the immediate labor market was. The OFCC said the labor market meant the Standard Metropolitan Statistical Area (SMSA), county, city, or recruitment area, or some combination thereof which reflected the highest minority population and work force. The reason for defining the labor market this way was to maintain maximum flexibility in putting pressure on contractors. Another difficulty was that contractors performing the eight-factor analysis had to convert statistical data from non-comparable sources into categories that could be compared to their own work force. They were given no guidance, however, in making the conversion. Furthermore, a contractor not deficient in minority hiring according to one standard—say, the labor market defined on the basis of city-wide data—was often forced to redefine the labor market area on some other basis that would show a deficiency. Agencies thus manipulated the availability analysis to make contractors appear non-compliant.[31]

Basing goals and timetables on under-utilization analysis was equally problematic. The logical way to develop a timetable was to consider the annual hiring or promotion rate or the projected rate of openings. A schedule could thus be established indicating how long it would take to reach the specified goal. Some contracting agencies, however, reversed the procedure, telling contractors arbitrarily to select a time for reaching a goal and making the annual hiring rate a function of the goal and the stipulated period of time. Furthermore, the idea of a good-faith effort, on which the distinction between goals and quotas depended, qualified the goal-reaching requirement and continued to be a confusing subject. Beyond advertising and recruitment, the OFCC gave little advice as to what constituted a good faith effort.[32]

Another problem was that contractors were required to have goals equal to or greater than the percentage of available minorities and females. Agencies justified this practice on the ground that discrimination should be eliminated as rapidly as possible. The use of inflated standards meant, however, that contractors were likely to be found non-compliant if they did not give preference to minorities. Because rates higher than availability could not be expected to be achieved except through racially preferential procedures, a contractor's agreement to try to reach such rates might be challenged as inherently discriminatory.[33]

In a formal procedural sense, the contract compliance program reflected arbitrariness, lack of uniformity, and uncertainty. In a substantive sense, it was intended to promote preferential hiring of minorities and women. The objective was proportionately equal employment of protected groups, rather than equal employment opportunity for individuals. Moreover, the theoretical distinction between goals and quotas, considered necessary for the political and social justification of affirmative action, in fact became meaningless. Personnel supervisors in private companies, aware that their job performance would be judged in part by their ability to meet a stipulated objective, tended to treat goals and timetables as inflexible instruments that had to be met. In an attempt to avoid being labeled "non-responsible," which was tantamount to practical debarment, managers did what was necessary to meet goals, even if they had to apply standards as rigid as these in a strict quota policy. Affirmative action in federal contract work was originally justified as an exercise of executive authority under congressional legislation intended to achieve economy and efficiency in providing goods and services to the government. A study of affirmative action under Executive Order 11246 in 1977 found the opposite result: "A program that requires preference for some at the expense of others simply does not accord with the contention that the program was undertaken to ensure that there be the fullest and most effective use of the nation's manpower resources."[34]

The contract program made quotas and preferential treatment an operative feature of private employment more effectively, with fewer legal controversies, than did the judicial establishment of quotas under Title VII. Compared to the executive order program, the judicial imposition of preferential treatment appears to be a restricted, measured, and temporary undertaking. In order to require quotas under Title VII, there had to be a complaint and proof of discrimination. Employers could invoke procedural guarantees; quota orders as a judicial remedy were exceptional, not routine. Under Executive Order 11246, by contrast, quotas were perfunctory; they were justified on a finding of under-utilization that was so easily manipulable as to be universal. Furthermore, the OFCC and the contract agencies took a more openly favorable view of affirmative action, rather than regarding it as something requiring elaborate justification in a defensive or apologetic manner.[35]

IV

Operating with broad discretion, the contract compliance program reflected the civil rights ideology of a small number of bureaucrats. If the government forced companies to adopt preferential practices, however, a substantial tendency toward race-conscious decision-making existed in the business world that facilitated the transformation of employment discrimination policy.

An industrial relations expert writing in the *Harvard Business Review* in 1968 advised that if recruiting efforts did not produce enough minority applicants, companies should consider preferential treatment. They could offer special training to bring blacks up to required standards, or simply accept poorer performance by minorities. Altruism or fear of adverse public reaction, in the view of this observer, led almost every major employer to retain blacks whose performance or attendance records would be unacceptable if made by whites. Herbert R. Northrup, an employment relations specialist, said many companies deliberately discriminated in favor of blacks to compensate for past failure to hire blacks or to persuade the civil rights agencies to relax their enforcement pressure. Northrup stated that employers were lowering their standards to hire unqualified workers. *U.S. News* reported that although employers were reluctant to admit it, reverse discrimination was being practiced more widely and was often the only way to obtain new black employees. Some personnel directors contended that reverse discrimination was required to convince blacks that the company wanted minorities to apply for work.[36]

A 1969 survey noted that 83 percent of *Fortune*'s 750 largest companies believed corporations should be doing more to solve the urban crisis by giving jobs to blacks. Almost as many persons involved in or affected by employment policy favored preferential treatment as opposed it. Fifty-two percent of professional persons thought companies had a responsibility not only to hire and train blacks, but also to educate and motivate them. Among managerial, blue-collar, clerical, and sales workers, the percentage favoring preferential treatment ranged from 44 to 49 percent. Among top-level executives, nearly 100 percent supported direct assistance to minorities and accepted lowered standards for blacks. First-line supervisors and foremen, however, were opposed to preferential policies because their performance was judged on the basis of productivity, and because they resented others getting through preference what they had had to work for.[37]

The idea of applying business management techniques to institutionalize affirmative action was a bridge between private employers and the civil rights agencies seeking to promote preferential treatment. Industrial relations consultant Theodore V. Purcell, S.J., cited the North American Rockwell Corporation to illustrate the use of "sophisticated systems engineering" for "advancing disadvantaged people." When conventional advertising and recruiting efforts yielded only meager minority hiring results, the company adopted a systems approach. It analyzed the racial composition of each unit, estimated new hires for the next year, ascertained the black labor market for each job category, and arrived at targets for minority hiring and upgrading. Unit managers were then responsible for reaching the goal. They were reported to like the system because it relieved them of uncertainty about how far and how fast affirmative action should be pushed. Although other firms considered this a reverse discrimination or quota system, North American Rockwell disagreed; its view was that only in this way could historical social disadvantage be changed. Purcell said many companies actually operated similarly, although they refrained from reducing the policy of preference to formal directives because of its controversial nature.[38]

As the civil rights agencies stepped up their efforts in the early 1970s, many businessmen continued to support preferential treatment. A St. Louis gas company executive told the EEOC at a public hearing: "I think our biggest job now is to give preferential or remedial treatment in whatever hiring we do to raise our percentage of minority employees and women employees." While explaining that its equal employment opportunity policy was not necessarily being reduced to numbers, a Louisville utility company official said the company aimed at having the same percentage of minority employees at every job level as the percentage of minorities in the local area population. Pointing out that OFCC Order No. 4 called, in effect, for preferential hiring, Theodore V. Purcell believed corporate executives faced the choice of either rapid integration and upgrading of blacks, or an escalation of racial strife.[39]

Purcell reported in 1974 that many managers took socially motivated actions not required by legislation or political pressure. Often, they set targets for black hiring in excess of the goals announced for compliance purposes. Noting that it was in the interest of companies and labor unions to prevent judges and government administrators from determining employment practices, Purcell said they could fight the agencies in court or develop programs more creative than those demanded by the government. Many corporations used an equal employment opportunity measurement system that offered rewards and penalties intended to change the behavior of managers, showing them how to arrive at an "ideal" number of minorities in the work force. Although middle-level managers often complained about the failure of blacks to show up for work, company executives increasingly included equal employment opportunity performance along with traditional business indicators as a standard in overall evaluation.[40]

Purcell observed in 1977 that preferential policies for qualified minorities and women were becoming commonplace. He argued that social justice required preference, provided it was rightly defined and carefully administered. Whether racial preference was justified or simply a form of reverse discrimination depended, in Purcell's view, on the circumstances. If the job in question was important and a significant difference existed between the skills of black and white applicants, then to choose the minority person was reverse discrimination. If, however, the job was not so important and the qualification level of blacks and whites was roughly the same, then preference for the minority candidate was appropriate and just.[41]

Despite considerable support for affirmative action in the business community, many executives criticized the new concept of equal employment and the coercive tactics of the civil rights bureaucracy. In a complaint to the Department of Labor, a Milwaukee executive expressed a widespread reaction against OFCC Order No. 4. The company in question had increased its minority hiring significantly, was training hard-core unemployed blacks, and had contributed to inner-city social reform projects. Now it was told by the OFCC that its equal employment opportunity record was inadequate. In order to keep its government contracts, it was required to analyze every department and job classification by race—a heavy and costly burden, considering the company's 300 departments and 450 job classifications. In one year alone, the company president complained, 37,000 job changes occurred; under OFCC regulations each one appeared to require an affirmative action reevaluation. The company protested that it was not prepared to make changes in its personnel program on such a great scale. "It is inconceivable to me," the executive wrote,

> that a corporation that has so sincerely and successfully applied its collective abilities to this important problem should find itself, on a basis of form alone, in a position of difficulty. I am certain you would

agree that the important objective is equal opportunity, and that has been, and will continue to be, our objective.[42]

C. Paul Sparks, an Exxon Corporation personnel officer and testing expert, stated in 1973 that employers did not object to the general philosophy of federal equal employment opportunity policy, but rather to the arbitrary definition of almost indefinable terms. Starting out as nondiscrimination, equal employment opportunity policy had gone beyond requiring affirmative action in the future to demanding remedies for past discrimination. Sparks observed that the results of employment practices had now become what counted, not the nature of the practices, with parity or proportionate representation for minorities and women the ultimate goal. He did not believe parity could be achieved, and he had "a gnawing feeling that at some point this [goal] can lead to a lack of freedom for individual self-determination." More serious, in Sparks's view, than the internal disruption caused by affirmative action planning was the fact that any difference of opinion about goals and timetables led to conciliation by government agencies or the courts. And no matter what language was used in conciliation agreements and consent decrees, the result was invariably a quota system.[43]

Government equal employment opportunity theory under Title VII and Executive Order 11246 emphasized voluntary compliance, a concept that civil rights bureaucrats clung to even as their methods became more coercive. Having filed affirmative action plans and having been found in compliance, contractors were still not secure against discrimination charges. Almost every contractor subjected to the conciliation or adjudication process, a business journal reported in 1975, had passed its compliance reviews. Nevertheless, the contractors were declared in violation of Title VII and forced into costly settlements on the ground that employers were responsible for the present effects of past discrimination. The Electronic Industries Association objected in congressional hearings in 1976 that the "rule of reason" had been abandoned and replaced by complex regulations and arbitrary procedures that were detrimental to achieving equal opportunity. For example, EEOC investigation and determination of whether reasonable cause existed to believe discrimination had occurred was described as the result of a subjective evaluation by untrained investigators who applied no consistent standard of judgment. Employers were precluded from contesting errors of fact, law, or interpretation, and conciliation agreements included demands going far beyond the original allegation. To call it a conciliation process was in fact misleading, the trade association testified, since it consisted in the presentation of adamant, often unreasonable demands. If the employer disagreed, the process was terminated.[44]

The defendants' attorney, Lewis J. Ringler, complained that consent decrees and conciliation agreements were "booby-traps." Employers who voluntarily entered an agreement made by the EEOC or a federal court found that the agreement could not be pleaded as a defense against Title VII actions that might subsequently be brought as a result of the implementation of the settlement. Ringler urged employers to fight back at the civil rights bureaucracy, resisting reverse discrimination and insisting that any agreements reached with the agencies be a final resolution of all issues and binding on all parties, including the government.[45]

Businessmen further complained that the civil rights bureaucracy refused to explain how minority hiring percentages should be determined. Many firms, therefore, set arbitrary preferential hiring goals in order to gain agency favor and acquire immunity from discrimination charges. Some set quotas without determining whether minorities with requisite skills were available. Moreover, many compliance officers using the eight-factor analysis stressed only the ratio of minorities to the majority population, without noting the other factors that were to be considered. Business writer Daniel Seligman pointed out that although Order No. 4 purported to be helpful in determining under-utilization, it offered no real guidance to contractors. A contractor trying to figure out a reasonable utilization rate for black mechanics, Seligman wrote, "might find himself utterly confused about the number of blacks in town who were already trained as mechanics, the number who were 'trainable,' the amount he was expected to spend on training, the distance he was expected to travel to recruit," and so on. Several years later the situation was no different. "Tons of paper are produced to prove or disprove a perception of either a government compliance officer or an industry AAP specialist," a person-nel expert observed. The failure to clarify the problem of availability analysis, however, did not deter the OFCC and the executive department contract agencies from exploring complex issues such as annual hiring and promotion rates. "More than 25 years of observing the cult development of government and industry specialists," he stated, "convinces me that we are moving more toward a preoccupation with the 'number of angels that can dance on the head of a pin' then toward progress in achieving effective equal employment opportunity."[46]

The major complaint among employers was that the civil rights bureaucracy proposed wholesale changes in basic business operations, while ignoring the problem of racial discrimination that Title VII and Executive Order 11246 were intended to ameliorate. According to industrial relations specialists Mary Green Miner and John B. Miner, most businessmen were prepared for and approved complaint conciliation as the essential element of anti-discrimination enforcement. They had no inkling that Title VII would be used to challenge basic personnel policies and practices that were fairly administered. Yet the EEOC and the OFCC viewed individual complaints mainly as an opportunity to review the whole spectrum of a company's employment practices. Instead of working out a settlement in an individual situation, which companies were willing to do, the EEOC insisted on agreements calling for fundamental changes in employment policy. Employers anticipated a quasi-judicial role for the EEOC in conciliation. The Commission, however, according to Miner and Miner, adopted an adversary role as well as a "missionary stance" against employers. The agency and its staff "are out to change the world, and often these people have little knowledge of or interest in how the business world operates." Many observers accused the EEOC staff of being against business, especially big business.[47]

Industrial relations writer Harold B. Hayes observed much the same thing. He stated that through conscious decision or lack of knowledge, some regulatory personnel did not recognize a number of realities in the operation of the private sector. Equal employment opportunity staff assumed an advocacy role that led employers to regard compliance monitoring as an adversarial relationship. According to Hayes, employers complained about the "guilty until proven innocent" attitude of the civil rights bureaucracy, its concern for form over substance, the lack of credibility of basic data on which elaborate affirmative action plans were established, and the "gun to your head" climate in which pre-award compliance reviews were conducted, leading to unrealistic and unattainable "promissory notes" for minority hiring. Contractors were held responsible for the inadequate supply of qualified minority applicants; hence, they engaged in the practice of "stealing" the same employees from each other to meet affirmative action goals. A "chaotic condition" existed in the equal employment opportunity field, marked by a polarization of attitudes. In effect, the government told employers: "We know you are guilty, and we'll catch up with you sooner or later." The employers' response was: "We are doing the best we can; we're being held for ransom for things beyond our control."[48]

By the mid-1970s, federal equal employment opportunity policy had departed radically from the letter, spirit, and intent of Title VII and Executive Order 11246. It was increasingly politicized, in that it was shaped by the policy demands of private interest groups in the civil rights lobby. Yet the equal employment opportunity system was protected against criticism by the non-political aura of the civil rights issue—the belief, that is, that the right of equal opportunity was not subject to political bargaining or judgments of political majorities. This made it exceedingly difficult to criticize equal employment opportunity policy and the actions of the civil rights bureaucracy. Furthermore, the longer affirmative action lasted and its legality was asserted, the more legitimacy it acquired. This, in turn, encouraged a tendency to forget about the arguably lawless and arbitrary character of equal employment opportunity policy and focus on its results. If affirmative action appeared to provide a solution to black unemployment, poverty, and related social ills, it might be justified in practical terms, if not as a public philosophy.

To determine the results of affirmative action was a complex problem in social science research that would take years to accomplish. The tentative findings, however, were not encouraging. A study published in 1978, perhaps betraying liberal expectations, concluded that federal equal employment opportunity policy "has not catapulted" minorities and women into business and industry. Although protected groups were more represented across all industries, they had not experienced a substantial increase in most industries since 1965. Minority and female participation rates increased most from 1966 to 1975 in larger firms in industries with lower average weekly earnings. The small improvement that may have occurred, the study suggested, was due to the expansion of the labor market rather than to equal employment opportunity enforcement by government or voluntary compliance by industry. The chief value of the actions of the civil rights bureaucracy appeared to be "in providing symbolic support for women and minorities who choose to assert themselves (i.e. 'do it yourself' affirmative action) in struggling for equal employment."[49]

Business observers, however, saw real consequences flowing from affirmative action, and they were predominantly negative. As early as 1973, Daniel Seligman wrote: "There is no doubt that between them, the EEOC and the contract compliance program have transformed the way big business in the United States hires people." The government had gone far toward eliminating "old-fashioned" racial discrimination, Seligman commented. It was clear, however, that "the government programs have undermined some other old-fashioned notions about hiring on the basis of merit." This result was evident mainly in the policies devised by the OFCC and EEOC for the use of testing and education standards in employee selection. Companies took the easy way out by playing the ratio game of hiring minorities, rather than attempting to validate their selection procedures.[50] This controversial issue, more than any other, displayed the conflict between affirmative action and the principle of individual rights and equal opportunity in bold relief.

5

Affirmative Action and
the War Against Testing

Of the many transvaluations of equal employment opportunity effected by the civil rights bureaucracy in the name of affirmative action, none displays more administrative cunning and audacity than the attempt to eliminate aptitude and intelligence testing as a legitimate employment practice in American business and industry. In order to prevent testing from being found unlawful for discriminating against socially and culturally deprived individuals, Congress included explicit approval of the use of professionally developed ability tests in Title VII. From its inception, the EEOC viewed this provision as a means of discouraging, if not preventing, employers from using tests as selection instruments. In its campaign against testing, the Commission was supported by numerous psychologists desiring to promote social justice and opposed by many other psychometric scholars and by a few government agencies, most notably the Civil Service Commission. A bitterly contested politico-scientific battle ensued as the several government agencies involved in employment discrimination policy struggled in the mid-1970s to carry out a congressional mandate to formulate a uniform approach to employee selection. When the Democrats returned to power under President Jimmy Carter, the Equal Employment Opportunity Commission finally prevailed, the beneficiary of an executive reorganization of civil rights policy that made it the preeminent civil rights enforcement agency. The EEOC adopted its anti-testing position in the Uniform Guidelines on Employee Selection Procedure (1978), regulations that continued to govern employment discrimination policy in the 1980s.[1]

I

During the debate on the Civil Rights Bill in 1964, a decision by an Illinois Fair Employment Practices Commission (FEPC) hearing examiner about culturally biased intelligence tests alarmed the opponents of Title VII. In *Myart v. Motorola*, the hearing examiner ordered the Motorola Corporation to discontinue the use of a test that black applicants failed because the test was "normed on advantaged groups" and failed to "reflect and equate inequities and environmental factors among the culturally disadvantaged and culturally deprived groups." Although the Illinois FEPC did not expressly affirm the hearing examiner's conclusion, it found an unfair labor practice. It also stated: "The commission does not foreclose the possibility that tests of this nature are inherently discriminatory against persons alien to the predominant middle-class white culture in this society."[2]

Senator John Tower, Republican from Texas, was one of the alarmed conservatives who were concerned to prevent *Motorola*-type discrimination charges from being brought under Title VII. During Senate consideration of the bill, Tower proposed an amendment stating that it was not unlawful to give a professionally developed ability test if the test was designed to determine or predict whether an applicant was suitable or trainable for employment and if it were given to all applicants irrespective of race. In Tower's view, the design or content of a test was the basis for determining whether or not it was discriminatory. The managers of the civil rights bill agreed that Title VII would prevent *Motorola*-type charges, but proposed to reach this end by asserting the merit principle as an exception to the rule of nondiscrimination. Their proposal stated that it was not an unlawful employment practice to apply different standards of compensation or different terms, conditions, or privileges of employment pursuant to a bona fide seniority or merit system, provided that such differences were not the result of an intention to discriminate because of race. This meant that it was not discriminatory to use a test to identify the best qualified applicants, no matter how unfavorable the results might be for minority candidates. Senator Tower subsequently modified his amendment to state that it was not an unlawful practice "to give and to act upon the results of any professionally developed ability test provided that such test, its administration or action upon the results is not designed, intended or used to discriminate because of race . . ." This language, plus the proposal of the bill's managers, formed Section 703(h) of Title VII. The authors of the law thus rejected an effects test under the disparate impact theory of discrimination and approved tests used to determine merit and ability.[3]

The testing question quickly became a divisive issue in relations between employers and the civil rights bureaucracy as well as within the professional community of industrial psychologists. Aptitude and ability testing, the basis of industrial psychology, had been practiced since the 1920s. Business firms used tests because they appeared to offer a rational and effective means of ascertaining whether applicants for jobs were capable of performing satisfactorily. Test developers conceived of their role as providing employers with an evaluation device to be used as the employer saw fit; they did not instruct test users in the problematic aspects of psychometrics, including the basic issue of test validation— that is, the question of whether performance on a test could be statistically shown to predict performance on the job. Indeed, psychologists disagreed on how to validate tests; in particular, they were troubled by the difficulty of finding a good indicator of job success to which the predictive power of the test could be compared. Nevertheless, tests had long been shown to predict job performance with at least some degree of accuracy, and it was considered common sense to use them to assess prospective employees' potential merit and productivity. Tests possessed what experts called "face validity"—that is, a self-evident rationality. Testing programs were therefore widely adopted in industry in the 1950s and 1960s. Studies showed that as many as 85 percent of companies surveyed used tests, although only 16 percent had evidence that testing actually improved the employee selection process.[4]

Although no one in the Title VII debate defended the notion of a culturally discriminatory test, the *Motorola* case touched a raw nerve precisely because many equal employment opportunity strategists were prepared to make this type of argument. At the White House EEOC start-up conference in August of 1965, much comment was directed to the issue of socially discriminatory tests. Numerous recommendations were made that tests be required to be specifically job-related and that employers modify their use of tests to expand black employment. In early conciliation efforts, the EEOC staff tried to persuade employers to eliminate or modify testing programs on the grounds that they were a pretext for discrimination. When that proved unsuccessful, the Commission staff moved for publication of EEOC guidelines on testing that would restrict employers' use of tests. The plaintiffs' bar and the civil rights lobby similarly argued that since testing programs were not generally adopted until desegregation began in the 1950s, tests were really an alternative form of discrimination and not a legitimate business practice. Sensitive to the racial implications of tests, many companies reevaluated their selection programs.[5]

Social criticism of testing reinforced a challenge to the discriminatory use of tests arising within the field of industrial psychology. Philip Ash, a leading authority in the field, published an analysis in 1966 that showed how tests could be found in violation of Title VII under a *Motorola* rationale. Ash noted that although the law required proof of intentional discrimination, intent could be proved by circumstantial evidence. If, for example, an employer knew that a test excluded more blacks than whites and nevertheless continued to use it, the EEOC and the courts could readily conclude the test was used to discriminate. Hoping to contribute to improved race relations, many psychologists tried to take race into account while upholding standards of scientific research. For example, Robert Guion, a highly respected psychometrician, proposed to treat race as a "moderator variable," or as something that explained why one person or group performed differently from another. In technical terms, a moderator variable identified a factor that defined differences between two or more groups having different patterns of validity with respect to test scores and job performance. According to Guion, race affected test performance in the same way that a personality characteristic such as compulsiveness might.[6]

To consider race as a moderator variable raised the issue of differential validity. This term referred to the essential idea behind the *Motorola*-type argument: namely, that a test that was valid for whites was not valid for blacks. In other words, it might predict job performance for whites, but not for blacks. This possibility did not lead psychologists who favored equal employment opportunity to reject the concept of validation. On the contrary, although Title VII did not require validation, equal employment opportunity strategists determined from the outset that a "professionally developed ability test," in the language of Title VII, meant a test that was validated, or shown to be job-related. How validation should be conducted, however, was an unresolved and controversial question.

There are three types of validity or methods of validation: criterion, content, and construct. In criterion validation (also known as predictive validation), all applicants are tested prior to employment, and the scores are subsequently correlated to some measure of job success to see whether those with higher scores do better on the job. The test is used to predict how well a person will do as measured against some external criterion of job performance. (If present employees are tested and their job performance is then measured, this slightly different method is called concurrent validation.) Content validity consists of systematic observation of the job and the content of the test with a view toward ensuring that the test contains a sampling of the knowledge, skills, and behavior required for successful job performance. A typing test for a job as a typist would illustrate content validity. Construct validation, the third type approved by industrial psychology, seeks to measure a trait such as verbal ability or spacial visualization that is believed to be important for successful job performance.[7]

The question of types of validation was related to the question of whether black and white applicants should be considered together as a single group, or separately as different groups. The civil rights lobby and many psychologists proposed separate validation studies and the establishment of different standards for blacks and whites. Psychologist Robert E. Krug held that in employment testing, treating people equally did not mean treating them identically. He reasoned that if whites scoring at the 55 level had a 50 percent success expectancy and blacks scoring at the 32 level had a 50 percent success expectancy, it was fair to set different predictor scores—at 55 and 32, respectively—for the two races. In other words, test scores meant different things for different groups. A stronger statement of this position questioned the significance of the concept of predictive validity. Psychologist Felix M. Lopez, Jr., contended that statistically valid instruments might be irrelevant to a selection situation and non-valid instruments relevant. To illustrate, he said a pencil and paper test might be a valid predictor for whites, whereas an unvalidated interview might be best for selecting blacks. Lopez believed test scores should be interpreted flexibly in light of the individual, organizational, social, and cultural dimensions of an applicant's situation. Critics believed the concept of differential validity was tantamount to advocating a double standard, but Robert Guion said this view showed an inability to distinguish between standards of test performance and of job performance. It was job performance that counted. Krug admitted that a double standard was being proposed, yet said this could be "masked" by the use of "prediction weights" and "conversion tables." Lopez declared that different standards were not only justified, but obligatory in order to make equal employment opportunity policy successful as a black placement and jobs program.[8]

The concept of differential validity figured prominently in the EEOC guidelines on testing issued in 1966. A report by EEOC staff psychologists established the agenda and viewpoint that drove the Commission's action. The report declared that inadvertent rather than intentional discrimination characterized professionally developed ability tests. "An aptitude test that fails to predict job performance in the same way for both Negroes and whites, or fails to predict performance at all is not a valid test," Commission psychologists argued. Asserting that the validity of a test interpretation was dependent on an adequate understanding of the social and cultural background of the group in question, they recommended that differential validation be conducted for different racial and ethnic groups. Moreover, inflexible minimum scores should be reexamined, and test results should be considered along with other data concerning motivation, experience, and dependability. "Differences in selection procedures for different ethnic groups do not mean a lowering of standards," the report concluded, "because the standards which count are standards of performance on the job, not the selection standards. Equally qualified persons may be selected from various ethnic groups by applying the standards which are appropriate to each group."[9]

The EEOC published *Guidelines on Employment Testing Procedures* in August of 1966. The brief document interpreted a "professionally developed ability test" to mean a test that fairly measures the knowledge or skills required by the particular job or class of jobs sought by the applicant, or that gives the employer an opportunity to measure the applicant's ability to perform a particular job. Employers had discovered that they might inadvertently be excluding qualified minority applicants through inappropriate testing procedures. The guidelines therefore declared that tests should only be one factor in "a total personnel assessment" system that was non-discriminatory "within the spirit" of the Civil Rights Act. Included in the system were job analysis, special efforts to recruit minorities, screening and interviewing related to job requirements, and tests selected on the basis of specific job-related criteria. The guidelines further stated that test performance should be compared to job performance. Employers were told that where applicants did not enjoy equal educational and developmental opportunities, their test scores might underestimate their job potential. "The ultimate standard . . . is not the test score but performance on the job," the Commission asserted. "Since cultural factors can so readily affect performance on so many tests," the EEOC "recommended that the test be judged against job performance rather than by what they [sic] claim to measure." Finally, only a test that had been validated for minorities could be assumed to be free of inadvertent bias.[10]

EEOC guidelines ignored the intent requirement of Title VII, substituting for it a *Motorola*-type concern with the effect of selection practices on minority hiring. The Commission's purpose was to attack "credentialism"—that is, the practice of setting qualifications for employment higher than was required for a particular job. "Total personnel assessment," including job analysis, was intended as a means of eliminating generalized merit requirements that might not be related to performance of a specific job in a specific work setting. Employers were further urged to consider candidates' potential abilities, and to hire persons who were "qualifiable." Although purporting to approve merit and ability testing, the guidelines actually constituted an attack on testing. The EEOC cited the American Psychological Association's *Standards for Educational and Psychological Tests and Manuals* (1966). It transformed the A.P.A.'s *Standards*, however, from a statement of the best professional judgment about testing that was intended to guide practitioners into rules for compliance with Title VII. Moreover, contrary to professional practice, which did not designate one method of validation as superior to the others, the Commission made criterion validity the preferred method of validation.[11] The EEOC made itself vulnerable to the charge that it was not interested in test validation, only in using the science of testing to make Title VII into a jobs program for blacks.[12]

William H. Enneis, chief psychologist for the EEOC, aggressively promoted the Commission's view of testing in papers to professional groups and in congressional hearings. Generally opposed to intelligence and aptitude tests, he favored "total personnel assessment." This was a euphemism for a selection process that subordinated test scores to other instruments, such as an interview or a record of personal biographical information. Urging total personnel assessment, Enneis did not recommend the elimination of tests. He argued instead for separate racial testing under the concept of differential validity, and advised hiring black applicants with lower test scores over whites with higher scores. This was justified on the ground that the lower minority test score predicted a higher job performance than did the higher non-minority score. Enneis acknowledged that many employers were "squeamish" about adjusting test scores because they thought it might constitute reverse discrimination. As a "pragmatic and scientifically defensible solution" to the problem, Enneis proposed to convert all applicants' test scores into predicted criterion scores (that is, prediction of job performance). "After all," he asked, "do we not give tests to predict what an employee will do on the job?"[13]

Published outside the procedures of administrative law, the EEOC guidelines in a legal sense were merely an expression of agency opinion that attracted little notice in the business community.[14] Yet some industrial psychologists were alert to their potential regulatory impact. John H. Kirkwood observed that since none of the tests commonly used in employee selection was validated for minorities, "the door of legal liability is wide open to any unwary employer." While the EEOC urged employers to eliminate inadvertent bias, test designers did not know what factors in tests contributed to cultural bias. Kirkwood believed the Commission should prescribe tests that it considered free of cultural bias, or at least show that it was possible to devise such a test. Testing expert Gerald A. McLain explained that since testing as a selection device was based on the "odds" of a prediction concerning an applicant's future success, the most that could be expected of a valid test was that the predictions would be correct more often than not. The EEOC's acceptance of the idea of cultural deprivation, however, showed that the agency was taking sides and giving the benefit of the doubt to the minority applicant. Asserting that the EEOC's position was incompatible with the statistical concepts implicit in testing, McLain predicted that employers would have difficulty applying the guidelines.[15]

II

The EEOC guidelines raised the question of whether there should be a general government policy on employee selection standards. The Department of Justice, the Office of Federal Contract Compliance in the Department of Labor, and the Civil Service Commission (CSC) were all concerned with the problem of testing. The CSC, statutorily charged with operating a non-discriminatory merit system, was then engaged in a study of the fairness of a number of employment tests. In 1967, it tried to join discussions held by the EEOC and the OFCC on the issue of testing guidelines. The two civil rights agencies rebuffed CSC, however, presumably because its concern for merit and efficiency caused it to appear not fully supportive of equal employment opportunity goals. Meanwhile, OFCC issued its own testing regulations in 1968. Just as the EEOC guidelines did, they required test validation by the criterion (that is, the predictive) method.[16] The CSC questioned the theory of disparate impact discrimination on which the OFCC guidelines rested, finding them to be inconsistent with professional testing standards. Moreover, the CSC believed that it should participate in any further discussion of testing guidelines, since the specific standards applied by the government to private employers would be compared to the government's own practices.[17]

In the politics of civil rights, the CSC's commitment to the merit principle placed it at odds with the OFCC and the EEOC. From the EEOC point of view, however, neither the CSC nor the OFCC was progressive enough to be relied upon in anti-bias matters. Thus, after participating for several months in an advisory committee on selection and testing formed by the OFCC, the EEOC withdrew when it appeared that the discussions might lead to revision of the Commission's 1966 guidelines. In a surprise move, the EEOC issued new Guidelines on Employee Selection Procedures in 1970. The OFCC, upstaged and excluded from a fundamental policy decision at a time when pressure to coordinate federal equal employment opportunity enforcement was increasing, was sharply critical of the EEOC action. It objected that the new EEOC guidelines contained material never considered by the advisory council and judged the regulations to be unworkable. Nevertheless, the political necessity of maintaining a united civil rights front prevented the OFCC from publicly criticizing the administratively irregular and scientifically unsupported action of the EEOC.[18]

The 1970 EEOC guidelines on testing were elaborate and stringent. The Commission said they were based on the finding that minority candidates frequently experienced disproportionately high rejection rates on tests that were not shown to be valid predictors of job performance. Although the guidelines declared that properly validated selection procedures could contribute to non-discriminatory personnel policies, the EEOC's real objective was to bring about equal employment results rather than equal employment opportunity. Achievement of identical rejection rates for minority and non-minority job applicants was expressly stated as a policy objective. If the disparate impact theory embodied in the guidelines was to be applied in any reasonable manner consistent with the merit principle contained in Title VII, it required comparison of the rejection rates of similarly qualified black and white applicants. Yet the guidelines did not stipulate a concern with *qualified* minority applicants. The implication was that disparate impact should be determined by the use of pass-fail ratios among a pool of applicants in an external hiring situation, where anyone is permitted to apply regardless of qualifications. In this situation, however, the use of the pool-of-applicants standard all but guarantees that the validity of the selection standard will be questioned.[19]

In pursuit of the goal of equal employment, the EEOC defined discrimination according to disparate impact theory. Discrimination was the use of any test which adversely affected hiring, promotion, and transfer of Title VII protected classes, unless the test was validated and showed a high degree of utility and the person giving the test could demonstrate that alternative suitable hiring procedures were not available.[20] Thus an employer had to prove validity, utility, and lack of a suitable alternative in order to use a test that adversely affected minority groups. Each of these technical burdens requires explanation.

In order to show that a test was valid, an employer had to present empirical evidence derived from a criterion-related validity study as prescribed by the A.P.A.'s *Standards for Educational and Psychological Tests*. Again, the Commission stated its preference for—and practical requirement of—criterion or predictive validation over the other two legitimate, A.P.A.-approved methods, content and construct validity. Only where criterion-related validity was shown to be infeasible could another method be used. The guidelines did not explain, however, how infeasibility was to be determined.[21]

The EEOC continued to endorse the concept of differential validity. The guidelines stated that data had to be generated and results separately reported for minority and non-minority groups. Where a test was validated for only one group, its use for other groups was provisional pending a separate validation study. Where a test was valid for both groups, but one group scored higher without a higher job performance, the guidelines said cutoff scores had to be adjusted—in other words, lowered—for the group with the lower scores so as to predict the same probability of job success in both groups. The EEOC further required scrutiny of the "fairness" of a test. "Fairness" was a technical concept; it referred to the possibility that a test might have equal validity for blacks and whites, but because of statistical problems fail to predict job performance for the two groups with equal accuracy. Employers were therefore required to provide evidence of test fairness—that is, its ability to predict performance equally for blacks and whites. If a test was found to be unfair, further lowering of the cutoff scores for the minority group was required.[22]

Employers routinely tested entry-level applicants for abilities that might be needed for job advancement. In order to discourage this practice, the EEOC required "functional" job performance criteria. The 1970 guidelines stated that the attainment of a higher-level job was a relevant consideration only when there was a "high probability" that persons would attain that level within a reasonable period of time. In other words, entry-level performance criteria had to be used, and the EEOC would decide what a high probability of advancement and a reasonable period of time were. The Commission assumed that the more functional the job performance criterion, the more likely it was that minorities would do better than their test scores might predict.[23]

In addition to validation, the employer faced a "utility" requirement. In practical terms, utility concerned the importance of a test in selecting satisfactory employees. The guidelines stated that besides having statistical significance, the relationship between test scores and job performance had to have "practical significance."[24] This term was defined in

relation to economic and human considerations. The guidelines explained that the correlation between test scores and job performance
had to be higher where there was little economic or human risk in hiring
an unqualified applicant, as in a low skilled job. In highly skilled jobs,
however, a low correlation between test scores and job performance
might be useful and was permissible, as in the case of an airline pilot
where a high risk was involved in hiring an unqualified person. The
utility requirement was another way of putting pressure on employers
not to use tests.[25] The EEOC in effect took the position that as far as
relatively low-skilled jobs were concerned, it made no difference
whether employers hired qualified or unqualified applicants.

The third obstacle in test use was the alternative search requirement.
Recall that in a discrimination suit, the complainant establishes a *prima
facie* case by showing a test or selection device to have disparate impact,
shifting the burden of proof to the employer to show that the practice is
job-related. If he succeeds, the charge is dismissed. Under the EEOC
guidelines, however, an employer who proves the validity of a test still
has the burden of demonstrating that "alternative, suitable hiring . . .
procedures are unavailable for his use."[26] Of the many instances where
the EEOC imposed a requirement without accompanying guidance on
how to meet it, the alternative search provision—in which the employer
had to prove a negative—was perhaps the most egregious.

The EEOC test guidelines constitute one of the most remarkable
examples of unwarranted bureaucratic policymaking in the history of
affirmative action. Title VII declares race an illegitimate factor in
employment decisions and expressly approves the use of ability tests.
The EEOC regulations made race the critical consideration in employment practices and attempted to discourage professional ability testing.
William A. Gorham, a CSC staff psychologist, stated that the EEOC's
interjection of race into Title VII enforcement, effected chiefly by
adopting the concept of differential validity, lacked even minimal
scientific support. "Based upon an untested hypothesis," Gorham
wrote, "tests were presumed guilty of being anti-equal employment
opportunity until proven innocent." Gorham also questioned the administrative legitimacy, if not the legality, of the EEOC test policy. Courts
had held that "great deference" was due the EEOC guidelines as an
interpretation of Title VII, yet the administrative process behind the
Commission's action was unknown and uncriticized. Only one EEOC
staff psychologist and one lawyer worked on the guidelines, and no
opportunity was given for public comment. "Did Congress intend that
its will be interpreted by only a few people (perhaps as few as two)?"
Gorham asked. Very few challenged the "suspect administrative proc-

esses" that produced the guidelines, however, because to do so might appear anti-civil rights, and because an employer who opposed the agency directive risked political and economic retaliation.[27]

The courts promptly approved the EEOC test guidelines. In *Griggs* (1971), the Supreme Court made job-relatedness, which was never discussed in the congressional debate on Title VII, the principal criterion for determining the legality of a test or other selection instrument. Furthermore, the decision equated job-relatedness with technical validation of a test. In *Albemarle* (1975), the Court used the EEOC guidelines as the actual standard for evaluating the legality of the company's testing program. Thus test validation methods which were intended by professional psychologists to guide employers in using tests were transformed by the EEOC and the courts into legal rules governing employment practices.[28]

Although not subjected to direct legal challenge, the EEOC guidelines provoked criticism. According to N. Thompson Powers, a leading defendants' attorney and former executive director of the EEOC, the guidelines on testing were contrary to the weight of professional authority and imposed standards that generally were unattainable. Powers believed the guidelines negated Congress's intent that a test could be considered a professionally developed measure of ability even if it had a disparate impact on minorities. Exxon test psychologist C. Paul Sparks said the EEOC policy misconceived the nature of testing principles. Testing manuals defined idealized procedures for practitioners to follow; the EEOC used the procedures as the basis for legal regulations. Donald J. Schwartz, a staff psychologist in the Department of Labor, criticized the government for treating test validation as an all-or-nothing condition attaching to a selection instrument, like the validation of a parking ticket. Ideal standards of testing theory were misused, he said, when made into minimal legal requirements of government policy. Schwartz urged psychologists to get involved in determining minimal government standards to prevent courts from deciding cases on the basis of ideal principles of validity that were intended only as goals. Such a practice would effectively end all test use.[29]

Thaddeus Holt, a defendants' attorney in testing cases, observed that the EEOC was not a regulatory agency, but an advocate whose interpretation of the law was open to rebuttal because it originated in special-interest pleading on behalf of minorities. Citing the EEOC's acceptance of the concept of differential validity in contrast to the findings of psychological research, Holt warned against letting unproven theories be written into legal decisions for ideological reasons. Critics further objected to the EEOC's preference for criterion validation, the most difficult type of study to perform, and its insistence on the situational specificity of a test—the idea, that is, that a test found valid in one industrial setting could not be transported into a comparable setting. Some psychologists urged cooperative research that would pool separate studies into a larger study with high statistical power.[30]

Personnel administrators trying to keep their companies in compliance said the government should provide "truly operational" testing guidelines that described validation more clearly and gave examples of acceptable statistical procedures. Otherwise many small and medium firms, unwilling to pay the high cost of validation studies, would drop tests and revert to subjective methods of employee selection. "The use of . . . tests is so fraught with hazards," wrote a business lawyer in 1976, "that, at least at this juncture in the development of the law, one is best advised to stop using them for employee selection." Industrial relations consultant John B. Miner observed that many employers had stopped testing as a result of EEOC and OFCC enforcement and were moving toward random hiring. A 1975 survey of 2500 companies showed that 36 percent did no testing, while three-fourths of those that did were cutting back on test use and 14 percent intended to eliminate it. A Bureau of National Affairs survey of 200 companies in 1976 showed that only 42 percent used tests, compared to 90 percent in a 1963 survey.[31]

If the testing guidelines seemed unrealistic from the employer's point of view, the civil rights bureaucracy believed employers and their allies in the industrial psychology community were simply not responsive to the equal employment opportunity laws. According to Stephen E. Bemis, a former OFCC psychologist, management took a half-hearted approach to test research and wanted findings that were tailor-made to pass government inspection. Companies conducted sloppy validation work that few psychologists were willing to criticize. Bemis complained that validation was considered low priority work that received little support and was assigned to the least able staff in many companies.[32]

The reaction to the EEOC guidelines showed that the testing issue had become thoroughly politicized. Employers and many industrial psychologists believed that the civil rights agencies were trying to force companies into abandoning tests. Government officials and staff psychologists believed that employers and personnel managers were evading their equal employment opportunity obligation. All, no doubt, could agree with N. Thompson Powers that the challenge in applying the test guidelines was "to show that individual merit, equal opportunity and professional standards are compatible concepts and are not simply conflicting code words for racism, special preference or elitism."[33]

Whether this challenge could be met, however, depended in large part on the efforts of the government civil rights agencies to agree on uniform standards of employee selection.

III

The Title VII amendments of 1972 created the Equal Employment Opportunity Coordinating Council, comprising the Department of Justice, Department of Labor, Civil Service Commission, Civil Rights Commission, and the EEOC. Congress charged the Council with developing a uniform approach toward employment discrimination on the part of federal agencies enforcing Title VII and Executive Order 11246. In interagency negotiations from 1972 to 1976, political conflict within the civil rights bureaucracy prevented agreement on a unified federal policy.

The EEOC, supported by the Civil Rights Commission, defended its existing guidelines. Treating Title VII enforcement as a jobs program for minorities and women, the Commission put pressure on employers to hire protected groups in order to avoid discrimination charges. The Departments of Justice and Labor and the Civil Service Commission, while accepting the disparate impact theory of discrimination, tried to make test validation more realistic and compatible with merit and efficiency. These agencies wanted to make equal employment opportunity compliance an achievable goal and encourage genuinely voluntary efforts to hire minorities.[34]

The EEOC and the CSC were the leading antagonists in the struggle over the uniform guidelines. The EEOC's identity as an advocate of minority interests was clear. The CSC, charged with maintaining professional standards in federal employment, identified with the merit principle just as clearly. Responsible for enforcing equal employment opportunity within the federal government, the CSC was criticized by the EEOC and the civil rights lobby for an alleged lack of commitment to affirmative action. Only reluctantly, for example, did the CSC accept goals and timetables in 1971, and it rejected the EEOC guidelines on testing as unworkable and unsuitable for public employment. The EEOC retaliated by supporting a discrimination suit against the CSC's principal test for federal employment.[35]

Within this political context, the highly technical issues discussed by the Equal Employment Opportunity Coordinating Council lent themselves to continuing controversy. First, there was disagreement over the scope of the proposed uniform federal guidelines. The EEOC held that the validation requirement should apply to every step in the employment process that could be regarded as a selection instrument. The other agencies opposed subjecting every aspect of the hiring process, such as background investigations or the requirement of prior experience, to validation. The degree of disproportionate impact necessary for a finding of discrimination was a second issue in dispute. The EEOC wanted to retain the vague requirement of its 1970 guidelines that called for validation where the rejection rate was "disproportionately high." Other agencies wanted a four-fifths rule, under which validation would be required where the minority selection rate was less than 80 percent of that of non-minority candidates.[36]

The types of validation that an employer could use were also a matter of contention. As in its 1970 guidelines, the EEOC sought to make criterion or predictive validation the preferred method, permitting content and construct validation only when a criterion study was not technically feasible. The CSC and the Labor and Justice Departments approved all three validation techniques equally, with the choice depending on the situation. Similarly, the EEOC insisted on differential validity, proposing to retain a requirement of separate validation for racial groups despite the lack of scientific support for the idea of race as a moderator variable. At one point, the Commission admitted that it rejected the research findings on differential validity because they were not in the interest of the groups it was trying to protect. The other agencies rejected differential validity, citing research showing not only that tests predicted job performance for minorities as well as non-minorities, but also that if a discrepancy existed it was that tests tended to over-predict job performance of minorities.[37]

Another issue was the transportability of tests. The EEOC insisted that a test validated in one company could not be used in another, even if used to select for the same job. Because validation of a test for a specific job required a large number of employees, it placed an unrealistic burden on smaller employers. The other agencies wanted to relax the ban on test borrowing and encourage cooperative validation studies.[38]

One of the most controversial issues concerned the "bottom line" approach to equal employment opportunity enforcement. This term referred to the proposal that the government permit an employer to use a test or other selection device having disparate impact, provided that the outcome of the employment process as a whole was satisfactory with respect to minority hiring. Employers liked the bottom-line idea; it enabled them to maintain control over qualifications and protect selection procedures from EEOC scrutiny and interference. In practical terms equal employment opportunity policy since the early 1960s, which in the broadest sense used racial canvassing of the work force to indicate "deficiencies" to be rectified by voluntary hiring of blacks, was based on the bottom-line idea. It was a way of giving *de facto* preferential treatment to minorities while maintaining employer freedom to set qualifications and insist on merit. In the Equal Employment Opportunity Coordinating Council deliberations, however, the EEOC strongly opposed the bottom-line proposal because it conceded too much to employer autonomy. The EEOC was also unwilling to publicly support an approach that discouraged individuals from filing complaints against specific components of a selection process. The other agencies recommended explicit approval of the bottom line as a means of reconciling business autonomy and minority economic advancement.[39]

The search for alternatives was also debated in the Equal Employment Opportunity Coordinating Council. This referred to the 1970 EEOC requirement that an employer who validated a test had to show that no alternative selection method was available having less disparate impact. The CSC and the Labor and Justice Departments viewed this rule as unreasonable; all three believed the plaintiff should bear the burden of searching for an alternative selection instrument.[40]

From 1972 to 1976, the Equal Employment Opportunity Coordinating Council produced four drafts of the proposed uniform guidelines. At each stage, public comment was invited and received from employer groups, civil rights organizations, and industrial psychologists. The final draft, published in August of 1976, was significantly different from the 1970 EEOC guidelines. It recognized that validation might not be feasible or appropriate in all circumstances, approved the four-fifths rule for defining disparate impact and triggering the validation requirement, regarded the three types of validity determination as equally legitimate, adopted the bottom-line idea, and assigned the search for alternatives to the plaintiff. The draft guidelines retained the concept of differential validity, in the form of "fairness studies," as a concession to the civil rights lobby. The requirement was less onerous, however, than the existing EEOC differential validity rule.[41]

The proposed uniform guidelines reflected a moderate approach to equal employment opportunity enforcement. Employers in both the private and public sector supported the proposal as a more reasonable and practicable policy than the existing EEOC and OFCC guidelines. A committee of the American Psychological Association found the proposed guidelines professionally sound and flexible.[42] The civil rights lobby, however, condemned the draft guidelines as a retreat from civil rights enforcement. Defending the existing EEOC guidelines, the

NAACP argued against tests and said employees should simply be hired on a probationary basis, with on-the-job evaluation replacing tests.[43] The civil rights establishment thus acknowledged that the purpose of EEOC policy was to force the elimination of tests and adopt random or preferential hiring practices.

The EEOC, withdrawing from the interagency talks, took the position that its interpretation of Title VII had been upheld by the courts and should not be changed without a change in judicial opinion.[44] David Rose, the Justice Department representative to the Equal Employment Opportunity Coordinating Council, presented a different assessment in a widely publicized memorandum in 1976. Referring to the unreasonable burdens imposed by existing EEOC standards, Rose observed: "It is little wonder . . . that there had been little effort by industry or state or local governments voluntarily to comply with the EEOC Guidelines." According to Rose, the real reason that the EEOC refused to alter its position was that under the present rules, few employers were able to show the validity of any of their selection procedures. They, therefore, faced a high risk of being charged with discrimination. Rose concluded that "the thrust of the present Guidelines is to place almost all test users in a posture of noncompliance; to give great discretion to enforcement personnel to determine who should be prosecuted; and to set aside objective selection procedures in favor of numerical hiring."[45]

Acting independently, the EEOC reissued its 1970 guidelines in 1976. The CSC and the Labor and Justice Departments proceeded to publish the new regulations, the Federal Executive Agency Guidelines on Employee Selection. Although an improvement over EEOC policy, this step hardly constituted a satisfactory solution to the problem. Parties and employers faced "an overwhelming quagmire of duplicative and often inconsistent remedies," and employment practices could still be challenged in "literally an inexhaustible number of forums." A General Accounting Office report described the web of conflicting requirements in which employers were caught. The GAO said that small employers did not understand equal employment opportunity regulations well enough to comply. Consequently, they often dropped tests that had disparate impact and adopted hiring quotas to avoid the validation requirements and achieve a representative work force. The report supported the view of critics that test validation was primarily a smoke screen to promote minority hiring.[46]

The Democrats' return to power in the election of 1976 resolved the political struggle over employment discrimination policy in favor of the EEOC and the civil rights lobby. Approving an executive reorganization plan, Congress in the Reorganization Act of 1978 made the EEOC the pre-eminent civil rights enforcement agency in the federal government. The plan, which originated in a proposal of the Congressional Black Caucus and the civil rights lobby, abolished the Equal Employment Opportunity Coordinating Council and transferred its functions to the EEOC. Dividing the Civil Service Commission into a Merit Systems Protection Board and the Office of Personnel Management, it also transferred enforcement of equal employment opportunity within the federal service to the EEOC. Administration of the Equal Pay Act and the Age Discrimination Act were also shifted from the Department of Labor to the EEOC. In a separate executive order, the functions of eleven contract compliance agencies in the executive departments were consolidated under OFCC, which was then renamed the Office of Federal Contract Compliance Programs (OFCCP).[47]

The reorganization of civil rights policy was mainly intended to separate administration of the government merit system from, and subordinate it to, the internal federal equal opportunity function now conferred on the EEOC. "The civil rights community would rightly feel betrayed," said a spokesman of the civil rights establishment, "if a personnel oriented rather than a civil rights oriented board were given jurisdiction over discrimination."[48] A second major result of the reorganization was to ensure EEOC control over the formulation of a unified policy on employee selection.

IV

Criticized for administrative mismanagement in the Nixon-Ford period despite its advocacy of minority programs, the EEOC returned to favor under the protection of the Carter Administration. Asserting that a "magic opportunity" existed for civil rights enforcement, soon-to-be-Chairman Eleanor Holmes Norton said the EEOC was approaching "a watershed moment." "For the first time since its creation," she stated, "the Commission has attracted the combined attention of those forces which can bring fundamental change to this beleaguered agency." Norton promised to reduce the backlog of individual complaints and pursue systemic discrimination charges. She also said the EEOC would reassess test validation as the key element in uniform guidelines for selection procedures.[49]

At a Commission meeting in December of 1977, Chairman Norton said that validation was widely regarded in the employer community as an instrument for coercing employers into eliminating tests and hiring by racial quotas. She suggested that, in reality, it was a loophole by which companies avoided their equal employment opportunity responsibility. "I think validation gives them an A-1 out," she contended, "because if you validate your tests you don't have to worry about exclusion of minorities and women any longer." According to Norton, the employer community "has caught on to a nice new thing, and if . . . they continue to rely as heavily on validation, they could actually undercut the purposes of Title VII." The government told employers to validate tests, which they did often at great expense. "My hat is off to the psychologists," she said. "We do not see, however," she added, "comparable evidence that validated tests have in fact gotten black and brown bodies . . . into places as a result of the validation of those tests."[50]

The EEOC chairman candidly acknowledged the contradiction between the merit principle and the logic of affirmative action. In the administration of the EEOC testing guidelines, Norton explained, "we do not see the kind of causal relation that I think . . . we expected to see." The government was faced with "the possible anomaly that tests could be validated and no effect or no appreciable effect flow to minorities and women, and in particular minorities, because of, perhaps, reasons more complicated than any of us understand . . ." Norton therefore proposed a change in EEOC policy. When the Commission in effect told employers that if they validated tests it would not otherwise be concerned with them or the results of their employment practices, it was saying "that the presence of real people who are not in the work force, is not as important as making sure that the tests have been validated." A better approach would be to encourage an employer "to look at what the ultimate goal is." She contended that the EEOC should ask employers whether they had minorities in their work force before validating a test or whether they had any appreciable number after the test was validated. "And if you really don't want to go through that [validation procedure], but you are interested in getting excluded people into your work force," Norton advised, "we would encourage you to do that."[51]

Norton expressed the social reform imperative that guided equal employment opportunity policy in the 1970s and that was reflected in the Uniform Guidelines for Employee Selection Procedures adopted by the EEOC in 1978. Rejecting most of the measures contained in the 1976 Federal Executive Agency (FEA) Guidelines, the EEOC kept the pressure on employers to adopt affirmative action minority hiring as an alternative to tests.

The 1978 Uniform Guidelines accepted the 80 percent rule proposed by the FEA Guidelines to determine when disparate impact was significant enough to be considered discrimination. Unless even the slightest degree of disproportionate impact was to be found illegal, some such standard was necessary to make disparate impact theory intellectually plausible. As adopted by the EEOC, however, the 80 percent rule clarified very little because it did not specify the comparative basis on which minority selection rates were to be evaluated. The proper comparison, if disparate impact theory was to be in any way compatible with the merit principle of Title VII, was between the minority selection rate and the minority percentage of the qualified labor market. To compare the selection rate to the percentage of blacks in the local area population, or simply to compare minority and non-minority selection rates in an external pool of applicants, was to disregard qualifications. Yet the 1978 guidelines did precisely that. They defined discrimination as "a substantially different rate of selection in hiring, promotion, or other employment decision" without answering the question: different from what? Depending on the reference group chosen as the basis for comparison, an employer's selection rate could more or less easily be found to be discriminatory. The EEOC's 80 percent rule thus left employers vulnerable to manipulated charges of discrimination.[52]

The guidelines appeared to accept criterion, construct, and content validation as equally sound strategies for showing the job-relatedness of a test. In practical effect, however, the EEOC continued to prefer criterion over content validation, the type most favored by employers because it was generally more feasible. The Uniform Guidelines imposed requirements on the use of content and construct validity in excess of professional practices. They discouraged the use of content validation by requiring any employer who rank-ordered candidates by means of a test (as opposed to making a pass-fail distinction) to validate the ranking as a selection device. Intended to prevent the selection of the most qualified applicants, the guidelines conflicted with the argument of professional groups that employers who met the job-relatedness standards could select on the basis of relative qualifications, including ranking.[53]

The search for alternative selection procedures was another issue on which the EEOC took an anti-employer line. The guidelines contradicted the *Albemarle* decision in stating that where a validity study was required, the employer rather than the plaintiff should include an investigation of suitable alternative selection methods that were "substantially equally valid" and had less disparate impact. When professional comment pointed out the conflict with the Supreme Court ruling, the EEOC simply denied it.[54]

The bottom-line approach was the most controversial feature of the Uniform Guidelines. As noted, this concept summarized the practical meaning of affirmative action. While some companies chose to validate tests and other dropped them, many employers believed that a sensible middle position was to use tests or other selection devices that might have a disparate impact, while hiring a sufficient number of minorities outside the usual selection procedure to achieve a good bottom line and be in compliance. Proponents of the bottom-line approach wanted to formalize it as an agreement whereby business would promote minority hiring and government would protect companies against Title VII discrimination charges. The EEOC and the civil rights establishment opposed formal recognition of the bottom-line approach, however, insisting that the right of an individual to challenge any part of the selection process must be preserved.

Controversy over the bottom line reflected political and ideological differences within the civil rights policymaking establishment; it also showed how far to the left the debate over affirmative action had moved. Bottom line enforcement of Title VII confirmed the radical transformation of the nondiscrimination principle into a system of proportional representation based on disparate impact theory. Yet it was supported by moderates as a compromise between the social objective of improving minority economic conditions and employers' interest in merit, productivity, and efficiency. The bottom-line approach had strong support in the business community because it avoided burdensome record-keeping and scrutiny of employment procedures. It recognized that employee selection seldom depended on a single decisive component, but consisted of formal and informal elements of an overall process. It was a real incentive for minority hiring that, in the opinion of its supporters, prevented employment practices from being reduced to simply a "numbers game." For that reason, some pragmatic liberals supported the bottom line. The most vigorous proponent of the bottom-line approach was Alfred W. Blumrosen, a principal architect of affirmative action in the 1960s, who saw it as a means of achieving the goals of Title VII while avoiding permanent allocation of employment on the basis of race and sex. Approved in the 1976 Federal Executive Agency Guidelines, the bottom-line approach also appeared to receive recognition in several court decisions, including the Supreme Court's ruling in *Washington v. Davis*.[55]

Under pressure from employer groups and other government civil rights agencies, the EEOC adopted bottom-line language in the Uniform Guidelines. It qualified the concept to such an extent, however, that it was rendered practically meaningless. The guidelines stated that federal agencies "generally" would not examine the individual components of the selection process for disparate impact or validity evidence where there was no overall exclusionary effect. Any application of the bottom line was dependent on "administrative and prosecutorial discretion," and agencies reserved the right to examine individual components of a selection process even if it had a clean bottom line.[56] Although Eleanor Holmes Norton publicly supported the bottom-line approach as a government-business compromise, the EEOC had no intention of letting employers use it to avoid liability. "It is clear that in reserving its options through the use of the word 'generally,' " Norton said in agency deliberations, "this Commission has reserved its options if it wanted to sue in every case next year. . . . In other words, we're putting employers on notice without at the same time limiting ourselves." Despite superficial agreement among the federal agencies, therefore, employers could expect conflicting applications of the Uniform Guidelines.[57]

Since 1966, the underlying purpose of the EEOC test guidelines was to place enough obstacles in the way of employee selection so that employers would choose to hire by race rather than objective criteria of merit. The Uniform Guidelines of 1978 made this policy more explicit by emphasizing the achievement of equal employment opportunity results through affirmative action, rather than through validation of selection processes. Thus the guidelines stated that an employer could choose to utilize alternative selection procedures as part of an affirmative action program in order to eliminate disparate impact. Alternative procedures included measures of superior scholarship; factors of culture, language, or experience; selection from a pool of disadvantaged persons who had demonstrated their general competence; and use of registers limited to qualified persons who were economically disadvantaged. Furthermore, the guidelines were not intended to preclude the use of lawful selection procedures which assisted in remedying the effects of prior discrimination or the achievement of affirmative action objectives. The EEOC said the guidelines were "intended to encourage the adoption and implementation of voluntary affirmative action programs by users who have no obligation under Federal law to adopt them."[58]

Many employers and industrial psychologists criticized the Uniform Guidelines. The American Society for Personnel Administration objected to the affirmative action provisions as inappropriate in a document intended to assure the use of job-related and properly validated selection procedures. Employers observed that the guidelines showed the EEOC's intention to discourage test validation and encourage the use of racial, ethnic, and sex-conscious selection methods. Critics further pointed out that while employers always had the "option" of eliminating disparate impact, it was illegal to do so under Title VII using selection procedures in which race or sex was the controlling factor.

Psychologists saw the guidelines as going beyond the present state of the art in testing, specifying requirements and procedures beyond the capability of even the largest corporations. Without a workable framework of objective selection criteria, employers believed hiring would evolve into a quota system or a random process with negative effects on productivity. Private sector equal employment opportunity analysts believed the government was committed to the "numbers game" rather than to a real effort to achieve equal employment opportunity.[59]

Preliminary evaluation of the effect of the Uniform Guidelines in the late 1970s tended to confirm these predictions. Observers noted that applicants were hired who would previously have been considered unqualified and that the focus of employment policy shifted from the selection process to training and development, causing increased costs and possibly leading to declining performance. A study by the National Academy of Sciences stated that employment tests were being subjected to a degree of government scrutiny that few institutions could bear. Whatever interests were served by tests—efficiency, better matching of people and jobs, the sense of fairness resulting from the allocation of scarce jobs through objective selection—were not strong enough to compete with the government's commitment to minority economic advancement. The National Academy study concluded that the EEOC pursued the type of policy "that would be adopted if the desired effect were to force employers to a quota system to achieve a representative work force."[60]

The civil rights lobby supported the Uniform Guidelines, with the exception of the bottom-line approach to hiring.[61] Nevertheless, in the opinion of some militant liberals, the affirmative action revolution remained incomplete. One commentator noted, for example, that although the EEOC guidelines focused attention on group-based relief, they did not resolve the underlying conflict between the merit principle and the social necessity of equal results for blacks as a group. In the view of this critic, the very fact that the government retained the concept of validation showed that it was unwilling to subordinate the merit principle to remedial social goals.[62] Thus from the radical point of view, the logic of the *Motorola* decision remained to be fulfilled as affirmative action policy entered its third decade of development in the 1980s.

6

The Supreme Court and Affirmative Action: 1977 to 1982

In *Griggs v. Duke Power Co.* (1971), the Supreme Court embraced the views of the civil rights establishment by writing the disparate impact theory of discrimination into Title VII. If under pre-Title VII state anti-discrimination laws there had been a tendency to favor minorities, under the *Griggs* effects test employers were practically compelled to adopt preferential practices in order to avoid disparate impact discrimination charges. At the same time, government contract agencies forced federal contractors under Executive Order 11246 to adopt affirmative action plans giving preference to minorities. By 1976, therefore, race-conscious policies were widely established in public and private employment. And although the Supreme Court had yet to affirm explicit racial preference, its approval of racial remedies in school desegregation cases as well as its tolerance of lower court expansion of Title VII remedies suggested that such an affirmation was imminent.

Although widely implemented, race-conscious affirmative action was not a broadly popular policy. Controversy over preferential treatment, intermittent since 1964, flared up again in 1972 when the Department of Health, Education, and Welfare imposed goals and timetables on colleges and universities receiving federal aid; quotas were also an issue in the presidential election. By the mid-1970s, numerous reverse discrimination suits by white males expressed opposition to preferential treatment, and some appellate courts invalidated quotas previously imposed by district courts as inconsistent with Title VII. In the 1974

DeFunis case, the Supreme Court turned down an opportunity to decide a law school admissions reverse discrimination claim. In 1976, however, in *Washington v. Davis*, the Court stunned the civil rights community by refusing to extend the disparate impact theory into constitutional law and by insisting that proof of discriminatory purpose was necessary to establish a violation of the equal protection clause. Although the decision did not alter employment discrimination policy under Title VII, since it was not a Title VII case, the Court plainly had reservations about making disparate impact theory the basis of civil rights policy in general.

Furthermore, in 1976 the Court upheld a charge of employer discrimination against whites that had implications for the reverse discrimination issue. In *McDonald v. Santa Fe Trail Transportation Co.*, the Justices found that an employer had violated Title VII by firing two white employees who were charged with theft, while retaining a black employee who was similarly charged. Justice Thurgood Marshall declared for a unanimous Court that Title VII prohibited discrimination against white persons on the same standards that applied to blacks. The Court rejected the argument that occasional instances of employer discrimination in favor of minorities were permissible if they did not unreasonably burden whites as a class, saying that Title VII made no exceptions for isolated cases. "Title VII tolerates *no* racial discrimination, subtle or otherwise," Justice Marshall stated. Although the Court reserved the question of the permissibility of a "judicially required or otherwise prompted" affirmative action program, the decision appeared to support reverse discrimination claims against affirmative action.[1]

From 1977 to 1982, the Supreme Court shaped employment discrimination law more actively than in the early years of Title VII development; its decisions in three politically conspicuous and controversial reverse discrimination cases were significant. In *Regents of the University of the California v. Bakke* (1978), the Court tried to compromise on the issue of reverse discrimination by invalidating an absolute racial quota while approving the principle of racial classification. In *United Steelworkers of America v. Weber* (1979), it upheld an employment quota under Title VII, and in *Fullilove v. Klutznick* (1980) it affirmed minority set-asides in public contracting authorized by Congress. Accepting the concepts of group rights and equality of result, the Court generally held that racial preference was necessary to achieve equal employment opportunity. At the same time, in a series of obscure Title VII cases dealing with technical procedural issues, the Court weakened the theoretical basis of race-conscious affirmative action by making it harder to apply the disparate impact theory. In the latter cases, the Justices also took a more reasonable and realistic view of job-relatedness and business necessity, the judicially created standards on which disparate impact charges particularly depended.

The fundamental issue in civil rights policy was whether equality would be defined in racially impartial terms of individual rights, or in racially preferential terms aimed at achieving proportional representation of groups. The reverse discrimination cases raised this issue in the broadest sense in asking whether the constitutional equal protection principle was color-blind or race-conscious, and whether in any event it would be applied in defining employment discrimination policy.[2] Title VII interpretation presented the basic issue of individual vs. group rights in a more specific sense. Notwithstanding *Griggs*, the question continued to arise whether discrimination was the intentional denial of equal treatment for individuals or the unintended effects of institutional practices on racial and ethnic groups. Moreover, it was uncertain whether in proving discrimination it was necessary to identify specific practices that caused the alleged discriminatory result or only to show a pattern of statistically derived disparate impact.[3] Where unlawful discrimination was found, the question of a proper remedy arose. Was it the award of make-whole relief for individuals, or was it permissible to confer benefits on persons who were not injured by discriminatory practices but belonged to a protected group? Still another emerging question was whether preferential policies had to be a remedy for discrimination, or whether they could be adopted simply to create an integrated society.

It was a measure of the radical transformation of civil rights politics that a decade after the Civil Rights Act was passed, a major issue in domestic policy was whether the principle of equality applied to all individuals irrespective of race. The Supreme Court answered this question in the negative in its reverse discrimination decisions: blacks and other protected groups were entitled to preferential treatment. In other cases, though, the Court qualified the application of the disparate impact theory, the legal concept that provided the rationale and practical incentive for preferential treatment. The court thus dealt with affirmative action in a contradictory manner, reflecting the division within American society over the meaning of equality.

I

In its 1976-77 term, the Supreme Court surprised observers first by accepting a large number of employment discrimination cases, and second by deciding for the defendant (the employer) rather than the plaintiff. The cases dealt with procedural and substantive issues, including class actions, time limits on filing discrimination suits, the meaning of religious discrimination, the constitutional standards for unlawful sex discrimination, the requirements for a *prima facie* case and the order and allocation of burdens of proof under Title VII, and the nature of Title VII as a prospective statute in seniority cases. The decisions encouraged the defendants' bar to think the Court was moving toward a more mature and reasonable view of employment discrimination.[4]

For example, in *East Texas Motor Freight System, Inc. v. Rodriguez*, the Justices placed restrictions on across-the-board class actions after years of tolerating an almost cavalier attitude toward this matter in the lower courts. The plaintiffs in the case filed a personal as well as class action complaint on behalf of all blacks and Mexican-Americans who had been denied equal employment opportunities by the company. Although the plaintiffs failed to take the required steps to have the action certified as a class action, the circuit court certified it nevertheless. The Supreme Court reversed. It held unanimously that the plaintiffs were not members of the class they claimed to represent and hence could not be considered adequate class representatives. While asserting that discrimination was by definition class discrimination, the Court declared:

> . . . careful attention to the requirements of Federal Rules of Civil Procedure 23 remains nevertheless indispensable. The mere fact that a complainant alleges racial or ethnic discrimination does not in itself ensure that the party who has brought the lawsuit will be an adequate representative of those who may have been the real victims of that discrimination.[5]

Time limits on filing discrimination charges were at issue in *United Airlines Inc. v. Evans*. The Court rejected a female flight attendant's request for retroactive seniority on the ground that she had failed to file a charge within the required 90-day period; she had resigned her position in 1968 because of a rule against flight attendants being married. The no-marriage rule was arguably illegal at the time it was enforced: after its elimination, it still had an effect on the company's seniority system. Nevertheless, the Court decided that the airline could treat its past action as lawful because the flight attendant did not charge discrimination within the time limit specified in Title VII.[6]

The court dealt with religious discrimination under Title VII in *Trans World Airlines Inc. v. Hardison*. Faced with working Saturday hours under a schedule agreed on by the company and the union, an employee claimed discrimination on account of religion, in violation of a Title VII provision declaring it unlawful for an employer not to make "reasonable accommodations" for the religious practices of employees. The Supreme Court rejected the claim, stating that an employer did not have to deny the preferences and contractual rights of some employees in order to accommodate or prefer the religious needs of others. In language that conceivably had relevance to the problem of reverse discrimination, the Court said that Title VII proscribed discrimination when it was directed against majorities as well as against minorities.[7]

A major sex discrimination case, *General Electric Co. v. Gilbert*, raised the possibility of a retreat from the disparate impact theory. The Court decided that the exclusion of pregnancy from a private employer's disability plan was not a violation of the Title VII ban on sex discrimination. Justice Rehnquist reasoned for the majority that since Title VII did not expressly define discrimination, the statutory meaning was intended to be based on the constitutional concept of equal protection. He stated: "When Congress makes it unlawful for an employer to 'discriminate . . . because of . . . sex,' without further explanation of its meaning, we should not readily infer that it meant something different from what the concept of discrimination has traditionally meant." This evidently referred to the disparate treatment concept, in terms that applied to discrimination on grounds of race as well as sex.[8]

The disparate impact theory was so radically divergent from the popular view of discrimination that decisions like *Washington* and *Gilbert* caused apprehension in the civil rights establishment: might the Justices be contemplating a wholesale abandonment of the new doctrine? There was, perhaps, equal reason to be concerned with decisions that accepted the disparate impact theory but qualified or placed restrictions on its application.

As the basis for a policy of civil rights enforcement, the disparate impact theory assumes that group differences are caused by discrimination. In the rhetoric of affirmative action, the term 'discrimination' is permitted, or is intended, to carry the connotation of traditional discrimination—that is, an intentional act of denial or injury caused by racial prejudice. In reality, of course, proponents of disparate impact, invoking the concepts of societal discrimination and institutional racism, eliminate the intentional, individual act of discrimination. In an attempt to utilize the moral opprobrium associated with traditional discrimination in support of socially redistributive policies based on the disparate impact theory, they seek to obscure these realities. Federal judges should have been more intellectually rigorous and demanding in accepting the disparate impact theory; under the political and social pressures of the late 1960s and early 1970s, they were little inclined toward a critical view of the new approach to civil rights.

The utility of the disparate impact theory as a tool of public policy depends on technical questions about the establishment of disparate impact charges. In particular, two questions are pertinent: what degree of statistical disparity is required to make a *prima facie* charge of discrimination, and how may statistics be used in proving a Title VII discrimination charge? Disparate impact can be established in various ways. It can be shown by comparing the number of minorities in the employer's work force with the percentage of minorities in the local area population, the percentage in the local labor market, or the percentage of qualified minorities in the labor market. Disparate impact can also be established by comparing the pass/fail rates of applicants from different racial groups. Furthermore, the applicants whose pass/fail rates are compared can be from within an organization or company, in which case qualifications are necessarily taken into account to some extent, or they can be from outside the company, which would involve persons off the street who may be not even remotely qualified. In applying *Griggs*, the lower courts dealt with these issues unsystematically, if not casually or impressionistically. They did not really consider that statistical disparities might be explained by something other than discriminatory practices—differences in age, individual preferences, or education, for example—but rather tended to treat any disparity as discriminatory. As the Supreme Court took a more active role in employment discrimination law in the later 1970s, it took a more critical view of these basic issues.

In *International Brotherhood of Teamsters v. U.S.* (1977), the Court confirmed that statistics could be used to make a *prima facie* case of discrimination under Title VII. The government's pattern or practice discrimination charge was based on the fact that only 32 of 6472 employees of a southern trucking company, and only 8 of its 1828 line drivers, were black. Since these percentages were far below the percentage of blacks in the local area population, the Court accepted them as *prima facie* evidence of discrimination. Statistics showing racial or ethnic imbalance were probative, the Court said, because such imbalance was often a tell-tale sign of purposeful discrimination. Evidence of "long lasting and gross disparity" between the composition of the work force and that of the local area population could therefore be considered significant in proving discrimination. However, this comparison, the one most commonly employed in Title VII litigation, was probative only if the disparity was "gross" and unrebutted.[9]

In *Dothard v. Rawlinson* (1977), the Court accepted general population statistics as the basis of a disparate impact charge of sex discrimination against the state of Alabama for making minimum height and weight requirements a condition of employment as a correctional counselor. The state argued that comparative statistics concerning actual applicants, rather than general population data, should be the basis of a *prima facie* charge. The Court rejected this contention, reasoning that awareness of inability to meet the requirements discouraged otherwise-qualified persons from applying and thus caused the application process to be an inaccurate reflection of the true potential applicant pool. In this case, the Court found the height and weight requirements discriminatory. Although an affirmation of *Griggs*, the force of the decision was weakened by the finding that the sex-segregation of guards in the correctional system was a bona fide occupational qualification under Title VII.[10]

The first serious check on the simplistic use of the disparate impact theory came in *Hazelwood School District v. U.S.* (1977). The Court reversed a finding of discrimination and insisted on a more reasonable approach to the use of statistics in making a *prima facie* case. At issue was the probative force of a statistical disparity between the percentage of blacks employed by the school district (1.8 percent), and the percentage of black teachers in the qualified labor pool of the St. Louis metropolitan area (15 percent). The Court said the proper comparison for disparate impact analysis was between the racial composition of the school district staff and the percentage of blacks in the qualified teacher population in the relevant labor market. It denied, however, that the relevant labor market was the metropolitan St. Louis area. The relevant labor market was the county in which the school district was located, where blacks constituted 5.7 percent of the qualified labor pool. Moreover, in the period from 1972 to 1974, after coming under Title VII coverage, the school district hired 3.7 percent blacks. The Court found this close enough to the percentage of blacks in the labor market to signify the absence of discrimination. *Hazelwood* established the rule that comparison of the work force with the qualified labor market is the proper approach to disparate impact analysis.[11]

The use of statistics in making a disparate impact charge of discrimination was also at issue in *New York Transit Authority v. Beazer* (1979). A city policy denying employment to methadone users was found discriminatory by the lower courts under Title VII and the Fourteenth Amendment. The basis of the *prima facie* case was the fact that 81 percent of employees suspected of narcotics use were black or Hispanic, as were 63 percent of persons receiving methadone maintenance in public programs. Reversing, the Supreme Court held these statistics insufficient to make a *prima facie* case because they did not show meaningful comparisons reflecting the existence of discrimination. The numbers did not indicate the racial composition of employees suspected of using methadone, nor the percentage of persons on methadone maintenance who worked for or sought employment with the transit authority. Moreover, even assuming that the statistics made a *prima facie* case, the Court said the charge was rebutted by a showing that the rule against employing methadone users was job-related since it served the ends of safety and efficiency.[12]

In *Beazer*, the Supreme Court rejected the use of general population data to establish disparate impact, the method it had approved in *Griggs* and *Dothard*. It also limited the presentation of statistics to those of actual applicants and employees. It thus imposed a heavier burden on plaintiffs trying to make a *prima facie* case under the disparate impact theory and a correspondingly lighter burden on the employer. Moreover, the Court's discussion of job-relatedness, though in a strict sense not binding because no *prima facie* case was established, was potentially significant. The Court found that the anti-narcotics rule was job-related, although it required no data validating the rule in relation to job performance; this diverged from the doctrine of the *Griggs* line of decisions. *Beazer* suggested the possibility of a common sense or "rule of reason" approach to defining the job-relatedness standard that was far less demanding than previous rulings.[13]

If, in disparate impact cases, the Court took a more cautious view of the use of statistics in making a *prima facie* case, in disparate treatment cases it was concerned with the evidentiary burden on the defendant. Since the allocation of the burden of proof in employment discrimination litigation was often dispositive, this question had great practical importance.

In *Furnco Construction Corporation v. Waters* (1978), the Court considered a charge of discrimination brought by qualified black bricklayers against an employer whose main hiring policy consisted of selection by a job superintendent of persons known to possess proven competence and experience. All of the employees hired under this procedure were white. The employer also had a 16 percent minority hiring goal, and 13 percent of his employees, all hired outside the main hiring process, were black. In the local labor market, 5.7 percent of the qualified bricklayers were black. The issue to be decided was the scope of a *prima facie* disparate treatment case under the *McDonnell Douglas* precedent and the nature of the evidence necessary to rebut such a case.[14]

Finding the employer not guilty of discriminatory practices, the Supreme Court held that the burden on the defendant was to show his decision was based on legitimate, non-discriminatory considerations. For the 7-2 majority, Justice Rehnquist stated that the employer did not have to prove that his action would both serve his business interest and allow consideration of the greatest number of minority applicants. Title VII does not impose a duty to maximize minority hiring. After the defendant makes a showing of legitimate, non-discriminatory purpose, the plaintiff has an opportunity to prove the reason is a pretext for discrimination. In the *Furnco* case, the company's record of minority hiring showed that its practices were not a pretext for excluding blacks.[15]

The significance of the decision was its clarification of the fact that a disparate treatment *prima facie* case establishes only an inference of discrimination which the employer can dispel by providing legitimate, non-discriminatory reasons for the action in question. Justice Rehnquist said the burden on the defendant was "to prove" that a questioned action was based on legitimate considerations and "to show" a legitimate reason for the action. This varying language appeared to distinguish between a heavier burden of *proof* and a lighter burden of *articulation*. Apparently Justice Rehnquist meant the latter, the issue in question being the production of evidence in response to a *prima facie* charge.[16] The employer, he said, did not have to convince the court that his action was nondiscriminatory or lawful; the burden of proof or persuasion thus remained on the plaintiff. *Furnco* indicated that the burden on the employer in a disparate treatment case was lighter than in a disparate impact situation, where the job-relatedness or business necessity of a challenged practice had to be shown.[17]

The Court further clarified the burden on the defendant in a disparate treatment case in *Board of Trustees of Keene State College v. Sweeney* (1978). In a 5-4 *per curiam* decision, it reversed a circuit court ruling that required an employer to prove absence of discriminatory motive. While conceding that "articulate," "show," and "prove"—the terms used in previous opinions to describe the employer's burden—had similar meanings, the court said there was a significant difference between articulating a legitimate, non-discriminatory reason and proving the absence of discriminatory motive. Arguing that *Furnco* used "prove" and "articulate" interchangeably, four dissenting Justices denied any distinction between articulating a nondiscriminatory reason and proving absence of discriminatory motive.[18]

In still another disparate treatment case, *Texas Department of Community Affairs v. Burdine* (1981), the Court elaborated on the burden of proof. In a unanimous opinion, Justice Powell reiterated that the burden of proof did not shift to the defendant, but at all times remained with the plaintiff. After a *prima facie* case was made, the burden on the employer was to produce evidence that the plaintiff was rejected for a legitimate, non-discriminatory reason. In a practical (though not a technical) legal sense, said Powell, the defendant would seek to establish or prove the factual basis for the non-discriminatory explanation. But he was not required, said the Court, to prove the action was lawful. The practical effect was that the employer need not convince the court by a preponderance of the evidence that his reasons for preferring a non-minority over a minority applicant were valid, nor need he hire a minority or female applicant when the individual's qualifications were equal to those of a white male applicant.[19]

Since the Supreme Court by 1981 had decisively approved affirmative action preferences in the reverse discrimination cases, its scrupulous regard for employer prerogatives in these technical and obscure disparate treatment decisions appears to be a case of closing the barn door after the cows have gone. If, however, the Court was concerned in the long run with developing a unified framework for employment discrimination policy, as some commentators suggested, the disparate treatment opinions were potentially very important.

Arguably, the concepts of disparate impact and disparate treatment discrimination were linked in the Court's view by the idea that hiring a competent and trustworthy work force was a valid business reason justifying employment decisions that might otherwise appear discriminatory. The legitimate, non-discriminatory reasons that rebutted a *prima facie* disparate treatment case were functionally similar to the showing of job-relatedness or business necessity used to rebut a disparate impact charge. Although the job-relatedness standard under *Griggs* was onerous, in *Beazer* the court appeared to lighten it considerably while imposing a heavier burden on the plaintiff in using statistics to make a *prima facie* case. This tended to equalize the evidentiary burdens in a disparate impact case in a manner comparable to the equilibrium in disparate treatment cases, where the plaintiff was considered to have a light burden in making a *prima facie* case and the defendant a similarly light burden in articulating non-discriminatory reasons for his action. In substantive terms, moreover, the *Beazer* 'rule-of-reason' approach to defining job-relatedness moved toward the less demanding requirement in disparate treatment cases that an employer need only articulate non-discriminatory reasons. The Court had gone so far in the direction of placating the civil rights lobby by adopting the disparate impact theory in *Griggs* that any modification or qualification of the theory seemed to point toward a reassertion of the traditional disparate treatment concept.[20]

II

Legal technicalities concerning *prima facie* charges and evidentiary burdens defined, in a practical sense, the meaning of discrimination. In *Griggs*, as noted, the Supreme Court went far beyond the pre-Title VII understanding of discrimination based on state fair employment practice law in adopting disparate impact theory. In *McDonnell Douglas v. Green* (1973), the Court at least recognized the concept of disparate treatment discrimination, creating what civil rights lawyers called an artificial and untenable dichotomy in Title VII interpretation. *Washington v. Davis* (1976) provoked apprehension in the civil rights establishment by stopping the spread of the disparate impact theory into constitutional law, but the possibility that the Justices might actually reverse the "quantum leap" taken in *Griggs* seemed more distinct in view of the holding in *International Brotherhood of Teamsters v. U.S.* (1977). Although not a disparate impact case, *Teamsters* shocked the civil rights lobby by reconsidering the fundamental question of whether Title VII was prospective or retrospective in nature.[21]

Although Congress intended Title VII to be prospective, the civil rights bureaucracy and the courts applied it retrospectively, transforming it into a comprehensive remedial statute directed against historic societal discrimination. A decisive step in this transformation was judicial acceptance of the argument that while pre-act discrimination was not unlawful, the present and continuing effects of past discrimination violated Title VII. Starting with the *Quarles* case in 1968, numerous lower court decisions applied the present effects doctrine to find seniority systems unlawful in a way never intended by Congress. In the *Teamsters* case, the Supreme Court overruled this line of precedents.

The seniority system at issue in *Teamsters* denied credit for plant seniority; it required an employee transferring to the line-driver position to start at the bottom of the seniority ladder in that department. Adhering to precedent under the present effects doctrine, the district court held that since blacks had been discriminated against in line-driver hiring before the enactment of Title VII, the seniority system, although neutral on its face, locked black employees into inferior positions and perpetuated prior discrimination. Justice Stewart conceded for the 7-2 majority that the seniority system appeared to come within the *Griggs* rule that practices fair in form but discriminatory in effect were unlawful. However, Title VII specifically exempted seniority systems. Justice Stewart pointed out that the literal terms of Section 703(h) and its legislative history showed that Congress considered the "freezing" effect of desegregated seniority systems and protected them. It sought to prevent vested seniority rights of employees from being destroyed or watered down because of pre-act discrimination by their employers. An otherwise neutral, legitimate seniority system did not become unlawful, the Court concluded, simply because it might perpetuate pre-act discrimination.[22]

Teamsters also involved preferential treatment. The Court held that to apply Title VII against pre-act discrimination would require the union and employer to subordinate the rights of employees to the claims of persons without seniority who were discriminated against before the effective date of Title VII. The problem of racial preference also arose in relation to remedies for victims of hiring discrimination. Those who applied and were actually discriminated against were entitled to make-whole relief, including constructive seniority. The question was whether employees who did not apply for a line-driver job were also victims of discrimination on the theory that awareness of the company's discriminatory practices discouraged them from applying. The company argued that relief for non-applicants was preferential treatment because of race; as such it was inconsistent with the principle of make-whole relief. The Court decided that non-applicants were eligible for relief, but it required such persons to prove they should be treated as an applicant. They had to show they were qualified and would have applied for the line-driver job but for the discriminatory practices. Remanding the case, Justice Stewart said the trial court had the task of "recreating the past." It had to determine who were the actual victims of discrimination and decide their rightful place, adjusting their remedial interests and the legitimate expectations of other employees who were innocent of wrongdoing.[23]

In repudiating the present effects doctrine, the Supreme Court did what had been viewed as "almost unthinkable."[24] To the civil rights lobby, *Teamsters* was "a devastating setback" that could have a disastrous impact on Title VII litigation in general. Most significantly, the decision reasserted the theory of intentional discrimination in a situation thought to be governed by the *Griggs* effects test. It thus augured further possible retreat from the disparate impact theory of discrimination. With respect to remedies, *Teamsters* extended the liberal approach of *Franks* by declaring non-applicants eligible for relief. However, the court limited the chance of actually obtaining relief by requiring non-applicants to prove they were potential victims of discrimination. In the determination of this issue, employers could argue that a non-applicant was unqualified or that others were more qualified. The effect was to make the remedial enterprise more time-consuming and expensive.[25] It might be argued that the effect of *Teamsters* was limited, since the present effects doctrine had served its purpose in desegregating seniority systems and was no longer needed.[26] Nevertheless, if the Court could interpret Title VII literally and in accordance with the legislative intent in this case, it could do so in others; the structure of race-conscious affirmative action under the disparate impact theory might eventually be threatened.

Even if the decisions in the Supreme Court's 1976-77 term are seen as an attempt to preserve the disparate impact theory by reforming it, they may have portended a shift away from *Griggs* by holding that a more carefully defined and reasonably explained statistical disparity raised an inference of intentional discrimination. If this inference were rebuttable through a showing of legitimate business purpose based on a rule-of-reason standard (as in *Washington v. Davis* and *Beazer*) rather than on the unrealistic validation standards of the civil rights bureaucracy, the structure of incentives by which the government forced employers to take race-conscious affirmative action would be seriously weakened.[27]

Simultaneous with the Court's reconsideration of the legal framework of affirmative action, a series of reverse discrimination suits came before it that posed a more direct and fundamental challenge to preferential practices. Because the Justices desired to proceed more cautiously in resolving the contradictions in employment discrimination law, or, more likely, because they thought race-conscious policies were either too firmly established to be abruptly overruled or were intrinsically sound as public policy measures, the Court turned back the reverse discrimination challenge. In three highly publicized and politically charged cases in the late 1970s, the Supreme Court approved racial preference. It denied the fundamental principle that the meaning of unlawful discrimination does not depend on the race, gender, or ethnic origins of the individual claiming rights under the Constitution or Title VII.

III

Judged by the attention it received from the media, affirmative action became a paramount national issue in the late 1970s.[28] The manifest contradiction between racial preference and the plain tenor of the Civil Rights Act of 1964 was reason enough for controversy. It was exacerbated by the functional incentives employed by the civil rights bureaucracy to promote preferential practices. Although affirmative action in its outreach and recruitment guises was preferential, it was not objectionable because it expressed a genuine desire to give members of minorities an opportunity to compete and did not interfere with employment decisions. The affirmative action programs that provoked reverse discrimination claims were different. Defensive in nature, they were intended to avoid disparate impact liability rather than assist members of minorities.[29] This fact compromised the moral character of affirmative action and provoked resentment against what was widely perceived to be its underhanded nature.

After avoiding the issue in *DeFunis* (1974),[30] the Supreme Court agreed to decide a reverse discrimination question in *Regents of the University of California v. Bakke* (1978).[31] The case commanded extraordinary attention; 115 organizations filed 51 *amicus curiae* briefs seeking to influence the outcome.[32] And although it dealt with federally funded programs under Title VI of the Civil Rights Act, *Bakke* could be expected to reflect the Court's view of preferential policies under Title VII.

Alan Bakke, a thirty-eight-year-old white male, was denied admission to the medical school of the University of California at Davis for two consecutive years. During this time, the school reserved 16 of 100 places in its entering classes for minority group individuals. Bakke's academic record and qualifications were superior to those of the minority group candidates admitted under the affirmative action plan, which was not based on a finding of discrimination but was intended to increase the number of minority doctors. Bakke claimed he was discriminated against because of his race, contrary to the requirement of the equal protection clause of the Fourteenth Amendment and Section 601 of Title VI. The latter states that no person shall, on the grounds of race, be excluded from participation in or be denied benefits of or be subjected to discrimination under any program receiving federal financial assistance. The California Supreme Court upheld Bakke's claim. In a 5-4 decision, the U.S. Supreme Court affirmed this result, declaring the affirmative action plan unlawful. The political, legal, and moral impact of the decision was unclear, however, because deep divisions within the Court prevented the adoption of a majority opinion on central issues of affirmative action policy.

Five Justices voted to uphold Bakke's claim, but disagreed about why the affirmative action plan was unlawful. A second group of five Justices approved race as a legitimate factor in professional school admission policies, but disagreed on the constitutional reasoning to support this conclusion. Justice Powell, staking out a centrist position, belonged to both groups. He announced the judgment of the Court and delivered an opinion declaring the affirmative action plan an unconstitutional quota. His opinion also approved the use of racial classification as a matter of constitutional principle. No other Justice agreed with his reasoning, however. Chief Justice Burger and Justices Rehnquist, Stewart, and Stevens concurred in the judgment for Bakke, but joined in an opinion written by Justice Stevens justifying the result on narrow statutory grounds. The second group, consisting of Justices Brennan, Blackmun, Marshall and White, agreed with Powell that racial classification was constitutional, but used different reasoning to reach the conclusion that the Davis plan was constitutional.

The problem faced by Justice Powell and the Brennan group was how they might justify racial and ethnic classification under the Constitution and Title VI. Despite the broad extent of preferential policies in education and in public and private employment, and notwithstanding Supreme Court decisions approving racial remedies in school desegregation and voting rights cases, this task was formidable.[33] In the first place, *Bakke* did not arise in a context of historic southern racial discrimination, as the school and voting cases did. Second, Title VI (like Title VII) on its face protected any person against exclusion on racial grounds.

The question in *Bakke* was whether the rules and standards defining equality and unlawful discrimination were the same for blacks and whites. In dealing with desegregation, the Court had evolved the doctrine since the mid-1960s that racial and ethnic classifications, although not unconstitutional *per se*, were suspect. They could be used only if justified by a compelling state interest, if narrowly structured to serve that interest, and if no alternative non-racial means were available. This was called the strict scrutiny standard of review; whenever it had been employed, the questioned racial classification had been found unlawful. *Bakke* posed the issue of whether a racial classification intended to benefit blacks should also be subjected to strict scrutiny analysis.

Justice Powell held that the Davis plan should be examined under the strict scrutiny standard. Asserting that Title VI incorporated a constitutional standard,[34] he decided the case on constitutional as well as statutory grounds. Forcefully restating traditional equal rights theory, he said the guarantees of the Fourteenth Amendment were personal rights that had the same meaning for all persons irrespective of race. Rejecting the argument that strict scrutiny review should apply only to racial classifications deemed hostile to minorities, Justice Powell argued that such an approach would reduce civil rights law to a subjective political process. He further criticized the notion of giving preferences to overcome societal discrimination. "By hitching the meaning of the Equal Protection Clause to these transitory considerations," he warned, "we would be holding, as a constitutional principle, that judicial scrutiny of classifications touching on racial and ethnic background may vary with the ebb and flow of political forces."[35]

Justice Powell acknowledged the Court's recent approval of race-conscious measures. These were premised on findings of constitutional or statutory violations resulting in identified, race-based injuries to individuals. In *Bakke*, by contrast, there was no determination that the university had discriminated, and "[w]e have never approved a classification," he averred, "that aids persons perceived as members of relatively victimized groups at the expense of other innocent individuals in the absence of judicial, legislative, or administrative findings of constitutional or statutory violations." While conceding that the state had a legitimate interest in eliminating the effect of "identified discrimination," he said this was a far more focused goal than remedying the effects of societal discrimination—"an amorphous concept of injury that may be ageless in its reach into the past."[36]

Having argued cogently against preferential treatment, Justice Powell abruptly changed course and offered a justification for racial preference. He propounded the view that race was a legitimate factor to be taken into account in attaining the constitutionally permissible goal of a diverse student body. Student diversity promoted an atmosphere of speculation, excitement, and creativity; it was a goal protected by the First Amendment. Race or ethnic background, therefore, could properly be considered. The way to do so, however, was not by setting a racial quota, but by regarding race as a "plus" in a competitive process in which each individual would be evaluated as an individual and no one would be rejected simply because of race.[37]

Justice Powell's theory of diversity attempted to justify racial preference in a manner consistent with the merit principle. The Brennan bloc that voted to uphold the medical school admission policy was far more forthright in seeking to accommodate the demand for preferential treatment emanating from the civil rights establishment in the late 1970s.

The next stage of the civil rights revolution envisioned by supporters of affirmative action was to discard the make-whole theory of relief for individual victims of discrimination and adopt racial preferences as compensation for historic societal discrimination against blacks as a group. Although it was originally used to expand the scope of preferential policy, the make-whole theory now constituted a limitation on the new racism. The lower courts were divided on the question of whether remedies could be awarded only to identifiable victims of discrimination or also conferred on members of the protected group who had not suffered individual injury. In either case, the predicate for awarding relief was a finding of discrimination. The opinion of the Brennan group in *Bakke*, however, obviated the issue of make-whole relief by arguing that racial preference could be awarded in the absence of unlawful discrimination in order to counter the effects of societal discrimination.

The Brennan group accepted the equivalence of Title VI and the Constitution concerning the meaning of equality and unlawful discrimination. Neither in the Constitution nor the Civil Rights Act, however, did it find a requirement of racial neutrality. The school desegregation decisions were cited to show the constitutional permissibility of race-conscious remedies. To argue that Title VI permitted racial decision-making, when in fact it expressly prohibited it, challenged Justice Brennan's interpretive ingenuity.

In general, Brennan simply argued that the statute did not mean what it said. He stated that it was "inconceivable," in view of the legislative intent to encourage voluntary compliance with the Civil Rights Act, that Congress would forbid voluntary race-conscious remedies by recipients of federal aid "to cure acknowledged or obvious statutory violations." Recipients who were guilty of discrimination should not be expected to await a finding of unlawful practices by a court or administrative agency. The opinion then argued that although Congress prohibited discrimination in Title VI, it did not define it. Congress "specifically eschewed any static definition of discrimination in favor of broad language that could be shaped by experience, administrative necessity, and evolving judicial doctrine." The constitutional standard of discrimination was supposed to supply the content of Title VI, the Brennan bloc reasoned, but since this standard was in "a state of flux and rapid evolution," the inference followed that the meaning of discrimination in the statute, expressed as it was in "cryptic language," should "evolve with the interpretation of the demands of the Constitution." Therefore, "any claim that the use of racial criteria is barred by the plain language of the statute," the opinion stated, "must fail in light of the remedial purpose of Title VI and its legislative history." The Brennan group concluded:

> Congress did not intend to prohibit . . . the consideration of race as part of a remedy for societal discrimination even where there is no showing that the institution extending the preference has been guilty of past discrimination nor any judicial finding that the particular beneficiaries of the racial preference have been adversely affected by societal discrimination.[38]

Having disposed of Title VI, the Brennan opinion elaborated on the constitutionality of race-conscious measures. Although racial classification was suspect and required strict scrutiny, the Davis affirmative action plan was not suspect. To be sure, it designated minorities for special treatment and restricted whites. It did not, however, stigmatize whites, who as a class were not saddled with disabilities or subjected to unequal treatment. The admissions policy did not contravene "the cardinal principle that racial classifications that stigmatize—because they are drawn on the presumption that one race is inferior to another or because they put the weight of government behind racial hatred and separatism—are invalid without more." But if strict scrutiny was inapplicable, so was the more relaxed rational-basis standard, the test ordinarily applied in non-racial matters. The Brennan group proposed an intermediate standard of review under which the state could employ a racial classification that was shown to serve "important governmental objectives" and was "substantially related to achievement of those objectives."[39] The purpose of remedying the effects of past societal discrimination was sufficiently important to justify a race-conscious admission policy where there was a sound basis for concluding that minority underrepresentation was substantial and chronic, and the handicap of past discrimination impeded access of minorities to the school.[40]

In separate dissenting opinions, Justices Marshall and Blackmun defended compensatory racial preference. Justice Marshall reasoned that since the Constitution had been interpreted for 200 years as permitting the most ingenious and pervasive forms of discrimination against blacks, he could not "believe that this same Constitution stands as a barrier" to state measures attempting to remedy the effects of that discrimination. Dismissing the notion that unlawful discriminatory action was a necessary basis for preferential treatment, he declared: "It is unnecessary in 20th century America to have individual Negroes demonstrate that they have been victims of racial discrimination." Blacks' different experience entitled them to "greater protection" as "'special wards'" under the Fourteenth Amendment, where it was necessary to remedy the effects of past discrimination. Justice Blackmun, looking to a time when "persons will be regarded as persons," nevertheless believed it was impossible at present "to arrange an affirmative action program in a racially neutral way and have it successful." "In order to get beyond racism," he said, "we must first take account of race. There is no other way. And in order to treat some persons equally, we must treat them differently."[41]

Justice Stevens, joined by Justices Rehnquist, Stewart, and Chief Justice Burger, submitted the fifth opinion in *Bakke*. Concurring in the judgment that Bakke be admitted to the medical school, Stevens said the admission policy clearly violated Title VI. The law plainly prohibited the exclusion of any individual from a federally funded program because of race, regardless of whether the exclusion carried a racial stigma. The Stevens group, therefore, considered it unnecessary to examine the constitutional issue and inappropriate to ask whether race could ever be a factor in an admission program.[42]

IV

At one level, the result in *Bakke* could be considered a compromise. Critics of affirmative action claimed victory because the Court upheld the reverse discrimination charge and struck down the admission policy as a quota. Supporters of affirmative action claimed victory because a majority of the Justices approved race-conscious measures for remedial purposes. At the level of moral principle and political theory, however, *Bakke* was not a compromise because the competing principles—equal rights for individuals without distinction of color and compensatory preference for racial groups—were ultimately irreconcilable.

Because only one member of the majority voting to strike down the quota was willing to deal with the problem of affirmative action in constitutional and public policy terms, the deeper meaning of *Bakke* (as the Brennan group stated) was to confirm existing policies of racial preference in educational programs and in employment.[43] In this basic sense, *Bakke* was a victory for affirmative action, despite the appearance of a compromise and notwithstanding Justice Powell's attempt to reconcile equal rights and racial group preference. To be sure, Justice Powell's ingenious effort appealed to many observers, including some critics of affirmative action, as a prudent and pragmatic solution. It avoided broad condemnation of preferential treatment while withholding categorical approval of race-conscious measures, and possibly even casting a cloud over affirmative action by insisting on strict scrutiny of compensatory preferences.[44] Powell alone, however, required strict scrutiny review of affirmative action, and his defense of individual rights was nullified by his argument that race should be considered a "plus" in admission policies. It was obvious that race, once admitted to the decisional process, could be subjectively manipulated to reach any number, just as in a quota program.[45]

Justice Powell's "diversity" rationale, based on First Amendment considerations, was apparently intended to defuse the issue of preferential treatment by saying, in effect, that if institutions and employers were not too blatant about it, they could use race-conscious measures and work out their own compromise between the values in conflict. This approach lacked candor, if it did not rest on a complete fiction, and it trivialized the Constitution by making it easy to overcome the presumption against racial classification and discrimination. If there was much pretense and self-delusion in affirmative action policy already, Justice Powell's solution seemed to encourage more of it. Much as one might admire Justice Powell's conscientious quest, described by one commentator as "perhaps the grandest finesse of a searing legal issue in Supreme Court history," the fact remained that it rested on no consensus and no clear doctrinal foundation in anti-discrimination theory.[46]

In the context of widespread adoption of preferential policies, the Brennan group opinion, in conjunction with Justice Powell's approval of race as a legitimate consideration, emerged as the Court's principal teaching on the problem of reverse discrimination. Together, these opinions obscured the narrow and opaque opinion of the Stevens group. Although the Brennan group lost on the specific quota in question, it prevailed strategically by presenting a bloc of five Justices, including Powell, who supported race-conscious measures on constitutional grounds. This was a majority in favor of preferential treatment without the requirement of a finding of unlawful discrimination.[47] A more solid majority held preferential remedies constitutional to eliminate the effects of existing discrimination, pursuant to legislative, judicial or administrative findings of unlawful practices. Although in a formal sense *Bakke* resolved very little that was not already obvious—namely, that an absolute quota was unlawful—and thus technically could be said to stand for very little, it was generally seen as sanctioning existing affirmative action programs in higher education. Furthermore, although the decision had no direct effect on Title VII enforcement, in the opinion of one supporter of preferential remedies it "caused a surprisingly large number of people of good will to rethink their commitments to affirmative action and to express a more ready willingness to be forthright and open about efforts taken to cure problems associated with race and sex bias in this nation."[48]

The majority that supported Bakke's claim may have believed it would be counterproductive to hand down a decision clearly outlawing reverse discrimination. Such a result would expose educational institutions, corporations, and unions to reverse discrimination lawsuits and outrage the civil rights bureaucracy, minority groups, and liberal opinion in general.[49] Although in a sense *Bakke* might be said to have cast a cloud over affirmative action, the vision of proportional racial representation held out by the Brennan group seemed more likely to be advanced as a result of the decision.

If a university could use race-conscious remedies when required by a court after a finding of discrimination, a defender of affirmative action asked on the basis of Justice Powell's opinion, why could it not do so in a consent decree? And if that was permitted, why could the institution not simply adopt racially preferential measures on its own initiative, or at the suggestion of an injured party before it was sued? To forbid or discourage voluntary measures to correct violations of law, as Justice Powell proposed in requiring a finding of unlawful discrimination as a predicate for preferential remedies, was viewed as "a strange posture for a legal system."[50] The opinion of the Brennan group, in contrast, pointed the way beyond the unlawful discrimination make-whole relief barrier to the approval of racial preference based on societal discrimination. This step awaited to be taken in further reverse discrimination cases.

7

The Supreme Court and Affirmative Action:
Weber and *Fullilove*

If the divisions within the Court on the *Bakke* case did not reflect "chaos" in anti-discrimination law, as a future Justice of the Supreme Court suggested,[1] at the very least they revealed serious internal contradictions. These contradictions resulted from the adoption of disparate impact theory in *Griggs* and the acceptance of race-conscious remedies in voting rights and school desegregation cases in the 1970s. By the latter part of the decade, a majority of the Court apparently desired to restrict the application of the *Griggs* effects test as interpreted by the lower courts and the civil rights bureaucracy. This was the effect, in any event, of decisions concerning the use of statistics in disparate impact cases and the allocation of evidentiary burdens in disparate treatment cases. But, while qualifying the underlying theory of discrimination that rationalized (and, in practical legal effect, required) preferential practices, the Court rejected the equal rights argument advanced by opponents of affirmative action in the reverse discrimination cases. Thus, *Bakke*, although it struck down an absolute racial quota, confirmed most existing systems of preferential treatment by signaling approval of racial classification when used to promote minority interests.

If a majority of the Court thought it possible to retreat gradually from disparate impact theory in order to restore traditional equal rights principles, while acquiescing in the political demands of the government and the civil rights establishment for racial preference, the *Weber* case provided a further opportunity to develop this strategy. The second of three major reverse discrimination cases decided by the Court in the late 1970s, *Weber* had a more direct bearing on affirmative action policy than *Bakke* because it concerned the meaning of discrimination and the validity of equal rights claims under Title VII and Executive Order 11246.

I

In a practical sense, affirmative action under Executive Order 11246 had operated under disparate impact theory since the mid-1960s, when contract compliance officers began to pressure contractors to hire more minorities on the basis of work-force surveys showing low utilization of blacks but no evidence of unlawful discrimination. Meanwhile, racial measures, including quotas, were authorized in judicial decisions under Title VII as a remedy for unlawful discrimination. As opposition to quotas increased in the mid-1970s, many lower courts held that the fair way to resolve the conflict between the equal rights principle and the demand for compensatory group preference was to insist on a finding of unlawful employment practices as the legal justification for race-conscious affirmative action.

Under the conflicting sources of authority on which federal equal employment opportunity policy was based, the chief practical means of extending affirmative action was the contract compliance program. The principal legal justifications of affirmative action, however, were developed by the courts under Title VII. As the pressure to defend and rationalize race-conscious policies increased in response to reverse discrimination claims, the tendency to apply the legal standards developed under Title VII to affirmative action under Executive Order 11246 emerged. If preferential treatment was permissible only as a remedy for unlawful discrimination, as Title VII case law held, then the same rule should be applied to the contract compliance program. This tendency was based in part on the rational perception that the separate tracks on which equal employment opportunity policy operated should be merged. All corporate employers were subject to Title VII, and most of them were government contractors as well. It was confusing, impractical and unreasonable to have two sets of legal standards—EEOC Title VII guidelines and OFCCP executive order regulations—governing their employment practices.

The *Weber* case revealed the inherent contradiction in federal anti-discrimination policy. Under the *Griggs* disparate impact theory, employers were forced to engage in preferential hiring to avoid liability and the potentially heavy costs of litigation and remedial measures. Under Executive Order 11246, they were under pressure to prefer minorities in hiring in order to avoid being found out of compliance with the affirmative action obligation. At the same time, both measures expressly prohibited discrimination against individuals because of race. Moreover, under Title VII, race-conscious remedies could only be ordered upon a finding of unlawful employment practices. These conflicting imperatives and lines of development converged in *Weber*.[2]

Brian Weber was a white employee of Kaiser Aluminum and Chemical Corporation who claimed that he was discriminated against because of his race in violation of Title VII. At issue was a craft training program that allocated positions on a 1:1 ratio between black and white racial groups on the basis of relative seniority within each group. Weber failed to be admitted to the program, while black employees with less seniority than he were admitted.[3] The training program quota was established in 1974 under a collective bargaining agreement between the company and the United Steelworkers of America. At the time, blacks constituted 14 percent of the Kaiser work force and 1.83 percent of the skilled craft workers in the Grammercy, Louisiana, plant, an area where blacks constituted 39 percent of the labor market. The quota was to continue until blacks held 39 percent of the skilled craft jobs in the Grammercy plant work force.

The Kaiser-Steelworkers affirmative action plan was part of a general effort to hire minorities that began in the 1960s under contract compliance pressure. At the time the plan was adopted in 1974, the union faced race and sex discrimination charges under Title VII. Denying any prior discrimination and blaming the union for excluding minorities, the company defended the training program quota by pointing to its affirmative action obligation under Executive Order 11246. It argued that racial classification and preference were an indispensable means of ending the exclusion of blacks from craft jobs, and that no practical alternative existed as a mechanism for achieving compliance with the executive order. Kaiser also faced the prospect of Title VII discrimination suits at two other plants in Louisiana. Between the threat of Title VII liability on the one hand and the affirmative action obligation on the other, the company contended that it had to be race-conscious. Notwithstanding the prohibitions of Title VII, the union argued before the Supreme Court that employers should be permitted to adopt racial preferences "within a zone of reasonableness" because it simply was not feasible to have government agencies make specific findings of discrimination and prescribe remedial action. Disputing the notion that its quota policy was truly voluntary, Kaiser observed that in view of contract compliance pressure and the pending Title VII litigation which it faced, "voluntary action may in reality be a misnomer, for legal compulsion was present as surely as if a suit had been filed or a contract lost."[4]

The United Steelworkers of America blamed the company for the low percentage of minorities in craft jobs, asserting that the purpose of the affirmative action plan was to cure employer discrimination and eliminate the effects of historic societal discrimination. The union described the training program quota as purely private conduct that was permissible under Title VII. It argued that Section 703(j), the ban on preferential treatment, only prohibited government agencies from granting preferential treatment on account of racial imbalance; by implication, it permitted employers and unions to adopt preferential measures. The union furthermore declared: "It would be ironic if a law triggered by a Nation's guilt over centuries of racial injustice constituted the first prohibition of private endeavors to accelerate the elimination of the vestiges of that injustice."[5]

Weber won in the lower courts. The district court in Louisiana, rejecting the argument that the ban on preferential treatment permitted private preferences, held that the affirmative action plan violated the clear and unequivocal prohibitions against discrimination in Title VII. Adhering to Title VII case law, the court acknowledged that preferential treatment—including quotas—could be ordered for remedial purposes, but only after a finding of discrimination and only for persons who were victims of unlawful practices. Judge Jack M. Gordon noted that racial preference was lawful before the enactment of Title VII, and it should perhaps again be permitted in order to achieve a national social goal. However, "this Court is not sufficiently skilled in the art of sophistry," he said, "to justify such discrimination by employers in light of the unequivocal prohibitions against discrimination against any *individual*" contained in Title VII.[6]

The Fifth Circuit affirmed. In addition to the restrictions on affirmative action imposed by the requirement that Title VII relief be awarded only to individual victims of discrimination to make them whole and give them their rightful place, the court noted that the quota was adopted under contract compliance pressure. It therefore evaluated the Kaiser quota in light of the nondiscrimination requirement of Executive Order 11246. The court observed that quotas under the Philadelphia plan had been upheld against a Title VII challenge in 1971. In that case, however, there had been a finding of prior discrimination, so the racial quota was not prohibited by the Title VII rule of nondiscrimination. If Executive Order 11246 mandated a racial quota for admission to the Kaiser training program in the absence of any prior discrimination, the court declared, "the executive order must fall before this direct congressional prohibition."[7]

In a dissenting opinion, Judge John Minor Wisdom pointed out that employers faced the threat of Title VII disparate impact suits by minority employees on the one hand and—if they adopted preferential measures to avoid such liability—the threat of discrimination charges by white employees on the other. Employers were thus forced "to walk a high tight-rope without a net beneath them." Judge Wisdom argued that employers should be permitted to adopt race-conscious affirmative action when it appeared to be "a reasonable remedy for an arguable violation of Title VII." The court should create a "zone of reasonableness," he said, "within which the employer and the union would be sheltered from liability" as a means of encouraging private settlements. Dispensing with the requirement of a finding of unlawful discrimination, the dissent held the affirmative action plan to be justified by "societal discrimination."[8]

In effect regarding private employment as a public enterprise subject to regulation in the public interest, the civil rights agencies and the courts had used disparate impact theory for over a decade to force employers to engage in preferential practices in order to improve economic conditions for blacks.[9] *Weber* was a test of whether the government could pursue this policy to the point of explicit repudiation of the equal rights principle. As the Kaiser brief in the Supreme Court made clear, the affirmative action plan in reality was not voluntary. It was required by—indeed was all but indistinguishable from—government action. From the business point of view, it seemed only fair to limit employers' liability in return for carrying out the national policy. It was unethical and improper, from their perspective, for the government to force employers to engage in racial hiring or else lose government contracts without protecting them from being found guilty of discrimination under Title VII if they complied with the government policy.

A corporate equal employment opportunity attorney stated that *Weber* finally presented the conflict between Executive Order 11246 and Title VII that the courts had avoided since the start of affirmative action in the 1960s. Noting that the liberal Fifth Circuit had decided for Weber, Michael Farrell said that once a court faced the conflict, the result was obvious. "While some may disagree on the merits of quota or preferential hiring," he wrote, "most will agree that the President cannot require something that Congress has forbidden."[10] If the Supreme Court adhered to the rules of statutory interpretation integral to the rule of law, there was reason to think it would affirm the circuit court holding.

II

The Supreme Court surprised employment discrimination lawyers and the civil rights establishment by upholding the Kaiser-Steelworkers quota. But far from clarifying the nature of affirmative action, the *Weber* decision obscured the basic realities of federal anti-discrimination policy. In a tendentious and labored opinion, the Court interpreted the employment quota as private, voluntary action occurring in a kind of no man's land beyond the sphere of government, law, and public policy in general.

Writing for a 5-2 majority, Justice Brennan simply ignored the fact that the Kaiser quota was a response to contract compliance pressure.[11] The affirmative action plan, he wrote, did not involve state action; hence, it raised no constitutional considerations under the equal protection clause of the Fourteenth Amendment. Nor did it present a violation of Title VII that would raise the question of the scope of judicial remedial authority. Most astonishingly, Justice Brennan denied that the case raised any question about the requirements of Title VII. The only issue was whether Title VII left employers and unions free to take race-conscious steps "to eliminate manifest racial imbalances in traditionally segregated job categories."[12]

Justice Brennan conceded that Weber's claim, based on a literal interpretation of the anti-discrimination provisions of Title VII, was "not without force." Weber overlooked the fact, however, that the affirmative action plan was voluntarily adopted by private parties to eliminate traditional patterns of racial segregation. Disregarding the plain meaning of the law, Justice Brennan purported to find justification of racial discrimination against white employees in the legislative history of Title VII on the grounds that it was consistent with the spirit and intent of the Civil Rights Act. Congress was primarily concerned with "the plight of the Negro in our economy," he stated; its objective was to open opportunities for blacks in occupations traditionally closed to them. Furthermore, Congress wanted to encourage voluntary compliance. Therefore, Brennan reasoned, a literal interpretation of Title VII "that forbade all race-conscious affirmative action would 'bring about an end completely at variance with the purpose of the statute' and must be rejected." Quoting from the Steelworkers' brief, he declared:

It would be ironic indeed if a law triggered by a Nation's concern over centuries of racial injustice and intended to improve the lot of those who had 'been excluded from an American dream for so long,' constituted the first legislative prohibition of all voluntary, private, race-conscious efforts to abolish traditional patterns of racial segregation and hierarchy.[13]

The second part of Justice Brennan's opinion dealt with Section 703(j) of Title VII, the ban on preferential treatment. Weber's reliance on this provision was puzzling, for it had not generally been interpreted as a barrier to quotas, but rather as dealing mainly with the definition of a discriminatory violation. Most courts interpreted Section 703(j) to mean that an employer could not be charged with unlawful discrimination for having a racially imbalanced work force.[14] Moreover, civil rights lawyers had argued since 1965 that the language in Section 703(j) stating that preferential treatment is not *required* allows the inference that it is *permitted*. Justice Brennan adopted this reading. He used Section 703(j) as a statutory tool to justify the affirmative action plan, diverting attention from the Court's refusal to be bound by the obvious meaning of the nondiscrimination requirements in Title VII.[15]

Justice Brennan argued that if Congress had intended to prohibit all race-conscious affirmative action, it could have written Title VII to say that preferential treatment is neither required *nor permitted*. However, Section 703(j) prohibits only the former; it does not order that Title VII not be interpreted to permit preferential treatment. In the debate over Title VII, opponents of the bill mainly objected to the racial preference they believed would result from government intervention in the labor market. Distorting this legislative history, Justice Brennan emphasized opposition to government intervention, rather than to racially preferential hiring, as the central issue in the debate. He said Section 703(j) was added to the bill to reassure conservatives that the government's purpose was not to interfere with the free market. It was to prevent undue federal intervention into private business "because of some Federal employee's ideas about racial balance or racial imbalance."[16]

The majority opinion thus concluded that the refusal to admit Weber to the training program was not unlawful discrimination because of race. In other words, the rejection of Weber was a form of legalized discrimination. Justice Brennan acknowledged that the quota "trammeled," or restricted, the interests of white employees. It did not do so unnecessarily, however, nor did it require the discharge or replacement of whites. Furthermore, the plan did not absolutely bar the advancement of white workers, and it was temporary (even though it would take 30 years to reach the goal!).[17] The purpose of the quota was not to maintain a racial balance, but "to eliminate a manifest imbalance."[18] Although denying a need to draw the line between permissible and impermissible affirmative action, Justice Brennan nevertheless laid down broad criteria within which preferential practices could work against white employees.

In a concurring opinion, Justice Blackmun placed the majority opinion in perspective by discussing the theory of affirmative action proposed in the Fifth Circuit dissent and argued for by the company. This was the view that employers caught between discrimination charges by blacks and reverse discrimination charges by whites should be allowed to adopt "reasonable" measures of racial preference where there was an "arguable violation" of Title VII. Justice Blackmun believed this to be a better solution to the problem than the majority's approval of affirmative action based on "traditionally segregated job categories." It was less expansive and did not entirely abandon the concept of a nondiscrimination principle that would apply equally to black and white employees. Nevertheless, Blackmun accepted the majority's rationale. Although he conceded it was not supported by the legislative history, private and voluntary racial preference was justified by practical and equitable considerations not perceived by Congress in 1964. Most important, according to Justice Blackmun, preferential treatment permitted employers to redress discrimination that lay outside the bounds of Title VII—that is, pre-act societal discrimination.[19]

In a forceful dissenting opinion, Justice Rehnquist accused the majority of reversing the entire course of Title VII interpretation. In his view, the overriding purpose of the law was to eliminate race from employment decisions. The majority opinion of the Court, however, rewrote the statute to permit employers to "trammel" the interests of white employees and favor blacks in order to eliminate racial imbalance. Noting that the affirmative action plan was adopted under contract compliance pressure, Justice Rehnquist said Section 703(j) was intended to prevent government-required preferential treatment for racial balance where no finding of discrimination was made. Moreover, to interpret the provision as permitting employers to discriminate on racial grounds was "outlandish," in light of the flat prohibition of race-based employment decisions elsewhere in the law. It was true that Title VII was intended to open economic opportunities for blacks, but this did not create a warrant for discriminating against whites. Justice Rehnquist declared that the majority opinion "introduces into Title VII a tolerance for the very evil that the law was intended to eradicate, without offering even a clue as to what the limits of that tolerance may be."[20]

Chief Justice Burger charged the Court with rewriting Title VII to achieve what it regarded as a desirable result. He said the majority seized on "the very clarity of the statute almost as a justification for evading the unavoidable impact of its language." The Court amended the law to do precisely what both its supporters and opponents agreed it was not intended to do—permit discrimination because of race. "I fail to see how 'voluntary compliance' with the no-discrimination principle that is the heart and soul of Title VII," Chief Justice Burger wrote, "will be achieved by permitting employers to discriminate against some individuals to give preferential treatment to others."[21]

III

In one sense, *Weber* merely confirmed the course of Title VII development since *Griggs* and changed very little. This was true, observed N. Thompson Powers, the counsel for Kaiser, "in the same sense that the same could be said of one who had been shot at but missed, because affirmative action definitely dodged a bullet in the *Weber* decision."[22] At the level of principle, however, the case marked a fundamental turning point: it repudiated the explicit prohibition of unequal treatment because of race in Title VII and the concept of individual equality on which it rested. *Weber* elevated racial group equality and proportional representation to a paramount position in national civil rights policy. Although Title VII interpretation following *Griggs* in effect required racial preference, the courts had not expressly sanctioned racial discrimination against white employees in the absence of unlawful discrimination. *Weber* did precisely that. And while the Supreme Court might modify disparate impact theory in other cases to make it more reasonable, its explicit approval of racial preference at the expense of universal equal rights promised to have a far more important effect. It legitimized deciding by race in employment and elsewhere. In this sense *Weber* reinforced *Bakke*, despite the fact that virtually the same prohibition of racial discrimination was upheld in the latter case and repudiated in the former.

Title VII was intended to simplify the problem of defining the meaning of equal opportunity by outlawing the use of racial criteria in employment decisions. It is true that implementation of the law involved some consideration of race and even a measure of racial preference, as in the efforts to broaden the pool of minority applicants. The present effects doctrine carried this tendency farther in the early seniority cases, bringing pre-act discrimination within the scope of Title VII. The degree of preference that resulted was judged legal and proved to be politically acceptable. Administrative and judicial adoption of the disparate impact theory of discrimination followed as a more comprehensive means of encouraging or requiring race-conscious practices. Identified victims of discrimination were awarded make-whole relief; at times, under quota remedies, persons who were not victims of discrimination were given benefits by virtue of membership in a protected minority group. In each instance, however, there was a finding of discrimination, even if under disparate impact theory the unlawful practices might only be putative or inferred from statistics of racial imbalance.

In *Weber*, the Supreme Court dispensed with the remedial rationale that the courts had so carefully (if, at times, disingenuously) constructed to justify preferential treatment. Although disparate impact theory was intended to hold employers responsible for historic societal discrimination, it retained the notion of unlawful employment practices. However fictional this may have been, it provided a patina of moral justification and placed some limits on the scope of preferential measures. Yet this remedial strategy was inconsistent with the nature of affirmative action. Regarding group rights and equality of result as intrinsically sound political principles, supporters of preference seek to distribute social goods and resources according to a calculus of proportional representation. The logic of affirmative action looks forward to a racially balanced and integrated society, based on considerations of social utility and political expediency. As a public policy alternative to equal opportunity based on individual rights, it is prospective rather than retrospective in nature.

The essential character of affirmative action ideology emerged clearly in *Weber* as the Supreme Court, casting aside the concept of a discriminatory violation, held that societal discrimination is a sufficient basis for race-conscious preferences. The Court expressed this shift in strategy in references to "manifest" or "conspicuous" "racial imbalance" in "traditionally segregated job categories," "traditional patterns of racial segregation," "occupations which have been traditionally closed" to blacks, and "traditional" or "old" "patterns of racial segregation and hierarchy."[23] Justice Brennan referred to craft unions' exclusion of blacks in Louisiana, and some observers took this to mean that references to "traditionally segregated job categories" implied specific unlawful practices and thus indicated something different from societal discrimination. The more widely shared view, however, was that after *Weber*, racial imbalance justifying racial preference need not be directly or even indirectly attributable to an employer's practices.

Employers could take affirmative action to remedy whatever effects of societal discrimination were evident in their work force.[24] Societal discrimination as a justification of racial preference was retrospective and remedial only in a rhetorical sense. In reality, invoking this concept signified that affirmative action would be pursued as a prospective policy of minority group preference.

A second principal meaning of *Weber* was that discrimination against whites under an affirmative action plan could be practiced outside the sphere of legality and law enforcement. The decision was intended to nullify the Title VII rule of nondiscrimination and revert to the pre-act situation where employers could hire and classify employees on any basis they pleased, including that of race. This was only a fictional entrepreneurial liberty, of course, or one that was relevant only for the purposes of discriminating against white employees. In the larger picture, employers would continue to be forced by the threat of Title VII liability to adopt racial hiring practices. How to describe this circumstance in legal terms was difficult, since there was no intention of repealing Title VII. The Court chose to call the Kaiser program "private" and "voluntary," implicitly contrasting it to "public" and "coercive" affirmative action, which presumably was not permissible. In fact the race-conscious measures that had been approved, those in judicially ordered remedies for discriminatory violations and under the executive order program, were public and coercive.

Eleanor Holmes Norton, the Chairman of the EEOC, said the civil rights lobby was surprised at the Court's acceptance of the concept of societal discrimination in *Weber*. "The Court went off on a theory of private action to correct manifest racial imbalance," she wrote. Unlike *Bakke*, which focused on government involvement in discrimination, *Weber* held that private individuals may go farther than the government, which was bound by Title VII. According to Norton, the Court "carved out a corporate zone free from law enforcement" and from government regulation and interference.[25] The standard of societal discrimination was broader than the legal concept of an "arguable violation," which was tied to law enforcement. The EEOC itself did not go so far in its affirmative action guidelines, adhering to the "arguable violation" standard.[26]

The Court also went farther than Kaiser asked it to go in the company's argument for a judicially regulated "zone of reasonableness" under the arguable violation theory. N. Thompson Powers said corporate equal employment opportunity planners wanted a more rational and coherent bureaucratic framework for affirmative action. Powers recommended a rule-making procedure in which all interested groups would participate, leading to formal opinions extending immunity from liability to employers and unions. Meanwhile, the civil rights bureaucracy, according to Powers's proposal, should develop fairer standards for evaluating the job-relatedness of employee selection procedures. Powers thought employers and unions might see *Weber* as a mixed blessing, publicly applauding it yet privately regretting that federal enforcement efforts were not restricted to seeking relief for identified victims of discrimination.[27] Nevertheless, the decision provided the "net beneath" that had hitherto been missing: the protection that employers believed was a necessary *quid pro quo* for acquiescing to the government's demand for affirmative action.

The arguable violation rationale was ultimately unacceptable because it was likely to lead to an increase in discrimination suits by minorities, threatening employers with back pay liability claims. "Only a standard divorced entirely from legalities would seem to provide a way out of this dilemma," wrote one equal employment opportunity analyst.[28] By calling affirmative action private and voluntary and making it immune to Title VII attack, in effect the Court declared the motivating link between legal rules and employer conduct irrelevant. Under the theory of *Weber*, employers were given extraordinary latitude and left to their own devices, presumably motivated by the perceived need to eliminate the effects of traditional segregation. Their reward was to escape the cost of paying for the redress of past discrimination, possibly including their own unlawful practices, and to shift the cost to innocent white workers. *Weber* thus transformed Title VII from a law to protect individual employees irrespective of race into a law for the protection of employers who were forced to adopt racial hiring practices. Directed at the effects of societal discrimination, it ignored the injustice faced by minority individuals who might be the actual victims of discrimination. The expansive approach of *Weber* might incidentally compensate victims of past discrimination, Justice Blackmun observed, but benefits generally would go to those who had not suffered specific injury.[29] The affirmative action approved in *Weber*, therefore, was not truly remedial; rather, it conferred benefits on individuals because of their membership in a racial group.

How, we are compelled to ask after reading the opinion in *Weber*, could the equal opportunity principle become so distorted and contradictory? The question requires analysis at several levels, but the basic answer is that *Weber* was necessary if *Griggs* was to continue to provide the theoretical framework for affirmative action policy. As a justification for quotas, "societal discrimination" was preferable to "arguable violation" because it avoided any inquiry into the legitimacy of affirmative action. It was also preferable because it more effectively obscured the responsibility of the government in forcing employers to adopt preferential practices under disparate impact theory. As long as the Court remained committed to *Griggs*, *Weber* was the most efficient economic outcome and the best way to allocate judicial resources from the standpoint of industrial relations. It was irrational and unfair not to let employers discriminate in favor of blacks in order to dispel the appearance of discrimination in statistical disparities. If Weber had won, employers would still have lost disparate impact suits because of their inability to prove the job-relatedness of their selection procedures.[30]

From the perspective of public philosophy, *Weber* had a profoundly negative impact. In the words of one critic, it "formally lets loose the racial genie bottled with great difficulty in 1964."[31] Did the Court seriously intend to broaden the sphere of employer freedom in *Weber*? It is naive to think so, and if it did, it ignored the danger of racial decision-making that even Justice Brennan had warned against in a recent decision.[32] The Court's support for business freedom and its aversion to federal intervention were patently disingenuous. *Weber* completed the transformation of Title VII from a law protecting individual rights and equal opportunity to a statute recognizing and enforcing the right of racial groups to proportionate employment. It legitimated the structure of legal rules that necessarily caused employers to prefer certain racial groups. It also eliminated the legal obstacle to racial group recognition that Title VII erected by conferring on individuals the right not to be discriminated against because of race.[33]

It might be argued that racial preference had been government policy for so long that the Court saw no realistic alternative but to accept it, especially in the face of a reverse discrimination challenge. Some of the Justices may have thought it necessary to protect employers in their "devil's deal" with the government, adopting racial preference until disparate impact theory could be revised in less politically charged cases.[34] Such speculation is provoked by consideration of the voting alignment in *Weber*. The key vote, enabling the Brennan group that dissented in *Bakke* to form a majority, was that of Justice Stewart, who rejected the quota in *Bakke*. He may have been persuaded to join the Brennan group by the strategy of "privatizing" affirmative action, thereby avoiding an examination both of the government's role in creating the structure of racial preference and of constitutional considerations relating to Title VII. On policy grounds, moreover, Justice Stewart may have been willing to favor race (an arbitrary standard) over seniority (also an arbitrary standard) in *Weber* while being unwilling to favor race over academic qualifications in *Bakke*. In addition, Justice

Brennan stressed "the narrowness of our inquiry," and his statutory focus may have seemed sufficiently confined to gain majority approval.[35]

In actuality, the limits on affirmative action in *Weber* can scarcely be considered restrictive. The standard of "traditionally segregated job categories," the rationale which justified race-conscious measures, was in practice tantamount to existing racial imbalance.[36] In formulating affirmative action programs, employers were cautioned to avoid only two things: total exclusion/replacement of whites and permanent racial preference. Permanence, however, was not defined temporally; it referred to measures that were intended to maintain a racial balance. An affirmative action plan intended to *eliminate* a racial imbalance was by definition temporary, although it might last indefinitely. If an affirmative action program conformed to these criteria, it did not unnecessarily trammel the interests of white employees. The assumption behind this reasoning, explicitly stated by the Brennan group in *Bakke* (though only implicit in *Weber*), was that whites—by virtue of their majority political status—did not need legal protection for individual rights.

Under disparate impact theory—intellectually fallacious though it was—the possibility existed that a statistical disparity might actually give rise to a valid inference of racial discrimination. By contrast, *Weber*'s reliance on the standard of societal discrimination had no precise meaning. It merely created a license for racial irresponsibility. The remedial rationale that was the corollary of disparate impact theory at least had the virtue of giving semantic legitimacy to race-conscious measures and perhaps mitigating the racial tension resulting from preferential policies.[37] The "privatization" strategy of *Weber* seemed likely to encourage invidious racial judgments and decision-making.

It was true that improved job opportunities for blacks was a major purpose of Title VII, as Justice Brennan said. But surely the whole point of the statute's delineation of unlawful employment practices was to specify the legitimate means by which this purpose was to be achieved.[38] Congress did not provide that if, in the opinion of judges and administrators, the race-neutral enforcement structure prescribed in the law did not produce sufficiently rapid economic improvement, policies of racial favoritism could be adopted in their place. *Weber*, of course, was not the first judicial decision to ignore this basic fact. Nevertheless, it was the most flagrant repudiation of congressional intent that had occurred.

In *Weber*, the Court treated Title VII as virtually a separate constitution. Defining congressional intent at a high level of abstraction and generality, it assumed for itself the power to create a statutory policy in the absence of a direct prohibition of that policy (assuming that the ban on preferential treatment was not a conclusive proscription of quotas). The Court viewed Title VII as a broad, philosophical statute that left open questions about the proper application of the concept of color-blind individual rights.[39] According to Justice Blackmun, considerations of fairness and administrative practicality that justified racial preference were not understood by Congress when it enacted Title VII. This was patently untrue, as Justice Rehnquist pointed out. It was also erroneous of Justice Blackmun to say that if the Title VII prohibition of racial discrimination was read literally, "[e]ven a whisper of emphasis on minority recruiting would be forbidden."[40] It is hard to escape the conclusion that the Court, for political reasons, willfully rejected both the plain meaning and intent of Title VII as well as obvious facts about its implementation as an equal opportunity measure.

The significance of *Weber* in the struggle over American equality was apparent at the time to those critics who focused on the Court's denial of a plainly written statutory right: the right not to be discriminated against because of race. Among supporters of the decision, however, the pattern of denial that had become familiar since the start of affirmative action manifested itself. Justice Blackmun aptly illustrated it in disavowing any permanent departure from traditional equal rights principles. The Court's description of the racial quota as private rather than government action was accepted at face value. *Weber* was therefore considered not to possess constitutional significance.[41] The import of *Weber* was also obscured by the concern of equal employment opportunity managers with practical questions about affirmative action. As seen in the *prima facie* and burden-of-proof cases, there were many unresolved issues in Title VII law. Since *Weber* did not address these matters, the decision could be seen as Justice Brennan tried to present it—as having only a narrow focus.[42]

Assessing the impact of *Weber*, discrimination law specialists asked whether the doctrine of affirmative action preferences applied where sex, national origin, and religion were concerned. Were state and local governments permitted to adopt preferential measures? What degree of disparity between the percentage of minorities in the work force and the percentage of minorities in the local labor market could trigger a preferential policy? And was the proper comparison for a disparate impact analysis the one between the work force percentage of minorities and the percentage of minorities in the local area, or the number of *qualified* minorities in the labor market? Still more important, where was the line to be drawn between legitimate and illegitimate affirmative action? Saying it was not necessary to draw such a line, Justice Brennan nevertheless drew one in observing that the Kaiser quota was temporary and did not totally exclude whites. Employment law commentators were reluctant, however, to view this as a statement of the limits of affirmative action.[43]

In a sense, Justice Brennan's description of the Kaiser plan was not a considered statement about the permissible scope of affirmative action, for it said in effect that any preferential measure constituting less than an absolute racial preference was acceptable. This simply did not seem reasonable, fair, or realistic to equal employment opportunity observers, who did not believe affirmative action would be permitted to expand to such an extent. The large number of reverse discrimination suits filed in the aftermath of *Weber* indicated that the decision was not viewed as having settled the question of the limits of preferential treatment. Commentators suggested that the scope of affirmative action could be decided on an *ad hoc*, case-by-case basis, depending on the extent of past discrimination, the degree of racial imbalance, the type of affirmative preference at issue, and the impact on white employees.[44] It remained to be seen, finally, whether the *Weber* guidelines on affirmative action would be revised by the lower courts or the Supreme Court itself. Yet modification might merely signify the rationalization of racial preference as a permanent feature of civil rights policy.

To a considerable extent, the future of employment discrimination policy depended on the executive order program; in relation to this issue, the implications of *Weber* were unclear. The principal effect of "privatizing" the Kaiser quota was to prevent consideration of the federal contract program in relation to Title VII, thus approving *sub silentio* the government's preferential policy. N. Thompson Powers has written that if Weber had won his suit, the federal contract agencies would have lost much of their justification for insisting on affirmative action to correct underutilization without regard to actual evidence of past discrimination. From one point of view, then, *Weber* appeared to strengthen affirmative action under Executive Order 11246.[45]

However, the Court also criticized federal officials who interfered with employer freedom because of their ideas of racial imbalance. Regarding this as an accurate description of the contract compliance program, some analysts predicted a test case that would consider the legality of Executive Order 11246 against the requirements of Title VII. If the courts followed *Weber* and abandoned the "legal sophistry" of denying that OFCCP regulations required racial quotas, the decision could be used to strike down the executive order program. Yet it was hard to see what would lead the Supreme Court to adopt a candid and realistic view of federal contract compliance in the future, should a case involving it come before the Court. It was far from certain that government contractors would seek to challenge the executive order. Their actions depended on public perceptions of civil rights and the status of minorities, as well as changes that might be made in OFCCP regulations. In any event, only when the relationship between government demands and affirmative action quotas was acknowledged would the implications of *Weber* become fully apparent.[46]

IV

Government pressure for affirmative action far exceeding the federal contract program was at issue in *Fullilove v. Klutznick* (1980), the third of the reverse discrimination cases decided by the Supreme Court during the Carter Administration. Whereas *Bakke* concerned state action and *Weber* private employer action, *Fullilove* involved the constitutionality of an act of Congress that allocated public benefits on a racial and ethnic basis. In the Public Works Employment Act of 1977, Congress provided that ten percent of all federal grants awarded by the Department of Commerce should be given to minority business enterprises.[47] Although race was considered a suspect classification to be justified only on the demonstration of a compelling governmental purpose in cases at constitutional law, Congress ignored this requirement in exercising its constitutional powers to enact the minority set-asides. It basically dealt with the measure as a conventional interest-group demand. In desultory and limited debate, unassisted by committee hearings or a report detailing conditions in the construction industry, Congress approved the quota as a means of giving blacks "a fair share of the action" in public works contracting, rather than as a remedy for past discriminatory practices. Explaining the action as consistent with preferential policies long since established by the courts and administrative agencies, members of Congress showed no awareness of their historic role in enacting the first statute in modern American history creating on a racial classification.[48] White contractors immediately challenged the law as a violation of the equal protection component of the Fifth Amendment, and two lower federal courts rejected their claim.

In a 6-3 decision, the Supreme Court upheld the minority set-aside as constitutional. Chief Justice Burger announced the judgment of the Court and, joined by Justices Powell and White, wrote an opinion justifying the quota partly on the basis of a remedial rationale aimed at societal discrimination. But Burger also justified the act by reference to a prospective general legislative rationale unrelated to past discrimination. In taking this step, Chief Justice Burger, a dissenter in *Weber*, went beyond the majority justification of affirmative action established in that decision.

The remedial aspect of the minority set-aside received the greater emphasis in Burger's opinion. He held that Congress had power under the commerce and appropriations clauses as well as under the legislative implementation provision of the Fourteenth Amendment to remedy the "prevailing impaired access" of minority businesses to, and the denial of their "effective participation" in, public contracting opportunities. Congress could also prohibit practices that perpetuated the effects of pre-Title VII discrimination. No finding of contractor violation of anti-discrimination laws was necessary to justify the set-aside. Although he did not employ the term, Burger plainly regarded societal discrimination as a valid basis for race-conscious measures. Disparity in the award of public contracts, he asserted, resulted from the existence and maintenance of barriers to competitive access that were rooted in racial and ethnic discrimination but continued in its absence. Departing from this remedial approach, Burger went on to say that Congress could require the set-aside in order to ensure minority enterprises an equal opportunity to participate in the federal grant program. The racial preference was a means of enforcing the equal protection of the laws and the constitutional mandate for equality of economic opportunity.[49]

Finding the legislative goal legitimate, Chief Justice Burger considered whether the race-conscious means chosen to effect it were also permissible. He recognized that where racial classification was employed, careful judicial evaluation was necessary to ensure that the measure was narrowly tailored to the goal. He did not, however, apply the strict scrutiny standard of review proposed by Justice Powell in *Bakke*, nor the intermediate standard favored by the Brennan group. Without explaining the criteria for his evaluation, the Chief Justice found the racial classification to be legitimate in a remedial context. Blurring the distinction between the law's retrospective and prospective purposes, he said Congress exercised its remedial power to enact a measure that guaranteed equal protection of the law in the present and future.[50]

Chief Justice Burger extended the *Weber* analysis of the standards and criteria for permissible racial discrimination. Under the set-aside program, white contractors innocent of any prior discriminatory practices would be denied some contracts. This was an incidental consequence of the policy, however, comparable to the incidental impairment that minorities suffered under the system of "business as usual." The

Constitution permitted a sharing of the burden by innocent third parties under a narrowly tailored remedy, Chief Justice Burger said, and the actual burden on non-minority firms was light when considered in relation to the entire public works program. Moreover, Congress could assume that innocent white contractors might have benefited from the prior exclusion of minority businesses.[51]

In a concurring opinion, Justice Powell purported to apply the strict scrutiny standard of review he had used in *Bakke*. Under this standard, judicial inquiry focused on whether a governmental authority made a finding of a constitutional or statutory violation, identifying a compelling interest that justified a racial remedy. In the brief congressional discussion of the minority business enterprise set-aside, it was hard to see anything reasonably resembling a conclusive governmental finding of discrimination. Nevertheless, Justice Powell satisfied himself that Congress had met the requisite standard of finding "purposeful" private and governmental discrimination. He did so by assuming that Congress was not held to the record-keeping requirements that applied to courts and administrative agencies and that it did not have to make specific factual findings. The means chosen by Congress were equitable and reasonably necessary to rectify the "identified" discrimination. Justice Powell added that the impact of the racial preference on innocent whites was so widely dispersed and limited as to be "consistent with fundamental fairness."[52]

Justice Marshall, joined by Justices Brennan and Blackmun, upheld the minority business enterprise provision under the intermediate standard of review used by the Brennan group in *Bakke*. This standard considered whether the racial classification served "important governmental objectives" and was "substantially related" to achieving them. In Justice Marshall's opinion, the "question is not even a close one"; the set-aside was plainly constitutional.[53] Having disposed of this issue, Justice Marshall elaborated on the concept of equality under affirmative action that permitted racial discrimination.

Central to the concept was the idea of stigmatization, introduced in the dissenting opinion in *Bakke*. Justice Marshall acknowledged that the set-aside was a quota which created an absolute preference. In his opinion, however, this fact did not mean that it stigmatized anyone. The quota passed the new equal protection test by "avoiding stigmatization and penalizing those least able to protect themselves in the political process." It did not stigmatize as inferior either non-minority firms that were burdened by it or minority firms that benefited; the latter had to be qualified in order to get a contract. Justice Marshall said the minority business enterprise set-aside was the type of race-conscious remedy necessary to move the society beyond racism to "a state of meaningful equality of opportunity. . . ." [54]

Justice Stevens, presenting his constitutional view of affirmative action for the first time, wrote a dissenting opinion rejecting the set-aside as unconstitutional. Stevens saw compensatory racial preference as constitutional in principle. The wrong committed against blacks as a class in the form of slavery and racial discrimination, he stated, was so serious and pervasive that it would "constitutionally justify an appropriate class-wide recovery measured by a sum certain for every member of the injured class." However, because racial classifications were potentially harmful and usually irrelevant, they required clear and unquestionable justification. The ten percent set-aside failed to meet these criteria. Describing the quota as a "perverse form of reparation," Justice Stevens said it was "a random distribution to a favored few" that would not help the most disadvantaged blacks. Moreover, the minority business enterprise provision was not a proper remedy because it did not attempt to measure the recovery by the wrong, nor did it remove barriers to entry into the construction industry. It was simply a "legislative preference" resulting from the political strength of particular racial and ethnic groups. Terming it a "slap-dash statute" passed without procedural safeguards, Justice Stevens said the quota was an "accidental malfunction of the legislative process" that would increase rather than reduce racial prejudice and resentment.[55]

Justice Stewart, joined by Justice Rehnquist, also regarded the minority business enterprise provision as an unconstitutional racial preference. According to Justice Stewart, the Constitution was color-blind, and the equal protection provision had "one clear and central meaning—it absolutely prohibits invidious discrimination by government." Exceptions to this rule were permitted for the sole purpose of eradicating the effects of illegal racial discrimination, but the Public Works Employment Act set-aside failed to meet this criterion. Not only did it expressly bar a class from receiving a government benefit strictly on racial grounds, but it also exceeded proper remedial limits. The quota was directed at achieving a racial balance as an end in itself. Moreover, by compensating only some groups for the effects of social and economic disadvantage, it violated the equal protection guarantee. Justice Stewart warned that by making race once again a relevant criterion in public policy, "the Government implicitly teaches the public that the apportionment of rewards and penalties can legitimately be made according to race—rather than according to merit and ability—and that people can, and perhaps should, view themselves and others in terms of their racial characteristics."[56]

Fullilove was the most important of the reverse discrimination cases for political and legal theory. To begin with, it concerned constitutional principles rather than statutory interpretation. Six Justices in three opinions upheld the racial quota on broad constitutional grounds, while a seventh approved racial group compensation in principle. The chief significance for civil rights policy was the departure from the remedial rationale that had originally been used to justify preferential treatment and the adoption of a prospective rationale that justified preference in order to achieve racial balance or proportional representation. To be sure, Justices Burger, Marshall, and Powell employed rhetorical strategies that offered a remedial rationale for the quota under varying degrees of judicial scrutiny that were intended to be more demanding than the rational basis test.[57] In reality, however, the three opinions accepted the proposition that congressional legislation of a racial preference was justified by the history of slavery, segregation, and racial discrimination.

In a sense, of course, the choice of societal discrimination as the predicate for affirmative action was retrospective and remedial. The generality and imprecision of the remedial rationale, however, and the failure to specify unlawful practices and injury or denial of economic opportunity to individuals in applying it, permitted the distinction between past and present to become obliterated. The make-whole rationale that had been used with a view toward identifying intentional disparate treatment discrimination was transformed in *Fullilove* into a warrant for allocating resources on a racial basis in response to political pressures. As Justice Stevens observed, if the history of slavery "can justify such a random distribution of benefits on racial lines . . . , it will serve not merely as a basis for remedial legislation, but rather as a permanent source of justification for grants of special privileges."[58] Justices Stewart and Stevens rightly pointed out that no race had a monopoly on social disadvantages, and that American history could support a legislative preference for almost any racial, ethnic, or religious group with the political strength to demand "a piece of the action" for its members.[59] For blacks, the badge of slavery and discrimination under the rationale of *Fullilove* could become a permanent entitlement.

In essential respects, the opinions in *Fullilove* accepted a theory of national power to enforce civil rights that provided a constitutional justification for affirmative action. The theory held that the Reconstruction Amendments conferred on blacks not just ordinary civil rights, but specially sanctioned liberty and civil rights under exclusive national authority that Congress was uniquely empowered to enforce by race-conscious legislation.[60] Thus Chief Justice Burger cited section five of the Fourteenth Amendment, the implementation provision, as giving Congress power to adopt the ten percent quota to ensure that minority businesses were given equal opportunity to participate in federal grants. Arguing that section five had been interpreted to permit racially preferential legislation, he said Congress adopted the set-aside as a remedial measure that was intended to function prospectively.[61] Justice Powell reasoned that although the use of racial classification was fundamentally at odds with democratic ideals, Congress had a unique constitutional role under the Thirteenth and Fourteenth Amendments to make findings of discrimination and award race-conscious remedies. Justice Marshall's *Fullilove* opinion was a sequel to his historical argument in *Bakke* that Congress under the Fourteenth Amendment has the power to pass race-conscious measures. Finally, Justice Stevens in dissent said blacks as a class could be awarded monetary compensation for the historic wrongs committed against them.[62]

Thus seven Justices held it was constitutional for Congress to legislate on a racial basis for an ostensibly remedial purpose. This was a pivotal interpretation of the equal protection clause. In effect, the Court concluded that the standard of unlawful discrimination, and the test of whether government action was consistent with the equal protection requirement, was not whether it distinguished according to race and ethnicity but whether it stigmatized. Stigmatization, however, was a subjective, psychological standard that lent itself to political manipulation. Since Congress had made no attempt to identify unlawful discrimination in previous federal grant programs, the result in *Fullilove* simply meant that Congress could legislate according to race. The underlying principle revolved not around the problem of discrimination, but the power of Congress to pursue social policy. The program approved by the Court was not designed to identify minority individuals injured by past discrimination or help them compete more effectively in the construction business. It merely allocated resources on a racial basis.[63]

In cases dealing with the use of statistics to make a *prima facie* charge and the allocation of evidentiary burdens, the Court, as previously noted, was trying to rationalize basic employment discrimination law. *Fullilove*, however, represented a reversion to the simplistic application of disparate impact theory. According to Justice Powell, the ten percent quota was a reasonable number because it was midway between the percentage of blacks among all contractors (4 percent) and the percentage of blacks in the U.S. population (17 percent).[64] If *Weber* was intended to establish manifest imbalance in traditionally segregated job categories as justification for affirmative action, *Fullilove* asserted an even more lax standard of justification by shifting to a prospective rationale for preferential treatment. Like the affirmative action plan in *Weber*, the minority business enterprise quota was an absolute preference that excluded whites from a substantial category of grants. Furthermore, the Court seriously considered the effects of this monopolistic grant on either minority or non-minority contractors no more than Congress did.

Fullilove significantly broadened the emerging principle of race-conscious affirmative action. "What was hinted at in *Bakke* and permissible as private action in *Weber*," wrote equal employment opportunity analyst William J. Kilberg, "is now countenanced as a government requirement . . . ."[65] Yet this decision, the most important of the reverse discrimination cases from a constitutional standpoint, attracted much less attention than *Weber*. This was perhaps an indication that with the legalization of quotas, the popular debate over affirmative action was ending. Employment discrimination lawyers, however, saw *Fullilove* not as the end of the controversy, but as part of an unfolding story. Racial preference had been approved, but it was not clear from the employer's point of view under what circumstances preferential treatment could be utilized in the absence of a finding of discrimination.[66] Employers were reluctant to conclude that racial preference was permitted to combat societal discrimination in general, apparently because of a residual belief that racial discrimination of any sort was wrong.

Although affirmative action was greatly strengthened during the Carter Administration, it was the product of both Democratic and Republican efforts since the 1960s. This bipartisan support was threatened in 1980, however, by the election of Ronald Reagan, a conservative Republican who had publicly opposed racial preference and quotas. Liberal criticism of Republican administrations for inadequate enforcement of civil rights had become a standard feature of civil rights politics, but the alarm that swept the civil rights establishment at the prospect of Ronald Reagan in the White House appeared to have a more substantial basis. In a general sense, the election signified the persistence of public opinion supportive of individual rights and equality of opportunity and the rejection of preferential treatment. Whether this opinion would be translated into effective public policy restricting the spread of affirmative action, if not abolishing it, depended on a multitude of political, social, and legal factors, including the judicial decisions of the late 1970s. Despite a tendency to regard the quota controversy as settled by the reverse discrimination cases, seen in declining media coverage of the issue, the struggle to define the meaning of American equality continued in the 1980s.

8

The Reagan Administration
and Affirmative Action

The 1980 election of President Ronald Reagan presented the possibility of significant changes in national civil rights policy. The Republican platform criticized "bureaucratic regulations which rely on quotas, ratios, and numerical requirements to exclude some individuals in favor of others." During the campaign, the Republican candidate declared: "We must not allow the noble concept of equal opportunity to be distorted into federal guidelines or quotas which require race, ethnicity, or sex—rather than ability and qualifications—to be the principal factor in hiring or education."[1] After the election, the Reagan transition team for equal employment opportunity advised a basic shift in government policy. Attacking the civil rights bureaucracy for pursuing equality of result rather than equal opportunity, the transition team criticized disparate impact theory and urged a return to the intentional disparate treatment concept of discrimination.[2] Although it was easy to condemn quotas, as President Nixon showed by repeatedly doing so even as he established preferential policies, it appeared that the Reagan Administration might really oppose race-conscious affirmative action.

At the same time, there were enormous political obstacles to the reform of civil rights policy. Although polls showed large majorities opposed to preferential treatment, public opinion also supported civil rights enforcement and approved affirmative action in the weak sense of recruitment and training programs for minorities. With liberal Democrats and the civil rights lobby poised to go on the attack, proposals of changes in civil rights policy ran the risk of appearing opposed to civil rights enforcement. Reinforcing this political restraint was the fact that although race-conscious affirmative action contradicted the letter and spirit of the Civil Rights Act, it had been legalized under court decisions and agency regulations. Opposition to quotas could thus be presented as opposition to enforcement of the civil rights laws. Even without attempting to reform civil rights policy, moreover, the Reagan Administration's domestic budget-cutting goals were bound to provoke charges of insensitivity to the needs of the poor, especially minorities.[3]

President Reagan had the legal authority to alter or abolish affirmative action unilaterally, insofar as it consisted of mandatory goals and timetables under Executive Order 11246. Besides the political liability of appearing to be against civil rights, two other factors made the President's power problematic. The first was business opinion, especially that of large corporations. Although once hostile toward government-mandated preferences, corporate America had learned to live with quotas; its interests and point of view were important influences on civil rights policymaking. A second consideration in evaluating the prospects of civil rights reform was the political benefit that the Reagan Administration, like every previous administration, might derive from the federal contract program. Goals and timetables requiring affirmative action, and minority set-asides under federal legislation and executive orders, might be a means of gaining political support among blacks while protecting the administration against charges of being opposed to civil rights enforcement.

Faced with conflicting political and ideological pressures, in its civil rights policy the Reagan Administration acted as a "party of balance" rather than a "party of opposition," as it had appeared to be in the election of 1980.[4] In a general sense, this outcome can be explained by the fact that other domestic and foreign policy issues possessed greater political salience and had a higher priority than race relations. Furthermore, civil rights policy comprised such a sprawling array of bureaucratically- and judicially-managed programs and activities, backed by well-organized interest groups with established connections in Congress, as to defy systematic and coherent reform.

Education, housing, federally assisted programs, voting rights, and employment were the principal areas of civil rights enforcement. Although each presented special policy demands, in general the Administration tried to resist the expansion of group-based effects tests as a means of defining discrimination, and reasserted equal rights for individuals—including relief for actual victims of discrimination—as foundation principles of civil rights policy. Racially balanced school integration and employment preferences, the most politically provocative features of the civil rights revolution of the 1970s, commanded the most attention. By 1980, however, the busing issue had been defused, in part because Congress in 1976 and 1978 passed legislation restricting federal administrators from requiring busing as a remedy for school desegregation.[5] Affirmative action in employment, therefore, provided the major focus of civil rights reform at the start of the Reagan Administration.

Instead of consistently opposing race-conscious affirmative action throughout the government, the administration tried to limit its excesses and make it more politically and administratively palatable. No more than previous administrations was the Reagan government successful in coordinating employment discrimination policy among the departments and agencies involved in civil rights enforcement. Indeed, at the top level of administration it appears that no effort was made to unify equal employment opportunity policy. A split within the policymaking establishment therefore developed. The Department of Labor and OFCCP reformed the administration of the executive order goals and timetables policy in response to business criticism of the Carter Administration's overly aggressive affirmative action program. The Department of Justice, the government's chief law enforcement agency, vigorously pursued an anti-quota policy. The Equal Employment Opportunity Commission, the stronghold of militant affirmative action in the 1970s, was slower to change: in the second Reagan Administration, though, it opposed quotas and adopted a policy of full relief for individual victims of discrimination.

Differences within the Administration were exacerbated by relentless and indiscriminate congressional criticism. Through oversight hearings and control of appropriations, liberal lawmakers tried to preserve the radical policies of the Carter Administration. In a proximate sense, however, if not ultimately, the decisive voice in the cacophonous dialogue on affirmative action was that of the judiciary. In a series of cases in the mid-1980s, the Supreme Court further approved and rationalized racially preferential practices. Rejecting the anti-quota initiative of the Justice Department, the Court upheld affirmative action in terms similar in their scope and effect to the revised quota policy of the Reagan OFCCP and Department of Labor.

I

Any criticism of quotas in the early 1980s, no matter how moderate, would have been denounced by the civil rights lobby as opposition to civil rights. The appointment of William Bradford Reynolds as Assistant

Attorney General for Civil Rights demonstrated that the Reagan Administration was prepared to accept this risk. Reynolds was a Washington attorney who had served in the Solicitor General's office in the Justice Department in 1973-74. Not a Reaganite or a movement conservative, he had no particular background or experience in the area of civil rights; he initially was considered for a position in the Civil Division of the Department of Justice. A lawyer rather than a politician, Reynolds accepted the job as head of the Civil Rights Division and at the earliest opportunity made clear his support of individual rights and equality of opportunity and his opposition to preferential treatment and quotas.

Within the divided structure of equal employment opportunity authority under Title VII and Executive Order 11246, the Civil Rights Division in the Department of Justice was strategically situated to influence the development of anti-discrimination law. The Division enforced Title VII in state and local government and filed pattern or practice suits against federal contractors.[6] President Reagan's choice of Reynolds to head the most powerful civil rights unit in the government is evidence that despite his lack of familiarity with key issues in the field and subsequent unwillingness to resolve basic policy conflicts, he seriously desired to restore the traditional ideal of equal employment opportunity.[7]

Although William Bradford Reynolds quickly acquired the reputation of being a reactionary ideologue intent on rolling back the civil rights revolution, as head of the Civil Rights Division he accepted the judicial development of Title VII law based on the theory of disparate impact discrimination in almost every respect. The single exception was opposition to quota relief as preferential treatment prohibited by Title VII. This was a politically provocative if not radical position to assume. After the Supreme Court rejected it, it appeared only negative in retrospect, concerned more with protecting white males against reverse discrimination than with offering a positive approach to employment bias that would appeal to all Americans, including minorities. In the circumstances facing the administration in 1981, however, it is difficult to see what more moderate policy could have been adopted that would have redirected equal employment opportunity policy toward the traditional equal rights standard without conceding the then-unresolved question of the legality of quotas. Although the Supreme Court had approved minority set-asides based on race (*Fullilove*) and government-required "voluntary" affirmative action (*Weber*), it had not ruled on judicially ordered quota remedies under Title VII. It was reasonable for the Department of Justice to try to stop the expansion of preferential treatment and the corollary theory of proportional racial representation by opposing numerical remedies for Title VII violations.[8]

In Senate nomination and House oversight hearings, Assistant Attorney General Reynolds explained the Justice Department's litigation strategy. The government would apply the *Griggs* disparate impact concept of discrimination and the use of statistical evidence of racial imbalance to infer unlawful discriminatory intent. Under the make-whole theory of relief, it would support affirmative action as a remedy for discriminatory practices, demanding back pay, retroactive seniority, reinstatement and hiring, and promotional priorities for victims of discrimination. The Department of Justice would also seek relief for qualified persons who were discouraged from applying for a job because of an employer's reputation for discrimination. And, if necessary, in order to place an individual in the position he would have occupied but for discrimination, minorities and women would be given preference over white males shown to have been improperly favored.

The Assistant Attorney General declared, however, that the department would not support the use of quotas or any other numerical or statistical formula "designed to provide to non-victims of discrimination preferential treatment" based on race, sex, or ethnicity. Class-oriented relief aimed at achieving immediate numerical equality went beyond the accepted view that a racial or sexual preference was permissible only when necessary to make a victim of discrimination whole. It contradicted the proper understanding of a judicial remedy by aiding those who were not identifiable victims of discrimination at the expense of those who were innocent of any wrongdoing. Reynolds stated that preferential affirmative action elevated group rights over individual rights and was "at war with the American ideal of equal opportunity for each person to achieve whatever his or her industry and talents warrant." It was not the intent of Title VII or the Constitution, he said, to use anti-discrimination litigation "to go back and cure all the evils of past generations."[9]

Although the Department of Justice clearly supported Title VII law as it had developed down to *Weber*, critics charged that it was opposed to the enforcement of the civil rights laws in general.[10] In response, Reynolds pointed out that the Civil Rights Division was filing class actions under the *Griggs* effects test and seeking remedies for victims of discrimination under the make-whole concept of relief. "I am not out to dismantle the civil rights laws of this country," he insisted.[11] Employment law commentators subsequently confirmed his statement. The department initiated Title VII suits against state and local governments, negotiated consent decrees, and obtained back pay awards, retroactive seniority, and other remedial relief. By the standards used to measure civil rights enforcement, the Reagan Justice Department record was comparable to that of the Carter Administration's. The employment discrimination laws "are here to stay," observed an equal employment opportunity consultant, who said that while the Justice Department wanted to balance equities between protected groups and non-protected groups, affirmative action would continue to be enforced.[12]

Acceptance of disparate impact theory was evident in the Civil Rights Division's support of the bottom-line theory of Title VII enforcement. It will be recalled that the bottom-line concept permitted employers to use selection devices that had a disparate impact and were not validated under EEOC guidelines, provided that blacks and women were sufficiently represented in the work force. Favored by moderates, the bottom line was a compromise between the employer's interest in efficiency and productivity and the government's interest in promoting minority employment. In *Connecticut v. Teal* (1982), a case considered more fully below, the Department of Justice filed an *amicus* brief defending the bottom line as an interpretation of Title VII that upheld traditional employer freedom while fulfilling the ultimate statutory goals defined in *Weber*—namely, racial group equality in employment. The department's advocacy of the bottom line was hardly the action of an unreconstructed proponent of the intentional disparate treatment concept of discrimination.[13]

Nevertheless, the Department of Justice tried to stop the spread of quotas at points where the policy appeared legally vulnerable. In 1983, the Civil Rights Division intervened in a number of cases at the appellate level to argue that quota remedies were inconsistent with the make-whole theory of relief and were prohibited by Title VII. The strategy was first employed in *Williams v. City of New Orleans*, a Fifth Circuit case concerning a consent decree that included a 50 percent quota for promotion of blacks in the police department. In an *amicus* brief, the Department of Justice contended that Title VII did not authorize relief that conferred benefits on persons who were not identifiable victims of discrimination and that denied the interests of non-minority individuals. It argued that the promotion quota, and any preferential remedies not tied to the make-whole theory of relief, exceeded the remedial authority of federal courts under Section 706(g) of Title VII.[14] The Circuit Court ruled that the consent decree violated the rights of innocent non-minority employees, although only 4 of 13 judges accepted the Justice Department's statutory interpretation precluding judicial quota orders. Subsequently, the department's view of judicial remedial authority was rejected in two other circuits.[15]

Although initially unpersuasive to the courts, the Justice Department's litigation strategy had the effect of forcing judges to take a more rigorous view of remedies involving racial and sexual preference.[16] It appeared to gain a measure of acceptance in *Firefighters Local Union No. 1784 v. Stotts*, a Title VII case decided by the Supreme Court in 1984. In reversing a lower court ruling that upheld an affirmative action quota over a seniority layoff plan, the Court stated that it was the policy of Title VII and of Section 706(g) in particular to provide make-whole relief only to actual victims of illegal discrimination.[17] Although *Stotts* suggested that all court-ordered quotas might be regarded as illegal, its precedential value might also be limited to situations where quota orders conflicted with seniority rules. The Justice Department viewed the decision as a major victory. It promptly requested state and local governments involved in 51 consent decrees to reopen the cases and conform to the department's anti-quota interpretation of Title VII. It also filed motions to modify several consent decrees and submitted briefs in three circuits opposing remedial goals.[18]

The Department of Justice's anti-quota campaign based on *Stotts* was unsuccessful. State and local governments were opposed to reopening cases in which goals and timetables were being implemented; federal courts, confining *Stotts* to the particular facts of the situation in Memphis, rejected the Civil Rights Division's expansive view of the decision. More importantly, in a series of affirmative action cases in 1986-87, the Supreme Court upheld quotas and repudiated the department's argument that Title VII and the Constitution permitted only relief for identifiable victims of discrimination.[19] Although the Court continued to hold that quota agreements and judicial orders could not override the rights of non-minorities protected in bona fide seniority systems, this restriction on preferential treatment fell far short of the Justice Department's objective.[20] Department officials commented that the Supreme Court recognized the preferability of victim-specific remedies, while making narrow exceptions in order to permit egregious discrimination to be corrected. Although this assessment was not inaccurate, the department had argued for the absolute impermissibility of race-conscious relief for non-victims, not merely a preference for victim-specific remedies. After the court's affirmative action decisions, the Civil Rights Division abandoned its policy of seeking to remove goals and timetables from existing consent decrees.[21]

In addition to Title VII law, the Department of Justice tried to eliminate quotas from the federal contract program. With the support of Attorney General Edwin Meese, Reynolds was able to raise the issue of contract compliance quotas in the White House domestic policy council in late 1985. This effort, which will be examined more closely in relation to OFCCP policy, also ended in failure as the Department of Labor stood firm in defense of the executive order affirmative action program.[22]

II

With the failure of the Justice Department's anti-quota strategy, the EEOC assumed a more prominent role in employment discrimination policy. The Carter Administration elevated the EEOC to preeminence in the civil rights bureaucracy, and its Uniform Guidelines for Employee Selection Procedures and affirmative action guidelines represented a high point in the promotion of racial group preference. Because of the relative autonomy of the Commission as a so-called independent agency in the executive branch and the political difficulty of effecting regulatory reform by formal rule-making, the Reagan Administration initially made little use of the EEOC in reforming civil rights policy. The agency marked time as the nomination of William M. Bell as chairman, a black Republican businessman with little stature or experience in civil rights matters, was submitted and then withdrawn. Two acting chairmen served until a permanent appointment was made in 1982. The inconsistency in the administration's civil rights policy could be seen by comparing the Justice Department opposition to quotas against the EEOC's continued support of class-based numerical remedies.[23]

The appointment of Clarence Thomas as EEOC chairman in March of 1982 began a period of internal reform that improved EEOC morale and administrative competence. A free-market black conservative, Thomas disavowed the expansive approach of the Commission in the late 1970s. He said the EEOC would not try to develop new legal theories; it would concentrate on law enforcement rather than regulation by formal rule-making. Existing policies thus continued with little change. Using disparate impact theory, the EEOC made *prima facie* discrimination charges and sought appropriate remedies, including various forms of affirmative action. Emphasis on systemic class actions was reduced, and more attention was given to obtaining relief for individual victims of discrimination. Although Thomas expressed disapproval of quotas as a matter of statutory interpretation, he nevertheless said numerical standards were a useful measure of equal employment opportunity progress and were sometimes the only effective type of affirmative action. Moreover, in 1983 Thomas criticized the Justice Department's anti-quota litigation strategy as a radical departure from existing policy.[24]

In President Reagan's second term, the EEOC shifted to an anti-quota policy. In contrast to the straightforward and categorical approach employed by the Department of Justice, the EEOC adopted an incremental strategy that was less confrontational. Emphasizing enforcement of Title VII rights of minority group individuals under the direction of a forceful black chairman, the Commission was less vulnerable to the charge that its purpose was simply to protect the interests of white males. The EEOC also avoided controversy by eschewing highly visible and potentially costly administrative rule-making. Making policy through the relatively inconspicuous and inexpensive procedures of law enforcement, the agency made no attempt to revise existing guidelines on employee selection and affirmative action.[25]

In November of 1984, Chairman Thomas announced support of the concept of relief only for identifiable victims of discrimination. Further indications of a return to individual rights and equal opportunity principles were the elimination of a separate administrative unit for bringing charges of systemic constitutional discrimination based solely on statistics, the assignment of pattern or practice suits to the agency's trial division, greater emphasis on litigation, and less reliance generally on statistics to prove discrimination. Stating that it would "go all-out for anybody that was wronged," Thomas said the EEOC would consider court action in every case where a reasonable cause finding was made and conciliation failed. It would seek "full remedial, corrective and preventive relief" in conciliation agreements and in litigation. The new policy produced a dramatic rise in the number of suits initiated by the Commission and a large increase in the amount of back pay awards obtained through class actions for victims of discrimination. Although private actions continued to be the main source of federal equal employment opportunity cases, statistics of heightened EEOC enforcement activity indicated that the administration was not, despite critics' charges, insensitive to civil rights.[26]

The policy of full investigation and relief for individual victims of discrimination implied the abandonment of goals and timetables as a remedial device, and in 1985 the EEOC publicly assumed this position. It did so in a passive and indirect manner, apparently in the hope of averting criticism from the civil rights lobby. Acting General Counsel Johnny Butler announced the anti-quota policy in the form of internal instructions to staff attorneys not to include goals and timetables in new conciliation agreements and settlements. Butler based his action on his assessment of the views of the individual commissioners as reflected in votes on several cases, rather than on formal deliberation and decision by the agency as a whole. He said his intent was to concentrate agency resources on identifying victims of discrimination and obtaining make-whole relief.[27]

The EEOC's low-key approach to eliminating quotas was no less objectionable to the civil rights lobby than the Justice Department's high-profile tactics. Defending the new policy in hearings before hostile Congressmen, Chairman Thomas rejected the view that racial quotas were the only effective means of combating discrimination. He argued that goals and timetables did not in fact solve the problems of those who were discriminated against because they failed to bring about the practical changes that would ensure equal employment opportunities. Although reputed to be a "tough" remedy by affirmative action theorists, Thomas said goals and timetables were actually more lenient than make-whole relief for victims of discrimination. This was because they enabled employers to hide behind the number of minorities hired without truly providing equal opportunities for those individuals. "As long as minorities and women are treated as numbers, and not as individuals with unique combinations of education, experience and training to offer employers," Thomas testified, "they will not be able to reach their full potential in the professional world, and will not share fully in our national economy." Goals and timetables were also easy on employers because they were less expensive than back pay awards and other forms of make-whole relief. Quotas permitted employers who in many cases were guilty of unlawful practices to shift the cost of the remedy elsewhere. Actual victims of discrimination, who failed to receive the back pay and jobs to which they were entitled, bore the burden, as well as qualified individuals who were deprived of employment opportunity because those who had not previously been discriminated against were given preferences under affirmative action plans.[28]

After the Supreme Court approved affirmative action quotas in 1986-87, the EEOC accepted the legality of numerical remedies and withdrew its General Counsel directive against them. The Commission maintained that quotas were not an appropriate form of relief in the vast majority of cases, however, and were not as effective as other remedies in situations where they were permissible.[29] Goals and timetables had become "a sideshow in the war on discrimination," Clarence Thomas wrote in 1987. A more effective enforcement strategy would be to require employers to submit detailed information on all hiring and promotion decisions, impose fines and jail sentences on guilty employers who defied court injunctions, and appoint special masters to supervise a discriminatory employer's business in respect of employment practices.[30] The Commission thus remained philosophically opposed to quotas as a policy of group compensation for historic discrimination. Title VII "is not a reparations act," declared Commissioner William A. Webb.[31]

The EEOC's litigation strategy under Clarence Thomas made it less vulnerable than the Department of Justice to liberal charges of failure to enforce the civil rights laws.[32] Thomas was probably right, moreover, in contending that the main form of discrimination in the 1980s was that of "individual bigots in high places," and that quota remedies affecting entire classes of people were not warranted.[33] It was difficult to convince politicians, the media, and relevant interest groups of this fact, however, in view of the pervasive acceptance of disparate impact theory and the simplistic appeal of the idea that members of minority groups can be treated as fungible for social reform purposes. This circumstance was all the more apparent in the experience of the OFCCP, the third principal agency in the civil rights bureaucracy.

III

Although the Department of Justice and the EEOC, in conjunction with the courts, defined the legal concept of discrimination, the Office of Federal Contract Compliance Programs had a broader impact in requiring employers actually to adopt racially preferential practices. Because it was not a statutory law enforcement unit but an administrative agency operating largely beyond judicial oversight, the OFCCP had considerable latitude in dealing with the more than 325,000 companies that were subject to Executive Order 11246. Written affirmative action plans had been required since 1968, goals and timetables based on underutilization analysis since 1971. The Ford Administration modified the aggressive contract compliance program of the Nixon Administration, but the Carter government turned up the pressure again, provoking strong opposition in the employer community. Accordingly, the Reagan transition team targeted the OFCCP for reform. It proposed to eliminate OFCCP back pay awards, which the agency had adopted on its own initiative. Such awards were also of dubious authority, since Executive Order 11246 did not involve findings of discrimination. The transition team also urged restoring affirmative action to its original non-discriminatory purpose, provoking speculation that the contract program might be brought under the requirements of Title VII.[34]

Although the President had the legal authority to revise or abolish the quota system, the political risk of appearing opposed to civil rights led to a decision to leave Executive Order 11246 in place and concentrate on reforming the administration of the federal contract program. Opinion within the business community justified this course of action. While some employers supported and others opposed race-conscious practices, almost all federal contractors agreed that the executive order should be enforced in a less onerous and adversarial manner than it had been in the Carter Administration. Moreover, in view of the unresolved legal questions concerning affirmative action, most companies had little incentive to discontinue racially proportional employment plans that offered protection against Title VII liability.[35] In the area of anti-discrimination policy that affected the largest number of employers, therefore, the Reagan Administration acted as a party of balance from the outset. It maintained the policy of preferential treatment while trying to curb its bureaucratic excesses.

Undersecretary of Labor Malcolm Lovell presented this strategy in House oversight hearings in October 1981. Lovell testified that the contract compliance program inherited from the Carter Administration was run in a highly adversarial way that "produced paperwork, aggravation and contempt for the affirmative action concept" among contractors and the public. There was nothing wrong with the executive order, however; all that was needed was "a 'tuneup' of that enforcement vehicle that would continue to provide protection under the law [for enumerated minority groups] without the Government trying to dictate every detail of a contractor's personnel practices." In general, the OFCCP proposed to reduce the compliance burden on small contractors and adopt a more cooperative attitude that would encourage voluntary compliance. To this end, the agency had introduced regulatory changes which Lovell said emphasized substance over form and were intended to result in "real equal opportunity in the work place." Yet the OFCCP continued to define equal opportunity as proportional racial representation. The "mission of OFCCP," Lovell asserted, "is to insure [sic] . . . that the employment of protected groups does not vary to a major degree from the availability of their qualified, willing members in the work force."[36]

In effect, Undersecretary Lovell acknowledged the difference between the OFCCP concept of equal *employment* and the traditional concept of equal employment *opportunity*. The proposed agency regulations "will produce more jobs over time for minorities and women," he claimed, "while preserving the support of the American people for the goal of equal opportunity for all." The OFCCP further conceded that the difference between the administration and its critics concerned the degree of coercion to be employed in achieving equality of result for racial groups, not the end in itself. Liberal congressmen objected that the proposed regulations would simply ease the burden on employers rather than improve enforcement. Undersecretary Lovell, observing that "Social engineering is a very inexact science," responded: "We really don't know that well how various efforts work in this regard." But in "a free society," he said, it was necessary to depend on the will and determination of the corporations that were the targets of a social policy in order to achieve the goals of that policy. Instead of threatening contractors with punishment, the OFCCP was trying "to encourage people to follow the dictates of the national conscience." The Department of Labor did not intend to alter the basic premise of affirmative action, but was simply "making changes at the margin."[37]

In August 1981, the OFCCP published proposed regulatory revisions. Their principal effect was to relax the operation of the notorious eight-factor availability analysis—regarded in the employer community as "an intellectual joke"—as the basis for imposing goals and timetables.[38] A four-factor analysis was to be used, with contractors rather than compliance officers in effect determining the availability of minorities and women for each job group. The most important regulatory change concerned the point at which goals and timetables had to be set. Instead of requiring goals when the analysis showed "any difference" between the availability percentage and the contractor's actual utilization percentage, as the Carter OFCCP did, Reagan officials would require goals only when utilization was less than 80 percent of availability. While the OFCCP would continue to seek back pay, it would do so only for identifiable victims of discrimination. Individual complaints could be filed only by a person claiming to be a victim of discrimination, and third-party complaints of systemic violations had to identify alleged victims of discrimination. The OFCCP proposed to abandon pre-award compliance reviews, returning to the practice of reviewing affirmative action compliance after one contract was awarded. It also sought to raise the affirmative action threshold requirement from firms with 100 employees or $100,000 worth of federal contracts to 250 employees or $250,000 in federal contracts.[39]

The proposed revisions provoked widespread opposition. Congressional liberals and the civil rights lobby rejected the changes as a retreat from civil rights enforcement. The Department of Justice and the Office of Management and Budget objected to the retention of goals and timetables. Although business groups generally supported the revisions, they disliked the continued assertion of OFCCP back pay authority both in individual and class actions. While the combined opposition was strong enough to stop pursuit of reform by formal rule-making, the OFCCP was able to put the substance of the changes into effect by informal policymaking. Through internal directives, orders, and notices that were considered consistent with existing regulations, it modified the executive order program.[40] The OFCCP further eased pressure on contractors by providing that annual goals need not exceed availability and by permitting national corporations to adopt standardized affirmative action plans rather than single plans for each facility. The logic of the new policy was epitomized in agreements between the OFCCP and A.T. & T., General Motors, Hewlett-Packard, and I.B.M. for voluntary self-monitoring and compliance with their affirmative action plans rather than direct agency supervision.[41]

Formulated in consultation with industry groups, the OFCCP informal revisions were intended to enable employers to achieve easy-to-measure bottom-line results and to remove the threat of class back pay awards. (Back pay in individual cases of discrimination was still possible.) The revisions also brought the contract program into closer conformity with the legally defined character of affirmative action resulting from Supreme Court opinions.[42] The Court's decisions, in turn, confirmed the Department of Labor-OFCCP position in the struggle with the Department of Justice over revision of Executive Order 11246, referred to previously.

Arguing that informal administrative changes were an inadequate means of eliminating racial preference and reverse discrimination from the contract program, Attorney General Meese urged revision of the executive order to make goals and timetables voluntary. He introduced a new executive order into the White House Domestic Policy Council that revoked all regulations under Executive Order 11246 if they required federal contractors "to use numerical quotas, goals, ratios, or objectives." The proposal further declared:

> Nothing in this executive order shall be interpreted to require or provide a legal basis for a government contractor or subcontractor to utilize any numerical quota, goal, or ratio, or otherwise to discriminate against, or grant any preference to, any individual or group on the basis of race, color, religion, sex, or national origin with respect to any aspect of employment.[43]

Secretary of Labor William Brock, who had told the NAACP convention in July that some form of affirmative action would exist "for the foreseeable future," called revision of the executive order "politically crazy" as well as unnecessary. Brock was supported by Secretary of

Transportation Dole, Secretary of the Treasury Baker, and Secretary of State Shultz (who had instituted mandatory goals and timetables in the Philadelphia plan under President Nixon). Supporting the Attorney General were Secretary of Education Bennett, Secretary of the Interior Hodel, and Secretary of Energy Herrington. Opponents of the Justice Department proposal conceded that racial quotas were wrong, but said the issue was whether revision of affirmative action policy would help or hurt President Reagan in regard to other policy questions that had a higher priority. With opinion divided, Chief of Staff Donald Regan was unwilling to present the issue to the President. After a series of inconclusive meetings between Secretary Brock and Attorney General Meese, the latter withdrew the Justice Department's draft order.[44]

The Supreme Court's decisions upholding quotas in 1986-87 ended any prospect of reforming the federal contract program. Welcoming the rulings, the Department of Labor said they defined a middle ground between categorical opposition to race-conscious policies and the hard-line support of quotas that could be expected if a Democratic administration returned to power. Labor Department officials believed the Supreme Court's standard for requiring or permitting affirmative action was essentially that of the OFCCP. Secretary Brock stated that although color-blind non-preferential practices were desirable, "we are beyond the emotion of the early civil rights struggles and can now look dispassionately at the economic necessity of full participation of all minority groups in the work force."[45]

In addition to maintaining goals and timetables, the Reagan Administration expanded minority business enterprise quotas, or set-asides. Minority set-asides, begun in the Small Business Administration under the Johnson Administration, were institutionalized by the Nixon and Ford Administrations and ratified and expanded by Congress during the Carter period.[46] The Reagan government carried the minority business enterprise program still farther. In January of 1983, President Reagan approved the Surface Transportation Assistance Act, providing that not less than ten percent of funds spent under the law should go to business concerns owned and controlled by "socially and economically disadvantaged individuals." The Department of Transportation defined this class as the minority groups previously identified by the Small Business Administration for preferential treatment, namely, blacks, Hispanics, Native Americans, and Asian-Pacific Americans.[47] In 1983 President Reagan also issued Executive Order 12432, directing each federal agency with procurement or grant-making authority to develop plans for encouraging prime contractors to utilize minority business enterprises. The objective was to achieve "a reasonable minority business participation" in contracts awarded, and the program was expected to produce a ten percent annual increase in minority business procurement with a three-year goal of \$15 billion in goods and services obtained from minority business enterprises. President Reagan described the set-aside program as "a mighty engine for social progress," but it was also an attempt to use federal patronage to strengthen the Republican Party in the black business community.[48]

IV

Although the attention given to the Justice Department's anti-quota litigation strategy obscured the fact, employment discrimination policy under the Reagan Administration was characterized more by continuity than change. Like previous administrations, the Reagan presidency was unable to achieve coordination and consistency in equal employment opportunity policy. This internal disagreement in the 1980s was more significant than it had been before, for key agencies in the civil rights bureaucracy—for the first time since the start of affirmative action— opposed racial group preference. Insofar as the Reagan Administration pursued a policy of opposition, it expressed the continuing disapproval of public opinion for preferential treatment. On the whole, however, the administration rationalized and strengthened affirmative action more than it restricted it. In this respect it was particularly responsive to business opinion, which to a significant extent had accommodated itself to racial preferences in employment. By the 1980s most large companies, having institutionalized affirmative action as part of the corporate culture, had little inclination to stir up the employment discrimination pot once again by supporting the Justice Department's anti-quota policy.

Early in the Reagan Administration, business writer Daniel Seligman noted that the government was getting mixed signals from the corporate community. A significant portion of corporate opinion disapproved of preferential treatment, but was reluctant to say so for fear of being labeled opposed to civil rights. Organizations like the U.S. Chamber of Commerce and the National Association of Manufacturers wanted a reduction in the paperwork burden, Seligman reported, but it was hard to find major employers who desired an outright end to affirmative action. William J. Kilberg, an employment discrimination consultant and former OFCC official, commented on the change in business attitudes since the early 1970s. While the civil rights agencies used to argue that goals and timetables were different from quotas, Kilberg related, "I keep hearing all that mush from the business side." The

prevalent business attitude was toleration of affirmative action, provided it was modified to permit greater employer autonomy and self-regulation.[49]

Industry consultant George P. Sape, a former EEOC attorney, testified in Congress in 1981 that large companies had accepted the equal employment objective. Their main interest was to engage in profitable enterprise, however, and this purpose—so basic as to be "virtually beyond political motives"—was threatened in the Carter Administration by inflexible affirmative action policies. Sape said corporations wanted relief from excessive equal employment opportunity pressure. But reports that the Reagan Administration intended to dismantle affirmative action were equally disturbing. Corporate personnel management systems had been revised to include equal employment opportunity requirements, and it would be bad for business to interfere with this development.[50]

Affirmative action was good for business in the eminently practical sense that a corporation fighting discrimination charges faced enormous expenses that cut into company profits. From 1975 to 1980, about 5,000 discrimination suits were filed annually. Each year, the EEOC received about 75,000 complaints that warranted investigation. Forty-eight percent of the nation's largest companies were named in discrimination suits in this period, and half of those that were not had employees who filed formal discrimination charges. Afraid of being caught in the middle of a struggle between anti-quota forces in Congress and the civil rights lobby, corporate executives wanted to retain goals and timetables as a means of demonstrating compliance with the law. A reduction in equal employment opportunity paperwork and elimination of class action back pay awards would be a sufficient reform.[51]

By the time Executive Order 11246 revision became an issue in the mid-1980s, corporate affirmative action had become further institutionalized. Besides protecting against discrimination suits, an additional consideration supporting preferences was that any formal change in equal employment opportunity enforcement was likely to provoke grievances among workers who were beneficiaries of affirmative action. This fact was indirectly acknowledged in the argument that affirmative action fostered employee loyalty. Strictly on pragmatic grounds, moreover, the increasing number of minorities and women entering the work force led businesses to accept affirmative action. Goals and timetables were also justified as good for business for idealistic social reasons. Corporate equal employment opportunity officers and executives stated that affirmative action expanded the pool of available talent and led to increased productivity. Although hard evidence to support this claim was lacking, it appeared in the argument that the "multi-culturalism" of affirmative action had a creative and innovative effect, maximizing the contribution of individuals to their firms' success. "You have to feel it in your gut," explained a corporation vice-president for human resources, "I think we are a better company as a result of [affirmative action]."[52]

Affirmative action was also good for business in the sense that it improved a company's public image and customer relations. Some corporate personnel officers said there was value in making the mix of executives match the racial and ethnic composition of their customer base. Declared a General Motors executive: "I hate to think where this corporation would be today without these [affirmative action] programs. G.M. should be a reflection of the larger community and society around us." These justifications merged with the argument that quotas should be maintained because they had become part of the corporate culture. Surveys reported that many large firms believed affirmative action was simply a part of doing business, and that within two decades all companies would have irrevocably altered their business culture. One executive stated: "It's like showing up for work on time. Affirmative action is something the manager is expected to do as part of his job. If you can't show improvement [in EEO results], then your chances for advancement are decreased." Affirmative action in the mid-1980s was said to be so firmly established, according to a survey of the Fortune 500, that 88 percent of 197 corporations responding said they would maintain quotas even if not legally required to do so.[53]

Some business lobbyists justified affirmative action in the language of deregulation. Testifying against revision of Executive Order 11246, Peter C. Robertson, a former EEOC official, argued that quotas were instituted in the Nixon Administration "in essence as a deregulatory move" in the area of employment discrimination. It would be ironic, he stated, if the deregulation-minded Reagan Administration moved in the opposite direction, "eliminating an objective numerical measure and substituting bureaucratic examination of employers' practices to see if they meet government standards." In the world of affirmative action, employer acquiescence in government-mandated racial preference appeared as business freedom, and abandonment of preferential treatment requirements was seen as a form of government intervention![54]

Business support was thus the political reward administration pragmatists got for their conciliatory approach toward affirmative action. As former EEOC official Herbert Hammerman observed, OFCCP's affirmative action regulations began as a deal struck between big business and the government. When the Carter OFCCP changed the rules by pursuing a militantly preferential policy, employers appealed for relief.

The Reagan Administration restored the bargain whereby corporations accepted race and sex preferences within a framework of sufficient flexibility of enforcement to satisfy their need for business autonomy.[55]

Yet not all executives supported affirmative action or thought it was good for business. The Bureau of National Affairs noted in 1986 that although opposition to affirmative action was not as widespread as support for it, it was equally fervent where it existed. Pragmatic as well as principled reasons formed the basis for this opposition. For many companies, compliance costs were an "overwhelmingly expensive burden" that spurred resistance to OFCCP regulations.[56] Moreover, successful compliance might only be the start of costly legal involvement. For example, a construction company in an area where minorities were only 4.5 percent of the qualified labor force hired 19 percent black craft workers under an affirmative action plan. The company ignored deficiencies in background, skills, interests, and a higher failure rate among minority applicants compared to whites; further, it offered little training and support to those whom it hired. Frustrated by their failure to gain promotions and transfers, blacks engaged in work disruption and filed a class action suit that cost the company large legal fees.[57]

As this example shows, the effects of preferential practices on their supposed beneficiaries might be a reason for opposing affirmative action. Numerous observers reported that affirmative action programs often wasted the potential of persons they were intended to help as companies hired marginally qualified individuals simply to meet government requirements. Critics held that education and training, in the context of an expanding economy, were the most effective type of affirmative action. According to one equal employment opportunity consultant, companies with the fewest Title VII suits and largest increase in minority and women employees eschewed the "body count" approach. Using a "social contract" strategy, they hired employees with a view toward developing their talents and encouraged their participation in the goals of the organization.[58]

Business opposition to affirmative action also expressed concern for the merit principle and individual rights. Critics said preferential treatment created a spoils system that gave benefits to persons who were not discriminated against, while denying the rights of innocent white workers. Preferences bred bitterness and resentment; they were "an anathema in a free enterprise democratic society." Richard E. Hall, president of the Associated General Contractors, declared that to require employers to discriminate in favor of some and against all others was to undermine the fundamental belief that all Americans have the civil right to succeed or fail on their own merits.[59]

Support for affirmative action was much less prevalent among the nation's 500,000 small businesses, most of which lacked the technical and financial resources to absorb and socialize the costs of preferential treatment through the market. Nor were race-conscious practices as widely accepted in middle management as in the top executive echelon. As with social engineering schemes in general, those not directly affected by affirmative action were more inclined to support it, while those who were required to enforce it or pay the costs were more critical. Statements that affirmative action is part of the corporate culture were perhaps intended to counter the normal tendency of most employees and managers to think that the merit principle should govern employment practices, not race or other irrelevant considerations. To supporters of affirmative action, the Reagan Justice Department's arguments against quotas were particularly objectionable because they reinforced this natural tendency.

Equal employment opportunity consultant William Brown III, chairman of the EEOC in the Nixon Administration, told a House oversight committee in 1986 that the Reagan Administration introduced elements of uncertainty into a previously stable situation. Brown said it was much more difficult to talk to corporate executives, "and particularly people at the mid-level executive levels of corporations . . . when you hear the kinds of sounds coming out of EEOC that you hear now." The Bureau of National Affairs reported that race-conscious policies were harder to implement because of negative perceptions about affirmative action created by Reagan officials. An executive for a major pharmaceutical firm said that when employees who were well-educated and informed heard the subject discussed, "a lot of times they do question whether or not affirmative action is necessary." To counteract this effect, the company promoted "constant reinforcement" of affirmative action, emphasizing that it was "a way of life here and we still have the monitoring and the goal setting."[60]

The construction industry was the principal source of business criticism of affirmative action. Decentralized, subject to economic fluctuations, and characterized by competition among numerous small firms, the construction industry resisted the anti-competitive business and employment practices that racial group preference required. Complicating the picture was the weak employer-employee relationship that existed because of the nature of the industry, the difficulty of developing a skilled labor force, and the racial exclusiveness practiced by many craft unions in pre-Title VII days.[61] The construction industry was the target of the first mandatory quota policy, the Philadelphia plan of 1969, and was a constant source of criticism of racial preference thereafter. In the

1980s, its opposition to affirmative action was directed in particular at the minority set-aside programs favored by the Reagan Administration.

Minority business enterprise set-asides required a substantial portion of construction contracts to be awarded to a racially and ethnically defined sector of the industry that might not be large enough to meet the challenge of the work load. At the same time, they excluded non-minority contractors who claimed a right to compete for public contracts. Some specialty contractors were forced out of business or stopped bidding on federal work because of the requirements that prime contractors give ten percent of every contract to minority business enterprises. Prime contractors often could not find such businesses to give work to, or, finding them, were forced to beg them to accept a subcontract at an inflated price that distorted the competitive bidding process and increased the cost to the government. Private construction contractors, though not required to do so, were also reported to be setting aside work for minority firms. In addition, corruption frequently marked minority business enterprise programs. State and federal investigations revealed a quarter to a half of minority business enterprise firms surveyed to be ineligible or questionable because they were fronts for white owners.[62]

Set-asides were justified as necessary to overcome the exclusion of minority contractors by the "old boy" network of prime- and subcontractors. The argument carried additional weight when advanced by black Republican businessmen, several of whom testified at controversial hearings on minority business enterprise set-asides held by the U.S. Commission on Civil Rights in 1985. Pointing to dozens of preferential federal programs intended to achieve economic objectives through the procurement process, James H. Lowery stated that the development of a black economic and entrepreneurial base was essential to prevent the "time bomb" of ghetto deprivation and injustice from exploding. The executive director of the National Association of Minority Contractors, describing preferences for American construction firms bidding on overseas military construction projects, argued that the same preferential approach should be applied to benefit minority contractors in the domestic market. Black Republican businessman Theodore A. Adams defended the minority business enterprise program by citing Supreme Court decisions upholding set-asides and by invoking a directive of President Reagan stating that "[g]oals and set-asides are necessary to right past wrongs."[63]

The fundamental contradiction in the affirmative action policy of the Reagan Administration was evident in the conflict between black businessmen, defending quotas in the name of the President, and the

Civil Rights Commission, opposing quotas under a black chairman appointed by the White House after a bruising fight with the civil rights lobby.[64] To complete the picture, the NAACP Legal Defense and Education Fund, an organization that had reason to support the minority business enterprise program because it gave benefits to minorities, boycotted the hearings on set-asides in protest against the Civil Rights Commission.[65] The situation illustrated the administration's dilemma. It was unable to formulate a coherent policy because of internal disagreement on affirmative action, yet it was denied credit by groups whose constituents benefited from the preferential treatment that it promoted. In part, this was the result of unremitting liberal accusations that the Reagan Administration was opposed to civil rights enforcement.

V

Liberals attacked the civil rights record of the Reagan Administration with an ideological fervor almost impervious to reality. They objected fundamentally to reassertion of the principle of equal rights for individuals without distinction of color. Although perhaps knowing better than anyone that racially preferential practices contradicted Title VII and Executive Order 11246, liberal critics treated employment discrimination policy as it had developed by 1980 as a fixed and unalterable body of legal rules that allowed no deviation from the logic of racial group equality of result. Accordingly, they defended race-conscious remedies as the only effective, if not the only permissible, method of dealing with discrimination. Regarding attempts to stop the spread of quotas as tantamount to opposing civil rights enforcement, they denied Reagan officials any interpretive latitude in enforcing Title VII and Executive Order 11246. Having rewritten Title VII on the basis of proportional group representation, liberals resorted to doctrinaire formalism to prevent any restriction of racial preference.

Congressional defenders of affirmative action, for example, reacted with indignation at the assertion of make-whole relief for victims of discrimination and opposition to quotas in 1981. Representative Augustus F. Hawkins called the administration policy "a shocking departure" from the bipartisan equal employment opportunity policy followed since the presidency of Franklin D. Roosevelt. Former EEOC chairman Eleanor Holmes Norton testified on behalf of the civil rights lobby that regulatory reform of affirmative action was viewed as "a general declaration of war by the new administration against firm enforcement in civil rights." Illinois Democrat Harold Washington advised Assistant

Attorney General Reynolds: "Your concept of non-victims escapes me. There is no such thing . . . If you say that the redress or the relief should be individually focused, you are getting away from the entire problem." "Why should the remedy have to be individual if discrimination is against a group?" asked Representative William Clay of Missouri.[66]

While promoting racial proportionalism, liberal critics concentrated on the charge that the Reagan Administration opposed civil rights enforcement. An analyst in the highly respected *National Journal*, voicing the complaints of civil rights groups, speculated on "whether the Administration wants to reform civil rights machinery or dismantle it gear by gear." The Washington Council of Lawyers, a legal arm of the civil rights lobby, criticized the Justice Department's focus on recruitment as an ineffective remedy that was contrary to established case law upholding quotas. The Council attacked the Department's *amicus* brief in *Connecticut v. Teal* as evidence that the Civil Rights Division always supported the employer. Assistant Attorney General Reynolds's application of the *Stotts* decision was even more provocative. Asserting that the Reagan Administration "has launched a systematic attack on the constitutional and statutory rights of minorities and women," the National Lawyers Guild contended before a House subcommittee that the Justice Department's attempt to reopen consent decrees to eliminate quotas was an abdication of law enforcement responsibility. The Leadership Conference on Civil Rights summed up liberal criticism in stating that the Department of Justice was "the locus of anti-civil rights activity in the federal government," and that it "subverted the federal civil rights laws."[67]

Liberals contended that prior to the Reagan Administration, employment discrimination policy was made and enforced in a bipartisan, non-political manner.[68] Not only was this assertion historically inaccurate, but insofar as Reagan officials tried to alter equal employment opportunity policy, they acted lawfully within the same administrative regulatory framework that previous administrations used. A test of the rule of law is whether the same forms and procedures are relied on to make public policy, irrespective of partisanship and ideology. Having shaped affirmative action policy to their satisfaction, liberals argued that opposition to racial preference and insistence on the color-blind equal rights principle were unlawful.[69] This was manifestly untrue. Although not intending to do so, some critics of the administration showed the fallacy of the unlawfulness argument.

Joel L. Selig, a Justice Department attorney who resigned in protest against William Bradford Reynolds's litigation policy, subsequently wrote a critical analysis of law enforcement by the Civil Rights Division.

Selig charged Reynolds with irresponsible management, not unlawful or unconstitutional actions. He said the Civil Rights Division departed from ten principles of responsible law enforcement, including regard for the facts, historical and institutional continuity, positive public image, separation from politics, and—most importantly—respect for the law. On this first count, Selig argued that while an executive department had some discretion with which to try to persuade Congress or the courts to change the law to accord with its policy preferences, it must enforce the law as declared by Congress and the courts. A department could not decline to enforce existing law because of disagreement with it. Significantly, Selig concluded that Reynolds's position on quotas "does not generally transgress allowable discretionary bounds." Although "unwise" and "regressive," the anti-quota policy was "not susceptible to the same administration of justice criticisms" as the department's anti-busing policy. Similarly, Reynolds's use of *Stotts* to reopen consent decrees to eliminate quotas, while extreme and irresponsible as a matter of statutory interpretation, was not contrary to law. Selig said the Civil Rights Division showed a lack of humility and self-restraint in trying to promote a major policy change without a definitive Supreme Court ruling on which to rely. Thus, at bottom, Selig's attack was directed at the political judgment and values of the Civil Rights Division. Selig wrote that Reynolds was "an aggressive point man in the divisive politics of racial backlash" whose top priority was to eliminate reverse discrimination as an unacceptable burden on the white majority.[70]

Drew S. Days III, Assistant Attorney General for Civil Rights in the Carter Administration, criticized the Reagan Department of Justice on essentially the same political grounds. Before 1980, Days wrote, the momentum of the civil rights movement was basically forward. The Reagan government "has shown an inclination to move in precisely the opposite direction from former administrations."[71] Days was correct in one sense: the Reagan Justice Department tried to reverse the legal and political tendency toward racial group preference that began after the enactment of Title VII. Yet if the Civil Rights Act guaranteed equal rights without distinction of color, as seems indisputable, then the Reagan policy gave forward momentum to civil rights enforcement by restoring this purpose.

Days complained further that because the Department of Justice proposed to use remedies that had been tried and found ineffectual in the past, it could be charged with less than good-faith efforts to protect the victims of discrimination. The Reagan Justice Department took "categorical positions against settled principles of civil rights law, irrespective of the principles of any particular case." This too was true:

the Civil Rights Division held that racial quotas were never permissible under Title VII. It was proper to advance this argument in view of the fact that, prior to *Stotts*, the Supreme Court had not ruled on quotas as a remedy for unlawful discrimination. Subsequently, the Justice Department interpreted *Stotts* broadly, and perhaps imprudently, in trying to eliminate quotas. However, the Department cannot fairly be charged with refusal to enforce the civil rights laws, nor did Days so contend. He criticized Assistant Attorney General Reynolds for stating publicly that *Weber* had been wrongly decided. He protested the fact that Reagan officials stopped supporting voluntary efforts to adopt quotas. Ultimately, Days objected to the attempt to change policies of previous administrations with which he agreed, and which he said a substantial number of citizens had come to accept. "The spirit of voluntary compliance with civil rights laws engendered by so many years of 'carrot and stick' federal enforcement," he concluded, "is integrally threatened by an administration which upholds the civil rights laws only grudgingly."[72]

VI

If the charge of Reagan Administration lawlessness is unfounded, is it then true—as liberal critics also claim—that employment discrimination policy in the 1980s consisted of an ideologically inspired backlash that undermined a consensus on affirmative action principles and politicized the civil rights question?[73] The essence of a legal or constitutional right is that its exercise not be conditioned on partisan or ideological considerations. In the era of segregation, black citizens' civil rights were denied because of fundamental racial purposes embedded in the structure of southern and national politics. Intended to repudiate this tradition, the Civil Rights Act of 1964 guaranteed a personal right not to be discriminated against in employment because of race.

When federal judges and bureaucrats redefined equal employment opportunity as a right of group equality under the disparate impact theory of discrimination, they politicized equal employment opportunity law and policy. The establishment of racial group preference against the express provisions and plain legislative intent of the Civil Rights Act repudiated the fundamental consensus on which the law rested. It allocated and redistributed public and private resources according to racial criteria as a means of eliminating societal discrimination. Affirmative action confers benefits on specific racial and ethnic groups for political reasons, then protects those interests by declaring them to be civil rights beyond the political control of the majority. The process by which this transformation in employment discrimination law occurred was political in nature; it ought to have been debated openly. Race-conscious affirmative action was not subjected to public scrutiny, however, because its proponents believed it could not be approved in the legislative arena.

When the Reagan Administration took office, affirmative action was widely established. Yet significant legal questions were unresolved. The Supreme Court had approved the disparate impact theory of discrimination, the framework and practical instrument for promoting racial preference. Consistent with this theory, the Court upheld voluntary private quotas in *Weber*, and it approved minority set-asides authorized by Congress in *Fullilove*. Lower court approval of quotas, although not unanimous, was sufficiently widespread that it might have been prudent and realistic for the administration to assume that the Supreme Court would never reverse such a line of decisions and hence should not even be asked to do so. Yet the same thing might have been said of the "present effects" doctrine in Title VII seniority cases before the Court overturned that seemingly irreversible line of precedents in the *Teamsters* case in 1977. It was not unreasonable, therefore, in order to restore civil rights policy to the statutory basis intended by Congress in Title VII, to pursue a litigation policy based on the concept of make-whole relief for identifiable victims and to oppose group based quota relief.

To the consternation of supporters of affirmative action, this was what the Reagan Department of Justice did. The principal charge in critic Selig's case against the Civil Rights Division was that it disregarded the fact that "the entire federal government for years had supported the same kind of affirmative action [i.e. racial quotas] in countless interactions with employers, unions, and state and local governments."[74] But was the affirmative action quota policy established in the period before 1981 legally and constitutionally sound? And did the decision to challenge it politicize a previously non-political area of public policy? The Reagan Administration answered no to both questions, apparently with ample justification. Affirmative action racial preference had existed for over a decade, but that fact did not conclusively resolve its legality or constitutionality. If equal employment opportunity law were as clear as the civil rights lobby said it was, a Department of Justice official observed in 1982, most of the civil rights questions dealt with in the courts would not be litigated. "Some of these issues are debatable," he said, "and to debate them doesn't mean you're trying to roll back civil rights."[75]

There is no reason to think President Reagan was not true to his principles and convictions in professing opposition to quotas. It was nonetheless true that his protestations conformed to a pattern which saw Republican presidents criticize quotas, even as their administrations established or maintained systematic racial preference.[76] The conclusion to be drawn is that while the Reagan Administration sought to resolve crucial legal questions in an already politicized field of public policy, its internally inconsistent approaches to affirmative action under the circumstances led to a compromise.

Affirmative action was probably too deeply entrenched to be radically eliminated by "a stroke of the pen," as some thought could be done.[77] The administration's appointments in the Department of Justice showed a serious desire to pursue civil rights reform. Reasserting the equal rights principle, the Department tried to reorient judicial, bureaucratic, and public sector managerial opinion toward traditional anti-discrimination concepts. Because affirmative action was so widely established, however, especially under Executive Order 11246, it was also prudent to maintain the system while reforming it administratively to accommodate employer interests as well as looking to economic development on free-market principles as a means of obviating racial preference and reviving traditional equal employment opportunity practices. Of course, the possibility existed that administrative reform would merely strengthen affirmative action in the long run, causing it to appear the reasonable means of achieving equal opportunity that its defenders claimed it was.

In any event, the Reagan Administration alone could not determine the outcome of the affirmative action controversy. The executive branch might propose civil rights policies, but in the modern American state it is the Supreme Court that often disposes of them. Partly in response to pressures generated by the Justice Department's litigation policy, the Supreme Court in the mid-1980s decided a series of affirmative action cases that further defined the meaning of American equality.

9

The Supreme Court and Affirmative Action in the 1980s

In the affirmative action cases of the late 1970s, the Supreme Court approved racially preferential practices adopted in response to the inherent logic and incentives of the disparate impact theory of discrimination. The rejection of the reverse discrimination challenge in *Bakke*, *Weber*, and *Fullilove* significantly clarified the politics of affirmative action, while leaving many legal questions unanswered. Although the Reagan Administration enforced the substance of employment discrimination law, its reassertion of traditional anti-discrimination principles altered the political environment in which preferential treatment had long flourished. Internal conflicts notwithstanding, the Administration's civil rights policy gave urgency to critical and unresolved legal and constitutional issues concerning the scope and effect of race-conscious measures adopted under Title VII and Executive Order 11246.

Although in reality the racial quota upheld in the *Weber* decision was tantamount to a government policy, in legal theory it was private and voluntary affirmative action. The question remained whether judicially imposed quota orders that were the model for private affirmative action were legal under Title VII. It was unclear, moreover, whether voluntary minority preferences in public employment, widely adopted after *Weber*, were constitutional under the equal protection guarantee. More broadly, the coexistence in equal employment opportunity law of two distinct if not antithetical concepts—the disparate impact and disparate treatment theories of discrimination—raised the question of whether sound public policy required a more coherent and unified conception of equality. From the standpoint of the public philosophy, it was pertinent to consider whether civil rights policy should continue to be developed according to racially defined legal principles and rules divorced from the persistent belief of most Americans that discrimination was an intentional act intelligible only within a framework of individual rights and personal responsibility.

In the early 1980s, the Supreme Court refrained from deciding any affirmative action cases comparable in their political impact to the reverse discrimination rulings during the Carter Administration. This restraint reflected division within the Court and its sensitivity to the controversial nature of the issue. For the time being, the Justices were content to let the lower federal courts determine the limits of affirmative action on a case-by-case basis. In the mid-1980s, however, the Court decided a series of cases that confirmed and expanded the scope of race-conscious affirmative action. Whatever doubts might have existed about the legitimacy of racial preference were dispelled by the Court's clear rejection of the Justice Department's anti-quota litigation policy.

The affirmative action decisions affirmed the proposition that the exercise of individual rights can be conditioned by racial considerations. Having decided this basic issue, the Court in the late 1980s returned to the problem of employment discrimination theory and technical questions concerning evidentiary burdens. Continuing a tendency seen in earlier cases, it modified disparate impact theory to closer align it with the disparate treatment concept of discrimination. Affirmative action was so widely established, and so well supported by organized political interests, however, that the Court's action—if, indeed, it was not overruled by congressional legislation—was likely to have little impact.

I

The philosophical contradictions in employment discrimination law and the Court's continued support of minority plaintiffs as the guiding principle of affirmative action jurisprudence were apparent in the first important Title VII case during the Reagan Administration, *Connecticut v. Teal* (1982). At issue was the validity of the bottom-line concept, the method of Title VII enforcement favored by equal employment opportunity moderates as a compromise between the government's interest in promoting minority employment and the employer's interest in maintaining control over the employee selection process. The case concerned a discrimination charge by four black employees against the state for using a test for promotion that had a racially disparate impact and was not job-related. The state denied the charge, pointing to the fact that 22.9 percent of the black candidates had been promoted, compared to 13.5 percent of the white candidates. This was a disparate impact case, yet the plaintiffs, who failed the test, inconsistently claimed disparate treatment discrimination on the basis of statistics showing the disparate impact of one part of the promotion process.[1]

In a 5-4 decision, the Supreme Court rejected the bottom-line defense and found the employer guilty of unlawful practices. Justice Brennan held for the majority that the result of using the test was to create a barrier to individual opportunity. Denying the manifest practical consequence of the *Griggs* disparate impact theory of liability, he said the Court had never interpreted Title VII as requiring the focus to be placed on the overall number of minority applicants hired. The purpose of the law, he declared, was to achieve equality of opportunity and root out arbitrary barriers that had a discriminatory impact on individuals. It protected the individual employee, not the minority group as a whole. Contending that the bottom-line defense contradicted the basic nature of Title VII, Brennan stated that favorable treatment of the racial group as a whole did not justify discrimination against an individual member of the group.[2]

Justice Powell, in dissent, objected that the majority used disparate impact analysis while reaching a conclusion inconsistent with the nature of a claim advanced under that theory. The decisive fact in a disparate impact case was the effect on the group. Where the group was not adversely affected, the individual could not claim discrimination, whereas in a disparate treatment case an individual could claim discrimination despite the absence of injury to the group. Justice Powell said the Court conflated the two methods of proving discrimination. However, the plaintiffs "cannot have it both ways," he argued. "Having pleaded a disparate impact case," he reasoned, "the plaintiff cannot deny the defendant the opportunity to show that there was no disparate impact." Powell believed the decision would force employers either to engage in expensive and difficult validation or to resort to quota hiring.[3]

Teal showed the pro-plaintiff bias of the Burger Court. Having effectively required preferential treatment through the use of disparate impact analysis, it refused to apply the theory in an even-handed way. It reneged on the implicit bargain by which government and business agreed to promote minority employment within a context of substantial employer autonomy. The decision thoroughly confused Title VII law. It contradicted the voluntary affirmative action upheld in *Weber*, reducing the incentive for employers to support preferential goals beyond what they were legally required to do. Moreover, by ignoring the distinction between disparate treatment and disparate impact discrimination, the Court merged the two theories for the first time. Even some liberals criticized Justice Brennan's strategy for weakening the logic and persuasiveness of disparate impact theory. Justice Brennan used the rhetoric of individual rights in a purely expedient manner to justify a decision that could not be reached by a fair application of the statistical disparity standard for evaluating employment practices that the Court had invented to secure benefits for minority plaintiffs. By failing to adhere to the disparate impact theory of discrimination, the Court called into question the purpose of the theory and invited reconsideration of the basic premises of Title VII law.[4]

Although the Court was willing to place some limits on the use of statistics in making disparate impact charges, it was too divided on affirmative action to undertake a systematic reassessment of equal employment opportunity policy. The only part of Title VII it was inclined to interpret in accordance with the intent of Congress, and the only political value it was willing to assert against the rule of racial preference, involved the seniority principle. In seniority cases, the Supreme Court upheld the interests of employers and innocent third parties against expansive discrimination claims. It affirmed the principle of the *Teamsters* case that discriminatory impact was not enough to invalidate a seniority system; rather, discriminatory intent must be proved.[5] It was within this decisional trend that the Court made its first pronouncement concerning the validity of judicial quota orders under Title VII.

In *Firefighters Local Union No. 1794 v. Stotts* (1984), the Court considered the validity of a district court order modifying a consent decree between the city of Memphis and a class of black firefighters. The consent decree provided for hiring and promotion ratios for blacks without regard to whether they were actual victims of discrimination. It said nothing about layoffs. Subsequently, the city laid off firefighters in accordance with a "last hired, first fired" rule stipulated by the seniority system agreed on by the city and Local 1784, a predominantly white organization. Recently hired blacks were laid off. The district court, declaring the seniority system not bona fide, modified the consent decree to prevent black layoffs and maintain minority employment ratios.

In a 6-3 decision, the Supreme Court held that the district court exceeded its authority under Title VII. Justice White stated for the majority that the district court disregarded Section 703(h) of Title VII, protecting bona fide seniority systems. According to the majority, this provision permitted the award of competitive seniority to persons who could show they were actual victims of discrimination; mere membership in a disadvantaged class did not qualify a person for relief. The black employees protected from layoffs by the lower court, however, were not victims of discrimination. Justice White went on to say that the limitation on the relief available in seniority cases was consistent with the policy behind Section 706(g), which governed the award of judicial relief generally under Title VII. "That policy," Justice White asserted, was "to provide make-whole relief only to those who have been actual victims of illegal discrimination."[6]

In a dissenting opinion, Justice Blackmun rejected the limitation of relief to actual victims of discrimination. Citing lower court quota orders and opinions in the *Bakke* case, he said a consensus existed that race-conscious relief was appropriate under Title VII as a remedy for "the present class-wide effects of past discrimination."[7]

Stotts conformed to the line of decisions since *Teamsters* protecting seniority systems against discrimination charges. Although Justice White might have decided the case strictly on the basis of the seniority provision, quotas were involved insofar as the district court order was intended to preserve the minority hiring ratios of the consent decree, which were not awarded on a victim-specific basis. Justice White's statement of the make-whole theory of Title VII relief was so limited, however, as virtually to ignore the scope and depth of the quota controversy to which it appeared to respond. Although the Supreme Court had approved only make-whole relief, a national policy of preferential remedies existed as a result of lower court quota orders. Yet Justice White made no reference to this fact. Supporters of quotas said his assertion of the policy of victim-specific relief did not prohibit preferential treatment as a remedy for past discrimination in non-seniority cases. Critics of quotas saw *Stotts* as a signal that the Court was troubled about the use of race-conscious remedies where there was no finding of discrimination.[8]

The Justice Department's aggressive use of *Stotts* in its anti-quota litigation policy forced the Supreme Court to take a more comprehensive view of affirmative action. The basic issue was whether preferential treatment defined by race or ethnicity was a valid means of enforcing the nondiscrimination principle. For two decades the government in varying degrees had assumed that it was, yet neither Congress nor the Supreme Court had addressed this question squarely. Moreover, if preferential practices were to be confirmed, who was to bear the cost? To what extent would the rights and interests of individuals who were not members of protected groups be restricted as a result of affirmative action? Still another fundamental question had to do with the means or agency by which racial group preference was to be implemented. Responding to the government's legal incentives and pressures, private employers had "voluntarily" adopted preferential measures in order to avoid liability for discrimination. If proportional racial representation was to be fixed permanently in the public philosophy, as many supporters of affirmative action desired, it was necessary to consider whether it was feasible for the government to continue to force preferential treatment on society, or whether private individuals and associations could be brought to accept the racial group conception of equality in a genuinely voluntary way. The fact that private employers could lawfully discriminate for or against individuals on account of race before the enactment of Title VII ironically provided a model for affirmative action strategists.

The relationship between Title VII and the Constitution also remained crucially ambiguous. The Constitution establishes the primary rules regulating the government, and legislation under the Constitution provides the rules of action governing the conduct of private individuals. Did the Fourteenth Amendment and the civil rights laws have the same meaning with respect to equality, or did equal protection of the law mean different things depending on the source of authority used to define unlawful discrimination? Did the Constitution prohibit the government from using race-conscious measures except under strict standards—to achieve a "compelling governmental interest"—yet permit it to condone or encourage race-based practices in the laws it enacted for the regulation of private conduct?

The Supreme Court began to answer these questions more systematically in its 1985-86 term. In general, it confirmed the policy of preferential treatment based on group rights and equality of result while claiming that it was protecting the rights of individuals who were not members of protected groups from undue infringement.

II

In *Local 28 Sheet Metal Workers International Association v. EEOC* (1986), the Court upheld a judicial quota order in a Title VII private discrimination suit for the first time. The quota order had its origins in charges filed under the New York state fair employment practice law more than twenty years earlier. After desegregation efforts failed in the New York courts, in 1975 a federal court found the sheet metal workers union guilty of discrimination under Title VII and ordered it to adopt a

29 percent minority membership goal. When the union failed to meet the goal, it was found in civil contempt and ordered to pay a $150,000 fine, which would be used as a fund for increasing minority membership. In the Supreme Court, the union argued that the membership goal and fund exceeded the scope of available remedies under Title VII by giving race-conscious preferences to persons who were not identifiable victims of discrimination. The Justice Department submitted an *amicus* brief making the same argument.

In a 5-4 decision, the Supreme Court upheld the goal and fund order as a valid exercise of Title VII judicial remedial authority. Justice Brennan declared for the majority that quota relief was appropriate where an employer or union "has engaged in persistent or egregious discrimination, or where necessary to dissipate the lingering effects of pervasive discrimination." The Court stated that in addition to make-whole relief, race-conscious class relief was available as a remedy under Title VII. In this type of remedy no individual was entitled to relief, and beneficiaries did not have to show they were victims of discrimination. The purpose of race-conscious relief was "to dismantle prior patterns of employment discrimination and to prevent discrimination in the future."[9]

Justice Brennan held quota relief valid on the grounds that because Congress did not prohibit it in Title VII, it was within judicial equitable powers. The standard argument against quotas had long been that they are prohibited by the statement in Section 703(j) that "nothing in the act" shall be interpreted to require any employer or union to grant preferential treatment to any individual or group on account of racial imbalance. Opponents also cited numerous statements by the sponsors of Title VII denying that quotas could ever be ordered or adopted under Title VII. As he had done in *Weber*, Justice Brennan answered these arguments by appealing to the purpose of Title VII—to open opportunities for blacks. He conceded that, in most cases, Title VII could be enforced by an order to stop discrimination. But in cases of "long-standing or egregious discrimination," he said, "requiring recalcitrant employers or unions to hire or to admit qualified minorities roughly in proportion to the number of qualified minorities in the work force may be the only effective way to ensure the full enjoyment of the rights protected by Title VII." Brennan dismissed the textual and legislative history argument against quotas by interpreting Section 703(j) as dealing only with the definition of a violation under Title VII. It simply meant, he held, that employers could not be found in violation of the law on account of racial imbalance; it did not affect judicial remedial authority.[10]

But under what circumstances could quota relief be ordered? Justice Brennan gave no clear answer to this question. Conceding that a preferential remedy was not always proper, he said courts should be guided by the congressional concern that such a remedy not be invoked "simply to create a racially balanced work force," but to deal with "persistent or egregious discrimination." In the instant case, a numerical goal was justified for this reason; it was not used to achieve or maintain a racial balance. Justice Brennan said the goal was a way of measuring efforts to remedy past discrimination. Furthermore, it did not unnecessarily encroach upon the interests of white union members, since none of them was laid off and no absolute bar to white membership was imposed.[11]

Four dissenting Justices believed the goal exceeded Title VII limitations on judicial remedial authority. Justice O'Connor viewed the goal as a quota extending preferential treatment on account of racial imbalance in violation of Section 703(j). Justice Rehnquist said the quota order disregarded Section 706(g), barring judicial relief to persons who were not victims of discrimination at the expense of innocent whites. The minority believed that to meet the 29 percent membership quota, white journeymen would have to be replaced by apprentices on a racial basis.[12]

Local 93 v. City of Cleveland (1986) was the second decision of the term to uphold affirmative action. At issue was the validity of a consent decree entered by a district court giving relief to persons who were not victims of discrimination.[13] Writing for a 6-3 majority, Justice Brennan said the court action was valid because the limitations on judicial authority in Title VII did not apply to relief awarded in a consent decree. In essence, the Court viewed the consent decree as a form of voluntary affirmative action on the *Weber* model, rather than as a judicial order. According to Justice Brennan, there was no reason to distinguish between voluntary action taken in a consent decree pursuant to litigation and action taken outside of the context of litigation. Whatever the limits on judicial quota orders might be, he reasoned, they did not restrict employers' ability to make voluntary agreements providing for race-conscious remedies. Justice Brennan stressed the narrowness of the decision; he noted that it did not address the issue of judicial relief for non-victims, the circumstances and limits of voluntary affirmative action by a public employer, or the showing of prior discrimination needed to defeat a reverse discrimination charge.[14] Justices White and Rehnquist objected in dissent that the consent decree violated the rights of innocent white firefighters and should have been invalidated under the *Stotts* decision.[15]

The third affirmative action case of 1986, *Wygant v. Jackson Board of Education*, resulted in the rejection of preferential treatment by a public employer acting under the Constitution. At issue was the constitutionality of an agreement between the board of education in Jackson, Michigan, and the teachers' union that protected minority employees against layoffs. White teachers who were displaced as a result of the affirmative action plan claimed discrimination in violation of the Fourteenth Amendment. District and circuit courts approved the racial preference as a permissible remedy for societal discrimination that provided "role models" for minority students. The Supreme Court reversed the lower courts, 5-4.

A plurality opinion by Justice Powell and a concurring opinion by Justice O'Connor discussed the constitutional problems of affirmative action. The principal issue was the extent to which race-conscious measures by public employers needed to be justified by a finding of unlawful discrimination. Justice Powell held that a racial preference plan, like any other racial classification, was inherently suspect and subject to strict scrutiny review. It had to be justified by a compelling government interest and narrowly tailored to achieve that interest. Justice Powell rejected the school board's use of role model theory to overcome societal discrimination as a justification that was so amorphous as to have no logical stopping point. In his view, the proper predicate for race-conscious measures was "convincing" and "sufficient evidence" that prior discrimination had occurred. The school board had made no finding of discrimination, however; even if it had, laying off white teachers was an excessive remedy. Unlike preferential hiring, where the burden was diffused among society generally, layoffs too intrusively disrupted settled expectations of innocent individuals.[16]

Justice O'Connor required a less demanding predicate for public sector affirmative action. In her opinion, it was not necessary to have "contemporaneous findings of actual discrimination" or instances of "identified discrimination" in order to justify race-conscious measures. A state or local government need only have "a firm basis for believing that remedial action is required." This might consist of a disparity between the percentage of qualified blacks on a school staff and the percentage of qualified minorities in the relevant labor pool sufficient to make a *prima facie* discrimination charge. To go farther and insist on a finding of illegal discrimination would destroy the incentive to voluntary compliance and prevent public employers from doing under the Constitution what private employers were permitted to do under Title VII to correct apparent violations. Justice O'Connor rejected the school board's affirmative action plan mainly because it was not based on a sufficiently important governmental purpose. She held that the layoff provision, pegged to the number of minority students rather than to the percentage of qualified minority teachers in the labor market, had no relation to remedying employment discrimination.[17]

In a dissenting opinion, Justice Marshall argued that the layoff plan was justified both by societal discrimination and underrepresentation of minorities. Affirmative action hiring goals served no purpose, he reasoned, if they were nullified by layoffs.[18] In a separate dissent, Justice Stevens shifted the rationale for preferential treatment even farther from the concept of a remedy for discrimination. He viewed the layoff plan as calculated to serve the public interest by creating an integrated faculty that provided benefits not attainable by an all-white staff. According to Stevens, the plan was inclusionary and reinforced the principle of equality. And although the plan caused grave loss to white teachers, their injury was "not based on any lack of respect for their race."[19]

Local 28 was the most important of the three 1986 decisions. Although affirmative action had progressed to the point where Supreme Court Justices were advocating it as a reasonable social policy to counter racial imbalance, it was legally and politically necessary for proponents to win Court approval of the initial idea of racial group preference as a remedy for unlawful discrimination. *Local 28* belatedly legitimized the defining element of affirmative action—the notion of preference for some minority individuals who were not victims of discrimination—after a finding that other members of the racial group had been discriminated against. The Court thus rectified the anomalous situation created in *Weber*, where it approved voluntary quotas before upholding the judicial quota orders that had prepared the way for them.

Nevertheless, because affirmative action had gone so far beyond the original remedial concept, *Local 28* was a disappointing victory for proponents of racial preference in some respects. By the 1980s, the operational focus of affirmative action had shifted to the question of the factual circumstances justifying race-conscious measures. Justice Brennan emphasized that courts could order racial remedies only where "egregious" and "persistent" discrimination was evident. Court-ordered preferences were thus a remedy of last resort. As a practical matter, however, preferences ordered on this basis would not be very pertinent because most unions and employers did not engage in this type of overt discrimination. Because *Local 28* established such a high burden of proof before preferential relief could be ordered, and because the judicial outcome might be less onerous than the result plaintiffs could demand in a consent decree, it might encourage employers to go to trial rather than accept a voluntary settlement. Requiring a history of discrimination before awarding quota relief was also seen as a form of protection for white workers' interests.[20]

Although *Local 93* offered no further support for judicial remedial authority, it was more responsive to the issues of the 1980s insofar as it treated the city's affirmative action plan as an essentially private and voluntary matter on the *Weber* model. Whereas civil rights strategists previously argued that private parties should be allowed to take preferential measures comparable to what a court could order after a finding of discrimination, they now sought to avoid tying voluntary preferences to court-ordered relief lest the Supreme Court restrict judicial remedial authority.[21]

As *Local 28* was not an unqualified victory for affirmative action, so *Wygant* was not an unqualified defeat. The Court followed *Stotts* in confirming the inviolability of seniority system rights. More important was the attempt to set constitutional limits on affirmative action. According to Justice Powell's plurality opinion, something close to a conclusive finding of unlawful discrimination by a public employer was required to justify race-conscious measures, while Justice O'Connor would require evidence sufficient to support a *prima facie* case. At the same time, the Court's rejection of preference in layoffs suggested that hiring quotas would be permitted.[22] From the standpoint of industrial relations, moreover, *Wygant* lacked relevance because the affirmative action plan it struck down was atypical, pegging minority teacher appointments to the number of minority students rather than to the percentage of qualified blacks in the labor market.[23]

The Supreme Court's 1986 affirmative action decisions mark a major turning point in the struggle to define American equality. More clearly than in school desegregation and voting rights cases, the Court accepted the proposition that individual rights are contingent upon racial identity. Although the Court rejected the argument of the civil rights lobby that societal discrimination was a sufficient justification for affirmative action, it firmly defended preferential measures against the anti-quota policy of the Reagan Administration. In this respect, the decisions were politically as well as legally clarifying.[24]

III

In its 1986-87 term, the Supreme Court expanded the scope of race-conscious affirmative action. In *U.S. v. Paradise* (1987), the Court upheld a judicially imposed 50 percent promotion quota under the Constitution that had a severe impact on white employees. In *Johnson v. Transportation Agency, Santa Clara County* (1987) it approved a public employer's voluntary affirmative action plan under Title VII on the basis of underrepresentation of women and minorities. Together, the decisions went far toward insulating preferential treatment from criticisms of reverse discrimination; they shifted the rationale of affirmative action from that of a retrospective remedy for discrimination to a prospective instrument of social engineering to achieve racial balance.

U.S. v. Paradise began in the early 1970s as a hiring discrimination case, in which a quota was ordered as a means of breaking down employment practices that excluded blacks from the Alabama state police.[25] Blacks were then hired, but none was subsequently promoted. A district court in 1983 therefore ordered a 50 percent promotion quota for qualified blacks until 25 percent of the police corporals were black and until the state developed a promotion plan free of disparate impact on minorities. In *Paradise*, the Supreme Court affirmed the district court quota order by a 5-4 margin.

In a plurality opinion, Justice Brennan analyzed the quota order under the standard of review required by the Constitution. Acknowledging that the Court had not agreed on whether ultra-strict or only moderately strict scrutiny was appropriate for reviewing a remedial racial classification, Justice Brennan said the issue was immaterial because the quota order passed even the most stringent test. The court order served a compelling governmental interest—to remedy past discrimination—and was narrowly tailored. According to Justice Brennan, the promotion quota was the only effective means of achieving the government's purpose. It was flexible, since it could be waived if there were no qualified blacks; it was temporary, since it would remain in effect only until an acceptable promotion plan was devised. Furthermore, the order was fair to white employees. It did not dismiss them or absolutely bar their advancement, but merely postponed their promotion. Finally, Justice Brennan asserted that the 50 percent goal was not really a goal, but a procedural device for measuring the speed at which the 25 percent minority promotion level would be achieved. Therefore, the government was wrong to argue that the goal was a "catch up" quota intended to achieve racial balance rather than remedy unlawful discrimination.[26]

In a dissenting opinion, Justice O'Connor objected that the quota was unconstitutional because it was excessively broad. To be acceptable under strict scrutiny, she argued, the goal must be tied more closely to the percentage of blacks eligible for promotion. The purpose of this requirement was to protect the rights of non-minority employees. Justice O'Connor also noted that the district court failed to consider alternatives to the quota, such as appointing a trustee to develop a promotion policy or finding the state in contempt of court and imposing stiff fines. The minority thus accused the Brennan plurality of adopting a "standardless view" of the constitutional requirement that affirmative action be narrowly tailored.[27]

In *Johnson v. Transportation Agency*, the Court considered a reverse discrimination charge under Title VII against a public employer's selection of a female candidate according to a voluntary affirmative action plan. Twenty-two percent of the agency's employees were women, but not one of their 238 skilled craft workers was a woman. The affirmative action plan adopted a goal of 36.4 percent female employees in every job category, based on the percentage of women in the area labor market. The plaintiff, a male, lost out to a woman in his bid for promotion, despite his higher qualification rating (which was based on testing and interviews). The agency's plan set aside no specific number of positions for women or minorities; rather, it authorized gender or race to be considered as a factor in evaluating qualified candidates for jobs in which members of such groups were poorly represented. Johnson charged the agency with discrimination and was upheld by the district court. The Ninth Circuit reversed, and the Supreme Court affirmed, 6-3.

Justice Brennan, writing for the majority, applied the *Weber* analysis to this long-awaited test of the justifiable basis for voluntary affirmative action by a public employer under Title VII.[28] After *Wygant*, it was reasonable to argue that racial preferences in public employment must be predicated on evidence of past discrimination. Elaborating on the societal discrimination rationale of *Weber*, Justice Brennan rejected the *Wygant* remedial criteria. He held that the use of race or sex as a consideration in job selection was "justified by the existence of a 'manifest imbalance' that reflected an underrepresentation of women 'in traditionally segregated job categories.'" In unskilled jobs, he said, manifest imbalance was established by comparing the percentage of women and minorities in the work force with the percentage in the local labor market. In skilled jobs, it was shown by comparing the work force percentage with the percentage of qualified women and minorities in the area labor market. The disparity need not be such, however, as would support a *prima facie* charge against the employer. Justice Brennan argued that although the Constitution required evidence of a *prima facie* disparity before race-conscious measures could be taken, Title VII demanded less so that employers would have an incentive to adopt affirmative action plans.[29]

Satisfied that the agency's plan to correct underrepresentation was sound in principle, Justice Brennan found it valid as applied to the facts of the case. The plan was not really aimed at the ultimate goal of 36 percent; rather, the desired outcome lay in annually adjusted short-term goals indicating the extent to which sex should be taken into account. This kept the plan from being reduced to blind hiring by the numbers, which Justice Brennan implied would have made it illegal. The fact that ability qualifications were taken into account, in addition to sex, also strengthened the plan. Furthermore, the plan did not unnecessarily trammel the rights of male employees or absolutely bar their advancement. No specific number of jobs was set aside for women; all eligible employees could compete; and denial of promotion to Johnson "unsettled no legitimate, firmly rooted expectation," since he had "no absolute entitlement" to the position. Finally, Justice Brennan said the affirmative action plan was temporary, since it was intended to achieve a balanced work force, not maintain one. Taking the language of the plan at face value, he concluded that the agency "has no intention of establishing a work force whose permanent composition is dictated by rigid numerical standards."[30]

Justice Stevens wrote a concurring opinion that explained the real significance of the non-remedial theory of affirmative action upheld in *Johnson*. With unusual candor, Justice Stevens stated that in *Bakke* and *Weber*, the Court interpreted Title VII "in a fundamentally different way" from the "absolute blanket prohibition against discrimination" intended by the authors of the Civil Rights Act, which neither required nor permitted preferences for any group. Since a majority of the Court decided to permit preferences, however, Stevens would go along with it. Revealing the direction in which affirmative action policy was moving and its underlying objective, Justice Stevens observed further that the logic of anti-discrimination legislation required interpretations of Title VII that leave "breathing room" for employer initiatives to benefit members of minority groups. If Title VII had never been enacted, he pointed out, an employer would be free to hire members of minority groups for any reason that might seem sensible from a business or social point of view. That was the logic of *Weber*. It was now carried forward in *Johnson*, a decision which Justice Stevens emphasized did not establish the permissible outer limits of voluntary affirmative action. The point of the whole policy, Stevens said, was to give managerial prerogatives as much scope as possible. He saw no reason, under the *Weber* and *Johnson* decisions, why an employer had any duty, before granting a preference, to determine whether his past conduct might constitute even an arguable violation of Title VII. Instead of scrutinizing past discrimination, he believed employers should consider forward-looking reasons to give racial preferences, such as improving services to minority communities. Justice Stevens saw affirmative action as a means of achieving "a racially integrated future" without becoming " 'racial balancing for its own sake.' "[31]

Concurring in the judgment, Justice O'Connor proposed more exacting criteria for voluntary affirmative action by public and private employers.[32] Trying to reconcile the Court's diverse affirmative action holdings, she claimed that *Weber's* requirement of "manifest imbalance in traditionally segregated job categories" was essentially the same as the *Wygant* plurality's demand for "a firm basis" for believing remedial action was needed. In neither case did the Court approve societal discrimination alone as an acceptable predicate for race-conscious preference. Nor did *Johnson*, in her opinion, signify acceptance of such an amorphous standard. In order not to discourage voluntary affirmative action, however, Justice O'Connor said employers should not be required to prove they had discriminated before adopting preferential practices. She believed an appropriate intermediate standard, between societal discrimination and a judicial finding of unlawful discrimination, was that of a work force imbalance sufficient for a *prima facie* charge. In the instant case, the complete absence of women in the road dispatcher category, compared to the figure of 5 percent of women in the skilled labor market, was enough to permit the affirmative action plan.[33]

In a strongly worded dissent, Justice Scalia underscored the significance of the new justification of preferential treatment approved by the majority. He stressed that the affirmative action plan was not a remedy for discrimination, but a method of establishing proportionate representation in employment. It "imposed racial and sexual tailoring," in defiance of normal expectations and laws of probability, in order to overcome societal attitudes limiting the entry of racial and sexual groups into certain jobs. According to Justice Scalia, the plan was intended to "give each racial and sexual group a governmentally determined 'proper' proportion of each job category." He believed there were no women road dispatchers because women did not generally desire to do that kind of work. Yet the Court now approved affirmative action in order to change "societal attitudes," not to remedy or eliminate unlawful discrimination or even to overcome the effects of prior societal discrimination. Employers, subject to liability where there was a "noticeable imbalance" in the representation of minorities or women in the work force, were not only free to discriminate—they were required to in order to avoid charges of unlawful practice under Title VII. Stating that the decision transformed Title VII into "a powerful engine of racism and sexism," Justice Scalia called for the overruling of *Weber* and the application of constitutional standards of equal opportunity to restore Title VII to its true anti-discrimination purpose.[34]

The Court's 1987 decisions went well beyond previous affirmative action holdings. *Paradise* extended judicial authority to order quotas in promotions as well as hiring. The notable feature of Justice Brennan's opinion was his conclusion that a "catch-up" quota that was greater than availability was permissible. Used by the Carter OFCCP, this type of extreme pressure on employers was discontinued by the Reagan Administration; its resurgence in the late 1980s came in part from congressional liberals. It had never been discussed in any of the Supreme Court's affirmative action opinions. If a 50 percent quota far beyond labor market availability was permissible, on Justice Brennan's reasoning there was nothing to stop a court from ordering a 100 percent quota.[35] *Paradise* suggested that extreme remedies for unlawful discrimination would be upheld and that remedial orders did not need to be the most narrowly tailored ones conceivable. In an area of law where social and political opinions had broad influence, *Paradise* showed how subjective the concept of a "narrowly tailored" remedy was. Apparently any remedy that did not dismiss or replace innocent white male employees was narrowly tailored.[36]

In *Johnson*, the Court finally acknowledged the true purpose of disparate impact theory: to justify affirmative action as a means of achieving proportional representation. Although *Weber* was intended to shift affirmative action from a remedial basis to a less restrictive rationale of societal discrimination, its reference to "manifest imbalances in traditionally segregated job categories" permitted it to be read as consistent with the Court's previous remedial approach. In *Johnson*, the Court dropped the idea of preferential treatment as a remedy for discrimination and introduced the concept of "underrepresentation." For years the civil rights bureaucracy had employed the concept of under-utilization in the federal contract program, and disparate impact theory assumed that in the absence of discrimination the percentage of blacks in any social institution or activity would equal that of the general population. As thus used, the idea of underrepresentation at least retained some connection—however tenuous or fictitious—with the concept of unlawful discrimination. In *Johnson*, however, the Court severed race and gender preference from any plausible understanding of discrimination, even under disparate impact theory.[37] Race and gender balance was declared to be a legitimate and sound policy, as Justice Stevens's concurring opinion made clear.

Avoiding the larger implications of the decision, most equal employment opportunity analysts greeted *Johnson* with a sense of relief that the Court had finally settled the basic issue: whether employers would be protected in the policy of preferential treatment that the government in effect forced them to adopt. Although the precise degree of underrepresentation would be determined in future cases, it was clear that large disparities between minorities and women in the work force and in the relevant labor market would not be necessary to justify race-conscious measures. According to one commentator, the Court drew "a dotted yet clearly recognizable line" between acceptable and unacceptable affirmative action that was far more permissive than the *prima facie* standard required for an orthodox discrimination suit.[38]

Johnson was especially important to the corporate equal employment opportunity community because the affirmative action plan it approved was so typical. It avoided hard numbers or specific allocation of positions for minorities, referred to qualifications, and sidestepped adjudication and any findings of discrimination. Employers were now free to create a balanced work force, and had more latitude to achieve that end than courts did in their broad remedial power. Finally, *Johnson* broadened the extent to which the rights of white males could be denied. The decision approved the type of sharply focused, individualized, and personalized disappointment of an innocent party that was found unconstitutional in *Wygant*.[39]

In *Johnson*, the Court went a great deal farther in transforming Title VII from a law guaranteeing the individual right of equal employment opportunity into a grant of immunity for employer discrimination. How clear and reliable the new standards of affirmative action would be remained to be seen. That a genuine consensus was forming on the controversial issue was even less clear. According to veteran equal employment opportunity observer William J. Kilberg, the shifting majority in the affirmative action decisions consisted largely of "Justices who are willing to reach results derived much more by sentiment than principled legal analysis . . ." Kilberg concluded: "We do not yet have a cohesive theory of affirmative action."[40]

IV

Affirmative action policy lacked consistency and coherence insofar as the Supreme Court applied two antithetical theories of employment discrimination, upheld quotas in hiring and promotion while prohibiting them in layoffs, and used some form of strict scrutiny review to analyze discrimination under the Constitution while forsaking any such review under Title VII—and only then asking whether a race-conscious measure promoted the goal of minority employment. From the standpoint of the public philosophy, however, the decisions of the mid-1980s were consistent in substantially rejecting reverse discrimination challenges to racial preference and vindicating the principles of group rights and equality of result inherent in disparate impact theory. Lawyers advising corporations on how to avoid discrimination charges, of course, can find problematic features in the rules of affirmative action; politically, however, the decisions appear to be clarifying and decisive. They give the civil rights establishment additional reasons to argue that affirmative action is the law of the land, as well as providing the essential meaning of civil rights enforcement.[41] The rejection of Judge Robert Bork's nomination to the Supreme Court in 1987 signaled, among other things, the determination of the forces of contemporary liberalism to preserve affirmative action jurisprudence as an essential element in American law.

If the affirmative action decisions eliminated any doubt about the political legitimacy of racial preference in civil rights policy, they nevertheless failed to resolve some technical legal issues concerning the nature of employment discrimination that had persisted since the *Griggs* case. In the late 1980s, the Supreme Court resumed consideration of these issues, especially the problem of the *prima facie* charge and the order and allocation of evidentiary burdens. Having protected affirmative action against conservative attack, the Court appeared to veer sharply to the right by revising key elements in the disparate impact theory of discrimination. Furthermore, the Justices reconsidered constitutional dimensions of affirmative action with respect to the minority set-aside policy approved a decade earlier in the *Fullilove* case.

The replacement of Lewis Powell, a moderate conservative essentially sympathetic to race-conscious remedies, by Anthony Kennedy, a conservative apparently more opposed to preferential treatment, may help partially to explain the Court's action. More broadly, the defeat of the Justice Department's anti-quota policy, the declining political fortunes of the Reagan Administration during its second term, and the Senate rejection of the Bork nomination altered the political situation. Affirmative action no longer may have appeared to be a burning political issue, but rather one that could be dealt with as a matter of interest to lobbyists, bureaucrats, and legal professionals at a level similar to the one that labor law has assumed. The reaction of the civil rights lobby to the 1988-89 decisions suggests that the well-organized constituencies of affirmative action will resist any judicial tampering with the group-equality legal theories that provide the incentives for preferential treatment.

The Court's rightward shift began with a reconsideration of the relationship between the disparate impact and disparate treatment concepts of discrimination in *Watson v. Fort Worth Bank* (1988). At issue was the question of whether subjective evaluation devices—for example, a job interview or a supervisor's assessment of an employee's performance—had to be validated under the Uniform Guidelines for Employee Selection Procedures. The scientific difficulty and the expense of validating this type of instrument, as well as the principle of employer autonomy and free enterprise, argued against the application of the validation requirement to non-objective selection under disparate impact theory.[42] Such devices had generally been dealt with under disparate treatment analysis and were not validated. For a unanimous Court, Justice O'Connor held that disparate impact analysis, with its validation requirement, applied to subjective selection criteria. Otherwise, a selection process that combined objective and subjective standards would be considered subjective and dealt with under disparate treatment analysis. The objective part of the process could be given the greatest weight and be made decisive, Justice O'Connor said, yet if it had disparate impact, it would escape liability and the *Griggs* effects test would be rendered useless and irrelevant.[43]

It was generally assumed among personnel administrators that since validation of subjective selection devices would be either impossibly expensive or simply infeasible, the application of disparate impact analysis in this situation would provide yet another incentive for quota hiring. Justice O'Connor contended, however, that the use of proper evidentiary standards could prevent such a "perverse" result. In a part of her opinion that was supported by a plurality of the Court, she drew on earlier decisions concerning the burden of proof in disparate treatment cases to revise the procedure used in a disparate impact case.

First, Justice O'Connor held that in making a *prima facie* charge, the plaintiff must identify the specific employment practice claimed to be the cause of the disparate impact. Second, she redefined the concept of job-relatedness and business necessity that provided a defense against a disparate impact charge. Under *Griggs*, an employer had to show that an employment requirement had a manifest relationship to the job in question. This did not mean, Justice O'Connor said, that the ultimate burden of proof shifted to the defendant. The burden of proof always lay on the plaintiff. The defendant's burden was to produce evidence that its practices were based on "legitimate business reasons," whereupon the plaintiff could try to prove the reasons were a pretext for discrimination. This was disparate treatment analysis applied to a disparate impact case, in effect unifying the two concepts.[44] Dissenting from this part of O'Connor's opinion, Justice Blackmun accused the plurality of failing to understand the distinction between disparate treatment and disparate impact analysis. In disparate impact cases, he stated, the burden of proof shifted to the defendant.[45]

Although the extension of disparate impact analysis to subjective selection devices was a formal victory for the civil rights lobby, the revision of disparate impact analysis was the key part of the opinion. The Court confirmed and approved this revision in *Wards Cove v. Atonio* (1989). In this case, minority employees asserted a disparate impact claim against two Alaska canneries; their claim was based on racial stratification in the work force that they alleged was caused by subjective employment practices. The issues were whether a *prima facie* case could be based solely on statistics showing a high percentage of minority workers to be in unskilled cannery jobs and a low percentage in skilled office jobs, as well as the burden of proof in a disparate impact case. Justice White held for the 5-4 majority that the statistical comparison between minorities in unskilled and skilled jobs, which the circuit court had accepted, was insufficient to make a *prima facie* charge. The proper comparison was between the racial composition of the jobs at issue and the racial composition of the qualified population in the relevant labor market. In showing a statistical disparity, moreover, the plaintiff had to identify a specific employment practice as the source of the disparity.[46]

The Court also held that the standard of business necessity as a defense to a disparate impact charge could be satisfied outside the validation requirement contained in the Uniform Guidelines for Employee Selection Procedures. The purpose of that standard was to determine whether a challenged practice served the legitimate goals of the employer in a significant way. "The touchstone of the inquiry," declared Justice White, "is a reasoned review of the employer's justification for his use of the challenged practice." While the justification could not be insubstantial, White said "there is no requirement that the challenged practice be 'essential' or 'indispensable' to the employer's business for it to pass muster." He added that an overly rigorous standard would be practically impossible to meet and would lead to quota hiring to avoid liability. White went on to say that the burden on the defendant was to produce evidence of a business justification. The burden of persuasion, as in a disparate treatment case, always remained with the plaintiff.[47]

Wards Cove expressed a tendency toward a unified theory of discrimination more consistent with pre-Title VII state anti-discrimination law in which the burdens between plaintiff and defendant were roughly equal. The court further sought to restore equilibrium in employment discrimination policy in *Martin v. Wilks* (1989). The issue in this case was whether white firefighters in Birmingham, Alabama, could claim racial discrimination as a result of the city's promotion of less qualified blacks. The promotions came about under a consent decree between the city and a class of black firefighters to which the whites were not a party. The Supreme Court held that the white employees were not bound by the consent decree, but were entitled to a trial of their claim. Avoiding discussion of the substance of the consent decree, Chief Justice Rehnquist held for the 5-4 majority that the purpose of the ruling was to assure that the claims of various interested parties be brought before the court in the negotiation of an affirmative action settlement.[48] For the minority, Justice Stevens argued that the district court had considered the interests of white firefighters while arriving at the consent decree stage and had properly dismissed them.[49]

In its 1988-89 term, the Supreme Court also took a more critical view of constitutional limitations on minority set-aside programs. In *City of Richmond v. J.A. Croson Company* (1989), it considered a set-aside plan that required prime contractors to give 30 percent of each contract to minority firms. Intended to eliminate the effects of past discrimination, the policy was adopted by a black majority on the city council and was modeled on the congressional set-aside approved in *Fullilove*. In a 6-3 decision, the Court struck down the Richmond set-aside plan as an unconstitutional interference with the rights of white contractors.

Distinguishing *Fullilove*, Justice O'Connor said in a plurality opinion that Congress could identify and redress the effects of discrimination in ways not permitted to the states under the Fourteenth Amendment. Since racial classifications carried "a danger of stigmatic harm" in violation of the equal protection guarantee, remedial measures were subject to strict scrutiny review to determine whether they were truly benign or motivated by illegitimate notions of racial inferiority or simple racial politics. The Richmond plan failed to pass strict scrutiny review. It was premised on a generalized assertion of discrimination in public contracting, rather than on a showing of prior discrimination by either the city government or private construction companies. Borrowing from Title VII jurisprudence, Justice O'Connor said the set-aside was a "rigid racial quota" unrelated to any individual injury or to any circumstances approaching a *prima facie* case of a constitutional or statutory violation.

The disparity between the small number of contracts awarded to minority firms and the city's 50 percent black population, cited by the city, had no probative value in establishing a justification for the plan. The relevant statistical pool for purposes of justifying preferential remedies was the number of qualified minorities. Since there was no identified discrimination, Justice O'Connor concluded, the city had no compelling interest to justify the preference, which was aimed merely at racial balance. The plan thus violated the equal protection guarantee.[50]

In a dissenting opinion, Justice Marshall asserted that the states had authority under the police power—the traditional source of states' rights—to take race-conscious remedial measures. He argued that the Richmond plan was predicated not merely on societal discrimination, but on evidence used by Congress to justify the minority set-aside upheld in *Fullilove*. Opposing the use of strict scrutiny review of preferential remedies, Justice Marshall particularly objected to the use of Title VII standards for evaluating unlawful discrimination under the Constitution. In his view the relevant constitutional principle, to be protected against Title VII revisionism, was that "all persons have equal worth, and it is permissible, given a sufficient factual predicate and appropriate tailoring, for government to take account of race to eradicate the present effects of race-based subjugation denying that basic equality."[51]

The 1988-89 affirmative action cases, along with a decision restricting the use of the Civil Rights Act of 1866 (Section 1981 of the U.S. Code) as a prohibition against private discrimination in non-employment matters, sent shock waves through the civil rights establishment.[52] The legal issues raised by these decisions are obviously of great significance. They involve nothing less than the meaning of unlawful discrimination, the procedure for proving and rebutting discrimination charges, and the scope and effect of race-conscious remedies. *Watson* and *Wards Cove* point toward a unification of the disparate impact and disparate treatment theories of discrimination, using the more reasonable and evenly balanced allocation of burdens stipulated under the disparate treatment concept. If carried further, the effect could be to overrule *Griggs*. The *Wilks* decision threatens the permanence of "temporary" affirmative action plans adopted to avoid liability under the one-sided *Griggs* effects test. *Croson* is perhaps the most theoretically significant holding, because a majority of the Court voted for the first time to apply a strict scrutiny standard of review to preferential measures. This in effect introduced Title VII evidentiary principles into constitutional discrimination cases.[53]

Whether the Court's most recent decision will have the consequence of curtailing or reversing the spread of race-conscious affirmative action, however, seems doubtful. In *Croson*, Justice O'Connor warned that if unjustifiable racial preferences were not prohibited, "the dream of a Nation of equal citizens in a society where race is irrelevant to personal opportunity and achievement would be lost in a mosaic of shifting preferences based on inherently unmeasurable claims of past wrongs."[54] In *Watson*, she cautioned: "If quotas and preferential treatment become the only cost-effective means of avoiding expensive litigation . . . such measures will be widely adopted."[55] One wonders where Justice O'Connor has been, or whether this is the same judge who voted to uphold the affirmative action plan in *Johnson*. Race, sex, and ethnic preferences have become so widely institutionalized in corporate, private associational, and government practices and so reflexive in the thinking of political elites and the media culture as to render Justice O'Connor's belated admonitions irrelevant, if not ludicrous.

In the next session of Congress after the court's 1989 term, legislation was introduced to amend Title VII to preserve race-conscious affirmative action. Republican representatives proposed a bill declaring that a *prima facie* case under Title VII can be made by showing a statistical underrepresentation of minorities in comparison to the qualified applicant pool. The bill also places the burden on the employer of proving that each part of the selection process in question is a business necessity.[56] Senate liberals expressing the views of the civil rights lobby introduced a far more comprehensive "civil rights restoration bill." In addition to fixing the burden of proof in disparate impact cases on the employer (without any stipulation that disparate impact must be shown by reference to a qualified applicant pool), the bill reverses *Martin v. Wilks* by preventing challenges to affirmative action consent decrees, provides for compensatory and punitive damages in cases of intentional discrimination, and redefines the right to make and enforce contracts under the Civil Rights Act of 1866 (Section 1981 of the U.S. Code) to include all benefits, privileges, terms, and conditions of employment.[57] The political interests that support affirmative action appear to be strong enough to override the Supreme Court's revisionist decisions, as they have on previous occasions.[58] As in the case of the Voting Rights Act of 1982, which reversed a Supreme Court decision that was a barrier to proportional representation in voting, there appears to be no organized political constituency seeking to resist a congressional override or oppose race-conscious affirmative action.[59] And a major factor in the political support that affirmative action enjoys is the Supreme Court's approval of quotas in the decisions of the mid-1980s.

In those decisions, the Court confirmed the legitimacy of racial group preference as an instrument of public policy. More significantly, in

Johnson the Court approved voluntary preferences in public and private employment in order to achieve racial balance—defined as proportional representation—rather than approving those preferences as a remedy for unlawful discrimination. This completed the rewriting of Title VII begun years earlier. The law was now a prospective statute, as originally intended, but the comprehensive ban on race-based employment practices that it was the purpose of the act to impose had been eliminated.

One attempt to justify and rationalize affirmative action asserted that the Court's decisions of the mid-1980s restored the legal situation that existed before Title VII was passed, when employers could select employees according to their own preferences. The Court advanced this view in *Weber* and *Johnson*, arguing that those decisions upheld the Title VII goal of leaving employers free to choose employees without the federal government telling them whom to hire in accordance with some scheme of racial proportionality. Even some critics of affirmative action lent support to this rationalizing strategy. Charles Fried, former Solicitor General in the Department of Justice under President Reagan, observed that when a private employer acted voluntarily he was permitted to prefer women and minorities. "After all," Fried wrote, "before the Civil Rights Act, private employers could discriminate against women and minorities with impunity."[60] Yet the Court, and commentators like Fried, were advancing a legal fiction—an unconvincing and pernicious fiction that was intended to obscure the racial discrimination lying at the center of affirmative action policy. Under the Court's decisions, private employers do not really prefer minorities voluntarily; they are forced to do so, and to discriminate against white males, by the government's interpretation of Title VII. There was no essential difference between former Solicitor General Fried's benign evaluation of the Court's affirmative action decisions and the claim of the civil rights lobby that discrimination against white males is "simple justice."[61] The attempt to rationalize affirmative action as a legitimate consequence and expression of market freedom and entrepreneurial liberty illustrates the perverse consequences of anti-discrimination law enforcement divorced from a commitment to equal rights principles.

10

The Affirmative Action Debate
and the Future of American Equality

In its modern form, the problem of civil rights came into existence after Reconstruction, when the newly conferred rights of black citizens were systematically denied because of political interests, civic prejudice, and personal racial bias. The goal of the twentieth-century civil rights movement was to resolve what Gunnar Myrdal, in his historic study of race relations, called the American Dilemma: the profound gap between the promise of equality and the reality of black subordination in American society. In the broadest sense, the purpose of civil rights enforcement was to realize the principles of democratic self-government. The Civil Rights Act of 1964 and the Voting Rights Act of 1965 were intended to promote this end by removing racially discriminatory barriers and creating equality of opportunity. In implementing these measures, however, federal officials and the civil rights organizations decided that equal opportunity was an inadequate principle on which to base the pursuit of genuine equality. Under what was really a new concept of civil rights—the disparate impact theory of discrimination—government policymakers and political elites reconceived equality on the basis of group rights and proportional racial representation.

In employment relations (as this study has shown) and in other areas of civil rights, intent to discriminate ceased to be an essential element in defining unlawful conduct.[1] Social institutions in general and business practices in particular were held to discriminate against blacks and other minority groups. Civil rights activists and officials claimed to discover a perverse and paradoxical fact: that equality of opportunity under the traditional disparate treatment concept of discrimination makes the achievement of substantive racial equality impossible. This contention led to the perception of a new American dilemma. Radical civil rights ideologists asserted that it was democratic self-government as practiced by a racist people, not the failure to practice democracy, that prevented the attainment of true equality. Race-conscious affirmative action, a judicially and administratively created structure of legal rules for the allocation of public goods, was intended to achieve substantive racial equality and resolve the new American dilemma.

Affirmative action racial preference was adopted mainly in reaction to the black riots of the 1960s. Subsequently, as black political participation increased with the elimination of discriminatory exclusion, affirmative action gained political support. It was defended by government policymakers as a transitional step toward the ultimate goal of a color-blind society and as a necessary means of enforcing equal opportunity laws. The corollary of this argument is a reluctance to acknowledge the origins of affirmative action as an expedient response—if not a capitulation—to political (if not simply criminal) violence.[2] The reason for such reluctance is that constitutional government and the rule of law repudiate force and violence as legitimate methods of political persuasion. Because of its origins, therefore, the question of providing a philosophical justification and rationale for affirmative action has been a continuing problem of considerable practical importance. This study of equal employment opportunity, then, will conclude with an analysis of this problem, the debate it has fostered, and its implications for the future of American equality.

Supporters of affirmative action initially justified its practice as compensation for slavery and segregation. This argument continues to be invoked by many advocates of racial preference, as is seen in the bill introduced into Congress in 1989 to establish a commission to study the effects of slavery and make recommendations on appropriate remedies.[3] The central argument for affirmative action, however, in accordance with the logic of the disparate impact theory of discrimination, posits the ideal of a racially balanced society organized on the principles of group rights and equality of result, regulated by government policies aiming at proportional racial representation. Opponents of affirmative action, on the other hand, argue for color-blind individual rights and equality of opportunity as sound principles of civil rights policy that enable individuals to pursue their diverse interests within a framework of law that promotes the common good.

I

Analysis of the affirmative action debate begins with the idea of equality of opportunity on which traditional anti-discrimination law rests. Based on the natural rights principles of the Declaration of Independence, equal opportunity rejects distinctions of legal status and privilege defined by race, religion, ethnicity, language, sex, and family inheritance that formed the basis of premodern societies. Defined by the guarantee of equal treatment regardless of superficial differences such as race, it is a means by which individuals, through talent, ability and other personal attributes, take responsibility for themselves and pursue their interests. The rule of equal opportunity does not guarantee equal results. Because it values liberty and gives scope to differences among individuals with respect to interest and ability, it recognizes the impossibility of achieving perfect equality in the distribution of social and economic goods.[4]

In comparative historical terms, the promise of equal opportunity inherent in the American Revolution was broadly realized in nineteenth-century America. Even in a country like the United States, however, where feudal or aristocratic institutions were never firmly established, equal opportunity was seriously restricted by the existence of slavery. Nevertheless the idea of equality of opportunity possessed unquestioned political legitimacy, even among groups that were excluded from its full benefits. This fact explains why equal opportunity was the aim of democratic political reformers, abolitionists, and women's rights advocates in the nineteenth century as well as progressive reformers in the early twentieth century.

In race relations, equal opportunity—long denied by the system of legalized segregation—was guaranteed in the Civil Rights Act of 1964. The law commanded indifference to race in private employment in order to reinforce the government's own constitutionally required indifference to race under the equal protection clause of the Fourteenth and (by judicial construction) Fifth Amendments.[5] In a political sense, Title VII reflected an interest-group outlook, insofar as the right of individuals not to be discriminated against because of race was intended to improve economic conditions for blacks in general. Under the law, however, the rights of individuals were the basis for any group concern. The Civil Rights Act recognized that individuals are morally prior to rather than dependent upon groups.[6]

The civil rights establishment and the equal employment opportunity bureaucracy in the 1960s, as we have seen, rejected equal opportunity because it did not lead to equality of condition. In their view, the legal capacity to participate and the right to equal treatment in a procedural sense—the central meaning of equal opportunity—were insignificant compared to the socially determined meaning of opportunity. The social and cultural deprivation suffered by blacks and other minority groups was seen as constituting an inseparable obstacle to the advancement of their interests and socioeconomic status. Civil rights policymakers therefore infused the equal opportunity law with the new meaning of group-based equality of result.

The theory of disparate impact discrimination provided the means for this transformation. Under pre-Title VII fair employment practice legislation, an inference—though not a conclusive finding—of intentional discrimination could be drawn from statistics of racial imbalance or exclusion. In enforcing Title VII, civil rights strategists persuaded the courts to accept statistical racial disparity, completely apart from an employer's intent, as *prima facie* evidence of unlawful discrimination. The *prima facie* evidence became a conclusive finding of discrimination if the employer could not prove that the employment practice that caused the disparate impact was a business necessity. Accordingly, in order to avoid discrimination charges under the disparate impact theory of liability, employers were forced to have a sufficient number of blacks in their work force. This method of enforcing or complying with Title VII focused attention on the results of the employment process, or on the 'bottom line', rather than on equality of opportunity defined as the removal of procedural barriers to the equal treatment of individuals. The civil rights lobby argued that focusing on bottom-line results was a way of monitoring the extent to which an employer was providing equal opportunity in employment. In reality, employers were forced to guarantee equal or racially proportionate results in disregard of equal opportunity for individuals irrespective of race—as was required by Title VII.

Under disparate impact theory routine business practices could be found unlawful. The theory served the liberal purpose of expanding government regulation of business and forcing private employers and white workers to bear the cost and responsibility of compensating blacks for societal discrimination. Liberals were able to pursue the goal of restricting the operation of the labor market for social redistributive purposes while justifying it simply as a means of securing equal opportunity.

Disparate impact theory also provided a rationalization for preferential treatment, whether voluntary or coerced, as a remedy for unlawful discrimination. Preferential treatment as public policy was adopted in the absence of informed national discussion of the remedial concept or of the theory of disparate impact discrimination on which it rested. No one in Congress supported quotas in the Title VII debate; when affirmative action preferences were introduced, policymakers deliberately obscured their coercive, race-conscious character. Objections had been raised against compensatory preference since the idea was first proposed in the early 1960s; not until the early 1970s, however, when defenders of the new civil rights ideology undertook to justify race-conscious measures, did the affirmative action debate really take shape.

Affirmative action preferences were initially justified as a legal remedy for past discrimination. Since pre-act conduct was not illegal, the first step in pursuing this strategy was to revise Title VII to prohibit the present effects of past (lawful) discrimination. The early seniority cases effected this revision, preparing the way for the disparate impact theory of discrimination as a means of attacking historical societal discrimination. Courts proceeded to exercise broad remedial authority and elaborate the remedial rationale as an instrument of social reform. From the standpoint of public opinion, remedying past unlawful discrimination remains the principal justification of preferential treatment.

In the debate that began in the 1970s, however, the logic of affirmative action was shown to be that of extending racial preference based on social utility and political expediency, rather than as a legal remedy for discrimination. The essential element in race-conscious affirmative action is the conferral of a benefit on members of a racial group who have not been discriminated against in order to compensate injuries suffered by other members of the group at the expense of innocent third parties, rather than that of the employer charged with illegal practices. This type of transaction does not conform to the established legal meaning of a remedy, which requires that the injured party (the victim) be given something in the nature of a substitute or equivalent in place of his original rights that have been violated or denied.[7] To use racial preference prospectively might be said to be a more honest and straightforward approach to public policy than the continued distortion of the concept of a legal remedy, which has the further consequence of permanently expanding the judicial authority used to order affirmative action remedies. By making racial balance an end in itself, however, and by redefining equality to mean racial group diversity, affirmative action inflates the importance of race and exacerbates racial consciousness. This is done for the avowed purpose of eliminating racial classification and achieving equal opportunity for individuals. To complete the contradiction, affirmative action is justified politically by the social pathology of ghetto life, which recalls the historic degradation of slavery.

Liberal theories rationalizing preferential treatment lagged behind government actions ordering preferential practices. By the late 1960s many critics of race relations concluded that merely to establish equality before the law for blacks would prevent the achievement of real equality. How to overcome the bias toward individual rights in the legal system, and what to substitute for it, posed difficulties. While reparations for American Indians could plausibly be defended, the case for group compensation for blacks was harder to make. Pointing out that, in a legal sense, it was difficult to identify proper black plaintiffs in the absence of broken treaties or other discrete events, Graham Hughes said it was impossible to make a viable argument for compensation in existing legal theory. In a study of the reparations question, Boris Bittker reasoned that although the concept of indemnity or remedy could be stretched to cover state-ordered segregation, despite the fact it was legal at the time it occurred, there were problems with group reparations since millions of blacks were not directly affected by segregation. Insofar as they were indirectly affected, it would be unfair to exclude them, yet to include them would cause other problems—including the task of formulating an official racial code.[8]

Nevertheless, quota preferences appealed to many civil rights advocates as a simple and just solution to a complex social problem. Black psychologist Kenneth Clark saw quotas as a derivative issue compared to the inefficiency of segregated schools, but he was prepared to accept quotas as a way of ensuring representation to blacks. Many affirmative action supporters no doubt believed, as did federal judge J. Skelly Wright, that individual responsibility could be maintained under a system of racially preferential remedies. Yet in asserting that anti-discrimination law was not color-blind, and that simply to detect and seek to remedy racial discrimination was to regulate by race, Judge Wright accepted the redefinition of equality in result-oriented, racial group terms. Defenders of affirmative action concluded, as civil rights attorney Robert Belton expressed it, that although neither the anti-discrimination laws nor their legislative histories expressly provide for preferential treatment, "this concept is implicit in the enactment of laws prohibiting discrimination . . ."[9]

The shift from a remedial individual rights justification of racial preference to a prospective one based on group equality began in the early 1970s, when the first judicial quota decisions were handed down and goals and timetables were imposed in the federal contract program. Liberal theorist Owen Fiss said it was unclear whether the basic goal of the anti-discrimination principle was equal treatment of individuals or equal achievement for racial groups. Fiss observed that while there was no evidence that Congress in Title VII intended affirmative action as a remedy for unlawful discrimination to be used to increase black employment, preferential treatment as a means of achieving social redistribution for blacks was increasingly common. In a legal sense, affirmative action had a purely remedial meaning. To ignore race in employment practices, however, Fiss argued, was to allow inequality to persist. The anti-discrimination principle should therefore not be confined to a remedial focus; rather, it should be redefined as a strategy for conferring benefits on blacks as a racial class.[10]

According to Fiss, even when redefined as preferential treatment, the anti-discrimination principle expressed too much concern for economic efficiency and individual fairness. He sought a "more robust strategy" for equal employment opportunity law, based on the idea that "[t]here are natural classes . . . in American society and blacks are such a group." Although conceding the difficulty of defining racial groups and determining individual racial identity, Fiss saw a greater threat in permitting individualist principles to obscure the reality of group rights. Indeed, he rejected anti-discrimination as the basic meaning of the equal protection principle, because the anti-discrimination idea was identified in the public mind with the concept of equality of treatment or opportunity. According to Fiss, the equal protection principle did not suffer from this association. It was therefore the proper instrument for preventing group disadvantage and ending the subordination of blacks as a natural class.[11]

Although the anti-discrimination principle was too deeply embedded in the civil rights laws to be superseded, liberals gave it a non-remedial interpretation. Kenneth L. Karst and Harold W. Horowitz contended that the purpose of affirmative action was not to remedy discrimination, but to serve contemporary social needs. Quotas, they pointed out, were intended to achieve racial balance in employment. It was expedient for courts to use the concept of a remedy for unlawful discrimination to justify racial distinctions, but properly understood (Karst and Horowitz wrote in 1974), judicial quota orders did not rest on a narrow remedial doctrine. They reflected a compelling governmental interest in creating an integrated society.[12]

The logical fallacy of regarding racial group preference as a true remedy for discrimination may have led apologists for affirmative action to defend it on expedient grounds as a prospective social policy measure. Questioning whether groups rather than individuals could be wronged so as to deserve redress, philosopher George Sher noted that preferential treatment as compensation for past discrimination was unfair because it deprived innocent individuals of legitimate expectations. Sher justified reverse discrimination as a means of giving blacks the ability to compete on equal terms for social goods that were competitively distributed. Thomas Nagel observed that since it was not genuinely remedial to compensate wrongs done to some members of a group by benefiting other members, the notion of group compensation concealed an element of unfairness. Moreover the perpetrator of the injustice, the employer, was not held liable for compensation under a system of quota remedies; further, not all blacks had suffered nor all whites benefited from discrimination, as the argument for preferential treatment implied. Nagel believed race-conscious policy was justified because it improved the position of excluded groups and gave them a reasonable share of power in society. Social utility rather than retributive justice was the basis for preferential treatment.[13]

Robert Sedler, a professor of constitutional law, contended that affirmative action preferences could not be justified solely by the make-whole theory of compensation for past discrimination. The real issue was "the interest of blacks as a group in having a 'fair share' of an employer's jobs." Edwin Dorn, a political scientist, asserted that affirmative action as a remedy for illegal discrimination, or even as compensation for the present effects of past lawful discrimination, was inadequate for dealing with the problem of substantive racial inequality. He urged a system of compensatory inequality to eliminate current inequality. Social philosopher Robert Fullinwider, noting that compensatory affirmative action was not truly compensatory or remedial, viewed social utility as the most persuasive argument for racial preference. Quotas should be supported, he argued, as a means of achieving racial integration unrelated to individual rights, not as a form of restitution.[14]

When the Reagan Administration tried to limit affirmative action by insisting on the make-whole, victim-specific theory of Title VII remedies, liberals justified preferential treatment all the more emphatically on the grounds of expediency and social utility. Indeed, they now abandoned the fundamental distinction between lawful and unlawful discrimination. In 1981 the U.S. Commission on Civil Rights, dominated by Carter Administration appointees, stated that it was no longer useful to distinguish between illegal and legal discrimination. The Civil Rights Act disapproved of all discriminatory acts while actually prohibiting only some of them, the Commission noted. Therefore, while government agencies and the courts could order affirmative remedies only on the basis of a violation of law, employers subject to enforcement action could remedy all forms of discrimination. In this analysis the concept of a remedy was still used, but obviously not in the sense intended in the Civil Rights Act. Neither was the discrimination to be eliminated that against which Congress had directed Title VII. In the Commission's view, discrimination was "an interlocking" and "self-perpetuating" "process involving the attitudes and actions of individuals and the organizations and social structures that guide individual behavior." If the civil rights law were applied only to illegal acts, essential components of the process of discrimination would be unaffected. It was necessary, in order to avoid perpetuating discrimination, to "carefully assess the context and consequences of our everyday actions."[15]

Contending that the victim-specific view of discrimination was too narrow, NAACP Legal Defense Fund attorney Ronald Ellis proposed a broader definition that transcended questions of the guilt and innocence of individuals. On the theory that everyone was a victim when certain groups were excluded from society's benefits, Ellis argued that the goal of creating a pluralistic society could only be achieved by policies based on group wrongs and remedies. Similarly, Paul J. Spiegelman defended true quotas, which he defined as benefits dispensed strictly according to group membership rather than being contingent on discriminatory injury. He criticized references to goals because they obscured the central issue in the affirmative action debate: "the justification for allocating opportunities by group." Civil rights lobbyist Linda S. Greene asserted that to achieve meaningful equality, it was necessary to reject the concept of individual victimization and socialize the cost of guaranteeing basic needs under a concept of group rights. Black law professor Randall Kennedy, rejecting the anti-discrimination principle as a rationale, said the purpose of affirmative action was to end blacks' subordination by making a rational calculation about the most socially beneficial use of limited resources.[16]

Although the concept of discriminatory victimization might be nominally retained, it lost any recognizable remedial connotation. According to affirmative action supporters, all members of protected groups were victims, by definition entitled to preferential treatment. Moreover, the status of victim was a permanent one, unaffected by the conferral of preferential benefits. Penda D. Hair, an NAACP Legal Defense Fund lawyer, argued that affirmative action theory should be expanded to include the idea of blacks as "third-party" victims of discrimination. This was a variation on the theme that all blacks regardless of circumstance were victims of discrimination. For example, Hair said that minority employees in jobs where the supervisor was white, or a black woman who was hired but was deprived of the benefit of minority co-workers, were third-party victims of discrimination.[17]

The shift from a remedial rationale to a prospective justification of social utility based on group rights reflected a tendency to define the goal of affirmative action in a way that was perpetually incapable of realization. Rooted in the political requirements of the civil rights lobby, this tendency appeared in renewed calls for forward-looking justifications for racial preference after the Supreme Court upheld affirmative action for remedial purposes in 1986. Kathleen M. Sullivan, for example, faulted the Court for approving quotas as a "precise penance for the specific sins of racism" committed in the past. Sullivan observed that the remedial theory was politically attractive because it viewed preferential treatment as something other than arbitrary social engineering for racial balance. As a long-range justification for racial preference, however, it was flawed because it made affirmative action contingent on the factual circumstances in which discrimination could be alleged. It invited claims that non-victims should not benefit and non-sinners should not pay. Sullivan argued for a forward-looking rationale that would regard race-conscious measures as presumptively valid to achieve social goals, such as improved education and community services, workplace peace, and increased racial diversity in the work force.[18]

In *Johnson*, the Supreme Court adopted the forward-looking rationale for preferential treatment that liberal equal employment opportunity theorists had long advocated. Although the Court said that affirmative action could be used to achieve rather than maintain a racial balance, the requirement of temporariness was not considered a temporal limit but a means of assuring that whites' interests were not unduly disregarded. Liberal analysts saw *Johnson* as requiring proportionate representation indefinitely, in order to stabilize the position of minorities and women. One optimistic account viewed racial balance in the work place as a means of increasing productivity that benefited everyone, including white males. The forward-looking affirmative action of *Johnson* appeared as a positive force that would transform society in general.[19]

In the transformation from a remedy for unlawful discrimination to a prospective instrument for achieving racial balance, two basic elements of affirmative action have remained constant. The first is the idea that individual merit should be defined in social terms, in relation to the principle of racial group equality of result. The second is the idea that reverse discrimination differs from traditional racial discrimination in being non-stigmatic.

In their seminal analysis of preferential treatment in 1974, Karst and Horowitz argued that the idea of individual merit was a subjective construct concealing the fact that an individual's claim to equal treatment rested on his membership in a group. The content of the merit principle, they contended, was defined by reference to community needs. In an early study of institutional racism, Joe R. Feagin and Clairece B. Feagin asserted that successful affirmative action required modification of the concept of merit in order to take the demands of social justice into account. Denying that merit could be objectively measured, they urged that the concept be broadened to include indicators of individual potential and ability other than the traditional intellectual ones.[20]

The affirmative action vision identifies race as a major component of the concept of merit. According to sociologist Benjamin Ringer, in a true merit society each group will be represented at each occupational level according to its numbers in the total work force. Most defenders of affirmative action reject the traditional idea of individual merit as culturally biased and redefine it in terms of racial and ethnic diversity. Psychologist Craig Haney contends that test-based selection should be supplemented by "recognition of the special merit that racial minorities bring to the work place by virtue of their unique perspectives and experiences." Linda S. Greene views individual merit as "a visionary ideal" that should not be embodied in legal doctrine before it is actually realized in social practice. Asserting that the concept of merit is political, Randall Kennedy reasons that since the elevation of blacks is a response to pressing social needs, race is rightly to be considered one of the primary traits that constitutes merit. Jeffrey Prager explains that under affirmative action, race *per se* is a merit deserving of reward, expressed in the rhetoric of diversity and representation rather than intelligence and achievement. Affirmative action rejects the idea of a hierarchy of merit: instead, it argues for the concept of a pool of candidates who are equally qualified—that is, who are all equally likely to succeed on the job. Prager contends that companies operating under affirmative action plans should be permitted to set an absolute minimum standard of merit, rather than in effect be forced to accept the higher standards set by the abilities of candidates competing under a rank-ordered free-market concept of qualifications. Affirmative action merit is thus collectivistic, sociological, and relativistic.[21]

The non-stigmatic nature of affirmative action preferences is a second feature of the policy that is consistently asserted. This argument rests on the presumption that in a democratic political system governed by a white majority, it is not possible for policy outcomes to be antagonistic to the interests of members of the dominant group. Because of this fact, racial classifications may be used in relation to whites without the suspicion of unconstitutionality that ordinarily attaches to racial criteria.[22]

Because denial of the rights of some white persons by white policymakers is not considered invidious or stigmatizing, preferential treatment for blacks is not viewed by its supporters as a denial of equal opportunity for whites possessing superior qualifications. According to Thomas Nagel, blacks were excluded because they were thought to be inferior and undesirable, while whites who are excluded by an affirmative action plan are not being told this. The Carter Administration Civil Rights Commission contended that what distinguishes preferential treatment from past quota practices is "the fact that the lessened opportunities for white males are incidental, temporary, and not generated by prejudice against those who are excluded." Noting that affirmative action plans are adopted in situations where white males hold powerful positions, the Commission declared that only the use of racial criteria to stigmatize entire groups of peoples is unlawful. In numerous opinions, Supreme Court Justices on both sides of the affirmative action debate have accepted stigmatization as a test of the lawfulness and constitutionality of race-conscious measures.[23]

II

Analyzing the quota controversy, a defender of affirmative action in a judicious moment said there were two major reasons for opposing preferential treatment: it denied basic rights, and it might not serve the good of the community.[24] This comment aptly summarizes the position of critics of preferential treatment through two decades of controversy.

Opponents of preferential treatment argued, to begin with, that the Constitution guarantees equal protection of the laws to all persons, and that Title VII prohibits discrimination against any individual on account of race, color, religion, national origin, or sex. In their view, the anti-discrimination principle of the Civil Rights Act was effective in eliminating racial barriers to equal opportunity, enabling blacks to achieve social and economic gains. Urging that the policy of individual rights and equal opportunity be continued, critics held that preferential treatment did not address the problem of unlawful discrimination and economic deprivation. On the contrary, they contended, it exacerbated racial tension, impeded the formulation of sound social policy, and undermined equality of opportunity.

An early account by business writer Daniel Seligman, a consistent critic of affirmative action, provides insight into the anti-preferential point of view. In 1973, Seligman wrote that it was reasonable to believe that the Nixon Administration would at some point abandon goals and timetables because they led to preferential hiring. Taking seriously the statements of Administration officials that quotas were temporary, Seligman was skeptical about the long-range future of a program with so many anomalies. "For a democratic society to systematically discriminate against 'the majority' seems quite without precedent," he observed. "To do so in the name of non-discrimination seems mind-boggling. For humane and liberal-minded members of the society to espouse racial discrimination at all seems most remarkable."[25]

A more systematic argument against affirmative action developed in the later 1970s. Its fundamental premise is that the constitutional equal protection principle prohibits the distribution of benefits and costs by government on racial and ethnic grounds. Richard A. Posner states that to use race for constructive social purposes in non-stigmatizing or non-invidious ways, as affirmative action policy professes to do, requires courts to decide whether race-conscious measures harm a group. This involves weighing competing claims of racial groups on a subjective political scale that deprives the equal protection principle of its precision and objectivity. According to William Van Alstyne, determining that racial classification favoring certain groups can be justified under the Fourteenth Amendment by a compelling governmental interest rests on questionable judgments about motive and purpose. "That is not . . . a constitutional standard at all," Van Alstyne declares. "It is, rather a sieve . . . that encourages renewed race-based laws, racial discrimination, racial competition, racial spoils systems, and mere judicial sport."[26]

Critics of preferential treatment hold that the exercise of constitutional and statutory rights should not be conditioned on social pressures or political expediency. Richard Posner denies that racial preference should be accepted as the price that whites must pay to avoid ghetto violence. "If a constitutional right means anything," he states, "it means that infringement is not permissible merely because desired by the political organs." Alan H. Goldman argues that a basic purpose of constitutional government founded on rights was to remove certain interests from utility-maximizing calculations based on political motives. In the view of Robert G. Dixon, Jr., the obligation of government to treat persons equally and respect their dignity cannot be avoided by creating a non-constitutional concept called "stigma," and telling an individual whose rights are denied that he is not "stigmatized" because his racial group is adequately represented. "The function of constitutional law is not to abdicate to politics," Dixon reasons, "but to force majorities to deal fairly even with their own kind." The Fourteenth Amendment does not declare that "no person shall be denied the equal protection of the laws, except by members of his own group." In the view of critics, affirmative action rejects the liberal principles that rights inhere in individuals and that no natural distinction exists between the races that can justify the use of racial criteria in public policy.[27]

Opponents contend that preferential treatment is not only wrong in principle, it is also ineffective for achieving its intended purpose. It does not provide a remedy for discrimination, as its legal justification asserts. Anglo-American jurisprudence holds that where the law creates an injury, the law must afford a remedy. The corollary, reflecting the principle of individual moral autonomy, is that no one can be made part of the remedy who is not part of the injury. Under quota orders, however, those who receive preferential treatment often are not victims of discrimination, and those who are victims receive no benefit. In addition, members of excluded non-minority groups are unlikely to have perpetrated or benefited from the discrimination, while the employer guilty of discrimination bears none of the burden. The idea of group discrimination implies that individual members of the group suffer injury because of their race. Yet compensation to the group as a whole in the form of preferential hiring is directed at the wrong target. If past discrimination is the reason for giving compensatory preference, the recipients are deserving because they are victims of discrimination, not because of their race. And assuming that personal qualifications count even minimally in affirmative action, the beneficiaries of racial preference are those who suffer the least discrimination and are most qualified. Race-conscious affirmative action is thus over-inclusive. Any reason given for group preference, Alan Goldman points out, such as compensating for injury or giving opportunity to persons in need, provides grounds for defining the preference more narrowly than race.[28]

Critics further aver that insofar as preferential remedies are aimed at attaining racial balance or proportional representation, affirmative action rests on erroneous social science. Disparate impact theory holds that racial group differences in income, occupation, educational achievement, test scores, and other indicators are the result of discrimination. Opponents of preference contend, on the contrary, that to a considerable extent group differences are based on aptitude, ability, taste, and opportunity. Questioning the notion that members of minority groups can actually be placed in the position they would have occupied but for discrimination, critics claim that education, cultural values, age, geographical location and the character of the labor market are causes of racial group disparities. Moreover, it is false to assume that without discrimination, one can expect a nearly random distribution of women and minorities in all jobs. Economist Walter Williams says there is no known theory indicating the "correct" number of minorities that should be found in an activity or organization.[29]

Affirmative action not only contradicts social science, it disregards the lesson of history that race and ethnicity as principles of social organization result in hostility and repression. If discrimination along racial lines divides societies into oppressors and oppressed, observes Barry Gross, "it is scarcely reasonable to hope to heal the split and redress the wrongs by further reference to those things." In his view, the main argument against preferential treatment is the historical fact that racial, religious, and ethnic discrimination have led to social disorder, war, and mass slaughter. Alan Goldman notes that whereas the historic achievement of liberalism was to eliminate native differences like race as determinants of social roles and benefits, affirmative action reversed this trend. According to critics, the affirmative action strategy of using racial criteria to eliminate racial discrimination is inherently contradictory and futile. "We shall not now see racism disappear by employing its own ways of classifying people and of measuring their rights," declares William Van Alstyne. Douglas Rae expresses the fallacy of affirmative action thus: "The trouble with compensatory inequality—'inequality in the name of equality'—is that it is akin to 'killing for peace' or 'lying in the name of the truth.' "[30]

Still another argument against affirmative action is that it obscures the genuine achievement of those who receive preferential treatment. In 1973, Seligman reported the observation of a black corporate equal employment opportunity officer that all minorities are stigmatized when less qualified applicants are hired. Reverse discrimination denies minorities the satisfaction of having their ability validated if they otherwise would have made it on their own.[31] Criticism of this feature of affirmative action gained force as the policy spread. According to Charles Murray, under affirmative action a market premium attaches to race, with the result that every black professional, no matter how able, is tainted.[32] Some black supporters of preferential treatment concede its stigmatizing effect, but believe it is less than the stigma associated with exclusion.[33] Other blacks insist on standards that judge individuals by ability and achievement. If the worst feature of slavery was the dishonor it imposed on blacks, Glenn C. Loury asserts, then affirmative action preferences will not resolve but only prolong this destructive legacy.

Neither white guilt, special favors, nor racial proportionalism decreed by government can secure the freely conveyed respect of one's peers that signifies real equality, Loury concludes.[34]

Against the argument that racial preference is necessary to achieve the goal of Title VII, critics have insisted that equality of opportunity enables minorities to make progress toward substantive equality. Barry Gross says it is wrong to assume that the rules of equal opportunity do not lead to changes in the status quo. Alan Goldman holds that enforcement of the nondiscrimination principle achieves the purposes of equal employment opportunity policy as well as preferential treatment, but without the corruption and injustice that result from the latter practice.[35]

As this comment suggests, critics believe affirmative action should be evaluated not strictly on the basis of workplace results, but also in relation to the basic principles of the American political tradition. Posner asserts that proportional representation, the ultimate logic of affirmative action, has no stopping point short of perfect equality. Insofar as it tends toward this goal, it requires perpetual government intervention that distorts the allocation of labor, separates individual merit from economic and professional success, and undermines the system of incentives on which a free society depends. Goldman says the allotment of positions according to racial group percentage produces universal disutility that ignores socially productive effort as a basis for social rewards. Many critics have attacked the means by which preferential treatment was written into law and public policy—namely, judicial activism that rejected the plain meaning of the Civil Rights Act—as a threat to limited government and the rule of law. And the deliberate deception required by affirmative action has been seen as corrupting public morality. Reiterating the familiar charges against preferential policies, Morris B. Abram pleads for candor in the debate over affirmative action. "I ask only that the social engineers be open and candid about their vision for America," he writes, "and desist from camouflaging their redistributive goals behind the label of civil rights."[36]

According to Harvey C. Mansfield, Jr., the most obvious meaning of affirmative action is that certain groups of people are not sufficiently capable of helping themselves and so require assistance. In order not to hurt the pride of the minority groups, however, this fact cannot be publicly admitted. It is not the injustice of preferential treatment that is its worst feature, Mansfield contends, but its evil and underhanded means. In essence, affirmative action categorically accuses the American people of racial discrimination in order to avoid telling the truth that minorities, in the eyes of the civil rights bureaucracy, are incapable of competing in society. By focusing on equality of result instead of equal opportunity, Mansfield charges, preferential treatment encourages indifference to means as long as the end is achieved. The consequence is indifference to morality. This is seen in the "immoral moralism" of the consent decree, wherein a defendant employer who does not admit he is guilty agrees under compulsion to act as if he were. Mansfield warns that under the rule of affirmative action, government by consent decree threatens to replace government by consent.[37]

The ultimate criticism of race-conscious affirmative action, therefore, is that it lacks political legitimacy. While it purports to enforce civil rights and remedy discriminatory injury, it is in reality a policy of resource allocation and social redistribution that in a substantial sense has not been approved by democratic decision-making. Although most Americans supported the goal of bringing minority groups into the economic mainstream, they were divided on the problem of means. The question of whether measures going beyond the anti-discrimination principle were needed, the identification of alternative principles on which preferential treatment rested, and the reconciliation of conflicting values and interests provoked by affirmative action proposals were political questions that should have been decided by representative institutions. It is true that some preferential programs were adopted by legislative bodies, but these were by far the exception rather than the rule and occurred long after the courts and administrative agencies had fundamentally installed a new policy in place of the Civil Rights Act.[38]

By the start of the 1980s, the essential arguments in the affirmative action controversy had coalesced into the form they have maintained to the present day. Critics condemned racial preference as a contradiction of the requirements and intent of Title VII and a denial of individual rights and equality of opportunity. Defenders claimed affirmative action was legitimate on the grounds of historical justice, the necessity of flexible administrative policymaking in modern government, and expedient political considerations arising from the fact that 62 percent of the population were potential beneficiaries of preferential treatment.[39] As the Reagan Administration assumed responsibility for civil rights policy, the possibility of dismantling the quota system shifted the focus of debate from the wisdom and propriety of affirmative action to its impact and effects. In 1980, Alan Sindler stated that affirmative discrimination had "a sort of tenuous existence between the lines of the Constitution." A few years later, Harvey Mansfield, Jr., observed that "[a]ffirmative action is settling down in our constitutional polity like a determined guest seeking to establish squatter's rights."[40] In the 1980s, systematic study of the results of preferential treatment was undertaken in the hope that it could help decide the political controversy provoked by the Reagan Administration over whether affirmative action should be continued and further legitimized or restricted and placed on the road to extinction.

III

The stated goal of affirmative action is to create substantive racial equality by putting blacks into jobs from which they have previously been excluded, thereby reducing racial group differences of income, occupation, and other aspects of the employment process. The general objective is to promote the socioeconomic advancement of minority groups. System-wide or macro-level economic studies, focusing on factors such as education, mobility, and labor market conditions, examine the extent to which affirmative action contributes to these broad purposes. The pertinent question is the impact of preferential policies on the economic condition of minorities and women. A second type of study, pursuing micro-level analysis, focuses on the individual firm and considers the impact of affirmative action on the composition of the work force. Micro-level study examines the results of goals and timetables, judicial quota orders, and voluntary affirmative action plans. The general conclusions of impact studies are that it is hard to prove decisive economic effects of affirmative action and that government-enforced preferential treatment has caused a change in the racial composition of the work force.

The macro-economic effects of affirmative action have the most direct bearing on the goal of substantive equality. They have also been the most difficult to demonstrate. Several early studies claimed to show that equal employment opportunity laws do not improve the economic position of minorities because of a basic contradiction between the employment and wage provisions in the laws. For example, the requirement of wage equality for blacks was found to cause employers to substitute white for black labor, contradicting the requirement to hire more blacks relative to whites. To avoid compliance costs of the employment provision, employers might migrate to areas with a smaller black population or shift to less labor intensive production methods. As a result, black earnings and employment relative to whites remained unchanged.[41] To take another example, blacks and whites might be paid the same current wage, but employers raised the observed wage for blacks while decreasing the unobserved on-the-job training component of earnings. The effect was to preserve the racial group differential since blacks' and whites' jobs offered different prospects for growth and development of the employee.[42] James P. Smith and Finis Welch conclude that affirmative action has had no impact on the male racial wage differential, but that it has raised the incomes of young educated black males and especially black females.[43]

James E. Jones, Jr., a leading defender of affirmative action, accepts the conclusion of macro-level studies that race-conscious measures have had minimal impact on the employment status of blacks within a general pattern of slow economic improvement for minority groups. Affirming that it is difficult to establish causal links between specific policies and the overall economic condition of a group, Jones observes that blacks are moving up the economic ladder. He nevertheless argues that given the history of racism, it is counterintuitive to hold that affirmative action has not affected blacks' upward progress.[44]

A study of affirmative action at the level of the individual firm, funded in part by the Department of Labor and published in 1983, is the major source of information to date on which discussions of the impact of preferential policies are based. The study compared employment of protected groups in firms covered by Executive Order 11246 as against non-covered firms. Conducted by labor economist Jonathan S. Leonard and based on 16 million employees in a sample of 68,690 establishments, it showed that from 1974 to 1980 black employment increased more in federal contractor firms than in non-contract companies. The employment growth rate was 3.8 percent faster for black males, 7.9 percent for other minority males, 2.8 percent for white females, and 12.3 percent for black females. Gains were greater in more highly skilled occupations, and employment benefits were described as not transient, based on the lower proportion of terminations relative to hirings among blacks compared to other workers. Leonard also claimed that the productivity of females and minority males relative to the marginal product of a white worker did not significantly decline and that company profits were not affected. He estimated the costs of affirmative action compliance to be $78 per employee.[45]

Another study appearing in the mid-1980s confirmed the effect of affirmative action on the proportion of employed blacks in federal contractor firms. James P. Smith and Finis Welch reported that from 1966 to 1970, the percentage of employed blacks in the overall black labor force who were working in covered firms increased from 48.4 percent to 60.2 percent, reached 66 percent in 1974, and declined to 61.5 percent in 1980. Even more dramatic increases occurred among employed black females in the black labor force, 75 percent of whom worked in monitored companies in 1974, and in managerial ranks, where the proportion of black managers in the black labor force who were employed in federal contract firms rose from 20 percent in 1970 to 50 percent in 1980. Smith and Welch found, however, that at the macro-economic level, black income trends were similar to those in the 1960s, when affirmative action appeared not to have significant impact. Whether these trends would have been maintained without affirmative action could not be determined. Smith and Welch principally observed a "run for cover" by contractor firms which resulted in an absolute decrease in black male employment in non-covered firms. A relocation or shuffling of black employment thus occurred.[46]

Micro-level analysis examines the enforcement of affirmative action by the civil rights bureaucracy, not the effect of preferential treatment on blacks' economic condition. The studies show that when the government forces employers to hire minorities, employers hire minorities. Referring to affirmative action as "a set of vague and self-contradictory regulations" that left the OFCCP "virtually unrestrained" in telling contractors what they had to do, Leonard aptly describes it as the largest and most successful federally mandated job placement and training program ever created, "with the most intimate relation to the private sector." Leonard notes that although OFCCP affirmative action enforcement has consistently been criticized, the policy is nevertheless effective on the whole. He explains that while preferential goals are inflated, they are not hollow, because contractors who promise more deliver more. This result is "an overall response to pressure."[47]

Studies of shifts in black employment do not prove that affirmative action policy accomplishes the equal opportunity goals of Title VII, or even the social reform purposes of its supporters. Leonard claims that for the period he studied, preferential treatment did not exact efficiency costs.[48] Not only is this conclusion subject to dispute, but evaluating the effect of race-conscious practices involves more than strictly economic calculations. Leonard recognizes a broader dimension of the problem in conceding that while affirmative action promoted integration of the work place, "the delicate question of how to swiftly remedy the harm done by discrimination without distorting the democratic process is still with us . . ."[49] This points to the political and moral effects of preferential treatment, which are even more controversial and unclear.

Affirmative action reinforces and places a premium on racial consciousness and prejudice. It encourages an attitude of victimization among blacks and other protected groups whom it regards as dependent and—if not inferior—then at least incapable of competing on their own. Moreover, it requires that anti-bias and civil rights progress be denied in the face of clear evidence to the contrary. A deeply dialectical intelligence is required to conclude that affirmative action has not had a corrupting effect on the American political tradition.

Although the legal justification of affirmative action has shifted from a remedial rationale to a prospective argument for proportional representation, its broad political justification continues to be the historical identification of American blacks with slavery and racial segregation. The ultimate logic of preferential treatment, if it is intrinsically sound, would be to write it into the Constitution, as has been done in countries such as India, Indonesia, Malaysia, and Nigeria.[50] This has not happened in the United States, although the approval in constitutional law of racial classifications justified by a compelling governmental interest points in that direction. Because affirmative action is a means of enforcing the Civil Rights Act, it can be evaluated for its effectiveness in creating individual equal opportunity and enabling blacks in particular to exercise their constitutional rights and attain a greater measure of substantive equality in the society. Evidence of civil rights progress and social advancement would not be an argument for repealing the civil rights laws, but it would be a reason for ending racial preferences in employment, which are regarded by the general public as special measures needed to overcome the effects of segregation and discrimination. The question of whether blacks have achieved civil rights and social progress in the past three decades therefore has a critical bearing on affirmative action policy and the political understanding that supports it.

There is much evidence of black civil rights progress in the past several decades. Critics of affirmative action believe this progress shows that the American Dilemma—the contradiction between the promise of equal rights and the reality of pervasive discrimination against blacks—has been resolved. Blacks enjoy access to and attain status and recognition in political and social institutions to an extent that signifies a transformation of race relations in the United States. In a real sense, equality of opportunity exists in law and public policy as well as in the political culture.[51] Some liberal supporters of affirmative action agree that blacks have made substantial progress and are moving into upper-level managerial and technical positions, achieving greater income parity, and generally experiencing equal opportunity.[52]

Nevertheless, despite substantial progress, many blacks continue to live in conditions of severe disadvantage and demoralization. Criminal activity, drug dependency, illegitimate teenage pregnancies, and high unemployment among young black males are some of the problems that constitute the social pathology of ghetto existence, for which affirmative action does not appear relevant. These conditions define a problem of fundamental moral, political, and social reconstruction that transcends civil rights. The conservative social scientist Glenn Loury urges that the civil rights agenda be redefined to focus on means of ameliorating the conditions of lower-class black life. The liberal equal employment opportunity lawyer Alfred W. Blumrosen, a pioneer architect of affirmative action, asserts that the civil rights lobby "will have to join—or rejoin—those who are concerned with the enhancement of individual freedom, dignity and opportunity in fields which are 'new' to the civil rights movement."[53]

How to deal with the social pathology of lower-class black life is a troublesome and vexing question. Affirmative action, however, is an impediment to a clear-headed attack on this problem. Insofar as the civil rights lobby and its liberal allies persist in the belief that the goal of Title VII remains unfulfilled, that racism and discrimination remain dominant, and that affirmative action is needed to secure basic civil rights for all blacks, attention is diverted from the really pressing issue of black community reconstruction. Yet for the civil rights organizations to acknowledge progress in ending discrimination and the transformation in race relations would undercut the principal rationale for affirmative action in the public mind. It would allay the sense of historical responsibility for racism that many whites feel, thus weakening the political basis for preferential treatment.[54]

The civil rights lobby tends to deny black progress because it has a vested interest in the continuation of prejudice and discrimination. As Harvey C. Mansfield, Jr., points out, affirmative action does not eliminate prejudice; it triumphs over it. Despite civil rights legislation, prejudice is said to continue in new and more subtle forms. Civil rights rhetoric declares that prejudice must be abolished, yet in attempting to abolish prejudice affirmative action inflates it. Although disparate impact theory formally disavows prejudicial motive and intent as relevant factors in Title VII enforcement, the tendency to associate racism with any finding of unlawful discrimination is irresistible. The beneficiaries of preferential treatment are thus encouraged to think their jobs are a form of punitive compensation, while the guilty are humiliated by the presumption that they are too prejudiced to treat blacks equally. Although the goal of affirmative action is said to be the elimination of race from employment procedures, this is to be accomplished by practicing race consciousness. Since the means used promotes prejudice, affirmative action contradicts the professed goal and makes progress unlikely.[55]

Defenders of affirmative action recognize that it does not deal with the problems of the unskilled and uneducated poor.[56] Ironically, however, inner city slums are the most potent symbol of the historical injustice suffered by blacks which provides the main political justification for race-conscious preferences. "These [ghetto] masses and their miserable condition," Loury observes, "sustain the *political capital* that all blacks enjoy because of their historical status as victims." Nathan Glazer agrees: "It is thus the condition of the black population of the United States, not the state of their rights or the practices that affect them, that lends the strongest support to affirmative action." The "mass of misery characterizing their poor," he emphasizes, "stands as the great argument for affirmative action."[57]

That affirmative action limits the outlook of the civil rights lobby to the horizon of slavery and discrimination, creating a political interest in denying black progress, is confirmed in some liberal and black analyses of the question. Blumrosen comments concerning the issue of civil rights progress that "there seems to have been a 'conspiracy of silence' about this development." He notes that supporters of affirmative action fear recognition of success will justify a reduction in its support. Earl Picard observes that the strategy of the civil rights lobby is grounded in the legacy of slavery; it regards blacks as an oppressed caste. On this view, the nation is called upon to fulfill its moral obligation, and it becomes a tactical necessity to stress the worst conditions of black life. Social science data on black mobility and occupational gains are rejected as insignificant, and race is reported to be of "enduring significance."[58]

Jonathan Leonard's study of the results of affirmative action makes clear why the black lobby has a political interest in maintaining the policy. "In terms of redistributing income," Leonard states, "the OFCCP acts as an ideal union: it increases wages without decreasing employment for its members." Furthermore, he notes, "a history of discrimination pays the dues for the group." James E. Jones, Jr., argues that even if it cannot be proved that preferential treatment causes black economic progress, preference should be retained "to assure that progress is not lost." Randall Kennedy avers that even if the facts showed that affirmative action was not good social policy and ought to be eliminated, blacks would still support it because it has come to symbolize racial progress. As long as the motives of critics of affirmative action remain suspect, Kennedy warns, the merits of the policy will have little bearing on the controversy.[59]

The most radical analysis of affirmative action politics disavows the very goal of civil rights progress as it has been conceived in the black protest movement. Kimberle Crenshaw argues that civil rights reforms are actually harmful because they cause a decline in the commitment of courts and many whites to fight discrimination. Urging attention to the question of whether "limited gains hamper efforts of Afro-Americans to name their reality and to remain capable of engaging in collective action in the future," she warns against weakening black political consciousness by engaging in legal reforms based on the anti-discrimination principle. Kristin Bumiller similarly criticizes civil rights policy on the ground that it prevents the radical restructuring of society needed to eliminate hierarchies that oppress minorities. She concludes that "antidiscrimination law serves to reinforce the victimization of its 'beneficiaries.'"[60]

If blacks have not made substantial progress, or if the politics of affirmative action require that progress be denied, the guarantee of civil rights and the reform of democratic government that it signifies point to a new American dilemma. Arguing that American democracy has depended on and reinforced racism from its very inception, Jennifer Hochschild says the problem blacks and minorities face is the majoritarian tradition itself. Since democracy is symbiotic with racism, all policies in liberal democratic society favor whites. Therefore, racism and discrimination have not been eliminated. Hochschild writes: "if most citizens choose not to grant the rest of the citizens their full rights, then perhaps democracy must give way to liberalism." Only "substantial, authoritatively imposed change" for the purpose of protecting rights (which is her definition of liberalism) can eradicate racism, Hochschild advises.[61] What methods of policymaking are implied in this cryptic and portentous warning are not clear, but it points to the problem of racial attitudes broadly considered as the context in which the affirmative action controversy persists.

IV

Discussing the future of affirmative action policy, Edward W. Jones, a black employment consultant, asks:

> What kind of nation do we want to create? A nation in which competence and character will be the criteria for success? Or a nation in which psychologically based insecurities perpetuate predesignated places based upon color, gender, or other non-performance criteria?[62]

The issue transcends race and goes to fundamental questions of political theory and constitutional principle. Will individual liberty and freedom of association, within a framework of democratic decision-making and limited government, continue to provide the organizing and informing principle of the American polity? Or will government intervention and control, aimed at establishing equality of condition for racial and ethnic groups against the principles of market freedom and democratic politics, constitute the basis of our political life?

Although empirical observation suggests a transformation of race relations has occurred in the past three decades, the dominant social science research finds that racism persists as a major force in American society. It exists in a new form, however, according to the theory of symbolic or modern racism. This theory contends that overt, bias-based racism has been superseded by a more subtle and complex type, consisting mainly of economic self-interest, traditional American values, and a desire to preserve the existing social order.[63] Manifesting itself in opposition to busing and affirmative action, those guilty of symbolic racism are said typically to perceive blacks as rejecting the white, middle-class values of self-reliance, the work ethic, individualism, and the discipline of delayed gratification. The argument from symbolic racism discounts survey research and observed social practice indicating greatly increased levels of racial tolerance; such ostensible indicants do not really constitute a true expression of whites' racial outlook. The argument asserts that whites, believing that discrimination has ended, view blacks as responsible for their own situation and conclude that the position of blacks is caused by lack of effort or failure to adopt middle-class values.[64]

The thesis of symbolic racism emphasizes the discrepancy between high approval of equality norms in public opinion surveys and less consistent application of the norms in social practice. It fails to take into account, however, the fact that implementation of principles always receives less support than professions of them. To some extent, this is true even among blacks on civil rights issues, suggesting that opposition to government intervention is an independent variable in the affirmative action enforcement situation.[65] Furthermore, the theory ignores the fact, found in all societies and among all racial groups, that opposition to implementation of rights claims increases as the size of the minority group making the claim increases. Moreover, symbolic racism theory begs the question of a basic definition of racism by assuming that support of values leading to resistance to affirmative action is racist. Yet whether such support *is* racist is precisely the question to be answered.[66]

The more serious charge against the thesis of symbolic racism is that it is not really about race relations and civil rights. In fact, it is a political strategy for constitutional revolution which uses the race question as a rationale for rejecting individual rights and equality of opportunity as valid political and social principles. As it has been understood in modern history, racism refers to the attribution of innate biological inferiority to a group and the willingness to deny basic rights on the basis of that belief. In the 1960s and 1970s, the courts and the civil rights bureaucracy redirected the purpose of civil rights policy from the goal of ending racial prejudice and discrimination in order to create equality of opportunity to the goal of effecting social redistribution in order to create substantive equality. Affirmative action was to be the means of achieving this new goal. When opposition to preferential treatment emerged, supporters of affirmative action declared it was racist. Racism was thus redefined in strictly political terms: it had been transformed into opposition to liberal government policies that were presumed to help blacks.[67]

Contemporary liberalism uses the civil rights ideology of historical victimization and institutional racism, applied through the legal theory of disparate impact discrimination and the concept of symbolic racism, to promote its vision of the welfare state. If traditional middle-class values, individualism, and opposition to government intervention are barriers to substantive racial equality, then these barriers must fall. Resistance to efforts to achieve racial equality is said to be rooted in a commitment to "a distinctively American conception of equality."[68] Affirmative action as a policy of social reform becomes the model for liberal policymaking in general. In fields as diverse as foreign affairs and environmental protection, sound public policy is conceived of strictly as a matter of enforcing positive rights or entitlements. Presumed to be non-political because they are intended to protect people's "rights," these policies are typically developed, like affirmative action, by courts and administrative agencies acting beyond the reach of popular democratic control. In fact, however, this type of rights-driven policymaking, which involves claims on the resources of others insofar as it guarantees remedies in a substantive rather than procedural sense, is preeminently political.[69] The question is whether substantive rights-based remedial policies will be recognized as essentially political and dealt with through the institutions of representative democracy.

If, as Mansfield argues, affirmative action works only when it is concealed and lied about, and if the existence of a black underclass provides a permanent justification for preferential policies regardless of their effects, it will be difficult to change affirmative action by telling the truth about it.[70] The need to dissemble about affirmative action has produced a kind of censorship that has facilitated the development of preferential treatment. For over twenty years, public opinion survey data consistently have shown large majorities to be opposed to special treatment for minority groups.[71] Yet during this time, racially preferential programs have steadily expanded. A benign explanation of this paradox, advanced by supporters of affirmative action, holds that the best way to preserve color-blind individual rights is to accept racial preference as a means of accomplishing needed social change, without openly affirming it as a universal principle.[72] A less charitable view is that the idea of collective white responsibility for racism and the potency of the civil rights shibboleth have obscured the realities of affirmative action, enabling the civil rights bureaucracy to pursue its race-conscious policies.

Despite the political controversy it has stirred, affirmative action has been a relatively unexplored subject in social science research, with the exception of the economic studies noted previously. Since preferential treatment rests on concepts such as disparate impact theory that are the product of liberal social science, liberal scholars may be reluctant to investigate its effects. Noting the paucity of studies, William R. Beer writes: "It is as if affirmative action has assumed the status of a religious article of faith, and professionals choose to avoid studying its effects for fear of what they might find." According to Thomas Sowell, advocates of preference assume that such policies will benefit the disadvantaged and be at the expense of the privileged, but they neither offer evidence of these effects nor examine the consequences of affirmative action programs. Sowell notes that despite abundant statistical evidence concerning racial and ethnic matters, no one has collected data on the actual losers under affirmative action.[73]

Using communications theory, Frederick R. Lynch explains the acceptance of preferential treatment partially as the result of a process of "mass, semiconscious, intrapersonal and interpersonal censorship." Lynch refers to the concept that he labels the "tyranny of the majority syndrome," whereby those who feel they are the minority in any social group, whether or not they actually are, remain silent out of fear of disapproval. Carl Auerbach, examining the adoption of quotas in colleges and universities, concludes that affirmative action was established by a small minority of faculty and students against large majorities in both groups who were opposed to preferential treatment. A "spiral of silence" took effect, enabling those who were convinced they were right to act in the belief that others would agree with them, and causing dissenters to keep quiet lest they be seen as opposing equality.[74] It is possible that the introduction of racial preference against majority opinion is a reminder that majorities are not always right. It is more reasonable to see it as evidence of the persistence of racial politics and the intimidating effect of racism, redefined as opposition to policies that are presumed to be beneficial to blacks.

Whether or not an organized political opposition to affirmative action will emerge when Congress considers legislation to overrule the Supreme Court's 1989 rulings, the passionate attack on those decisions by the civil rights lobby shows the persistence of a philosophical impasse between support of individual rights and equality of opportunity on the one hand and group rights and equality of result on the other. In the face of this conflict, some observers believe the controversy over affirmative action will be resolved by practical economic and professional considerations. In the field of public administration, for example, it has been suggested that efficiency must be given a higher priority than it received in the Supreme Court's affirmative action decisions of the mid-1980s. In this view, it will be necessary to place greater emphasis on efficiency as a balance to social equity in order to maintain the legitimacy of preferential treatment.[75] In private employment, increased job availability is seen as a practical solution to the philosophical conflict over affirmative action. Many corporate equal employment opportunity consultants optimistically predict that the challenge of maintaining economic expansion will make worker qualifications and productivity, rather than simple racial or ethnic identity, the focus of equal employment opportunity policy.[76]

A report prepared in 1988 for the Department of Labor views the changing nature of the labor market as the decisive factor in resolving the affirmative action controversy. It states that because traditional sources of labor are shrinking, the potential new work force will comprise larger percentages of women, minorities, older workers, the disabled, the economically disadvantaged, and immigrants. One-third of all new entrants into the labor market are expected to be black or Hispanic, a figure double the present proportion. Greater skills will be required and companies will undertake more intensive education and training programs. Under these circumstances, asserts Assistant Secretary of Labor Fred W. Alvarez, the opportunity exists "to 'mainstream' affirmative action." Employers who want to remain competitive, he states, "will need to engage in affirmative action techniques to ensure an adequate supply of qualified, well-trained employees."[77] The labor market approach is essentially the old idea that economic expansion and full employment are the best equal employment opportunity policy. This approach is accompanied by the politically obligatory references to cultural diversity as a source of creativity and productivity, and it has been advanced by President George Bush as marking the "new frontier of civil rights."[78] A still broader strategy for equal opportunity centers on entrepreneurial liberty as the most effective basis for civil rights progress, supplemented by educational improvement and anti-crime measures.[79]

If competition and efficiency are to be emphasized, standardized tests may well assume renewed importance in employment relations policy.

Throughout the 1980s, the testing issue was relatively quiet, not because it had lost its salience but because the government was largely successful in the 1970s in forcing employers to eliminate objective tests. Compliance was extremely difficult, even for the companies with psychological testing staffs. The government's position was that employers dropped tests because they were shown to be imperfect and were costly to validate.[80] The Uniform Guidelines for Employee Selection Procedure, adopted by the EEOC in 1978, were seriously flawed, however, and in the 1980s these flaws came to be more clearly understood.

To begin with, the guidelines conformed neither to Title VII judicial decisions nor to accepted professional testing practices.[81] On the premise that tests were culturally biased, the guidelines required employers to conduct "fairness" studies. Yet psychometric research showed that tests predicted accurately for all racial groups. In fact, the model of separate regression lines used by EEOC as a standard of fair selection overpredicted black performance and had the perverse consequence of eroding minority employment. Not having the capability to conduct validity studies, most employers needed to transport evidence of validity of tests or engage in cooperative studies in order to comply with the Uniform Guidelines. For all practical purposes, however, the guidelines prohibited test transportability. Government regulations also limited the use of content validity, the most feasible method of test validation for most employers, and expressed a preference for criterion validity, a more technically difficult method. The American Society for Personnel Administration concluded in 1981 that the federal equal employment opportunity agencies had abandoned professional integrity and created a system purposely designed to prevent any employer from validating a selection device. Many test analysts, including a committee of the National Academy of Sciences, feared that testing was in danger of being abandoned entirely, with a consequent decline in productivity.[82]

The key feature of the government's testing policy was the requirement that every test used by an employer must be validated or shown to be job-related in the specific employment situation in question. That a test might be validated in one plant did not mean it could be considered valid in a comparable plant in the same industry. If most general ability tests were valid, however, as much research indicated, and if there was a general intelligence factor in human beings, then it was reasonable to aggregate or generalize test validity.[83] As the fallacies in the Uniform Guidelines have become more apparent in the 1980s, there has accordingly been a tendency to recognize validity generalization as a reasonable concept in test use.

Despite political and social pressure, a number of scholars in the 1980s have studied general intelligence testing and its relationship to economic productivity. They have found that general intelligence exists, that cognitive ability tests possess validity in the .5 range (meaning they accurately predict performance half the time), and that test validity is not situation-specific. At the same time, group differences in testing remain considerable. The debate has therefore shifted from whether tests are valid to the question of what to do when valid or fair tests create disparate impact. The main significance of the research is to establish the concept of validity generalization as a general rebuttal to the presumption of discrimination in test use based on statistical disparity.[84]

In practical terms, validity generalization means that cognitive ability tests which significantly predict performance are valid in a general sense and may be used for different work forces in different locations. Whether or not tests will be used more widely in the future, or how they will be used, are policy questions that ultimately concern the type of society the United States will become. Test practitioners claim that by identifying individual ability, tests promote equal opportunity and economic efficiency. Critics argue that tests are unfair, that a coefficient of correlation in the .3 to .5 range is not economically useful, and that employers who have dropped tests have substituted methods of determining workers' qualifications that have no discriminatory effect. Defending the existing government regulations on testing, critics contend that validity generalization, if accepted, would undermine the disparate impact theory of discrimination and lead to re-segregation of the work force.[85]

The question of test use may be resolved with greater attention to scientific research than was true in the 1970s. Several federal district court decisions have approved reliance on validity generalization in Title VII testing cases, and the Supreme Court in *Watson* and *Wards Cove* stated that employers are not required to use formal validation studies.[86] A compromise between science and politics on testing policy has also been proposed that seeks to reconcile merit selection and minority preference through a ranking system known as "race-norming."

Race-norming refers to the practice of ranking candidates within racial or ethnic groups rather than in a single group by pure rank-ordering. Used since the early 1980s by the U.S. Employment Service of the Department of Labor in its administration of the General Aptitude Test Battery (GATB), the practice has recently been endorsed by the National Research Council of the National Academy of Sciences. The Council does not claim that the GATB is scientifically unfair or biased in the sense of not being a valid predictor of job performance. It does contend, however, that the modest predictive accuracy of the test, combined with the lower average scores of minority applicants, results in proportionately more black and Hispanic test takers being falsely predicted to be unsatisfactory under a pure rank-ordering system, although their scores are high enough to predict success on the job.[87] Within-group scoring retains a substantial proportion of the productivity gains attainable through the non-preferential use of tests, which recommends it over quota hiring from a pool of applicants formed on the basis of a low cut-off score.[88] It does so, however, by reinforcing racial classification and stereotypes that militate against a policy of equal opportunity based on individual merit.

V

It is likely that the political, social, and moral consequences of affirmative action, rather than its strictly economic effects, will be the final determinants of the character of American equality. In 1981, the U.S. Commission on Civil Rights stated that the purpose of affirmative action was "to eliminate, not perpetuate, practices stemming from ideas of racial, gender, and ethnic inferiority or superiority."[89] If we apply the effects test which its supporters use to evaluate employment practices, however, we find that affirmative action reinforces and perpetuates notions of superiority and inferiority that the Civil Rights Act was intended to eliminate. This result is inherent in the theory of stigmatization that is central to the concept of discrimination and inequality underlying race-conscious practices.

An individual's rights are violated—in the language of the Supreme Court opinions, "unduly trammeled"—when the action in question is invidious and the individual is "stigmatized." According to affirmative action theory, however, whites cannot be stigmatized or made to feel inferior. As the Sixth Circuit expressed it: "The self-esteem of whites as a group is not generally endangered by attempting to remedy past acts militating in their favor. . . . In such instances the white majority is simply not being subjected to what amounts to a constitutionally invidious stigma."[90] Although the court did not say so explicitly, the implication is that whites cannot be stigmatized because they are dominant or superior. By the same token, while it is not intended to, affirmative action implies that blacks are inferior, in that they are not able to compete without compensatory assistance. To be sure, references to innate racial characteristics have disappeared from acceptable public discourse. Can the external and superficial racial classifications of affirmative action continue to be used in allocating resources and determining individual rights, however, without establishing a presumption about the superior qualities of character, mind, and ability attributed to those who cannot be stigmatized because of their dominant position, and the inferior qualities attributed to those whose victim status entitles them to preferential treatment?

Judge Damon J. Keith of the Sixth Circuit speaks for many blacks in urging that the legacy of slavery and discrimination be viewed as an important and viable factor in achieving a just accommodation of conflicting social interests in civil rights policy.[91] As Justice Thurgood Marshall said in *Bakke*, this means recognizing that it is unnecessary in twentieth-century America to require individual blacks to demonstrate that they have been victims of racial discrimination.[92] All blacks, by virtue of birth into the racial group, are presumed to be victims. As long as legal rights and social benefits are conditioned on racial victimization, however, it appears to be impossible for the beneficiaries of preferential treatment to achieve full equality. "One cannot be the equal of those whose pity, or guilt, one actively seeks," observes Glenn C. Loury. Nor is "coerced acquiescence to one's demands," satisfying though it may be in assuaging the resentment that blacks may naturally feel about their history, effective in gaining the peer respect that signifies genuine equality.[93] Moreover, if race is not a reliable indication of individual ability and worth, as is universally agreed, it is difficult to see how affirmative action as a means of bringing about racial balance, rather than as compensation for slavery, can be any more effective in achieving individual equality. Whether justified historically with reference to slavery or prospectively as intelligent social planning, the racial emphasis of affirmative action seems misplaced. Criticizing the civil rights lobby for its constant focus on racism as the source of the difficulties facing blacks, William Raspberry questions the strategy of trying to force whites to confess their racism and accept their guilt. Raspberry pertinently asks: "What would guilt-ridden white people be expected to do about black babies having babies, black children dropping out of school, black youths trafficking in drugs and murdering each other?"[94]

Affirmative action is often viewed as simply a strong means of enforcing traditional equal opportunity that can be used temporarily without weakening the principle of individual rights. Even so persistent a critic as Nathan Glazer says that preferential treatment has helped institutionalize nondiscrimination laws.[95] The longer racial criteria are employed, however, the more likely they are to become permanent. This result can only be at the expense of genuine equality of opportunity.

The chief historical significance of affirmative action has therefore been to promote statist intervention into the free market and weaken political and social institutions based on individual rights. In an era when proposals of social reform based on the rationale of class conflict have generally been rejected by the electorate, affirmative action attempts to achieve the redistributive and anti-capitalist purposes of contemporary liberalism by other means. Instead of promising liberty through social welfare and security, it promises substantial racial equality. To carry out its promise, it attacks individual liberty. Describing the obstacles to a policy of more far-reaching equality of result, Judge Damon J. Keith expresses the essential spirit of affirmative action when he critically observes: "Despite the progress of the past two decades, an entrenched belief in the sanctity of individual rights remains. Our courts have time and again explicitly or implicitly shied away from 'intruding' too far into the rights of private individuals."[96]

Affirmative action requires ever-expanding government regulation if the new American dilemma perceived by radical egalitarians—the unwillingness of democratic majorities to adopt measures necessary to achieve equality of condition for racial minorities—is to be resolved. Ultimately, then, the struggle to define American equality will determine whether the United States will remain a free society.

Notes

Introduction

1. "Civil Rights Forces Will Press Agenda," *Washington Times*, December 27, 1989, p. A3.
2. Eleanor Holmes Norton, "At Liberty," *Constitution*, vol. 1 (Fall 1989), p. 19; "Affirmative Action" (editorial), *Black Enterprise*, vol. 20 (September 1989), p. 42.
3. Robert Bork, "The Supreme Court and Civil Rights," *Wall Street Journal*, June 30, 1989, p. 12.
4. Bruce Fein and William Bradford Reynolds, "Putting Civil Rights on a Fair Course," *Legal Times*, June 19, 1989, p. 18.
5. *International Brotherhood of Teamsters v. U.S.*, 431 U.S. 324 (1977) at 372.
6. Norton, "At Liberty," p. 19.
7. Norman C. Amaker, *The Reagan Administration and Civil Rights* (Washington: Urban Institute Press, 1988), p. 157.
8. Ralph K. Winter, Jr., "Improving the Economic Status of Negroes Through Laws Against Discrimination: A Reply to Professor Sovern," *University of Chicago Law Review*, vol. 34 (Summer 1967), p. 847.
9. Alfred W. Blumrosen, "The Crossroads for Equal Employment Opportunity: Incisive Administration or Indecisive Bureaucracy?", *Notre Dame Law Review*, vol. 49 (October 1973), p. 9.
10. Norton, "At Liberty," p. 19.
11. V. Jon Bentz, "Comments on Papers Concerning Fairness in Employment Testing," *Journal of Vocational Behavior*, vol. 33 (December 1988), p. 396.
12. William J. Kilberg, "Title VII and the Supreme Court: Sowing the Seeds of a Profound Division," *Employee Relations Law Journal*, vol. 15 (Spring 1989), p. 3.

Chapter 1

1. Alex Elson and Leonard Schanfield, "Local Regulation of Discriminatory Employment Practices," *Yale Law Journal*, vol. 56 (February 1947), p. 431.
2. Lincoln Allison, *Right Principles: A Conservative Philosophy of Politics* (Oxford: Basil Blackwell, 1984), pp. 78-84; Douglas Rae, et. al., *Equalities* (Cambridge: Harvard University Press, 1981), pp. 65-73.

3. Jack Greenberg, "Race Relations and Group Interests in the Law," *Rutgers Law Review*, vol. 13 (Spring 1959), pp. 503-10.
4. *The Federalist*, ed. Edward Mead Earle (New York: Random House, 1938), p. 55.
5. Allison, *Right Principles*, p. 78.
6. The pertinent statutes are the Civil Rights Act of 1866, which was reenacted in the Enforcement Act of 1870 and is codified as 42 U.S.C. secs. 1981 and 1982; and the Civil Rights Act of 1871, codified as 42 U.S.C. secs. 1983 and 1985.
7. Eric Foner, *Reconstruction: America's Unfinished Revolution, 1863-1877* (New York: Harper and Row, 1988), pp. 77-175.
8. Public employers also discriminated, but this was arguably a violation of a right of equal employment opportunity under the Fourteenth Amendment that was recognized as early as 1880. In practice, of course, the right was consistently denied as states adopted policies of racial segregation and discrimination. Pauli Murray, "The Right to Equal Opportunity in Employment," *California Law Review*, vol. 33 (September 1945), pp. 391-92.
9. Quoted in Note, "Ives-Quinn Act—The Law Against Discrimination," *St. John's Law Review*, vol. 19 (April 1945), p. 171n.
10. Murray, "The Right to Equal Opportunity in Employment," pp. 388-89.
11. Paul H. Norgren and Samuel E. Hill, *Toward Fair Employment* (New York: Columbia University Press, 1964), pp. 205, 214; Herbert Hill, *Black Labor and the American Legal System* (Washington: Bureau of National Affairs, 1977), pp. 16-27, 173-74.
12. Norgren and Hill, *Toward Fair Employment*, pp. 205-7; Hill, *Black Labor and the American Legal System*, p. 40.
13. Michael I. Sovern, *Legal Restraints on Racial Discrimination in Employment* (New York: Columbia University Press, 1966), pp. 10-17; Hugh Davis Graham, *The Civil Rights Era: Origins and Development of National Policy* (New York: Oxford University Press, 1990), pp. 9-14.
14. Arthur E. Bonfield, "The Origin and Development of American Fair Employment Legislation," *Iowa Law Review*, vol. 52 (June 1967), pp. 1072-73; Michael I. Sovern, *Legal Restraints on Racial Discrimination in Employment* (New York: Columbia University Press, 1966), pp. 25-26.
15. *Engineering News-Record*, February 25, 1960, p. 116; March 17, 1960, p. 101; March 24, 1960, p. 330; April 21, 1960, p. 145; October 6, 1960, p. 106.
16. Note, "An American Legal Dilemma—Proof of Discrimination," *University of Chicago Law Review*, vol. 17 (Autumn 1949), pp. 107-25; Sovern, *Legal Restraints on Racial Discrimination*, p. 43.
17. This statement refers to voting rights before the rise of affirmative action and the elusive concept of vote dilution, in contrast to vote denial.
18. Note, "An American Legal Dilemma," p. 123; Norgren and Hill, *Toward Fair Employment*, p. 18; Irving Kovarsky, "Racial Discrimination in Employment and the Federal Law," *Oregon Law Review*, vol. 38 (December 1958), p. 60.
19. In *Hughes v. Superior Court of California*, 339 U.S. 460 (1950), the Supreme Court upheld a state court decision denying Negroes the right to picket in order to force an employer to establish a quota hiring system.
20. Note, "An American Legal Dilemma," pp. 111-23; Sovern, *Legal Restraints on Racial Discrimination*, pp. 41-43.

21. Sovern, *Legal Restraints on Racial Discrimination*, p. 124; Note, "An American Legal Dilemma," pp. 14, 31; Elson and Schanfield, "Local Regulation of Discriminatory Employment Practices," p. 447.
22. For example, Justice Blackmun, approving quotas in *United Steelworkers of America v. Weber*, said affirmative action was necessary to take into account "additional considerations, practical and equitable, only partially perceived, if perceived at all by the 88th Congress." 443 U.S. 193 (1979) at 209.
23. 3 CFR 1959-1963 Comp., pp. 448-54.
24. Under the National Labor Relations Act of 1935, the National Labor Relations Board was authorized to order an employer guilty of engaging in an unfair labor practice to cease and desist from the practice "and to take such affirmative action including reinstatement of employees with or without back pay, as will effectuate the policies of this Act." *U.S. Statutes at Large*, vol. 61, p. 147. The term was also used to described remedial measures that might be ordered in an employment discrimination suit, as well as voluntary measures by private employers to hire blacks. Note, "An American Legal Dilemma," p. 120; Elmer A. Carter, "Practical Considerations of Anti-discrimination Legislation under the New York Law Against Discrimination," *Cornell Law Quarterly*, vol. 40 (Fall 1964), p. 44; Note, "Civil Rights—Minnesota Fair Employment Practice Act—Supervision as Affirmative Action," *Minnesota Law Review*, vol. 42 (May 1958), pp. 1163-68.
25. John A. Wettergreen, "The Origins of Affirmative Action," unpublished ms., p. 6; Carl Brauer, *John F. Kennedy and the Second Reconstruction* (New York: Columbia University Press, 1978), pp. 147-50; Harris Wofford, *Of Kennedys and Kings: Making Sense of the Sixties* (New York: Farrar, Straus, Giroux, 1980), p. 142.
26. *Report to the President by the President's Committee on Equal Employment Opportunity* (Washington: 1963), pp. 5-6, 13-14, 28, 133-35.
27. William L. Taylor, Paper Presented to the International Conference on Public Personnel Administration, October 21, 1963, pp. 5-8. Leadership Conference on Civil Rights Collection, Manuscripts Division, Library of Congress.
28. 29 CFR 30.4(b)(1).
29. House Committee on Education and Labor, Hearings on Equal Employment Opportunity, 87th Cong., 1 sess., 1961, p. 190.
30. August Meier and Elliott Rudwick, *CORE: A Study in the Civil Rights Movement 1942-1968* (New York: Oxford, 1973), pp. 191-192, 232-235; Senate Committee on Labor and Public Welfare, Hearings on Equal Employment Opportunity, 88th Cong., 1 sess., 1963, pp. 204-205, 221-225; House Committee on the Judiciary, Hearings on Civil Rights, Subcommittee No. 5, 88th Cong., 1 sess., 1963, pt. III, p. 2239.
31. Joseph B. Robison, "Giving Reality to the Promise of Job Equality," *Law in Transition Quarterly*, vol. 1 (Spring 1964), pp. 105-17; Herbert Hill, "Twenty Years of State Fair Employment Practice Commissions: A Critical Analysis with Recommendations," *Buffalo Law Review*, vol. 14 (1964-65), pp. 22-69.
32. John Perry, "Business—Next Target for Integration?", *Harvard Business Review*, vol. 41 (March 1963), pp. 104-15; Charles Silberman, "The Businessman and the Negro," *Fortune*, September 1963, pp. 97-99; Stephen

Habbe, "Hiring Negro Workers," *The Conference Board*, vol. 1 (June 1964), pp. 16-19; Robert McKersie, "The Civil Rights Movement and Employment," *Industrial Relations*, vol. 3 (May 1964), pp. 1-21.

33. *New York Times*, July 18, 1963, editorial, p. 26; *U.S. News and World Report*, February 17, 1964, pp. 85-86; "Is Equality Unfair?", *America*, October 12, 1963, pp. 412-13; George Kelley, "Rights, Not Ratios," *America*, October 12, 1963, pp. 424-25.

34. Brauer, *John F. Kennedy and the Second Reconstruction*, p. 285.

35. Senate Committee on Labor and Public Welfare, Hearings on Equal Employment Opportunity, 88th Cong., 1 sess., 1963, pp. 73-74, 94, 137, 145.

36. Discrimination on account of sex was added in a floor amendment by Representative Howard Smith of Virginia in an attempt to make the bill unacceptably radical.

37. *Cong. Rec.*, 88th Cong., 2 sess., 1964, pp. 14191, 7207, 6549, 13899-900, 14225, 14239.

38. *ibid.*, pp. 22560, 2571, 2576, 2605, 8500.

39. *ibid.*, pp. 1518, 1540, 1547, 1600, 2560, 5863, 6000, 6001, 7204, 7213.

40. *ibid.*, p. 5808.

41. In 1990, after years of judicial interpretation of the evidentiary requirements of Title VII to require quotas to avoid liability, supporters of affirmative action continued to employ this logic in denying any intent to establish quotas. See the bill to amend Title VII, H.R. 3455, sec. 3, October 12, 1989, 101st Cong., 1 sess.

42. *White House Conference on Equal Employment Opportunity* (Washington: Equal Employment Opportunity Commission, 1965).

43. Herman Edelsberg, "Title VII of the Civil Rights Act: The First Year," *New York University Conference on Labor*, vol. 19 (1967), pp. 289-95; *Equal Employment Opportunity Commission First Annual Report* (Washington, 1967), pp. 7, 22; Herman Edelsberg to Herbert Hill, April 1, 1966, NAACP Papers, Group III, Series B, Box 333, Manuscripts Division, Library of Congress; Equal Employment Opportunity Commission, Utilities Industry Hearing, 1968, pp. 73-74.

44. Richard K. Berg, "Equal Employment Opportunity: Procedure under Title VII of the Civil Rights Act of 1964," *Illinois Bar Journal*, vol. 55 (April 1967), pp. 646-53; Cornelius J. Peck, "The Equal Employment Opportunity Commission: Developments in the Administrative Process 1965-1975," *Rutgers University Law School Symposium on EEOC*, vol. 2 (1975), Section II, p. 4.

45. Stephen Habbe, "Goals in Negro Employment," *The Conference Board Record*, vol. 2 (December 1965), p. 53; "The Unfinished Business of Negro Jobs," *Business Week*, June 12, 1965, pp. 84-87; Van H. Viot, "The Corporation and Title VII," *The Conference Board Record*, vol. 3 (April 1966), p. 16.

46. House Committee on Appropriations, Hearings, 90th Cong., 2 sess., 1968, pt. I, p. 880.

47. Richard P. Nathan, *Jobs and Civil Rights: The Role of the Federal Government in Promoting Equal Opportunity in Employment and Training*, reprinted in Senate Committee on the Judiciary, Hearings on Equal Employment Opportunity Procedures, 91st Cong., 1 sess., 1969, p. 288.

48. Although the legal relationship between Title VII and the executive order program remains unclear to this day, contract officials and employers assumed that the ban on preferential treatment applied to affirmative action in contract compliance.

49. House Committee on Appropriations, Hearings, 90th Cong., 2 sess., 1968, Pt. I, pp. 896-97; Nathan, *Jobs and Civil Rights*, in Senate Judiciary Committee EEO Hearings, 1969, pp. 288-89.

50. Alfred A. Gray, "Responsiveness v. Responsibility: Policy and Practice in Government Contracts," *Public Contract Law Journal*, vol. 7 (October 1974), p. 48.

51. Senate Committee on the Judiciary, Hearings on Equal Employment Opportunity Procedures, 91st Cong., 1 sess., 1969, pp. 27-31.

52. Philadelphia Federal Executive Board, Philadelphia Pre-award Plan, October 27, 1967, General Accounting Office, Philadelphia Plan File.

53. Nathan, *Jobs and Civil Rights*, in Senate Judiciary Committee EEO Hearings, 1969, p. 296.

54. *Decisions of the Comptroller General of the United States*, vol. 47 (Washington: GPO, 1969), pp. 666-70, vol. 48 (Washington: GPO, 1970), pp. 326-29.

55. *Cong. Rec.*, 90th Cong., 2 sess., 1968, p. 19506; Senate Committee on Public Works, Hearings on Equal Employment Opportunity, 90th Cong., 2 sess., 1969, pp. 115, 213-14, 223-31, 181, 286.

56. Lino A. Graglia, *Disaster by Decree: The Supreme Court Decisions on Race and the Schools* (Ithaca: Cornell University Press, 1976), pp. 46-66.

57. Abigail M. Thernstrom, *Whose Votes Count? Affirmative Action and Minority Rights* (Cambridge: Harvard University Press, 1987), pp. 1-30.

58. Stephen E. Ambrose, *Nixon: The Education of a Politician 1913-1962* (New York: Simon and Schuster, 1987), pp. 395-96, 396n., 434.

59. Senate Committee on the Judiciary, Hearings on Equal Employment Opportunity Procedures, 91st Cong., 1 sess., 1969, p. 193.

60. Comptroller General Staats to Secretary of Health, Education and Welfare, February 25, 1969, General Accounting Office, Philadelphia Plan File.

61. Revised Philadelphia Plan, Department of Labor Memorandum,, June 27, 1969, Senate Committee on the Judiciary, Hearings on the Philadelphia Plan, 91st Cong., 1 sess., 1969, pp. 26-28.

62. *Decisions of the Comptroller General*, vol. 49 (Washington: GPO, 1971), pp. 59-71.

63. *Opinions of the Attorneys General of the United States*, vol. 42 (Washington: GPO, 1975), pp. 405-16.

64. John D. Ehrlichman, Notes of Meetings with the President, Box 3, Nixon Papers, National Archives; *Cong. Rec.*, 91st Cong., 1 sess., 1969, p. 40749.

65. Comptroller General Staats to Newbold Noyes, January 8, 1970, Comptroller General Staats to Robert C. Byrd, December 24, 1969, General Accounting Office, Philadelphia Plan File.

66. *Engineering News-Record*, January 1, 1970, p. 12.

67. Robert J. Brown, Comments on Chairman Hampton's Report to the President, Ex Hu-2-2, Box 17, Nixon Papers, National Archives.

68. Wettergreen, "Origins of Affirmative Action," pp. 13-16.

69. Stanley R. Krakower, "The Constitutionality of 'Affirmative Action' to Integrate Construction Trades: The Philadelphia Plan," *Temple Law*

Quarterly, vol. 43 (Summer 1970), p. 338; Robert P. Schuwerk, "The Philadelphia Plan: A Study in the Dynamics of Executive Power," *University of Chicago Law Review*, vol. 39 (Summer 1972), p. 749.

70. *Eastern Contractors Association v. Secretary of Labor*, 311F. Supp. 1002 (1970).

Chapter 2

1. *U.S. v. Louisiana*, 380 U.S. 145 (1965) at 154.
2. EEOC was given enforcement authority in the sense of being charged with bringing about equal employment opportunity by receiving complaints and conciliating disputes. It had no rulemaking or adjudicatory power, however, and its interpretations of Title VII were opinions with no legally binding force.
3. *Hall v. Werthen Bag Co.*, 251 F. Supp. 184 (1966).
4. Alfred W. Blumrosen, "The Law Transmission System and the Southern Jurisprudence of Employment Discrimination," *Industrial Relations Law Journal*, vol. 6 (1984), pp. 313-52.
5. Alfred W. Blumrosen, *Black Employment and the Law* (New Brunswick: Rutgers University Press, 1971), pp. vii-x.
6. Section 706(g) states that judicial relief may be awarded when the court finds the respondent "has intentionally engaged in or is intentionally engaging in an unlawful employment practice."
7. Robert J. Affeldt, "Title VII of the Civil Rights Act of 1964: A Decade of Private Enforcement and Judicial Developments," *St. Louis University Law Journal*, vol. 20 (1975-76), pp. 225-307; Carl Rachlin, "Title VII: Limitations and Qualifications," *Boston College Industrial and Commercial Law Review*, vol. 7 (Spring 1966), pp. 480, 486-88; Blumrosen, *Black Employment and the Law*, p. 34; Sanford Jay Rosen, Book Review, *Harvard Law Review*, vol. 81 (November 1967), pp. 277-78.
8. William B. Gould, "Employment Security, Seniority and Race: The Role of Title VII of the Civil Rights Act of 1964," *Howard Law Journal*, vol. 13 (Winter 1967), pp. 1-50; Note, "Title VII, Seniority Discrimination and the Incumbent Negro," *Harvard Law Review*, vol. 80 (April 1967), pp. 1260-83; George Cooper and Richard B. Sobol, "Seniority and Testing Under Fair Employment Laws: A General Approach to Objective Criteria of Hiring and Promotion," *Harvard Law Review*, vol. 82 (May 1969), pp. 1598-1679.
9. *Quarles v. Philip Morris Inc.*, 279 F. Supp. 505 (1968) at 515-16.
10. Nathaniel R. Jones, "The Justification for Race-Conscious Remedies," *Harvard Journal of Law and Public Policy*, vol. 9 (Winter 1986), p. 72. The present effects doctrine was upheld in *Local 189 United Papermakers and Crown Zellerbach v. U.S.*, 416 F. 2d 980 (1969) and *U.S. v. Local 53 of International Association of Heat and Frost Insulators and Asbestos Workers v. Vogler*, 407 F. 2d 1047 (1969).
11. *Opinions of the Attorneys Generals of the United States*, vol. 42 (Washington: GPO, 1975), p. 411.
12. *Hicks v. Crown Zellerbach Corp.*, 319 F. Supp. 314 (1970). See also *Arrington v. Massachusetts Bay Transportation Authority*, 306 F. Supp. 1355 (1968) and *Penn v. Stumpf*, 308 F. Supp. 1238 (1970).

13. Robert Belton, "Discrimination and Affirmative Action: An Analysis of Competing Theories of Equality and *Weber*," *North Carolina Law Review*, vol. 59 (March 1981), p. 547.
14. *U.S. v. Sheet Metal Workers International Association No. 36*, 280 F. Supp. 719 (1968) at 728; *Dobbins v. I.B.E.W. Local 212*, 292 F. Supp. 413 (1968) at 444.
15. *Vogler v. Local 53*, 407 F. 2d 1051 (1969).
16. *U.S. v. I.B.E.W. Local No. 38*, 428 F. 2d 144 (1970) at 148-50.
17. Alfred W. Blumrosen, *Black Employment and the Law* (New Brunswick: Rutgers University Press, 1971), pp. 252-53.
18. U. S. Supreme Court, No. 124, 71-124, Oral Argument, *Griggs v. Duke Power Co.*, December 14, 1970, pp. 15, 26-27. Although in the district court the plaintiffs lost, they prevailed in the Fourth Circuit to the extent that six of the plaintiffs were found to have suffered unlawfully the present effects of past discrimination.
19. 401 U.S. 430 (1971) at 431-32.
20. *ibid.*
21. *ibid.*, p. 433.
22. *ibid.*, pp. 430-31, 436.
23. Interview with N. Thompson Powers, September 17, 1985. Alfred W. Blumrosen entitled his analysis of the decision: "Strangers in Paradise: *Griggs v. Duke Power Co.* and the Concept of Employment Discrimination," *Michigan Law Review*, vol. 71 (November 1972), pp. 59-110. Federal officials in EEOC and the Department of Justice considered *Griggs* a weak case and advised against obtaining a writ of certiorari. They noted the lack of evidence of actual disparate impact in the workplace and the fact that the company's tests were recommended by a professional psychologist and were widely used in industry. The NAACP Legal Defense Fund, Inc. weighed these factors against its interest in promoting "an institutional programmatic development of Title VII law," and decided to appeal the decision against the advice of its allies in the civil rights bureaucracy. Robert Belton, "A Comparative Review of Public and Private Enforcement of Title VII of the Civil Rights Act of 1964," *Vanderbilt Law Review*, vol. 31 (May 1978), pp. 937-43; Hugh Davis Graham, *The Civil Rights Era: Origins and Developments of National Policy* (New York: Oxford, 1990), p. 385.
24. Michael Evan Gold, "*Griggs'* Folly: An Essay on the Theory, Problems, and Origin of the Adverse Impact Definition of Employment Discrimination and a Recommendation for Reform," *Industrial Relations Law Journal*, vol. 7 (1985), p. 479.
25. James E. Jones, Jr., "The Development of the Law under Title VII Since 1965: Implications of the New Law," *Rutgers Law Review*, vol. 30 (Winter 1976-77), p. 2.
26. The case, *Gaston County v. U.S.*, 395 U.S. 285 (1969), concerned a literacy test that was struck down as indirectly abridging the right to vote because of race. The Court reasoned that although there was no intentional discrimination, the test in effect discriminated because inferior public education prevented blacks from acquiring the skills needed to pass the test. The opinion thus invoked a societal discrimination rationale.
27. Belton, "A Decade of Private Enforcement," p. 245; Hugh Steven Wilson, "A Second Look at *Griggs v. Duke Power Co.*: Ruminations on Job Testing,

Discrimination, and the Role of the Federal Courts," *Virginia Law Review*, vol. 58 (1972), pp. 844-74; Note, "Business Necessity under Title VII of the Civil Rights Act of 1964: A No-Alternative Approach," *Yale Law Journal*, vol. 84 (November 1974), p. 98.

28. See Chapter One.

29. Gold, "*Griggs*' Folly," p. 512.

30. Charles A. Sullivan, Michael J. Zimmer, and Richard F. Richards, *Federal Statutory Law of Employment Discrimination* (Indianapolis: Michie Co., 1980), p. 6.

31. *Carter v. Gallagher*, 452 F. 2d 315 (1971) at 324-25.

32. *ibid.*, pp. 329-30.

33. *Rios v. Enterprise Association Steamfitters Local 638*, 501 F. 2d 622 (1974) at 630-31.

34. *Castro v. Beecher*, 459 F. 2d 725 (1972) at 736.

35. See the discussion of this issue in Justice Scalia's dissenting opinion in *Johnson v. Transportation Agency, Santa Clara County*, 480 U.S. 616 (1987).

36. This was accomplished in the Equal Employment Opportunity Act of 1972. Congress exempted itself from the coverage of civil rights laws as a requirement of the separation of powers, to prevent the executive and judicial branches from encroaching on legislative prerogatives.

37. See, for example, *Chance v. Board of Examiners*, 458 F. 2d 1167 (1972) and *Bridgeport Guardians Inc. v. Members of the Bridgeport Civil Service Commission*, 354 F. Supp. 778 (1973).

38. *Morrow v. Crisler*, 491 F. 2d 1053 (1974) at 1057.

39. *NAACP v. Allen*, 493 F. 2d 614 (1974) at 621.

40. *Carter v. Gallagher*, 452 F. 2d 315 (1971); *Pennsylvania v. O'Neill*, 473 F. 2d 1029 (1973); *U.S. v. N.L. Industries Inc.*, 479 F. 2d 354 (1973); *Anderson v. San Francisco Unified School District*, 357 F. Supp. 248 (1972); *Harper v. Mayor and Council of Baltimore*, 359 F. Supp. 1187 (1973); *Harper v. Kloster*, 486 F. 2d 1134 (1973); *Kirkland v. New York State Department of Correctional Services*, 520 F. 2d 420 (1975).

41. *EEOC v. Local 638*, 532 F. 2d 821 (1976) at 828.

42. *ibid.*, p. 827.

43. *McDonnell Douglas Corp. v. Green*, 411 U.S. 792 (1973).

44. *Albemarle Paper Co. v. Moody*, 422 U.S. 405 (1975) at 421.

45. Based on the remedial principle of complete relief to the victim of discrimination, the special circumstances rule stopped short of categorically requiring back pay. It held that only under special circumstances, which were defined as not including or referring to good-faith compliance efforts of employers, would back pay not be awarded. In contrast, the equitable rule, as it was described in some circuits, tried to balance both sides of an employment discrimination suit, but placed special emphasis on fairness to the employer by taking into account good-faith compliance as a defense. Note, "Discrimination in Employment—Remedies—Standards for Violations of Title VII of the Civil Rights Act of 1964," *Cornell Law Review*, vol. 61 (March 1976), pp. 465-77.

46. Thaddeus Holt, "A View from *Albemarle*," *Personnel Psychology*, vol. 30 (Spring 1977), p. 67.

47. *Franks v. Bowman Transportation Company*, 424 U.S. 747 (1975) at 774-79.

48. *ibid.*, pp. 781, 791, 793.
49. William B. Gould, *Black Workers in White Unions: Job Discrimination in the United States* (Ithaca: Cornell University Press, 1977), p. 81.
50. Civil rights advocates in the early 1970s used adverse impact theory to challenge facially neutral laws that allegedly discriminated against minorities with respect to public services, housing, and employment. Robert G. Schwem, "From *Washington* to *Arlington Heights* and Beyond: Discriminatory Purpose in Equal Protection Litigation," *University of Illinois Law Forum*, vol. 1977, pp. 972-86.
51. *Washington v. Davis*, 426 U.S. 299 (1976) at 239-47.
52. See *Heart of Atlanta Motel v. U.S.*, 379 U.S. 241 (1964).
53. Abigail M. Thernstrom, *Whose Votes Count? Affirmative Action and Minority Voting Rights* (Cambridge: Harvard University Press, 1987), pp. 1-30.
54. Lino Graglia, *Disaster by Decree: The Supreme Court Decisions on Race and the Schools* (Ithaca: Cornell University Press, 1976).
55. Richard A. Posner, "The *DeFunis* Case and the Constitutionality of Preferential Treatment of Minorities," *Supreme Court Review*, vol. 1974, pp. 19-26.
56. Martin Slate, "Preferential Relief in Employment Discrimination Cases," *Loyola University Law Journal*, vol. 5 (Summer 1974), p. 315.
57. Alfred W. Blumrosen, "Quotas, Common Sense, and Law in Labor Relations: Three Dimensions of Equal Opportunity," *Rutgers Law Journal*, vol. 27 (Winter 1973-74), pp. 676-77.
58. Ellen Joseph, "Last Hired, First Fired Seniority, Layoffs, and Title VII: Questions of Liability and Remedy," *Columbia Journal of Law and Social Problems*, vol. 11 (Spring 1975), pp. 394-95; George P. Sape, "The Use of Numerical Quotas to Achieve Integration in Employment," *William and Mary Law Review*, vol. 16 (Spring 1975), pp. 481-506; Harry T. Edwards and Barry L. Zaretsky, "Preferential Remedies for Employment Discrimination," *Michigan Law Review*, vol. 74 (November 1975), pp. 1-13.
59. Slate, "Preferential Relief," pp. 321-22.
60. Michael J. Zimmer, Charles A. Sullivan, and Richard F. Richards, *Cases and Materials on Employment Discrimination* (Boston: Michie, 1982), p. 3.
61. Alexandra Wigdor, "Psychological Testing and the Law of Employment Discrimination," eds. Alexandra Wigdor and Wendell R. Garner, *Ability Testing: Uses, Consequences, and Controversies* (Washington: National Academy Press, 1982), p. 68.
62. Slate, "Preferential Relief," p. 348.
63. Gould, *Black Workers in White Unions*, p. 117.

Chapter 3

1. Edward J. Erler, "Sowing the Wind: Judicial Oligarchy and the Legacy of *Brown v. Board of Education*," *Harvard Journal of Law and Public Policy*, vol. 8 (Spring 1985), pp. 424-25.
2. House Committee on Education and Labor, Hearings on Equal Employment Opportunity Procedures, 91st Cong., 2 sess., 1970, p. 137.

3. Senate Committee on Labor and Public Welfare, Report No. 91-1137, 91st cong., 2 sess., 1970, p. 4.
4. House Education and Labor Committee Hearings on Equal Employment Opportunity, 1970, p. 107.
5. Senate Committee on Labor and Public Welfare, Hearings on Equal Employment Opportunity Enforcement Act S. 2453, 91st Cong., 2 sess., 1970, pp. 81, 87.
6. Mary T. Matthies, "Equal Employment Opportunity and the Business Community," *Journal of Contemporary Business*, vol. 2 (Summer 1973), p. 3.
7. House Education and Labor Committee Hearings on Equal Employment Opportunity, 1970, pp. 173-74; Senator Labor and Public Welfare Committee Hearings on S. 2453, 1970, p. 176.
8. House Education and Labor Committee Hearings on Equal Employment Opportunity, 1970, p. 116.
9. *ibid.*, pp. 35-36.
10. House Committee on Education and Labor, Hearings on Equal Employment Opportunity Enforcement Procedures, 92nd Cong., 1 sess., 1971, pp. 118, 304-306.
11. *ibid.*, pp. 68, 72; *Cong. Rec.*, 92nd Cong., 1 sess., 1971, pp. 31783, 31971, 31975, 31979.
12. Senate Committee on Labor and Public Welfare, Hearings on Equal Employment Opportunity Enforcement Act S. 2515, 92nd Cong., 1 sess., 1971, pp. 75-91.
13. *Cong. Rec.*, 92nd Cong., 1 sess., 1971, pp. 31970, 31973.
14. *ibid.*, p. 31979.
15. *ibid.*, pp. 32090, 32091, 32099, 32100.
16. *ibid.*, pp. 32111, 32113.
17. Senate Labor and Public Welfare Committee Hearings on S. 2515, 1971, pp. 346-347; Gerald R. Rosen, "Industry's New Watchdog in Washington," *Dun's Review*, vol. 103 (June 1974), pp. 83-85.
18. *Wall Street Journal*, September 15, 1971, quoted in Senate Labor and Public Welfare Committee Hearings on S. 2515, pp. 391-92.
19. *New York Times*, January 25, 1972, p. 34.
20. *Cong. Rec.*, 92nd Cong., 1 sess., 1972, p. 3979.
21. *ibid.*, pp. 6643-46.
22. *ibid.*, pp. 1661, 4917-18.
23. Katherine J. Thomson, "The Disparate Impact Theory: Congressional Intent in 1972—A Response to Gold," *Industrial Relations Law Journal*, vol. 8 (1986), pp. 105-16.
24. Michael S. Gold, "Reply to Thomson," *Industrial Relations Law Journal*, vol. 8 (1986), pp. 117-18; Note, "Business Necessity under Title VII of the Civil Rights Act of 1964," *Yale Law Journal*, vol. 84 (November 1974), p. 105.
25. Matthies, "Equal Employment Opportunity," p. 6.
26. William H. Brown III, "The Light at the Top of the Stairs: The Equal Employment Opportunity Act of 1972," *Personnel Administration*, vol. 35 (May-June 1972), p. 67.
27. Phyllis A. Wallace, "Employment Discrimination: Some Policy Considerations," eds. Orley Ashenfelter and Albert Rees, *Discrimination in Labor Markets* (Princeton: Princeton University Press, 1973), pp. 171-74.

28. Alfred W. Blumrosen, "The Crossroads for Equal Employment Opportunity: Incisive Administration or Indecisive Bureaucracy?", *Notre Dame Law Review*, vol. 49 (October 1973), pp. 46-62.

29. Dale L. Hiestand, "Comment on Wallace," in Ashenfelter and Rees, eds., *Discrimination in Labor Markets*, pp. 176-177.

30. *ibid.*, p. 180.

31. Nijole V. Benokraitis and Joe R. Feagin, *Affirmative Action and Equal Opportunity: Action, Inaction, Reaction* (Boulder: Westview Press, 1978), p. 17.

32. Phyllis A. Wallace, ed., *Equal Employment Opportunity and the A.T. & T. Case* (Cambridge: MIT Press, 1976), pp. 247-53.

33. "A.T. & T. Defends Record," *Public Utilities Fortnightly*, August 31, 1972, p. 34.

34. *U.S. News and World Report*, August 14, 1972, p. 66.

35. Wallace, ed., *Equal Employment Opportunity*, pp. 247-61.

36. *ibid.*, pp. 273-74, 277.

37. Theodore V. Purcell, S.J., "Management and Affirmative Action in the Late Seventies," in *Equal Rights and Industrial Relations* (Madison: Industrial Relations Research Association, 1977), p. 73; *U. S. News and World Report*, June 18, 1973, p. 88, October 8, 1973, p. 104; Lester A. Sobel, ed., *Quotas and Affirmative Action* (New York: Facts on File, 1980), pp. 106-7; Rosen, "Industry's New Watchdog," p. 83; Wallace, ed., *Equal Employment Opportunity*, p. 278.

38. Antonia Handler Chayes, "Make Your Equal Opportunity Program Court-Proof," *Harvard Business Review*, vol. 52 (September-October 1974), p. 81.

39. Rosen, "Industry's New Watchdog," pp. 83-84; Purcell, "Management and Affirmative Action," p. 90; *U.S. News and World Report*, June 18, 1973, p. 89.

40. *U.S. News and World Report*, June 18, 1973, p. 89; Rosen, "Industry's New Watchdog," pp. 83-84; *Air Conditioning, Heating, and Refrigeration News*, April 30, 1973; p. 17; Purcell, "Management and Affirmative Action," p. 89.

41. Purcell, "Management and Affirmative Action," p. 90.

42. *ibid.*, pp. 87-88; Rosen, "Industry's New Watchdog," pp. 83-85; *U.S. News and World Report*, June 18, 1973, p. 88.

43. John W. Kingsbury, "Business Realities and the Law," *The Conference Board*, vol. 10 (August 1973), pp. 55-57; "A.T. & T. Defends Record," *Public Utilities Fortnightly*, August 31, 1972, p. 34.

44. Rosen, "Industry's New Watchdog," pp. 83, 85.

45. Alfred W. Blumrosen, a labor lawyer who served the EEOC as a staff member or consultant from 1965 to 1968, described the regulatory process that produced affirmative action rules as a triumph of administrative ingenuity that was deliberately aimed at promoting the interests of the beneficiaries of Title VII while technically complying with the terms of the statute. Blumrosen acknowledged that EEOC regulations such as guidelines on testing were not dictated by statutory language or legislative history, but rather were "the product of the judgment of the original commissioners acting in response to the views developed by [a] small group of lawyers." Decisions were made "in an atmosphere where the choice is free, where judgment is unencumbered by immediate political pressures or judicial

precedent, where administrators can be either creative or cautious, and where the larger forces of the bureaucracy and the courts will support their decisions, whatever they may be." Particularly revealing is Blumrosen's account of how he persuaded EEOC to adopt a national reporting system to gather statistics of the racially disparate impact of employment practices, against the plain meaning of Title VII and the Senate compromise of 1964 which were intended to prevent a national system of reports by precluding EEOC reporting requirements in northern states which had fair employment practices commissions. Blumrosen kept pushing for a national reporting system, and sought the advice and approval of Senator Dirksen of Illinois, the principal architect of the 1964 compromise on Title VII. Senator Dirksen, supposedly the leading defender of states' powers and as critic of EEOC expansion, was reported to be unconcerned with the proposed statutory construction of Title VII and had no objections. Alfred W. Blumrosen, *Black Employment and the Law* (New Brunswick: Rutgers University Press, 1971), pp. 52, 66, 73.

46. Memorandum from Colston A. Lewis to Chairman William H. Brown III, February 16, 1971, Equal Employment Opportunity Commission Papers; Rosen, "Industry's New Watchdog," p. 83.

Chapter 4

1. Hugh Davis Graham, *The Civil Rights Era: Origins and Development of National Policy* (New York: Oxford University Press, 1990), pp. 342-43.
2. 41 C.F.R. (1971) Sect. 60-2.10.
3. *ibid.*, Sect. 60-2.11 As issued in February 1970, Order No. 4 contained a ninth consideration: the anticipated expansion, contraction, and turnover of the work force. This was deleted from the regulations the following year. 41 C.F.R. (1972) Sect. 60-2.11.
4. *ibid.*, Sect. 60-2.11 (b).
5. *ibid.*
6. *ibid.*, Sect. 60-2.24(e).
7. *ibid.*, Sect. 60-2.13.
8. Daniel Seligman, "How 'Equal Opportunity' Turned into Employment Quotas," *Fortune*, vol. 87 (March 1973), p. 162.
9. Robert W. Glover and Ray Marshall, "The Responses of Unions in the Construction Industry to Anti-discrimination Efforts," in *Equal Rights and Industrial Relations* (Madison: Industrial Relations Research Association, 1977), pp. 131-34. Glover and Marshall said that no significant results were achieved because the Philadelphia plan was restricted to federally funded projects—allowing contractors to ignore the plan on privately funded projects—and because no provision was made for recruiting and training minority craftsmen.
10. *New York Times*, March 16, 1972, p. 46, letter to the editor from Herbert Hill.
11. Byron E. Shafer, *Quiet Revolution: The Struggle for the Democratic Party and the Shaping of Post-Reform Politics* (New York: Russell Sage, 1983),

pp. 161-206, 464-522; "What's New in EEO," *EEO Today*, vol. 3 (August 1976), p. 138.

12. John H. Bunzel, "The Politics of Quotas," *Change*, vol. 4 (October 1972), pp. 25, 30-35; Geoffrey Wagner, "The New Discrimination or, A Race by Any Other Name," *National Review*, September 1, 1972, p. 951; Irving Kristol, "How Hiring Quotas Came to the Campus," *Fortune*, vol. 90 (September 1974), pp. 203-7.

13. President Nixon, strongly opposed to judicial busing orders to achieve racial balance, persuaded Congress in June of 1972 to pass a temporary, limited measure restricting the use of busing as a desegregation device. See Lester A. Sobel, ed., *Quotas and Affirmative Action* (New York: Facts on File, 1980), pp. 89-94.

14. *Public Papers of the Presidents of the United States: Richard Nixon, 1972* (Washington: Government Printing Office, 1974), p. 59.

15. Timothy Bates, "Minority Business Set-Asides: Theory and Practice," in *Selected Topics in Employment and Business Set-Asides* (Washington: United States Commission on Civil Rights, 1985), vol. 1, p. 143.

16. Sobel, ed., *Quotas and Affirmative Action*, p. 104.

17. *Public Papers of the Presidents: Richard Nixon*, p. 850.

18. Sobel, ed., *Quotas and Affirmative Action*, p. 104; *Engineering News-Record*, August 31, 1972, p. 7.

19. *Engineering News-Record*, September 14, 1972, p. 17; *Air Conditioning, Heating, and Refrigeration News*, September 11, 1972, p. 1, October 9, 1972, p. 8; Sobel, ed., *Quotas and Affirmative Action*, pp. 104-5.

20. Seligman, "How 'Equal Opportunity' Turned into Employment Quotas," p. 160.

21. House Committee on Education and Labor, Oversight Hearings on Federal Enforcement of Equal Employment Opportunity Laws, 94th Cong., 1 sess., 1975, pt. I, pp. 121-29.

22. House Committee on Education and Labor, Oversight Hearing on OFCC Proposed Non-Construction Regulations, 94th Cong., 2 sess., 1976, p. 41.

23. *ibid.*, p. 28.

24. *ibid.*, pp. 30-31, 38, 44.

25. House Committee on Education and Labor, Oversight Hearings, 1975, p. 154; House Committee on Education and Labor, Oversight Hearings, 1976, pp. 48, 92, 94, 96.

26. House Committee on Education and Labor, Oversight Hearings, 1976, p. 123.

27. This meant the agency found the contractor to be deficient in respect of the equal employment opportunity component of his general qualifications, comparable to a declaration that he had inadequate capital or technological competence for performing the work required. See *ibid.*, pp. 116-17.

28. In 1974, the OFCC issued revised Order No. 4, requiring contractors to provide relief for members of affected classes who suffered the present effects of past discrimination. 41 C.F.R. (1974) Sect. 60-2.1.

29. House Committee on Education and Labor, Oversight Hearings, 1976, pp. 117, 119-21.

30. Kevin S. McGuiness, *Government Memoranda on Affirmative Action Programs: A Study of Compliance Agency Documents Affecting Non-*

Construction Federal Contractors (Washington: Equal Employment Advisory Council, 1976), pp. 37-38.

31. *ibid.*, pp. 42, 51, 53-54.
32. *ibid.*, pp. 60, 62-63.
33. *ibid.*, pp. 67-68.
34. Kenneth C. McGuiness, ed., *Preferential Treatment in Employment—Affirmative Action or Reverse Discrimination?* (Washington: Equal Employment Advisory Council, 1977), pp. 2, 38, 44.
35. *ibid.*, pp. 105-9.
36. Richard S. Barrett, "Gray Areas in Black and White Testing," *Harvard Business Review*, vol. 46 (January-February 1968), p. 95; *U.S. News and World Report*, February 12, 1968, p. 6, October 14, 1968, p. 85.
37. Joseph R. Goeke and Caroline S. Weymar, "Barriers to Hiring Blacks," *Harvard Business Review*, vol. 47 (September-October 1969), pp. 144-49.
38. Theodore V. Purcell, S.J., "Break Down Your Employment Barriers," *Harvard Business Review*, vol. 46 (July-August 1968), pp. 67-68.
39. *Promise Versus Performance: The Status of Equal Employment Opportunity in the Nation's Gas and Electric Utilities* (Washington: Equal Employment Opportunity Commission, 1972), pp. 18, 32; Theodore V. Purcell, S.J., "Case of the Borderline Black," *Harvard Business Review*, vol. 49 (November-December 1971), p. 148.
40. Theodore V. Purcell, S.J., et. al., "What are the Social Responsibilities for Psychologists in Industry? A Symposium," *Personnel Psychology*, vol. 27 (Autumn 1974), p. 436.
41. Theodore V. Purcell, S.J., "Management and Affirmative Action in the Late Seventies," in *Equal Rights and Industrial Relations* (Madison: Industrial Relations Research Association, 1977), pp. 95, 97-100.
42. Urban T. Kuechle, President of A.O. Smith Corp., to Secretary of Labor Shultz, March 30, 1970, RG 174, Box 71, WF-2, National Archives.
43. C. Paul Sparks, "Changing Perspectives on Non-discrimination," *The Conference Board Record*, vol. 10 (August 1973), pp. 46-48.
44. Oscar A. Ornati and Edward Giblin, "The High Cost of Discrimination," *Business Horizons*, vol. 18 (February 1975), p. 36; House Education and Labor Committee Oversight Hearings, 1976, pp. 326-27.
45. Lewis J. Ringler, "EEO Agreements and Consent Decrees May Be Booby-Traps!", *The Personnel Administrator*, vol. 22 (February 1977), pp. 16-21.
46. David W. Pearson, "OFCC and EEOC Demands—Guidelines to Frustration," *The Personnel Administrator*, vol. 18 (November 1973), pp. 22-23; Seligman, "How 'Equal Opportunity' Turned into Employment Quotas," p. 163; Berwyn N. Fraguer, "Affirmative Action Through Hiring and Promotion: How Fast a Rate?" *Personnel*, vol. 56 (November-December 1979), pp. 69-70.
47. Mary Green Miner and John B. Miner, *Employee Selection Within the Law* (Washington: Bureau of National Affairs, 1978), pp. 11-13.
48. Harold P. Hayes, *Realism in EEO* (New York: John Wiley, 1980), pp. 8-13.
49. Nijole V. Benokraitis and Joe R. Feagin, *Affirmative Action and Equal Opportunity: Action, Inaction, Reaction* (Boulder: Westview Press, 1978), p. 116.

50. Seligman, "How 'Equal Opportunity' Turned into Employment Quotas," p. 165; Pearson, "OFCC and EEOC Demands," p. 24.

Chapter 5

1. 29 C.F.R. Part 1607.
2. Phil Lyons, "An Agency with a Mind of Its Own: The EEOC's Guidelines on Employment Testing," *New Perspectives*, vol. 17 (Fall 1985), pp. 20-21; *U.S. News and World Report*, December 14, 1964, pp. 83-84.
3. Phil Lyons, "Racial Discrimination vs. Equal Employment Opportunity: The Development of the Uniform Guidelines on Employee Selection Procedures," unpublished ms., 1985, pp. 8-18.
4. Alexandra Wigdor, "Psychological Testing and the Law of Employment Discrimination," eds. Alexandra K. Wigdor and Wendell R. Garner, *Ability Testing: Uses, Consequences, and Controversies* (Washington: National Academy Press, 1982), pp. 61-62; Dale L. Hiestand, "Comment on Wallace," eds. Orley Ashenfelter and Albert Rees, *Discrimination in Labor Markets* (Princeton: Princeton University Press, 1973), pp. 179-80; John E. Hunter and Frank L. Schmidt, "Ability Tests: Economic Benefits Versus the Issue of Fairness," *Industrial Relations*, vol. 21 (Fall 1982), p. 293.
5. *Business Week*, February 13, 1965, pp. 45-46; *White House Conference on Equal Employment Opportunity* (Washington: Equal Employment Opportunity Commission, 1965), Panel 1, p. 32, Panel 2, pp. 25-32, Panel 3, p. 17, Panel 7, pp. 13, 17; Alfred W. Blumrosen, "Strangers in Paradise: *Griggs v. Duke Power Co.* and the Concept of Employment Discrimination," *Michigan Law Review*, vol. 71 (November 1972), pp. 59-60; House Committee on Education and Labor, Oversight Hearings on Federal Enforcement of Equal Employment Opportunity Laws, 94th Cong., 1 sess., 1975, pt. I, p. 275; Harold Mayfield, "Equal Employment Opportunity: Should Hiring Standards Be Relaxed?" *Personnel*, vol. 41 (September-October 1964), pp. 8-9.
6. Philip Ash, "The Implications of the Civil Rights Act of 1964 for Psychological Assessment in Industry," *American Psychologist*, vol. 21 (August 1966), pp. 799-800; John H. Metzler, "Testing—Under Labor Contracts and Law," *Personnel*, vol. 43 (July-August 1966), p. 43; Robert M. Guion, "Employment Tests and Discriminatory Hiring," *Industrial Relations*, vol. 5 (February 1966), pp. 30-32.
7. Floyd L. Ruch, "The Impact on Employment Procedures of the Supreme Court Decision in the Duke Power Case," *Personnel Journal*, vol. 50 (October 1971), pp. 79-80; Lyons, "Racial Discrimination vs. Equal Employment Opportunity," pp. 24-26.
8. "Symposium: The Industrial Psychologist: Selection and EEO," *Personnel Psychology*, vol. 19 (Spring 1966), pp. 10-11, 18, 30-31; Guion, "Employment Tests and Discriminatory Hiring," pp. 31-33; Richard S. Barrett, "Gray Areas in Black and White Testing," *Harvard Business Review*, vol. 46 (January-February 1968), p. 93.
9. Phyllis A. Wallace, et.al., *Testing of Minority Group Applicants for Employment* (Washington: EEOC Office of Research and Reports, 1966).

10. *Guidelines on Employment Testing Procedure* (Washington: Equal Employment Opportunity Commission, August 24, 1966), pp. 2-4. The guidelines reflected confusion on the issue of differential validity. At one point, they said the sample population used in validating a test should include representative numbers of the minority groups to which the tests would be applied, implying that blacks and whites formed a single group for validation purposes. The guidelines thus inconsistently referred both to including minorities in a validation study and conducting separate validity studies—that is, differential validity. William A. Gorham, "Political, Ethical, and Emotional Aspects of Federal Guidelines on Employee Selection Procedures," eds. W. Clay Hammer and Frank L. Schmidt, *Contemporary Problems in Personnel*, rev. ed. (Chicago: St. Clair Press, 1977), pp. 160-61.

11. Under the A.P.A. *Standards*, criterion, content, and construct validity were all considered equally reliable and applicable. The choice of which method to employ depended on what the test user was trying to find out about prospective employees.

12. Lyons, "Racial Discrimination vs. Equal Employment Opportunity," pp. 22-24; Wigdor, "Psychological Testing and the Law of Employment Discrimination," pp. 44, 46.

13. Betty R. Anderson and Martha P. Rogers, eds., *Personnel Testing and Equal Employment Opportunity* (Washington: Equal Employment Opportunity Commission, 1970), pp. 18-20, 28; Lyons, "Racial Discrimination vs. Equal Employment Opportunity," p. 31.

14. The guidelines were not published in accordance with the requirements of the Administrative Procedure Act of 1946, as their subsequent importance would seem to have warranted. Notice was not given, nor was opportunity for public comment. The EEOC's reason for not conforming to the act was that the guidelines were not a substantive interpretation of Title VII, but rather dealt only with procedural matters.

15. John H. Kirkwood, "Selection Techniques and the Law: To Test or Not to Test?", *Personnel*, vol. 44 (November-December 1967), pp. 19-20; Gerald A. McLain, "Personnel Testing and the EEOC," *Personnel*, vol. 46 (July-August 1967), pp. 451-52.

16. Gorham, "Political, Ethical, and Emotional Aspects of Federal Guidelines," p. 161; *Iron Age*, October 3, 1958, p. 21. The OFCC order was largely ignored by industry and compliance officers, partly because it was not well understood and was considered unrealistic and partly because those affected by it hoped it would go away if ignored. Stephen E. Bemis, "Government Regulation of a Profession: Process and Implications," *Personnel Psychology*, vol. 29 (Winter 1976), p. 535.

17. John Macy to Secretary of Labor Wirtz, October 25, 1968, RG 174, Box 54, EEO-1, National Archives.

18. William A. Gorham, "Who Does the Government Listen To?", *Personnel Psychology*, vol. 29 (Winter 1976), pp. 528-29.

19. Lyons, "Racial Discrimination vs. Equal Employment Opportunity," p. 36; 29 C.F.R. 1607.4(a); Barbara Lerner, "Washington v. Davis: Quantity, Quality and Equality in Employment Testing," *Supreme Court Review 1976* (Chicago: University of Chicago Press, 1977), p. 272. In addition to the pool-of-applicants approach, another method of determining disparate impact is to compare the proportion of blacks hired with the racial

composition of the local area population. This was the approach initially employed by affirmative action proponents. It is even less rational than the pool-of-applicants approach, though, because it ignores the fact that it is not discriminatory to make a distinction between persons of different qualifications. Lerner, "Washington v. Davis," p. 274.

20. 29 C.F.R. 1607.3.22.

21. Lyons, "Racial Discrimination vs. Equal Employment Opportunity," p. 38; 29 C.F.R. 1607.4(c)(1). Validation is not technically feasible when the sample of minority individuals is not large enough to achieve statistically significant results. The guidelines do not specify how large a sample is required for this purpose.

22. Lyons, "Racial Discrimination vs. Equal Employment Opportunity," pp. 39-41; 29 C.F.R. 1607.5(b)(5).

23. Lyons, "Racial Discrimination vs. Equal Employment Opportunity," p. 37; 29 C.F.R. 1607.4(c)(2).

24. Statistical significance means that the relationship has to be high enough to have no more than a 1 in 20 (.05) probability of having occurred by chance.

25. 29 C.F.R. 1607.5(c)(2)(iii); Lyons, "Racial Discrimination vs. Equal Employment Opportunity," p. 41.

26. Lyons, "Racial Discrimination vs. Equal Employment Opportunity," p. 42; 29 C.F.R. 1607.3.

27. Gorham, "Political, Ethical, and Emotional Aspects of Federal Guidelines," pp. 162-63.

28. Wigdor, "Psychological Testing and the Law of Employment Discrimination," p. 57; Thaddeus Holt, "A View from *Albemarle*," *Personnel Psychology*, vol. 30 (Spring 1977), p. 71.

29. N. Thompson Powers, "Discussant's Comments," *Personnel Psychology*, vol. 29 (Winter 1976), pp. 552-53; C. Paul Sparks, "Discussant's Comments," *ibid.*, p. 557; Donald J. Schwartz, "Implications for Personnel Measurement," *ibid.*, pp. 521-25.

30. Thaddeus Holt, "Test Justification and Title VII," *The Personnel Administrator*, vol. 21 (January 1976), pp. 46-51; Frank L. Schmidt and John E. Hunter, "The Future of Criterion-related Validity Studies in Title VII Employment Discrimination Cases," *ibid.*, vol. 22 (September 1977), pp. 39, 42.

31. David E. Robertson, "Employment Testing and Discrimination," *Personnel Journal*, vol. 54 (January 1975), p. 21; Mary T. Matthies, "The Developing Law on Equal Employment Opportunity," *Journal of Contemporary Business*, vol. 5 (Winter 1976), p. 35; John B. Miner, "Psychological Testing and Fair Employment Practices: A Testing Program That Does Not Discriminate," *Personnel Psychology*, vol. 27 (Spring 1974), pp. 49, 61; *Wall Street Journal*, May 20, 1975, p. 1; Mary Green Miner and John B. Miner, *Employee Selection Within the Law* (Washington: Bureau of National Affairs, 1978), p. 56.

32. Stephen E. Bemis, "Government Regulation of a Profession; Process and Implications," *Personnel Psychology*, vol. 29 (Winter 1976), p. 539.

33. Powers, "Discussant's Comments," p. 554.

34. Lyons, "An Agency with a Mind of Its Own," p. 23; Lyons, "Racial Discrimination vs. Equal Employment Opportunity," pp. 49-50.

35. Robert E. Hampton, "The Response of Governments and the Civil Service

to Anti-discrimination Efforts," in *Equal Rights and Industrial Relations* (Madison: Industrial Relations Research Association, 1977), pp. 141-65; David H. Rosenbloom, "The Civil Service Commission's Decision to Authorize the Use of Goals and Timetables in the Federal Equal Employment Opportunity Program," *Western Political Quarterly*, vol. 26 (June 1973), pp. 236-51; Gorham, "Political, Ethical, and Emotional Aspects of Federal Guidelines," p. 162.

36. Lyons, "Racial Discrimination vs. Equal Employment Opportunity," p. 52.
37. Gorham, "Political, Ethical and Emotional Aspects of Federal Guidelines," p. 168; Joel T. Campbell, "Tests Are Valid for Minority Groups Too," *Public Personnel Management*, vol. 2 (January-February 1973), pp. 70-73; Robert G. Linn, "Single Group Validity, Differential Validity and Differential Prediction," *Journal of Applied Psychology*, vol. 63 (August 1978), pp. 507-12; Lyons, "Racial Discrimination vs. Equal Employment Opportunity," pp. 54-55.
38. *ibid.*, pp. 58-59.
39. *ibid.*, pp. 59-61.
40. *ibid.*, p. 61.
41. *ibid.*, pp. 51-62; Gorham, "Political, Ethical and Emotional Aspects of Federal Guidelines," p. 173n.
42. *ibid.*, p. 169.
43. House Committee on Education and Labor, Oversight Hearing on OFCC Proposed Non-Construction Regulations, 94th Cong., 2 sess., 1976, p. 194.
44. Gorham, "Political, Ethical and Emotional Aspects of Federal Guidelines," p. 169.
45. David Rose, Memorandum to Deputy Attorney General, *Cong. Rec.*, 94th Cong., 2 sess., 1976, p. 22589.
46. Matthies, "The Developing Law on Equal Employment Opportunity," p. 43; Comptroller General of the United States, "Problems with Federal Equal Employment Opportunity Guidelines on Employee Selection Procedures Need to be Resolved," *Report to the Congress,* Feb. 2, 1978 *(Washington: General Accounting Office, 1978), p. 29.*
47. *Congressional Record*, 95th Cong., 2 sess., 1978, p. 11332; Senate Committee on Governmental Affairs, Hearings on Reorganization Plan No. 1 of 1978, 95th Cong., 2 sess., 1978, p. 355.
48. *ibid.*, p. 666.
49. Senate Committee on Human Resources, Nomination Hearing of Eleanor Holmes Norton, 95th Cong., 1 sess., 1977, pp. 7, 19.
50. Quoted in Thomas P. Dhanens, "Implications of the New EEOC Guidelines," *Personnel*, vol. 56 (September-October 1979), p. 34, and in Barbara Lerner, "Employment Discrimination: Adverse Impact, Validity and Equality," *Supreme Court Review 1979* (Chicago: University of Chicago Press, 1980), p. 40.
51. *ibid.*
52. Lerner, "Washington v. Davis," p. 272; Lerner, "Employment Discrimination," p. 21; Lyons, "Racial Discrimination vs. Equal Employment Opportunity," p. 73.
53. Edward E. Potter, ed., *Employee Selection: Legal and Practical Alternatives to Compliance and Litigation* (Washington: Equal Employment Advisory Council, 1983), p. 11; Lyons, "Racial Discrimination vs. Equal Employment

Opportunity," p. 75; "Comment on the Proposed Guidelines on Employee Selection Procedures," *The Personnel Administrator*, vol. 23 (June 1978), pp. 45-46 (Comment of the American Society for Personnel Administration).

54. Analysis of Comments on Uniform Guidelines for Employee Selection Procedures, draft of December 30, 1977, 43 *Federal Register* No. 166, pp. 38293-38294, 38297.

55. Allan Sloan, "An Analysis of Uniform Guidelines on Employee Selection Procedures," *Employee Relations Law Journal*, vol. 4 (1978-79), p. 352; Alan M. Koral, "Practical Application of the Uniform Guidelines: What to Do 'Til the Agency Comes," *ibid.*, vol. 5 (1980), pp. 481-83; Alfred W. Blumrosen, "Equal Opportunity in the Eighties: The Bottom Line," *ibid.*, vol. 6 (1981), pp. 535-43.

56. 43 *Federal Register* No. 166, p. 38293; Miner and Miner, *Employee Selection Within the Law*, pp. 468-69; Lyons, "Racial Discrimination vs. Equal Employment Opportunity," p. 69.

57. *The Washington Post*, August 23, 1978, p. A6; Miner and Miner, *Employee Selection Within the Law*, pp. 468-69.

58. Miner and Miner, *ibid.*, pp. 55, 443, 471-473; Lyons, "Racial Discrimination vs. Equal Employment Opportunity," p. 84.

59. "Comment on the Proposed Guidelines on Employee Selection Procedures," *The Personnel Administrator*, vol. 23 (June 1978), pp. 41-46; Miner and Miner, *Employee Selection Within the Law*, pp. 52-53; Sloan, "An Analysis of Uniform Guidelines," p. 348.

60. Donald W. Myers, "The Impact of a Selected Provision in the Federal Guidelines on Job Analysis and Training," *The Personnel Administrator*, vol. 26 (July 1981), pp. 43-45; C.J. Bartlett, "Equal Employment Opportunity Issues in Training," *Public Personnel Management*, vol. 8 (November-December 1979), pp. 398-406; Wigdor, "Psychological Testing and the Law of Employment Discrimination," pp. 67-68; Potter, ed., *Employee Selection: Legal and Practical Alternatives*, p. 16.

61. 43 *Federal Register* No. 166, p. 38293.

62. Note, "The Uniform Guidelines on Employee Selection Procedures: Compromises and Controversies," *Catholic University Law Review*, vol. 28 (Spring 1979), pp. 632-33.

Chapter 6

1. 427 U.S. 273 (1976); *"McDonald v. Santa Fe Trail Transportation Co.—* Reverse Discrimination?", *EEO Today*, vol. 3 (Autumn 1976), p. 154.

2. William L. Kandel, *"Gilbert and the Ascent of Washington v. Davis,"* *Employee Relations Law Journal*, vol. 3 (1977), p. 138.

3. Robert Belton, "Burdens of Pleading and Proof in Discrimination Cases: Toward a Theory of Procedural Justice," *Vanderbilt Law Review*, vol. 34 (October 1981), p. 1286.

4. Michael Farrell, "Proposed EEOC Regulations," *The Personnel Administrator*, vol. 23 (November 1978), p. 56.

5. 431 U.S. 395 (1977), at 405-406. In 1982, the Supreme Court reaffirmed that a private party has to meet all the requirements of Rule 23, in contrast to

EEOC which under Title VII can seek class relief without conforming to the Federal Rules of Civil Procedure. Reversing lower court decisions that failed to consider Rule 23, the Court observed that across-the-board class actions had produced multiplication of claims and endless litigation. *General Telephone Co. of the Southwest v. Falcon*, 457 U.S. 147 (1982) at 163.

6. 431 U.S. 553 (1977) at 558.
7. 97 S.Ct. 2264 (1977) at 2275.
8. 429 U.S. 125 (1976) at 145. Justices Blackmun, Brennan, and Marshall objected to any inference that might be drawn from the decision that the *Griggs* effects standards was not valid law. Kandel, "*Gilbert* and the Ascent of *Washington v. Davis*," p. 135; Robert Belton, "Discrimination and Affirmative Action: An Analysis of Competing Theories of Equality and *Weber*," *North Carolina Law Review*, vol. 59 (March 1981), p. 555n.
9. 431 U.S. 324 (1977) at 339-40; Howard C. Hay, "The Use of Statistics to Disprove Employment Discrimination," *Labor Law Journal*, vol. 29 (July 1978), p. 434.
10. 433 U.S. 321 (1977) at 330.
11. 433 U.S. 299 (1977) at 308, 310, 312; Hay, "The Use of Statistics," pp. 438-439; Farrell, "Proposed EEOC Regulations," p. 56.
12. 440 U.S. 568 (1979) at 584-85.
13. Belton, "Burdens of Pleading and Proof," pp. 1245-47; Joel William Friedman, "The Burger Court and the Prima Facie Case in Employment Discrimination Litigation: A Critique," *Cornell Law Review*, vol. 65 (November 1979), p. 50; Hannah Arterian Furnish, "A Path Through the Maze: Disparate Impact and Disparate Treatment Under Title VII of the Civil Rights Act of 1964 after *Beazer* and *Burdine*," *Boston College Law Review*, vol. 23 (March 1982), pp. 427-33.
14. In *McDonnell Douglas v. Green* (1973), the Court held that a plaintiff could make a *prima facie* case of disparate treatment discrimination by showing that he was a member of a minority group, applied for a job and was qualified, and was rejected, and that the employer continued to try to fill the job after the rejection.
15. 438 U.S. 567 (1987) at 577.
16. In a discrimination case, the burden of proof is on the plaintiff or complainant, meaning that he will lose if he does not prove his case or convince the court by a preponderance of the evidence. The burden of proof also includes a burden of producing evidence, which the plaintiff initially meets by presenting facts sufficient to make a *prima facie* charge. The burden of producing evidence shifts to the defendant after a *prima facie* case is made, but the burden of proof in the first sense—that is, convincing the court by a preponderance of the evidence—remains on the plaintiff. The burden of producing evidence, having shifted to the defendant, can be met by showing or articulating legitimate business reasons for the action in question. Steven H. Gifis, *Law Dictionary* (Woodbury: Barron's Educational Series, 1975), pp. 27-28.
17. 438 U.S. 567 (1987) at 576-78. The decision also lent support to the bottom-line theory of Title VII enforcement since the employer's high minority work force representation, compared to the percentage of blacks in the local labor market, appeared to be a factor in the Court's rejection of the discrimination charge.

18. 439 U.S. 24 (1978) at 27-28.
19. 450 U.S. 248 (1981) at 253-59.
20. Belton, "Burdens of Pleading and Proof," p. 1243; Furnish, "A Path Through the Maze," pp. 435-44; Friedman, "The Burger Court and the Prima Facie Case," pp. 50-55.
21. N. Thompson Powers, "EEO: Significant Recent Developments and Predictions for the Future: Private Employment as a Public Utility," *Annual Institute on Labor Law*, vol. 24 (1978), p. 283; Belton, "Burdens of Pleading and Proof," p. 1230.
22. 431 U.S. 324 (1977) at 350, 353.
23. *ibid.*, pp. 353, 367, 372, 375.
24. Powers, "EEO: Significant Recent Developments," p. 280.
25. Harry R. Edwards, "Preferential Remedies and Affirmative Action in Employment in the Wake of *Bakke*," *Washington University Law Quarterly*, vol. 1979 (Winter 1979), p. 119; Note, "The Supreme Court, 1976 Term," *Harvard Law Review*, vol. 91 (November 1977), pp. 252, 254, 264; Note, "Exemption of Seniority Systems under Title VII," *Louisiana Law Review*, vol. 38 (Fall 1977), p. 259; 431 U.S. 267.
26. Alfred W. Blumrosen, "The Law Transmission System and the Southern Jurisprudence of Employment Discrimination," *Industrial Relations Law Journal*, vol. 6 (1984), p. 344; Staughton Lynd, Book Review, *Harvard Civil Rights-Civil Liberties Law Review*, vol. 12 (Summer 1977), p. 773.
27. Paul N. Cox, "The Question of 'Voluntary' Racial Employment Quotas and Some Thoughts on Judicial Role," *Arizona Law Review*, vol. 23 (1981), p. 141.
28. Frederick R. Lynch, "Affirmative Action, the Media, and the Public: A Look at a 'Look-Away' Issue," *American Behavioral Scientist*, vol. 28 (July-August 1985), pp. 807-27.
29. Powers, "EEO: Significant Recent Developments," p. 289.
30. 416 U.S. 312.
31. 438 U.S. 265.
32. Timothy J. O'Neill, *Bakke and the Politics of Equality: Friends and Foes in the Classroom of Litigation* (Middletown: Wesleyan University Press, 1985), p. 89.
33. In *United Jewish Organizations of Williamsburgh Inc. v. Carey*, 430 U.S. 144 (1977), the Court in upholding the Voting Rights Act of 1965 said the use of race in districting and reapportionment was permissible, and was not confined to eliminating the effects of past discriminatory actions.
34. In *Washington v. Davis* (1976), in contrast, the Court held that Title VII does not embody the constitutional standard of discrimination. This discrepancy in the relationship between two similar provisions of the Civil Rights Act and the Constitution has never been satisfactorily explained by the Court.
35. 438 U.S. 265 (1978) at 288, 294, 298.
36. *ibid.*, pp. 301-2, 307.
37. *ibid.*, pp. 311, 318.
38. *ibid.*, pp. 337, 339-40, 348.
39. *ibid.*, p. 359. This standard had been defined in gender discrimination cases.
40. *ibid.*, pp. 357, 359, 362.
41. *ibid.*, pp. 387, 400-401, 407.

42. *ibid.*, p. 421.
43. The Brennan group said the central meaning of the opinions was that "[g]overnment may take race into account when it acts not to demean or insult any racial group, but to remedy disadvantages cast on minorities by past racial prejudice, at least when appropriate findings have been made by judicial, legislative, or administrative bodies with competence to act in this area." *ibid.*, p. 325.
44. Nathan Glazer, "A Viable Compromise on Minority Admissions," *Washington University Law Quarterly*, vol. 1979 (Winter 1979), pp. 93-104; Richard A. Posner, "The *Bakke* Case and the Future of 'Affirmative Action,' " *California Law Review*, vol. 67 (January 1979), p. 172; Henry J. Abraham, "Some Past-*Bakke*-and-*Weber* Reflections on 'Reverse Discrimination,' " *University of Richmond Law Review*, vol. 14 (Winter 1980), p. 375.
45. Robert M. O'Neil, "*Bakke* in Balance: Some Preliminary Thoughts," *California Law Review*, vol. 67 (January 1979), p. 147; Alan H. Goldman, *Justice and Reverse Discrimination* (Princeton: Princeton University Press, 1979) pp. 201-2.
46. Guido Calabresi, "*Bakke* as Pseudo-Tragedy," *California Law Review*, vol. 28 (Spring 1979), pp. 430-31; Antonin Scalia, "The Disease as Cure: 'In order to get beyond racism, we must first take account of race,' " *Washington University Law Quarterly*, vol. 1979 (Winter 1979), p. 148; Robert G. Dixon, "*Bakke*: A Constitutional Analysis," *California Law Review*, vol. 67 (January 1979), p. 69.
47. The Brennan group approved racial preference as a remedy for societal discrimination. Although Justice Powell would require a governmental or judicial finding of discrimination before awarding a race-conscious remedy under Title VI or Title VII, under his 'diversity' rationale race could be a legitimate factor without a showing of unlawful discrimination. Edwards, "Preferential Remedies and Affirmative Action," p. 117.
48. *ibid.*; Kent Greenawalt, "The Unresolved Problems of Reverse Discrimination," *California Law Review*, vol. 67 (January 1979), p. 88; Terry Eastland and William J. Bennett, *Counting by Race: Equality from the Founding Fathers to Bakke and Weber* (New York: Basic Books, 1979), pp. 172-77.
49. Posner, "The *Bakke* Case," p. 172.
50. Greenawalt, "The Unresolved Problems of Reverse Discrimination," p. 128.

Chapter 7

1. Antonin Scalia, "The Disease as Cure: 'In order to be beyond racism, we must first take account of race,' " *Washington University Law Quarterly*, vol. 1979 (Winter 1979), p. 147.
2. Michael Farrell, "Proposed EEOC Regulations," *The Personnel Administrator*, vol. 23 (November 1978), p. 58; Harry T. Edwards, "Preferential Remedies and Affirmative Action in Employment in the Wake of *Bakke*," *Washington University Law Quarterly*, vol. 1979 (Winter 1979), p. 129.
3. Weber claimed that the affirmative action plan violated Sections 703(a) and (d) of Title VII, which declared it unlawful to discriminate against any

individual with respect to the terms, conditions, or privileges of employment, or to discriminate against any individual because of race in admission
to any apprenticeship or other training program. Weber argued further that
the employer and union action violated Section 703(j), stating that nothing
in Title VII should be interpreted to require any employer or union to grant
preferential treatment because of race on account of racial imbalance.

4. Petition for a Writ of Certiorari to the United States Court of Appeals for
the Fifth Circuit, *Kaiser Aluminum and Chemical Corporation v. Weber*;
Brief for Petition, *Kaiser Aluminum and Chemical Corp. v. Weber*, Supreme
Court Records and Briefs, vol. 72, Part 2, pp. 8, 19, 50.

5. Brief for Petitioners, United Steelworkers of America, in the Supreme
Court of the United States, *United Steelworkers of America v. Weber*,
Supreme Court Records and Briefs, vol. 72, Part 2, p. 84.

6. *Weber v. Kaiser Aluminum and Chemical Corp. and United Steelworkers of
America*, 425 F. Supp. 761 (1976) at 769.

7. *Weber v. Kaiser Aluminum and Chemical Corp.*, 563 F. 2d 216 (1977) at 227.

8. *ibid.*, p. 235.

9. Thompson Powers, "EEO: Significant Recent Developments and Predictions for the Future: Private Employment as a Public Utility," *Annual
Institute of Labor Law*, vol. 24 (1978), pp. 271-303.

10. Farrell, "Proposed EEOC Regulations," p. 58.

11. Justices Brennan, Blackmun, Marshall, Stewart, and White formed the
majority. Justice Rehnquist and Chief Justice Burger dissented. Justices
Powell and Stevens did not participate, the former because of illness, the
latter reportedly because his former law firm did legal work for Kaiser.

12. 443 U.S. 193 (1979) at 197.

13. *ibid.*, pp. 201-4.

14. Of course, under the *Griggs* disparate impact theory of discrimination,
employers *were* charged with unlawful practices because of a racially
imbalanced work force.

15. William J. Kilberg and Stephen E. Tallent, "From *Bakke* to *Fullilove*: The
Use of Racial and Ethnic Preferences in Employment," *Employee Relations
Law Journal*, vol. 6 (Winter 1980-81), p. 368.

16. 443 U.S. 205-206.

17. Thompson Powers, "Implications of *Weber*—'A Net Beneath,' " *Employee
Relations Law Journal*, vol. 5 (Winter 1979-80), p. 329, calculates the
duration of the quota.

18. 443 U.S. 208.

19. *ibid.*, pp. 209, 212, 214.

20. *ibid.*, pp. 221, 225, 229, 254.

21. *ibid.*, pp. 216-18.

22. Powers, "Implications of *Weber*," p. 326.

23. 443 U.S. 197, 201, 203-4, 208-9.

24. Burt Neuborne, "Observations on *Weber*," *New York University Law
Review*, vol. 54 (June 1979), p. 550; Powers, "Implications of *Weber*," p.
328.

25. *A Conversation with Commissioner Eleanor Holmes Norton* (Washington:
American Enterprise Institute, 1979), pp. 4-5, 17. This was a spurious
argument intended to obscure the fact that employers were still subject to
liability under Title VII for discrimination against minorities.

26. EEOC guidelines stated that although an employer should not be forced to admit a violation, he ought to feel there was some basis for believing there was a violation in order to create an affirmative action program, or that if he did not create such a program it might be successfully sued. Eleanor Holmes Norton, "Comment on the *Bakke* Decision," *The Personnel Administrator*, vol. 23 (August 1978), p. 28.

27. Powers, "EEO: Significant Recent Developments," p. 292; Powers, "Implications of *Weber*," p. 327.

28. William E. Boyd, "Affirmative Action in Employment—The *Weber* Decision," *Iowa Law Review*, vol. 66 (October 1980), p. 12; 443 U.S. 211, 214.

29. Paul N. Cox, "The Question of 'Voluntary' Racial Employment Quotas and Some Thoughts on Judicial Role," *Arizona Law Review*, vol. 23 (1981), p. 143; Neuborne, "Observations on *Weber*," p. 550; 443 U.S. 211.

30. Michael Evan Gold, "*Griggs'* Folly: An Essay on the Theory, Problems and Origin of the Adverse Impact Definition of Employment Discrimination and a Recommendation for Reform," *Industrial Relations Law Journal*, vol. 7 (1985), p. 509.

31. Cox, "The Question of 'Voluntary' Racial Employment Quotas," p. 145.

32. *United Jewish Organizations of Williamsburgh Inc. v. Carey*, 430 U.S. 144 (1977) at 172.

33. Cox, "The Question of 'Voluntary' Racial Employment Quotas," p. 145.

34. Michael W. McConnell, "Affirmative Action after *Teal*: A New Twist or a Turn of the Screw?" *Regulation*, vol. 7 (March-April 1983), p. 41.

35. Boyd, "Affirmative Action in Employment," p. 41; Richard K. Walker, "The Exorbitant Cost of Redistributing Injustice: A Critical View of *United Steelworkers of America v. Weber* and the Misguided Policy of Numerical Employment," *Boston College Law Review*, vol. 21 (November 1979), p. 49; John J. Gallagher, "The *Weber* Decision: Summary and Analysis," *EEO Today*, vol. 6 (Autumn 1979), p. 235.

36. Dennis H. Vaughn, "Employment Quotas—Discrimination or Affirmative Action?" *Employment Relations Law Journal*, vol. 7 (Spring 1982), p. 560.

37. Cox, "The Question of 'Voluntary' Racial Employment Quotas," p. 146.

38. Bernard Meltzer, "The *Weber* Case: Double Talk and Double Standards," *Regulation*, vol. 3 (September-October 1979), p. 37.

39. Cox, "The Question of 'Voluntary' Racial Employment Quotas," pp. 176-77; Neuborne, "Observations on *Weber*," pp. 553-54.

40. 443 U.S. 209, 211, 222.

41. Terry Eastland and William J. Bennett, *Counting by Race: Equality from the Founding Fathers to Bakke and Weber* (New York: Basic Books, 1979), pp. 197-98.

42. 443 U.S. 200.

43. Powers, "Implications of *Weber*," pp. 331-32; *A Conversation with Eleanor Holmes Norton*, p. 19; David H. Rosenbloom, "Kaiser v. Weber: Perspectives from the Public Sector," *Public Personnel Management*, vol. 8 (November-December 1979), pp. 392-96; David P. Callett and Berton S. Klein, "Affirmative Action after *Weber*," *EEO Today*, vol. 9 (Summer 1982), pp. 138-40; Gallagher, "The *Weber* Decision," p. 235.

44. Callett and Klein, "Affirmative Action after *Weber*," p. 138; Gallagher, "The *Weber* Decision," p. 237.

45. Powers, "Implications of *Weber*," p. 327; Meltzer, "The *Weber* Case," p. 42.

46. George E. Sape, "Use of Quotas after *Weber*," *Employee Relations Law Journal*, vol. 6 (Autumn 1980), p. 244; Andree Kahn Blumstein, "Doing Good the Wrong Way: The Case for Delimiting Presidential Power under Executive Order No. 11246," *Vanderbilt Law Review*, vol. 33 (May 1980), pp. 945-46; Gallagher, "The *Weber* Decision," p. 238; Callett and Klein, "Affirmative Action after *Weber*," p. 143.

47. The minority groups were blacks, Spanish-speaking, Orientals, Indians, Eskimos, and Aleuts.

48. *Cong. Rec.*, 95th Cong., 1 sess., 1977, pp. 5327-30.

49. 49 U.S. 448 (1980) at 475, 477-78, 489.

50. *ibid.*, pp. 480-82, 491.

51. *ibid.*, pp. 484-85. The $4.2 billion set aside for minorities was 2.5 percent of the $170 billion spent on construction in 1977.

52. *ibid.*, pp. 502-503, 514.

53. *ibid.*, p. 519.

54. *ibid.*, pp. 521-22.

55. *ibid.*, pp. 537-39, 543, 545, 550.

56. *ibid.*, pp. 527-32.

57. Under the rationality test, a racial classification would be regarded as presumably legitimate, like any other classification a legislature would employ, and would be upheld as constitutional if found to be rationally related to carrying out a legitimate governmental purpose.

58. 448 U.S. 539.

59. *ibid.*, pp. 529, 539.

60. For scholarly development of the theory, see Arthur S. Kinoy, "The Constitutional Right of Negro Freedom," *Rutgers Law Review*, vol. 21 (Spring 1967), pp. 387-441.

61. 448 U.S. 478, 481; Michael J. Phillips, "Reverse Racial Preferences Under the Equal Protection Clause: Round II," *American Business Law Journal*, vol. 19 (Summer 1981), pp. 197-213.

62. 448 U.S. 516-17, 537.

63. "The Supreme Court Permits Legislated Preferences: *Fullilove v. Klutznick*," *EEO Today*, vol. 7 (Autumn 1980), p. 177; Phillips, "Reverse Racial Preferences," pp. 197-213.

64. 448 U.S. 513.

65. Kilberg and Tallent, "From *Bakke* to *Fullilove*," pp. 373-74.

66. *ibid.*, pp. 365, 374.

Chapter 8

1. Quoted in Gary L. McDowell, "Affirmative Inaction: The Brock-Meese Standoff on Federal Racial Quotas," *Policy Review*, No. 48 (Spring 1989), p. 32.

2. "Excerpts from Final Report on EEOC Prepared by Transition Team of Reagan Administration," *EEO Today*, vol. 8 (Summer 1981), pp. 173-74.

3. Rowland Evans and Robert Novak, *The Reagan Revolution* (New York: Dutton, 1981), p. 222.

4. The term "party of opposition" is used by Aaron Wildavsky to describe opposition to the expansion of government and support of limited government, deregulation, and expansion of the private sector. The "party of government," on the other hand, is dedicated to constant expansion of government based on taxing and spending. The "party of balance" occupies a middle ground. It is reactive and conservative, tending to preserve the policies that exist when it assumes responsibility for administration of the government. Following a period of big government created by the party of government, the party of balance seeks to eliminate excess and slow down government expansion. Aaron Wildavsky, "The Party of Government, Party of Opposition, and the Party of Balance: An American View of the Consequences of the 1980 Election," ed. Austin Ranney, *The American Elections of 1980* (Washington: American Enterprise Institute, 1981), pp. 329-50.

5. Norman C. Amaker, *Civil Rights and the Reagan Administration* (Washington: Urban Institute Press, 1988), p. 36-47. The 1978 amendment to Title VI of the Civil Rights Act, concerning federally funded activities, forbids the Department of Education from adopting regulations that require busing of students beyond the school geographically nearest their homes in order to carry out a desegregation plan involving grade restructuring, pairing, or clustering. This amendment was subsequently reenacted by Congress annually. The Department of Education could still refer cases to the Department of Justice for prosecution in federal court, but the Reagan Administration Justice Department took a narrow approach to defining violations and sought to limit remedies to schools in which racial imbalance was the product of intentional segregation. The Justice Department also opposed mandatory reassignment of pupils, especially through forced busing. In general, the Reagan Administration policy on school desegregation and busing as a remedy for discriminatory practices by school districts conformed to the anti-busing policy established by Congress in the late 1970s.

6. Under Department of Labor regulations issued in 1977, the Department of Justice was authorized to initiate investigations and civil actions against federal contractors, subject to the approval of OFCCP. *Federal Enforcement of Equal Employment Requirements*, Clearinghouse Publication 93 (Washington: U.S. Commission on Civil Rights, 1987), p. 46.

7. Asked at a press conference in December 1981 whether he agreed with Assistant Attorney General Reynolds that the *Weber* decision should be overturned, President Reagan said he could not recall what the case dealt with. Informed that it authorized voluntary affirmative action training programs for minorities, the President stated that if it meant giving more opportunities for blacks under a voluntary agreement with employers and unions, he supported it. Emphasizing economic growth as the best means of providing equal employment opportunities for blacks, President Reagan denied that his administration would retreat from advocating affirmative action programs and minority hiring. In a press conference in January 1981, however, he said that while there had been civil rights progress, "there are some things . . . that may not be as useful as they once were or that may even

be distorted in the practice, such as affirmative action programs becoming quota systems." *Public Papers of the Presidents of the United States: Ronald Reagan, 1981* (Washington: GPO, 1982), Vol. I, pp. 58, 573-78, Vol. II, p. 1169.

8. In 1983, the Heritage Foundation outlined the policy that many conservative civil rights advocates would pursue in the second Reagan term when it recommended opening economic opportunities for minorities. It proposed to eliminate legal barriers to entry into trades, occupations, and businesses in the form of unreasonable fees, license, and certification practices. At the same time, the Heritage Foundation urged the Justice Department to resist goals and numerical remedies and recommended that Executive Order 11246 be amended to outlaw quotas. Richard N. Holwill, ed., *Agenda '83: A Mandate for Leadership Report* (Washington: Heritage Foundation, 1983), pp. 208-11.

9. House Committee on Education and Labor, Oversight Hearings on Equal Opportunity and Affirmative Action, 97th Cong., 1 sess., 1981, pp. 132-56; Senate Committee on the Judiciary, Hearings on the Nominations of Rex E. Lee and William Bradford Reynolds, 97th Cong., 1 sess., 1981, p. 81.

10. Reynolds said he would enforce *Weber* because it was improper not to support a Supreme Court decision, but he noted that the opinion was concerned with private rather than public sector employment and was narrowly drawn. Oversight Hearings on Equal Opportunity, 1981, p. 155.

11. Remarks of William Bradford Reynolds before the Southern Education Foundation, February 10, 1983, pp. 1, 3; William Bradford Reynolds, "The Justice Department's Enforcement of Title VII," *Labor Law Journal*, vol. 34 (May 1983), pp. 259-65.

12. *Federal Enforcement of Equal Employment*, pp. 45-46; Ronald M. Green, "A Washington Update: Compliance with Employment Law When the 'Regs' Are on 'Hold,'" *Employee Relations Law Journal*, vol. 9 (Summer 1983), pp. 113-17.

13. Brief for the United States as *Amicus Curiae*, Connecticut, et. al., Petitioners v. Winnie Teal, et. al., in the Supreme Court of the United States, October Term, 1981, p. 13.

14. The Justice Department reasoned that a clause in Section 706 (g), stating that no court shall order the admission or reinstatement of an individual or other relief if the individual was rejected for any reason other than discrimination on account of race, showed the intent of Congress to confine relief only to individuals who were victims of discrimination. The counter-argument was that this language was simply intended to clarify the fact that an employment decision based on reasons other than race was not unlawful. To justify quota relief, proponents of affirmative action cited language added to Section 706(g) in 1972 authorizing courts to award "any other equitable relief as the court deems appropriate," in addition to reinstatement and back pay.

15. Robert R. Detlefsen, "Civil Rights, the Courts, and the Reagan Justice Department," *Journal of Contemporary Studies*, vol. 8 (Spring-Summer 1985), pp. 107-8; "Current Developments in EEO Law," *Employment Relations Today*, vol. 10 (Spring 1983), pp. 23-27.

16. James H. Coil, III, "Action Needed on Affirmative Action," *Employment Relations Today*, vol. 10 (Winter 1983-84), p. 354.

17. 467 U.S. 561 (1984) at 579. See below, ch. 9.
18. Neal Devins, "Far-Reaching Title VII Effects of Supreme Court's *Stotts* Ruling," *National Law Journal*, July 30, 1984, p. 22; *Toward an Understanding of Stotts*, Clearinghouse Publication 85 (Washington: U.S. Commission on Civil Rights, 1985), pp. 48-49.
19. James H. Coil III, "Affirmative Action Reaches a Crossroads—Not a Dead End," *Employment Relations Today*, vol. 13 (Autumn 1986), pp. 211-12. The cases were *Local 93 v. City of Cleveland* (1986) and *U.S. v. Paradise* (1987). See below, ch. 9.
20. *Wygant v. Jackson Board of Education* (1986). See below, ch. 9.
21. *Federal Enforcement of Equal Employment*, p. 53; *Engineering News Record*, July 10, 1986, p. 52.
22. McDowell, "Affirmative Inaction," pp. 32-37.
23. House Oversight Hearings on Equal Opportunity, 1981, pp. 388-91; *Business Week*, December 14, 1981, p. 31; Jeremy Plant and Frank J. Thompson, "Deregulation, the Bureaucracy, and Employment Discrimination: The Case of the EEOC," eds. Michael W. Combs and John Gruhl, *Affirmative Action: Theory, Analysis, and Prospects* (Jefferson: McFarland and Co., 1986), pp. 147-51.
24. Green, "A Washington Update," pp. 120-21; *Federal Enforcement of Equal Employment*, pp. 16-20; *Business Week*, August 9, 1982, pp. 54-55; *U.S. News and World Report*, March 14, 1983, p. 68; Clarence Thomas to Attorney General William French Smith, April 5, 1983, Statement of Clarence Thomas before the House Committee on the Judiciary, May 6, 1983, Subcommittee on Constitutional and Civil Rights, Minority Counsel EEO File.
25. Plant and Thompson, "Deregulation, the Bureaucracy, and Employment Discrimination," p. 147.
26. *Federal Enforcement of Equal Employment*, pp. 21, 23, 35-37; Adin C. Goldberg, "The EEOC's New Aggressive Stance," *Employment Relations Today*, vol. 12 (Summer 1985), pp. 113-15; Clarence Thomas, "Affirmative Action Goals and Timetables: Too Tough? Not Tough Enough!", *Yale Law and Policy Review*, vol. 5 (Spring-Summer 1987), p. 405; Green, "A Washington Update," p. 123. The number of suits filed by EEOC increased from 195 in fiscal 1983 to 411 in 1985 and over 500 in 1986. Back pay awards increased from $16.2 million in 1981 to $46 million in 1986. The percentage of pattern or practice cases compared to individual cases decreased from 70 percent to 55 percent from 1983 to 1986.

   Elimination of the unit for systemic discrimination did not mean abandonment of class actions, which though often based on disparate impact theory and statistical imbalance, by no means always employ that approach. Class actions are often based on the disparate treatment concept of discrimination. The systemic discrimination unit was abolished in part because of budgetary considerations. In 1984 the unit spent $500,000 on six cases, compared to a litigation budget for cases brought by the General Counsel that amounted to $3.6 million. R. Gaull Silberman, "EEOC Is Meeting the Challenge: Response to David Rose," *Vanderbilt Law Review*, vol. 42 (November 1989), pp. 1641-46.

27. House Committee on Education and Labor, Hearings on Equal Employment Opportunity Commission Policies Regarding Goals and Timetables in Litigation Remedies, 99th Cong., 2 sess., 1986, pp. 3-4.
28. *ibid.*, pp. 33, 86; Thomas, "Affirmative Action Goals," pp. 405-7.
29. Thomas, "Affirmative Action Goals," p. 402. For the EEOC response to the Supreme Court rulings, see James H. Coil III, "EEOC's General Counsel Offers Insights," *Employment Relations Today*, vol. 14 (Winter 1987-88), pp. 321-29, and Douglas S. McDowell, *Affirmative Action After the Johnson Decision: Practical Guidance for Planning and Compliance* (Washington: National Foundation for the Study of Employment Policy, 1987), pp. 90-91. The EEOC said it would seek goals and timetables in accordance with a narrow reading of the rules for affirmative action set forth by the Supreme Court, and would continue to pursue its full relief policy.
30. Thomas, "Affirmative Action Goals," pp. 407-8.
31. House Hearings on EEOC Policies on Goals and Timetables, 1986, p. 97.
32. Amaker, *Civil Rights and the Reagan Administration*, pp. 109-13, says the EEOC enforcement record under Thomas was mixed, unlike the Department of Justice. He charges the latter with complete failure to enforce the civil rights laws.
33. Thomas, "Affirmative Action Goals," p. 405.
34. David P. Callet, "The OFCCP Raises the Back-Pay Issue Again," *EEO Today*, vol. 9 (Autumn 1982), pp. 223-32; "The Reagan Transition: Regulatory Reform and EEO Policy," *EEO Today*, vol. 8 (Summer 1981), pp. 93-101; "Excerpts from Final Report on EEOC Prepared by Transition Team of Reagan Administration," *EEO Today*, vol. 8 (Summer 1981), p. 174.
35. Jeremy Rabkin, "The Stroke of a Pen," *Regulation*, vol. 5 (May-June 1981), pp. 17-18; *Business Week*, May 25, 1981, p. 123; McDowell, "Affirmative Inaction," p. 33; Daniel Seligman, "Affirmative Action is Here to Stay," *Fortune*, April 19, 1982, p. 162.
36. House Oversight Hearings on Equal Opportunity, 1981, pp. 282-83, 287.
37. *ibid.*, pp. 289, 294, 301, 303.
38. Seligman, "Affirmative Action is Here to Stay," p. 105.
39. Susan A. Cahoon and James H. Coil III, "OFCCP Finally Adopts New AAP Rules," *Employment Relations Today*, vol. 10 (Summer 1983), pp. 123-33; Green, "A Washington Update," pp. 117-19.
40. The threshold for coverage remained at 100 employees or $100,000 in federal contracts.
41. David A. Copus, "OFCCP Quietly Adopts Major Policy Changes," *Employment Relations Today*, vol. 10 (Spring 1983), pp. 31-33; *Federal Enforcement of Equal Employment*, pp. 82-83; Green, "A Washington Update," p. 119; *Affirmative Action Today: A Legal and Practical Analysis* (Washington: Bureau of National Affairs, 1986), pp. 18-19.
42. *Affirmative Action Today*, p. 17; Coil, "Action Needed on Affirmative Action," pp. 355-57; McDowell, *Affirmative Action After the Johnson Decision*, p. 92.
43. Anne B. Fisher, "Businessmen Like to Hire by the Numbers," *Fortune*, September 16, 1985, p. 27.

44. Daniel Seligman, "It Was Foreseeable," *Fortune*, July 22, 1985, p. 119; McDowell, "Affirmative Inaction," pp. 34-37; *Affirmative Action Today*, p. 16.
45. McDowell, *Affirmative Action After the Johnson Decision*, pp. 89, 95-96; *Affirmative Action Today*, p. 148.
46. The Public Works Employment Act of 1977 provided that ten percent of government contracts awarded by the Commerce Department to state and local governments should go to minority business enterprises. An amendment of the Small Business Act of 1978 authorized the suspension of normal competitive bidding in relation to businesses owned by socially and economically disadvantaged individuals. Under this law, the Commerce Department issued regulations stating that members of protected groups under affirmative action policies were presumed to be "socially and economically disadvantaged." Jeremy Rabkin, "Reagan's Secret Quotas," *The New Republic*, August 5, 1985, p. 17.
47. *Selected Affirmative Action Topics in Employment and Business Set-Asides* (Washington: U.S. Commission on Civil Rights, 1985), vol. 1, pp. 93-94.
48. Executive Order 12432, 3 C.F.R. 198 (1983); *Public Papers of the Presidents of the United States: Ronald Reagan 1982* (Washington: GPO, 1983), pp. 1613-15; Rabkin, "Reagan's Secret Quotas," p. 17.
49. Seligman, "Affirmative Action is Here to Stay," p. 162.
50. House Oversight Hearings on Equal Opportunity, 1981, pp. 246-50.
51. Herbert Hammerman, " 'Affirmative Action Stalemate': A Second Perspective," *The Public Interest*, No. 93 (Fall 1988), p. 133; *Business Week*, October 13, 1980, p. 46, May 25, 1981, p. 123.
52. Anna Cifelli, "Quotas Live On," *Fortune*, July 23, 1984, p. 95; Fisher, "Businessmen Like to Hire by the Numbers," p. 28; *Affirmative Action Today*, pp. 10, 93, 137.
53. Fisher, "Businessmen Like to Hire by the Numbers," p. 28; *Affirmative Action Today*, pp. 1, 5, 13, 89, 116-17, 137; Susan Vernon-Gerstenfeld and Edmund Burke, "Affirmative Action in Nine Large Companies: A Field Study," *Personnel*, vol. 62 (April 1985), p. 60.
54. House Hearings on EEOC Policies on Goals and Timetables, 1986, pp. 227-58, 263-65.
55. Hammerman, "A Second Perspective," p. 134; Fisher, "Businessmen Like to Hire by the Numbers," p. 28; *Engineering News-Record*, August 22, 1985, p. 10.
56. *Affirmative Action Today*, pp. 1, 11.
57. Carl C. Hoffman, "Reopening the Affirmative Action Debate," *The Personnel Administrator*, vol. 31 (March 1986), p. 36.
58. Jeanne C. Poole and E. Theodore Kantz, "An EEO/AA Program that Exceeds Quotas—It Targets Biases," *Personnel Journal*, vol. 66 (January 1987), p. 103; Hoffman, "Reopening the Affirmative Action Debate," pp. 37-38; House Hearings on EEOC Polices on Goals and Timetables, 1986, p. 152. The effects of affirmative action are examined more fully in Chapter 10.
59. *Affirmative Action Today*, p. 11; Paul S. Greenlaw, "Affirmative Action or Reverse Discrimination?", *Personnel Journal*, vol. 64 (Spring 1985), p. 87; House Hearings on EEOC Policies on Goals and Timetables, 1986, p. 151.

60. House Hearings on EEOC Policies on Goals and Timetables, 1986, p. 215; *Affirmative Action Today*, p. 128.

61. *Selected Affirmative Action Topics*, vol. 1, pp. 90-91.

62. *ibid.*, vol. 2, pp. 40, 143, 274; *Engineering News-Record*, February 28, 1985, p. 28; Michael Oreskes, "The Set-Aside Scam," *The New Republic*, December 24, 1985, p. 19.

63. *Selected Affirmative Action Topics*, vol. 2, pp. 42-43, 87, 156.

64. In 1983 the administration waged a bitter fight against congressional liberals to reorient the Civil Rights Commission against preferential treatment. The structure of the Commission was changed to allow four appointments each by the President and Congress. President Reagan named Clarence Pendleton as chairman.

65. *Engineering News-Record*, March 14, 1985, p. 58.

66. House Oversight Hearings on Equal Opportunity, 1981, pp. 99-100, 142-43, 147, 151.

67. Michael Wines, "Administration Says It Merely Seeks a 'Better Way' to Enforce Civil Rights," *National Journal*, vol. 14 (March 22, 1982), p. 536; Washington Council of Lawyers, "Reagan Civil Rights: The First Twenty Months," *Black Law Journal*, vol. 8 (Spring 1983), p. 81; Barbara Wolvovitz and Jules Lobel, "The Enforcement of Civil Rights Statutes: The Reagan Administration's Record," *Black Law Journal*, vol. 9 (Winter 1986), pp. 252, 257; Wines, "Administration Seeks a 'Better Way' " p. 537.

68. Richard T. Seymour, "Why Executive Order 11246 Should be Preserved," *Employee Relations Law Journal*, vol. 11 (Spring 1986), pp. 568, 584; House Hearings on EEOC Policies on Goals and Timetables, 1986, pp. 102, 178-79.

69. Amaker, *Civil Rights and the Reagan Administration*, pp. 124-30.

70. Joel L. Selig, "The Reagan Justice Department and Civil Rights: What Went Wrong?", *University of Illinois Law Review*, vol. 1985, pp. 789, 823-24, 826, 833, 835.

71. Drew S. Days III, "Turning Back the Clock: The Reagan Administration and Civil Rights," *Harvard Civil Rights-Civil Liberties Law Review*, vol. 19 (Summer 1984), p. 346.

72. *ibid.*, pp. 313, 341, 347.

73. Amaker, *Civil Rights and the Reagan Administration*, p. 124.

74. Selig, "The Reagan Justice Department," p. 827.

75. Wines, "Administration Seeks a 'Better Way'," p. 537. That the legality of quotas was debatable can be seen in the tentative arguments of its supporters. Asked whether Title VII was intended to authorize only remedies for identifiable victims of discrimination, or quotas as well, Clifford Alexander, former Chairman of the EEOC in the Johnson Administration, said: ". . . [Y]ou do not specifically see anywhere in the statute, nor in the intent, that there should not be goals and timetables in decisions and conclusionary decisions after cases have been investigated." Former Carter Administration EEOC general counsel Leroy Clark said in defending the legality of quotas: "There is nothing in the legislative history of Title VII which mandates the utilization of ineffective remedies." House Hearings on EEOC Policies on Goals and Timetables, 1986, pp. 101, 179.

76. Seligman, "It was Foreseeable," p. 119.

77. Seligman, "Affirmative Action is Here to Stay," p. 162.

Chapter 9

1. The black pass rate was 68 percent of the white pass rate.
2. 457 U.S. 440 (1982) at 450-51, 453-55.
3. *ibid.*, pp. 458-60, 463.
4. Michael W. McConnell, "Affirmative Action after *Teal*: A New Twist or a Turn of the Screw?", *Regulation*, vol. 7 (March-April 1983), pp. 42-44; Paul N. Cox, "Substance and Process in Employment Discrimination Law: One View of the Swamp," *Valparaiso University Law Review*, vol. 18 (Fall 1983), pp. 52-53; Alfred W. Blumrosen, "The Group Interest Concept, Employment Discrimination, and Legislative Intent: The Fallacy of *Connecticut v. Teal*," *Harvard Journal on Legislation*, vol. 20 (Winter 1983), p. 102; Note, "The Bottom Line Defense in Title VII Actions: Supreme Court Rejection in *Connecticut v. Teal* and a Modified Approach," *Cornell Law Review*, vol. 68 (June 1983), p. 747; Abram Chayes, "The Supreme Court, 1981 Term," *Harvard Law Review*, vol. 96 (November 1982), p. 281.
5. Marcia Graham, "Seniority Systems and Title VII—Reanalysis and Redirection," *Employee Relations Law Journal*, vol. 9 (Summer 1983), pp. 81-97.
6. 467 U.S. 561 (1984) at 579.
7. *ibid.*, pp. 617-18, 620.
8. *Toward an Understanding of Stotts*, Clearinghouse Publication 85 (Washington: U.S. Commission on Civil Rights, 1985), pp. 1, 56, 63; Douglas F. Seaver, "The *Stotts* Decision: Is it the Death Knell for Seniority Systems?" *Employee Relations Law Journal*, vol. 10 (Winter 1984-85), p. 502; Neal Devins, "Far-Reaching Title VII Effects of Supreme Court's *Stotts* Ruling," *National Law Journal*, July 30, 1984, p. 22.
9. 106 S.Ct. 3019 (1986) at 3034-35, 3049.
10. *ibid.*, pp. 3035-36, 3038, 3040, 3044.
11. *ibid.*, pp. 3050, 3052.
12. *ibid.*, pp. 3057, 3062, 3064.
13. Facing a Title VII suit, the city agreed to a settlement with black and Hispanic firefighters that provided for a 50 percent quota for promotion of minorities to corporal rank and promotion of ten qualified blacks among 52 other positions. Two lists were thus created, enabling the advancement of blacks who otherwise would not have been promoted. White firefighters argued that the consent decree exceeded judicial authority under Section 706(g) by giving relief to non-victims.
14. 106 S.Ct. 3063 (1986) at 3072-73, 3075.
15. *ibid.*, pp. 3086-87.
16. 106 S. Ct. 1842 (1986) at 1848, 1851.
17. *ibid.*, pp. 1853, 1865-67.
18. *ibid.*, pp. 1863-64.
19. *ibid.*, p. 1870.
20. Douglas S. McDowell, *Affirmative Action After the* Johnson *Decision: Practical Guidance for Planning and Compliance* (Washington: National Foundation for the Study of Employment Policy, 1987), p. 31; James R. Redeker, "The Supreme Court on Affirmative Action," *Personnel*, vol. 63 (October 1986), p. 14; *Affirmative Action Today: A Legal and Practical*

Analysis (Washington: Bureau of National Affairs, 1986), p. 158 (comment of Carolyn B. Kuhl).

21. McDowell, *Affirmative Action After the* Johnson *Decision*, p. 19.
22. *Wygant* was decided before *Local 28*.
23. William L. Kandel, "The Limits of *Wygant v. Jackson Board of Education*," *Employee Relations Law Journal*, vol. 12 (Autumn 1986), pp. 290, 303.
24. James H. Coil III, "Affirmative Action Reaches a Cross-roads—Not a Dead End," *Employment Relations Today*, vol. 13 (Autumn 1986), p. 215; Michael H. Beck, "The Supreme Court Decisions of the 1985-86 Term," *The Labor Lawyer*, vol. 3 (Winter 1987), p. 67.
25. *NAACP v. Allen*, 340 F. Supp. 703 (1972).
26. 107 S.Ct. 1053 (1987) at 1071. Justice Brennan was joined by Justices Marshall, Blackmun, and Powell. Justice Powell wrote a concurring opinion accepting the quota as a narrowly tailored remedy. Justice Stevens said in a concurring opinion that the quota was an acceptable remedy under the rationality standard.
27. *ibid.*, p. 1080-82.
28. Justice Brennan rejected the argument, advanced by Justice Scalia, that a public employer was subject to the same obligations under Title VII as under the Constitution. According to Brennan, Title VII was enacted under the commerce power and was not intended to incorporate the requirements of the Fourteenth Amendment. He held that the 1972 Title VII amendments extending the law to public employers did not change the substantive standard governing employment conduct. 107 S.Ct. 1442 (1987) at 1449-50n.
29. *ibid.*, p. 1453.
30. *ibid.*, pp. 1454, 1457.
31. *ibid.*, pp. 1458-60.
32. Justice O'Connor believed the same anti-discrimination concerns were addressed by both Title VII and the Fourteenth Amendment. Therefore, the standards for defining discrimination and the requirements of the equal protection principle were the same in both instruments. *ibid.*, pp. 1461, 1463.
33. *ibid.*, p. 1463.
34. *ibid.*, pp. 1467, 1471, 1475. Justice White dissented separately, explaining that the Court was revising *Weber*'s "traditionally segregated job categories" to mean not intentional and systematic exclusion of blacks, but rather "a manifest imbalance between one identifiable group and another in an employer's work force." He now believed *Weber* should be overruled. *ibid.*, p. 1465.
35. As Justice O'Connor pointed out. 107 S.Ct. 1081.
36. McDowell, *Affirmative Action After the* Johnson *Decision*, pp. 81-82; Michael W. Sculnick, "The Supreme Court's 1986-87 EEO Decisions: A Review," *Employment Relations Today*, vol. 14 (Autumn 1987), p. 216.
37. Paul N. Cox, *New Developments in Employment Discrimination Law*, vol. 1, issue 1 (New York: Garland, 1987), p. 5.
38. McDowell, *Affirmative Action After the* Johnson *Decision*, p. 41.
39. *ibid.*, pp. 41, 59; Barbara A. Brown, "Affirmative Action: The Emerging Consensus," *Employment Relations Today*, vol. 14 (Autumn 1987), p. 225; William L. Kandel, "Johnson v. Transportation Agency: A Revival for Affirmative Action," *Employee Relations Law Journal*, vol. 13 (Autumn

1987), pp. 124, 134-35; William A. Nowlin, "*Weber* Doctrine Extended to Governmental Employees," *Labor Law Journal*, vol. 38 (November 1987), pp. 711, 713.

40. William J. Kilberg, "Playing Dice with Affirmative Action," *Employee Relations Law Journal*, vol. 13 (Autumn 1987), pp. 193-95.

41. Norman C. Amaker, *Civil Rights and the Reagan Administration* (Washington: Urban Institute Press, 1988), p. 124.

42. Earl M. Maltz, "Title VII and Upper Level Employment—A Response to Professor Bertholet," *Northwestern University Law Review*, vol. 77 (February 1983), pp. 776-93.

43. 108 S.Ct. 2777 (1988) at 2785-86.

44. *ibid.*, pp. 2788-91. To support her argument, Justice O'Connor cited disparate impact cases in which the Court found employment practices to have a manifest relation to job performance even though they had not been validated. The cases were *Washington v. Davis* (1976) and *New York Transit Authority v. Beazer* (1979). See Chapter 6.

45. *ibid.*, pp. 2793, 2797.

46. 109 S.Ct. 2115 (1989) at 2121-23.

47. *ibid.*, pp. 2125-27.

48. 109 S.Ct. 2180 (1989) at 2183-84. The decision reversed the trend of decision in the circuit courts. Michael W. Sculnick, "Key Court Actions," *Employment Relations Today*, vol. 15 (Spring 1988), pp. 62-65.

49. 109 S.Ct. 2198.

50. 102 E.Ed. 854 (1989) at 880-81, 885, 893. Justice Stevens wrote a separate opinion agreeing that the Richmond plan could not be justified as a remedy for past discrimination, but asserting that racial preferences could be used to promote the public interest. In a concurring opinion, Justice Scalia insisted on a color-blind Constitution that permitted the use of race only to remedy the effects of a system of unlawful racial classification, as in the school desegregation cases.

51. *ibid.*, pp. 912, 922-24.

52. The Court provoked a storm of criticism in 1988 when it asked for reargument on whether *Runyon v. McCrary* (1976), which interpreted the Civil Rights Act of 1866 as prohibiting discrimination in private education under a general right not to be discriminated against in private contractual matters, should be overruled. In *Patterson v. McLean Credit Union* it declined to overrule *Runyon*, but held that racial harassment relating to the conditions of employment is not actionable under the 1866 Act. 109 S.Ct. 2363 (1989) at 2369.

53. Kay Ann Hoogland and Condon McGlothlen, "*City of Richmond v. Croson*: A Setback for Minority Set-Aside Programs," *Employee Relations Law Journal*, vol. 15 (Summer 1989), pp. 13-18; Charles Fried, "Affirmative Action After *City of Richmond v. J.A. Croson Co*: A Response to the Scholars' Statement," *Yale Law Journal*, vol. 99 (October 1989), p. 156.

54. 102 L. Ed. 890.

55. 108 S.Ct. 2787.

56. H.R. 3455, 101st Cong., 1 sess., October 12, 1989.

57. S. 2104, 101st Cong., 2 sess., February 7, 1990.

58. In 1988, Congress passed legislation reversing *Grove City College v. Bell* (1984), concerning the definition of a recipient of federal aid. In the Voting

Rights Act of 1982, Congress reversed the Supreme Court decision in *City of Mobile v. Bolden* (1980), requiring proof of intent to discriminate in voting rights cases. In 1978, Congress overruled *General Electric Co. v. Gilbert* (1976), concerning pregnancy disability under Title VII.
59. Abigail M. Thernstrom, *Whose Votes Count? Affirmative Action and Minority Voting Rights* (Cambridge: Harvard University Press, 1987), pp. 105-36.
60. Charles Fried, "High Court Restores Balance on Rights," *Boston Herald*, June 19, 1989, p. 19; Fried, "Affirmative Action after *City of Richmond v. J.A. Croson Co.*," p. 161.
61. Amaker, *Civil Rights and the Reagan Administration*, p. 157.

Chapter 10

1. See Abigail M. Thernstrom, *Whose Votes Count? Affirmative Action and Minority Voting Rights* (Cambridge: Harvard University Press, 1987).
2. In a review of a biography of Whitney M. Young, National Urban League Executive Director in the 1960s, David Garrow circumspectly observes: "The visible and noisy presence of militant—and sometimes violent—black activists and masses tremendously *increased* white establishment support for upper-middle-class black leaders and organizations." *Washington Post Book World*, December 17, 1989, p. 5.
3. H.R. 3745, 101st Cong., 1 sess., November 20, 1989.
4. Douglas Rae, et. al., *Equalities* (Cambridge: Harvard University Press, 1981), pp. 61-73.
5. Fred Baumann, "The Latest Apologies for Preferential Treatment," *New Perspectives*, vol. 18 (Winter-Spring 1986), p. 23.
6. W. R. Newell, "Affirmative Action and the Dilemmas of Liberalism," eds. Michael W. Combs and John Gruhl, *Affirmative Action: Theory, Analysis, and Prospects* (Jefferson: McFarland and Co., 1986), pp. 57-58.
7. Charles J. Cooper, "The Coercive Remedies Paradox," *Harvard Journal of Law and Public Policy*, vol. 9 (Winter 1986), p. 80.
8. Frank Askin, "The Case for Compensatory Treatment," *Rutgers Law Review*, vol. 24 (Fall 1969), p. 65; Graham Hughes, "Reparations for Blacks?", *New York University Law Review*, vol. 43 (December 1968), p. 1064; Boris Bittker, *The Case for Black Reparations* (New York: Random House, 1973), pp. 120-21, 135-36.
9. Kenneth B. Clark, "Racial Justice in Quota Employment," *The Conference Board Record*, vol. 10 (August 1973), pp. 49-51; J. Skelly Wright, "Color-Blind Theories and Color-Conscious Remedies," *University of Chicago Law Review*, vol. 47 (Winter 1980), pp. 221-22, 240n.; Robert Belton, "Burdens of Pleading and Proof in Discrimination Cases: Toward a Theory of Procedural Justice," *Vanderbilt Law Review*, vol. 34 (October 1981), p. 1286.
10. Owen M. Fiss, "A Theory of Fair Employment Laws," *University of Chicago Law Review*, vol. 38 (Winter 1971), pp. 238-40, 310-13.
11. *ibid.*, p. 313; Owen M. Fiss, "Groups and the Equal Protection Clause," *Philosophy and Public Affairs*, vol. 5 (Winter 1976), pp. 148, 150, 173.

12. Kenneth L. Karst and Harold W. Horowitz, "Affirmative Action and Equal Protection," *Virginia Law Review*, vol. 60 (October 1974), pp. 956, 964-65.
13. George Sher, "Justifying Reverse Discrimination in Employment," eds. Marshall Cohen, et. al., *Equality and Preferential Treatment* (Princeton: Princeton University Press, 1977), pp. 51-54; Thomas Nagel, "Introduction," *ibid.*, pp. ix-xiii; Nagel, "Equal Treatment and Compensatory Discrimination," *ibid.*, p. 14.
14. Robert Allen Sedler, "Beyond *Bakke*: The Constitution and Redressing the Social History of Racism," *Harvard Civil Rights-Civil Liberties Law Review*, vol. 14 (Spring 1979), p. 148; Edwin Dorn, *Rules and Racial Inequality* (New Haven: Yale University Press, 1979), pp. 61, 121, 140, 144; Robert K. Fullinwider, *The Reverse Discrimination Controversy: A Moral and Legal Analysis* (Totowa: Rowman and Littlefield, 1980), pp. 244-47.
15. *Affirmative Action in the 1980s: Dismantling the Process of Discrimination*, Clearinghouse Publication 70 (Washington: U.S. Commission on Civil Rights, 1981), pp. 3, 13-14.
16. Ronald Ellis, "Victim-Specific Remedies: A Myopic Approach to Discrimination," *New York University Review of Law and Social Change*, vol. 13 (1984-85), p. 604; Paul J. Spiegelman, "Court-Ordered Hiring Quotas After *Stotts*: A Narrative on the Role of Moralities of the Web and the Ladder In Employment Discrimination Doctrine," *Harvard Civil Rights-Civil Liberties Law Review*, vol. 20 (Summer 1985), pp. 339-40; Linda S. Greene, "Twenty Years of Civil Rights: How Firm a Foundation?" *Rutgers Law Review*, vol. 37 (Summer 1985), pp. 753-54; Randall Kennedy, "Persuasion and Distrust: A Comment on the Affirmative Action Debate," *Harvard Law Review*, vol. 99 (March 1986), pp. 1335-36.
17. *Affirmative Action Today: A Legal and Practical Analysis* (Washington: Bureau of National Affairs, 1986), pp. 148-49.
18. Kathleen M. Sullivan, "Sins of Discrimination: Last Term's Affirmative Action Cases," *Harvard Law Review*, vol. 100 (November 1986), pp. 80-81, 92, 96.
19. Note, "Rethinking *Weber*: The Business Response to Affirmative Action," *Harvard Law Review*, vol. 102 (January 1989), pp. 658-71.
20. Karst and Horowitz, "Affirmative Action and Equal Protection," p. 956; Joe R. Feagin and Clairece B. Feagin, *Discrimination American Style: Institutional Racism and Sexism* (Engelwood Cliffs: Prentice-Hall, 1978), p. 172.
21. Benjamin B. Ringer, "Affirmative Action, Quotas and Meritocracy," *Society*, vol. 13 (January-February 1976), pp. 12, 25; Craig Haney, "Employment Tests and Employment Discrimination: A Dissenting Psychological Opinion," *Industrial Relations Law Journal*, vol. 5 (1982), pp. 79-86; Greene, "Twenty Years of Civil Rights," p. 754; Kennedy, "Persuasion and Distrust," p. 1333; Jeffrey Prager, "Merit and Qualifications: Contested Social Meanings and Their Impact on Affirmative Action," eds. Combs and Gruhl, *Affirmative Action*, pp. 24-34.
22. John Hart Ely, "The Constitutionality of Reverse Racial Discrimination," *University of Chicago Law Review*, vol. 41 (Summer 1974), pp. 723-41.
23. Nagel, "Introduction," p. xii; *Affirmative Action in the 1980s*, p. 35; *Regents of the University of California v. Bakke*, 438 U.S. 265 (1978) at 357 (Justice Brennan); *Fullilove v. Klutznick*, 448 U.S. 448 (1980) at 521 (Justice

Marshall); *City of Richmond v. J.A. Croson Co.*, 102 L. Ed. 854 (1989) at 882 (Justice O'Connor).

24. Fullinwider, *The Reverse Discrimination Controversy*, p. 246.

25. Daniel Seligman, "How 'Equal Opportunity' Turned into Employment Quotas," *Fortune*, vol. 81 (March 1973), p. 168.

26. Richard A. Posner, "The *DeFunis* Case and the Constitutionality of Preferential Treatment for Racial Minorities," *Supreme Court Review 1974* (Chicago: University of Chicago, 1975), pp. 22-24; William Van Alstyne, "Rites of Passage: Race, the Supreme Court, and the Constitution," *University of Chicago Law Review*, vol. 46 (Summer 1979), pp. 793, 979.

27. Posner, "The *DeFunis* Case," p. 30; Alan H. Goldman, *Justice and Reverse Discrimination* (Princeton: Princeton University Press, 1979), p. 151; Robert G. Dixon, "*Bakke*: A Constitutional Analysis," *University of California Law Review*, vol. 67 (January 1979), pp. 85-86; Ralph A. Rossum, "*Plessy, Brown*, and the Reverse Discrimination Cases," *American Behavioral Scientist*, vol. 28 (July-August 1985), p. 798; Glen E. Thurow, "The Declaration of Independence and the Equal Protection of the Laws," in *Still the Law of the Land? Essays on Changing Interpretations of the Constitution* (Hillsdale: Hillsdale College Press, 1987), p. 117.

28. Edward J. Erler, "Sowing the Wind: Judicial Oligarchy and the Legacy of *Brown v. Board of Education*," *Harvard Journal of Law and Public Policy*, vol. 8 (Spring 1985), p. 417; Posner, "The *DeFunis* Case," p. 16; Barry R. Gross, *Discrimination in Reverse: Is Turnabout Fair Play?* (New York: New York University Press, 1978), p. 83; Robert Simon, "Preferential Hiring: A Reply to Judith Jarvis Thompson," eds. Cohen, et. al., *Equality and Preferential Treatment*, p. 41; Goldman, *Justice and Reverse Discrimination*, pp. 90, 195.

29. Posner, "The *DeFunis* Case," p. 17; Thomas Sowell, "*Weber* and *Bakke* and the Presuppositions of 'Affirmative Action,' " *Wayne Law Review*, vol. 26 (July 1980), pp. 1314-16; Nathan Glazer, *Affirmative Discrimination: Ethnic Inequality and Public Policy* (New York: Basic Books, 1978), p. 63; *Affirmative Action Today*, p. 163.

30. Gross, *Discrimination in Reverse*, pp. 121, 131; Goldman, *Justice and Reverse Discrimination*, p. 63; Van Alstyne, "Rites of Passage," p. 809; Rae, *Inequalities*, p. 56.

31. Seligman, "How 'Equal Opportunity' Turned into Employment Quotas," p. 168.

32. Charles Murray, "Affirmative Racism," *The New Republic*, December 31, 1984, p. 22.

33. Kennedy, "Persuasion and Distrust," p. 1331.

34. *Affirmative Action Today*, p. 157; Glenn C. Loury, "Beyond Civil Rights," *The New Republic*, October 7, 1985, p. 25.

35. Gross, *Discrimination in Reverse*, p. 60; Goldman, *Justice and Reverse Discrimination*, pp. 218-19.

36. Posner, "The *DeFunis* Case," p. 18; Goldman, *Justice and Reverse Discrimination*, p. 191; Richard K. Walker, "The Exorbitant Cost of Redistributing Injustice: A Critical View of *United Steelworkers of America v. Weber* and the Misguided Policy of Numerical Employment," *Boston College Law Review*, vol. 21 (November 1979), pp. 66-67; Paul N. Cox, "The Supreme

Court, Title VII and 'Voluntary' Affirmative Action—A Critique," *Indiana Law Review*, vol. 99 (March 1986), p. 1326.

37. Harvey C. Mansfield, Jr., "The Underhandedness of Affirmative Action," *National Review*, vol. 36 (May 4, 1984), pp. 30, 32.

38. Alan P. Sindler, "Racial Preference Policy, the Political Process, and the Courts," *Wayne Law Review*, vol. 26 (July 1980), pp. 1205-6, 1209, 1221-26; Gary Bryner, "Congress, Courts, and Agencies: Equal Employment and the Limits of Policy Implementation," *Political Science Quarterly*, vol. 96 (Fall 1981), pp. 425-29; Bernard D. Meltzer, "The *Weber* Case: Double Talk and Double Standards," *Regulation*, vol. 3 (September-October 1979), p. 40.

39. James E. Jones, Jr., "The Genesis and Present Status of Affirmative Action in Employment: Economic, Legal and Political Realities," paper presented to the American Political Science Association, 1984, pp. 1-2, 28.

40. Sindler, "Racial Preference Policy," p. 1207; Mansfield, "The Underhandedness of Affirmative Action," p. 26.

41. Andrea H. Beller, "The Economics of Enforcement of an Anti-discrimination Law: Title VII of the Civil Rights Act of 1964," *Journal of Law and Economics*, vol. 21 (October 1978), pp. 359-80; Richard Butler and James J. Heckman, "The Government's Impact on the Labor Market Status of Black Americans: A Critical Review," in *Equal Rights and Industrial Relations* (Madison: Industrial Relations Research Association, 1977), p. 248.

42. Edward Lazear, "The Narrowing of Black-White Wage Differentials Is Illusory," *American Economic Review*, vol. 69 (September 1979), pp. 653-64.

43. James P. Smith and Finis Welch, "Race and Poverty: A Forty-Year Record," *American Economic Review*, vol. 77 (May 1987), p. 154.

44. Jones, "The Genesis and Present Status of Affirmative Action," pp. 22-23, 25.

45. Jonathan S. Leonard, "What Was Affirmative Action?", *American Economic Review*, vol. 76 (May 1986), p. 359; Leonard, *The Impact of Affirmative Action* (Berkeley: National Bureau of Economic Research and the University of California School of Business Administration, 1983), pp. iii, 215, 219, 221.

46. James P. Smith and Finis Welch, "Affirmative Action and Labor Markets," *Journal of Labor Economics*, vol. 2 (April 1984), pp. 269-301.

47. Leonard, *The Impact of Affirmative Action*, p. 18; Leonard, "What Promises Are Worth: The Impact of Affirmative Action Goals," *Journal of Human Resources*, vol. 20 (Winter 1985), p. 19.

48. Jonathan S. Leonard, "Anti-discrimination or Reverse Discrimination: The Impact of Changing Demographics, Title VII, and Affirmative Action on Productivity," *Journal of Human Resources*, vol. 19 (Spring 1984), p. 156.

49. Leonard, *The Impact of Affirmative Action*, p. 8.

50. Fali Sam Nariman, "The Indian Constitution: An Experiment in Unity and Diversity," eds. Robert Goldwin, et. al., *Forging Unity Out of Diversity: The Approaches of Eight Nations* (Washington: American Enterprise Institute, 1989), pp. 7-37; Thomas Sowell, "Affirmative Action: A Worldwide Disaster," *Commentary*, vol. 88 (December 1989), p. 21.

51. Glenn C. Loury, "The 'Color Line' Today," *The Public Interest*, No. 80 (Summer 1985), p. 94; Nathan Glazer, "Response," *New York University Review of Law and Social Change*, vol. 13 (1984-85), pp. 313-15.

52. Alfred W. Blumrosen, "Expanding the Concept of Affirmative Action to Address Contemporary Conditions," *New York University Review of Law and Social Change*, vol. 13 (1984-85), p. 298; Christopher Jencks, "Affirmative Action for Blacks: Past, Present, and Future," *American Behavioral Scientist*, vol. 28 (July-August 1985), p. 758.

53. Glenn C. Loury, "The Moral Quandary of the Black Community," *The Public Interest*, no. 79 (Spring 1985), p. 9; Blumrosen, "Expanding the Concept of Affirmative Action," p. 297.

54. Loury, "The Moral Quandary of the Black Community," pp. 13-14, 20.

55. Mansfield, "The Underhandedness of Affirmative Action," pp. 28-30.

56. Jones, "The Genesis and Present Status of Affirmative Action," p. 25; Leonard, *The Impact of Affirmative Action*, p. 360.

57. Loury, "The Moral Quandary of the Black Community," p. 20; Nathan Glazer, "The Affirmative Action Stalemate," *The Public Interest*, no. 90 (Winter 1988), p. 108.

58. Blumrosen, "Expanding the Concept of Affirmative Action," p. 299; Earl Picard, "The New Black Economic Development Strategy," *Telos*, no. 60 (Summer 1984), p. 55; Melvin L. Oliver and Mark A. Glick, "An Analysis of the New Orthodoxy on Black Mobility," *Social Problems*, vol. 29 (June 1982), p. 520.

59. Leonard, *The Impact of Affirmative Action*, p. 335; Jones, "The Genesis and Present Status of Affirmative Action," p. 25; Kennedy, "Persuasion and Distrust," pp. 1338, 1345-46.

60. Kimberle Crenshaw, "Race, Reform, and Retrenchment: Transformation and Legitimation in Anti-discrimination law," *Harvard Law Review*, vol. 101 (May 1988), p. 1349; Kristin Bumiller, *The Civil Rights Society: The Social Construction of Victims* (Baltimore: Johns Hopkins University Press, 1988), pp. 19, 39.

61. Jennifer Hochschild, *The New American Dilemma: Liberal Democracy and School Segregation* (New Haven: Yale University Press, 1984), pp. 5, 145.

62. *Affirmative Action Today*, p. 157.

63. James R. Kluegel and Eliot R. Smith, "Affirmative Action Attitudes: Effects of Self-Interest, Racial Affect, and Stratification Beliefs on Whites' Views," *Social Forces*, vol. 61 (March 1983), pp. 797-824; Paul M. Sniderman and Philip E. Tetlock, "Symbolic Racism: Problems of Motive Attribution in Political Analysis," *Journal of Social Issues*, vol. 42 (Summer 1986), pp. 129-50.

64. Howard Schuman, Charlotte Steeh, and Lawrence Bobo, *Racial Attitudes in America: Trends and Interpretations* (Cambridge: Harvard University Press, 1985), p. 6; James R. Kluegel, "'If There Isn't a Problem, You Don't Need a Solution,'" *American Behavioral Scientist*, vol. 28 (July-August 1985), pp. 766, 772, 774-75.

65. Schuman, et. al., *Racial Attitudes*, pp. 104, 147-49, 200; Richard Jenkins and John Solomos, eds., *Racism and Equal Opportunity Politics in the 1980s* (Cambridge: Cambridge University Press, 1987), pp. 6-61, discusses the same phenomenon in England.

66. Schuman, *Racial Attitudes*, p. 204; Sniderman and Tetlock, "Symbolic Racism," p. 132.
67. Byron M. Roth, "Symbolic Racism: The Making of a Scholarly Myth," *Academic Questions*, vol. 2 (Summer 1989), p. 56.
68. Sniderman and Tetlock, "Symbolic Racism," p. 145.
69. R. Shep Melnick, "The Courts, Congress, and Programmatic Rights," in Richard A. Harris and Sidney M. Milkis, eds., *Remaking American Politics* (Boulder: Westview Press, 1989), pp. 188-212; Hugh Heclo, "The Emerging Regime," *ibid.*, pp. 299-300; Theodore J. Lowi, "The Welfare State: Ethical Foundations and Constitutional Remedies," *Political Science Quarterly*, vol. 101 (Spring 1986), p. 126.
70. Mansfield, "The Underhandedness of Affirmative Action," p. 28.
71. Schuman, *Racial Attitudes*, p. 117.
72. Timothy J. O'Neill, *Bakke and the Politics of Equality: Friends and Foes in the Classroom of Litigation* (Middletown: Wesleyan University Press, 1985), p. 262.
73. William R. Beer, "Resolute Ignorance: Social Science and Affirmative Action," *Society*, vol. 24 (May-June 1987), p. 63; Sowell, "'Affirmative Action': A Worldwide Disaster," p. 33.
74. Frederick R. Lynch, "Affirmative Action, the Media, and the Public: A Look at a 'Look-Away' Issue," *American Behavioral Scientist*, vol. 28 (July-August 1985), p. 818; Carl A. Auerbach, "The Silent Opposition of Professors and Graduate Students to Preferential Affirmative Action Programs: 1969 and 1975," *Minnesota Law Review*, vol. 72 (December 1988), pp. 1268-80.
75. John Nalbandian, "The U.S. Supreme Court's 'Consensus' on Affirmative Action," *Public Administration Review*, vol. 49 (January-February 1989), pp. 43-45.
76. Interview with Jeffrey Norris and Douglas S. McDowell, Equal Employment Advisory Council, January 25, 1989.
77. *Opportunity 2000: Creative Affirmative Action Strategies for a Changing Workforce* (Indianapolis: Hudson Institute, 1988), pp. vii-viii, 92.
78. Remarks by the President to the National Urban League Conference, August 8, 1989, p. 3.
79. Mark B. Liedl, ed., *Issues '88: A Platform for America*, vol. 1 (Washington: The Heritage Foundation, 1988), pp. 253-62.
80. Leonard, *The Impact of Affirmative Action*, p. 20.
81. With respect to legal interpretation, for example, the Guidelines requires the employer to search for an alternative selection method when a test with adverse impact is validated, whereas the *Albemarle* decision places this burden on the plaintiff.
82. James Ledvinka, Val H. Markos, and Robert R. Ladd, "Long-Range Impact of 'Fair Selection' Standards on Minority Employment," *Journal of Applied Psychology*, vol. 67 (February 1982), pp. 18-36; Edward F. Potter, ed., *Employee Selection: Legal and Practical Alternatives to Compliance and Litigation* (Washington: Equal Employment Advisory Council, 1983), pp. 9-13, 17; Kenneth McCulloch, Book Review, *Employee Relations Law Journal*, vol. 7 (Spring 1982), p. 702; John E. Hunter and Frank L. Schmidt, "Ability Tests: Economic Benefits Versus the Issue of Fairness," *Industrial Relations*, vol. 21 (Fall 1982), pp. 293-308.

83. Mary L. Tenopyr, "The Realities of Employment Testing," *American Psychologist*, vol. 36 (October 1981), p. 1122.

84. Linda S. Gottfredson, "Foreword: The g Factor in Employment," *Journal of Vocational Behavior*, vol. 29 (December 1986), pp. 293-96; Linda S. Gottfredson, "Societal Consequences of the g Factor in Employment," *ibid.*, pp. 379-410; Frank L. Schmidt, "The Problem of Group Differences in Ability Test Scores in Employment Selection," *ibid.*, vol. 33 (December 1988), pp. 272-92; Linda S. Gottfredson and James C. Sharf, "Foreword: Fairness in Employment Testing," *ibid.*, vol. 33 (December 1988), p. 226; James C. Sharf, "Litigating Personnel Management Policy," *ibid.*, vol. 33 (December 1988), p. 237. Validity generalization results from analysis of individual validation studies at the organizational level. When corrected for distortions caused by small study samples, these studies show substantial correlations with a wide variety of jobs. Constance Holden, "Academy Panel Joins the Fray Over Job Testing," *Science*, vol. 244 (June 2, 1989), p. 1036.

85. Richard T. Seymour, "Why Plaintiffs Counsel Challenge Tests, and How They Can Successfully Challenge the Theory of 'Validity Generalization,'" *Journal of Vocational Behavior*, vol. 33 (December 1988), pp. 331-64; Barry L. Goldstein and Patrick O. Patterson, "Turning Back the Title VII Clock: The Re-segregation of the American Work Force through Validity Generalization," *ibid.*, pp. 452-62.

86. Sharf, "Litigating Personnel Management Policy," p. 256.

87. Letter to the Editor by John Hartigan and Alexandra Wigdor, *Science*, vol. 245 (July 7, 1989), p. 14. The National Science Council says this "false negative" effect is not a function of race or ethnicity. Nevertheless, it seeks to compensate for the effect as though it were racial in nature.

88. Linda S. Gottfredson, "Reconsidering Fairness: A Matter of Social and Ethical Priorities," *Journal of Vocational Behavior*, vol. 33 (December 1988), p. 307; Schmidt, "The Problem of Group Differences in Ability Test Scores," p. 288.

89. *Affirmative Action in the 1980s*, p. 35.

90. Quoted in Erler, "Sowing the Wind," p. 413.

91. Damon J. Keith, "Should Color Blindness and Representativeness Be a Part of American Justice?" *Howard Law Journal*, vol. 26 (1983), p. 5.

92. 438 U.S. 400.

93. Glenn C. Loury, " 'Matter of Color'—Blacks and the Constitutional Order," *The Public Interest*, no. 86 (Winter 1987), p. 119; Loury, "Beyond Civil Rights," *The New Republic*, October 7, 1985, p. 25.

94. *Washington Post*, September 4, 1989, p. A27.

95. Nathan Glazer, "Affirmative Action as a Remedy for Discrimination: Strategies for the Future," *American Behavioral Scientist*, vol. 28 (July-August 1985), p. 833.

96. Damon J. Keith, "What Happens to a Dream Deferred: An Assessment of Civil Rights Law Twenty Years after the March on Washington," *Harvard Civil Rights-Civil Liberties Law Review*, vol. 19 (Summer 1984), p. 492.

Chronology

1865 Thirteenth Amendment ratified; prohibits slavery and by implication confers unspecified civil rights on freed slaves.

1866 Civil Rights Act declares all persons born or naturalized in the United States, excluding Indians not taxed, to be citizens; guarantees individual citizens the right to purchase, lease, sell, hold, and convey real and personal property, and to make and enforce contracts; does not prohibit private discrimination.

1868 Fourteenth Amendment ratified; prohibits states from abridging the privileges and immunities of citizens of the U.S., depriving any person of life, liberty, or property without due process of law, or denying to any person the equal protection of the laws; does not prohibit private discrimination.

1935 National Labor Relations Act prohibits private employers from discriminating against individuals because of labor union membership; provides model for legislation against discrimination because of race.

1941 President Roosevelt's Executive Order 8802 prohibits discrimination by private employers in defense industries and by the federal government because of race, creed, color, or national origin; President Roosevelt creates Fair Employment Practice Commission (FEPC) to enforce order.

1943 President Roosevelt's Executive Order 9346 prohibits discrimination in government contracts because of race, creed, color, or national origin; reorganizes and strengthens FEPC, which is later terminated by Congress in 1946.

1945 New York state law against discrimination creates State Commission against Discrimination with authority to prohibit discrimination in public and private employment; first of 26 state fair employment practice laws passed from 1945 to 1964.

1948 President Truman's Executive Order 9980 creates Fair Employment Board within the Civil Service Commission.

1951 President Truman's Executive Order 10308 creates Government Contract Compliance Committee.

1953 President Eisenhower's Executive Order 10479 creates Government Contract Committee.

1955 President Eisenhower's Executive Order 10590 prohibits discrimination in federal employment; removes Government Employment Committee from Civil Service Commission and places it in direct line of authority to the President.

1961 President Kennedy's Executive Order 10925 prohibits discrimination in government contract program and in government employment; requires federal contractors to take affirmative action to ensure that individuals are treated without regard to race, creed, color, or national origin; creates President's Committee on Equal Employment Opportunity.

1964 Title VII of Civil Rights Act guarantees every individual the right not to be discriminated against in employment because of race, color, religion, sex, or national origin; applies to private employers and unions with 25 or more employees or members; creates Equal Employment Opportunity Commission (EEOC) with power to conciliate disputes arising from individual complaints of discrimination.

1965 President Johnson's Executive Order 11246 prohibits discrimination on the basis of race, religion, or national origin in government contracts and in federal employment and confirms the affirmative action obligation imposed by Executive Order 10925; assigns federal contract program to Department of Labor and authorizes Secretary of Labor to create Office of Federal Contract Compliance (OFCC); abolishes President's Committee on Equal Employment Opportunity.

1966 EEOC's Guidelines on Testing embody the disparate impact theory of discrimination and require employers to validate tests for minorities under differential validation rule.

1967 President Johnson's Executive Order 11375 prohibits discrimination by sex in government contracts.

1969 Nixon Administration Department of Labor revised Philadelphia Plan requires explicit quota hiring in the construction industry in

Philadelphia and three other cities, in the form of goals and timetables.

1970   OFCC Order No. 4 extends goals and timetables requirement of Philadelphia Plan to nonconstruction contractors as part of written affirmative action plan which contractors are obligated to submit.

1970   EEOC Guidelines on Testing revise and extend 1966 guidelines into systematic policy imposing stringent validation requirements on employers who use tests that have disparate impact.

1971   *Griggs v. Duke Power Co.* Supreme Court adopts disparate impact theory of discrimination in first Title VII case; requires employer to prove that tests or selection devices that have discriminatory impact are justified by business necessity.

1972   Title VII amendments (Equal Employment Opportunity Act of 1972) extend Title VII to private employers and unions with 15 or more employees or members, to public employers in state and local government, and to educational institutions; authorizes EEOC to enforce Title VII by bringing suit in federal district court; creates Equal Employment Opportunity Council in federal government to formulate uniform policy on employee selection procedures.

1973   *McDonnell Douglas v. Green.* Supreme Court recognizes disparate treatment concept of discrimination in case which determines order and allocation of burdens of proof in individual discrimination suit under Title VII.

1975   *Albermarle Paper Co. v. Moody.* Supreme Court affirms disparate impact theory of discrimination in class action case involving back pay award; upholds broad remedial authority of federal district courts under make-whole theory of relief; finds tests with disparate impact unlawful because not validated in accordance with EEOC guidelines on testing.

1976   *Washington v. Davis.* Supreme Court rejects disparate impact theory of discrimination in a Fourteenth Amendment constitutional case, holding proof of intent to discriminate is required in bringing discrimination charges under equal protection clause; finds test with disparate impact is job-related despite not being validated under EEOC testing guidelines.

1978   Executive Reorganization Plan No. 1 expands EEOC authority as preeminent civil rights enforcement agency; transfers federal equal employment opportunity function from Civil Service Commission to EEOC and administration of Equal Pay Act and Age Discrimination Act from Department of Labor to EEOC; OFCC is reorganized and given more centralized authority over contract compliance as Office of Federal Contract Compliance Programs (OFCCP).

1978   Uniform Guidelines on Employee Selection Procedures issued by EEOC on behalf of all federal agencies; systematic pressure applied to employers for adoption of affirmative action hiring policies in response to disparate impact discrimination findings and as an alternative to tests.

1978   *Regents of the University of California v. Bakke.* Supreme Court declares affirmative action plan imposing quota for medical school admissions is in violation of Title VI of the Civil Rights Act of 1964; approves race as a legitimate factor in college and professional school admission policies.

1979   *Kaiser Aluminum and Chemical Corporation v. Weber.* Supreme Court upholds 50 percent minority quota under affirmative action plan against reverse discrimination claim; declares voluntary affirmative action plans by private employers do not violate Title VII ban on discrimination or Section 703(j) prohibition of preferential treatment on account of racial imbalance.

1980   *Fullilove v. Klutznick.* Supreme Court upholds 10 percent minority set-aside quota for public contracts awarded by Department of Commerce under Public Works Employment Act of 1977; holds Congress is authorized to enact racially preferential remedial measures under commerce clause and Fourteenth Amendment as a means of overcoming societal discrimination.

1984   *Firefighters Local Union No. 1794 v. Stotts.* Supreme Court declares district court affirmative action plan exceeds judicial remedial authority under Title VII; seniority rights of white employees are upheld against minority preference under court-ordered affirmative action plan.

1986   *Local 28 Sheet Metal Workers v. EEOC.* Supreme Court for the first time upholds district court remedial quota order under Title VII; confirms lower court remedial quota policy begun in 1969.

1987   *Johnson v. Transportation Agency Santa Clara County.* Supreme Court upholds voluntary affirmative action plan of public employer against reverse discrimination charge; declares racial and gender preferences are justified in order to overcome under-representation rather than as a remedy for past discrimination.

1989   *Wards Cove Packing Co. v. Atonio.* Supreme Court rejects disparate impact discrimination charge under Title VII because based on statistics improperly comparing unskilled and skilled workers; adopts relaxed "rule of reason" approach to *Griggs* requirement that employer demonstrate business necessity of employment practices having disparate impact.

1989 *City of Richmond v. J.A. Croson Co.* Supreme Court rejects 30 percent minority quota requirement for public contractors as an unconstitutional interference with the rights of white contractors.

Index

About the Author

Herman Belz is a professor of American constitutional history at the University of Maryland. He has written extensively about the history of civil rights in *A New Birth of Freedom: The Republican Party and Freedmen's Rights 1861–1866* and *Emancipation and Equal Rights: Politics and Constitutionalism in the Civil War Era.* He is the co-author of *The American Constitution: Its Origins and Development.*